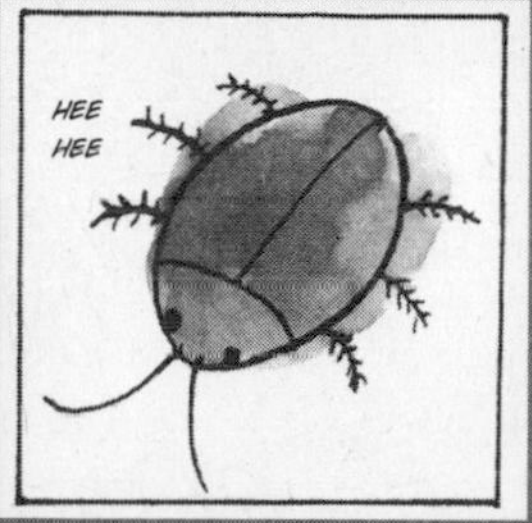
HEE
HEE

PRODUCTION REPORT 5: THE ANIME

I RECEIVED A TON OF LETTERS, BOTH SUPPORTING AND CRITICIZING THE VOICE ACTOR CHOICES. I WASN'T INVOLVED IN THE SELECTION PROCESS BECAUSE I DIDN'T HAVE ANY PRECONCEIVED NOTIONS OF HOW THE CHARACTERS SHOULD SOUND. I'M NOT FAMILIAR WITH THE PROCESS OF MAKING ANIME ON TV (OR THE CIRCUMSTANCES BEHIND THE SCENES), SO I HAVE NO IDEA WHAT THEY CAN OR CAN'T DO. ACCORDINGLY, I'M NOT INVOLVED IN THE ANIME AT ALL. THAT COULD SOUND EXASPERATING FOR THOSE OF YOU WHO ARE EMOTIONALLY INVESTED, BUT IT WAS ALWAYS MY OPINION, EVEN BEFORE I BECAME A MANGA ARTIST, THAT THE ORIGINAL MANGA AND THE ANIME ARE DIFFERENT ENTITIES.

—*YOSHIHIRO TOGASHI, 1992*

Born in 1966, Yoshihiro Togashi won the prestigious Tezuka Award for new manga artists at the age of 20. He debuted in Japan's WEEKLY SHONEN JUMP magazine in 1988 with the romantic comedy manga **Tende Showaru Cupid**. His hit comic **YuYu Hakusho** ran in WEEKLY SHONEN JUMP from 1990 to 1994. Togashi's other manga include **I'm Not Afraid of Wolves!**, **Level E**, and **Hunter x Hunter**. **Hunter x Hunter** is also available through VIZ Media.

YUYU HAKUSHO VOL. 10
The SHONEN JUMP Manga Edition

This manga contains material that was originally published in
English in **SHONEN JUMP** #39-43.

STORY AND ART BY
YOSHIHIRO TOGASHI

English Adaptation/Gary Leach
Translation/Lillian Olsen
Touch-up Art & Lettering/Elizabeth Watasin
Graphics & Cover Design/Courtney Utt
Editor/Michelle Pangilinan

Managing Editor/Frances E. Wall
Editorial Director/Elizabeth Kawasaki
VP & Editor in Chief/Yumi Hoashi
Sr. Director of Acquisitions/Rika Inouye
Sr. VP of Marketing/Liza Coppola
Exec. VP of Sales & Marketing/John Easum
Publisher/Hyoe Narita

Printed in the U.S.A.

Published by VIZ Media, LLC
P.O. Box 77010
San Francisco, CA 94107

SHONEN JUMP Manga Edition
10 9 8 7 6 5 4 3 2
First printing, August 2006
Second printing, August 2006

www.viz.com

PARENTAL ADVISORY
YUYU HAKUSHO is rated T for Teen and
is recommended for ages 13 and up.
This volume contains fantasy violence.

THE WORLD'S
MOST POPULAR MANGA

www.shonenjump.com

SHONEN JUMP MANGA

YuYu HAKUSHO ™

Vol. 10
Unforgivable!!

STORY AND ART BY
YOSHIHIRO TOGASHI

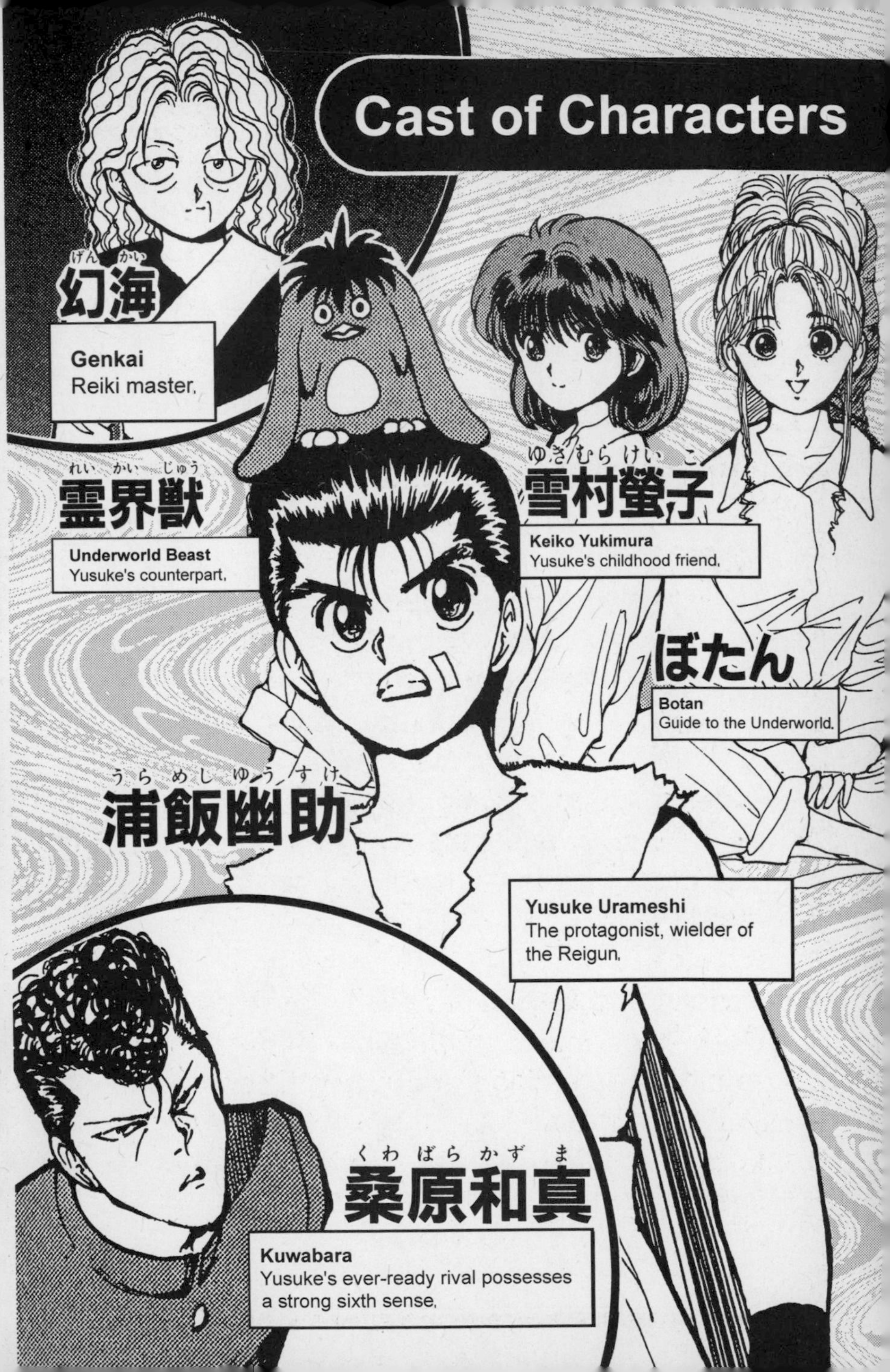
Cast of Characters
ゆきむら けいこ
雪村螢子
Keiko Yukimura
Yusuke's childhood friend.
ぼたん
Botan
Guide to the Underworld.
げんかい
幻海
Genkai
Reiki master.
れいかいじゅう
霊界獣
Underworld Beast
Yusuke's counterpart.
うらめしゆうすけ
浦飯幽助
Yusuke Urameshi
The protagonist, wielder of the Reigun.
くわばらかずま
桑原和真
Kuwabara
Yusuke's ever-ready rival possesses a strong sixth sense.

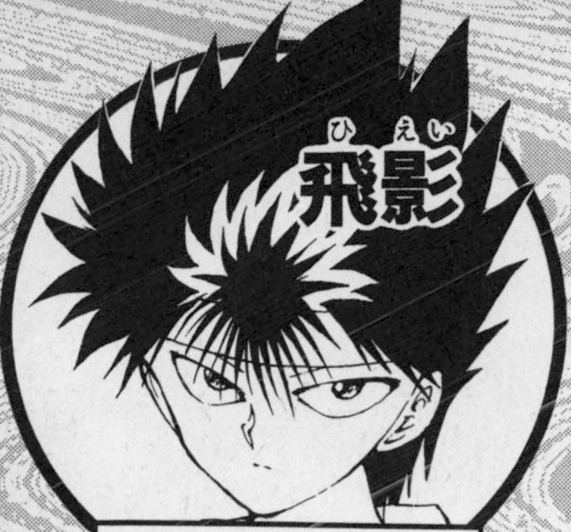
飛影

Hiei
A thief with abilities enhanced by the Evil Eye.

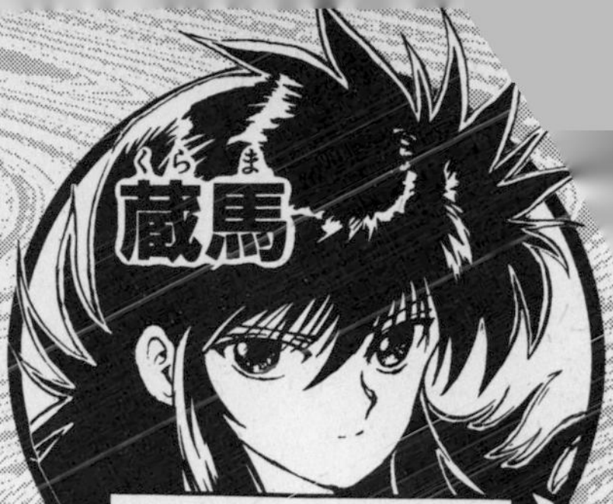
蔵馬

Kurama
A former fox demon now living in human society. He has suppressed his demonic powers.

This is the story of the hapless Yusuke Urameshi, hit by a car while attempting to save a little kid. For a while he was a ghost, but earned his way back to life through a series of ordeals set up by King Enma. He now works as an Underworld Detective, which means that demons everywhere want him dead—again!

Yusuke and friends have been entered in the Dark Tournament, and have won the third round by defeating the Shadow Channelers. Will they be able to do the same to the Fractured Fairy Tales and advance to the finals? How will it all turn out...?

YUYU HAKUSHO VOLUME 10 UNFORGIVABLE!!

CONTENTS

THE FOX DEMON AWAKENS!!

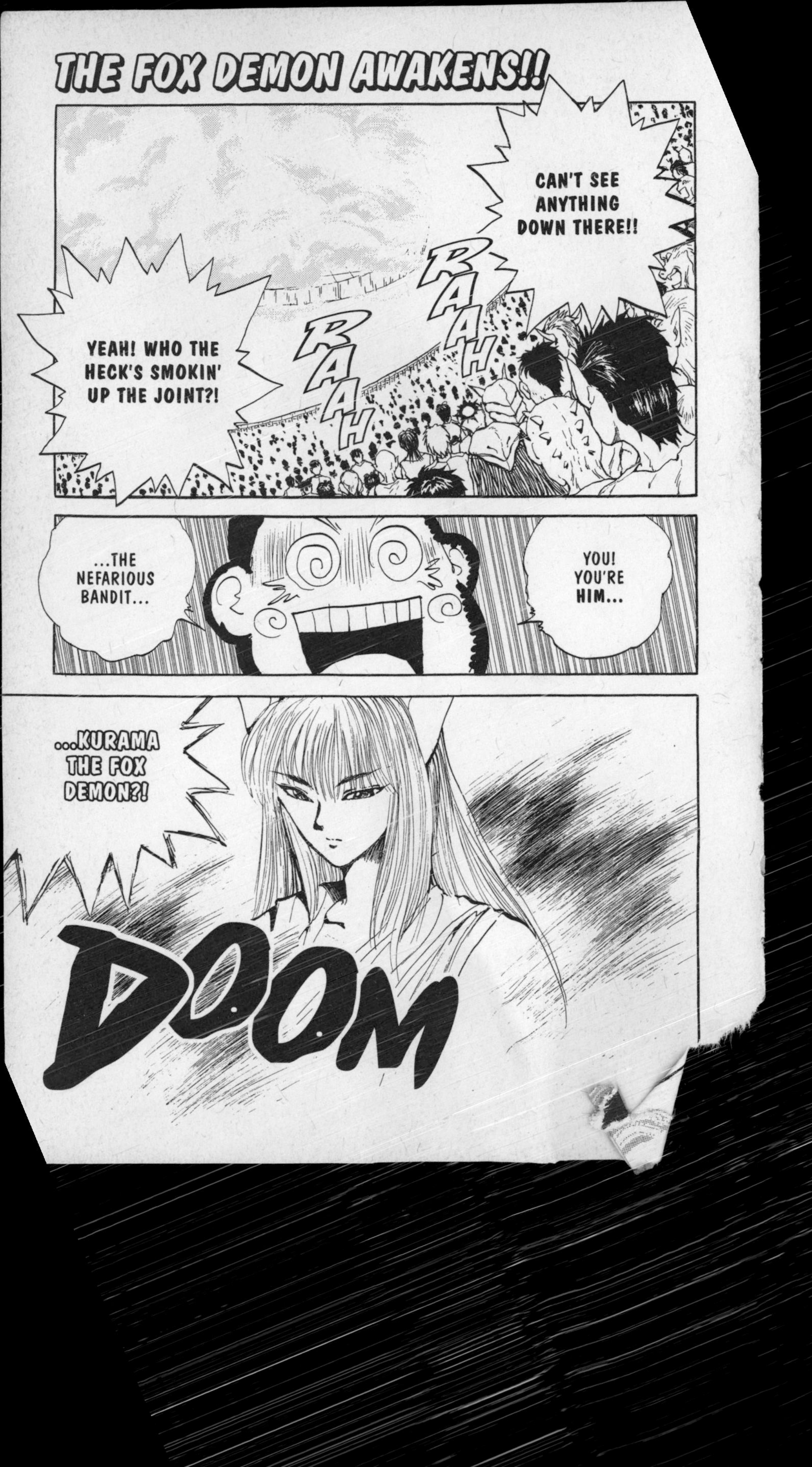
CAN'T SEE ANYTHING DOWN THERE!!
RAAH
RAAH
YEAH! WHO THE HECK'S SMOKIN' UP THE JOINT?!
YOU! YOU'RE HIM...
...THE NEFARIOUS BANDIT...
...KURAMA THE FOX DEMON?!
DOOM

THE FOX DEMON AWAKENS!!

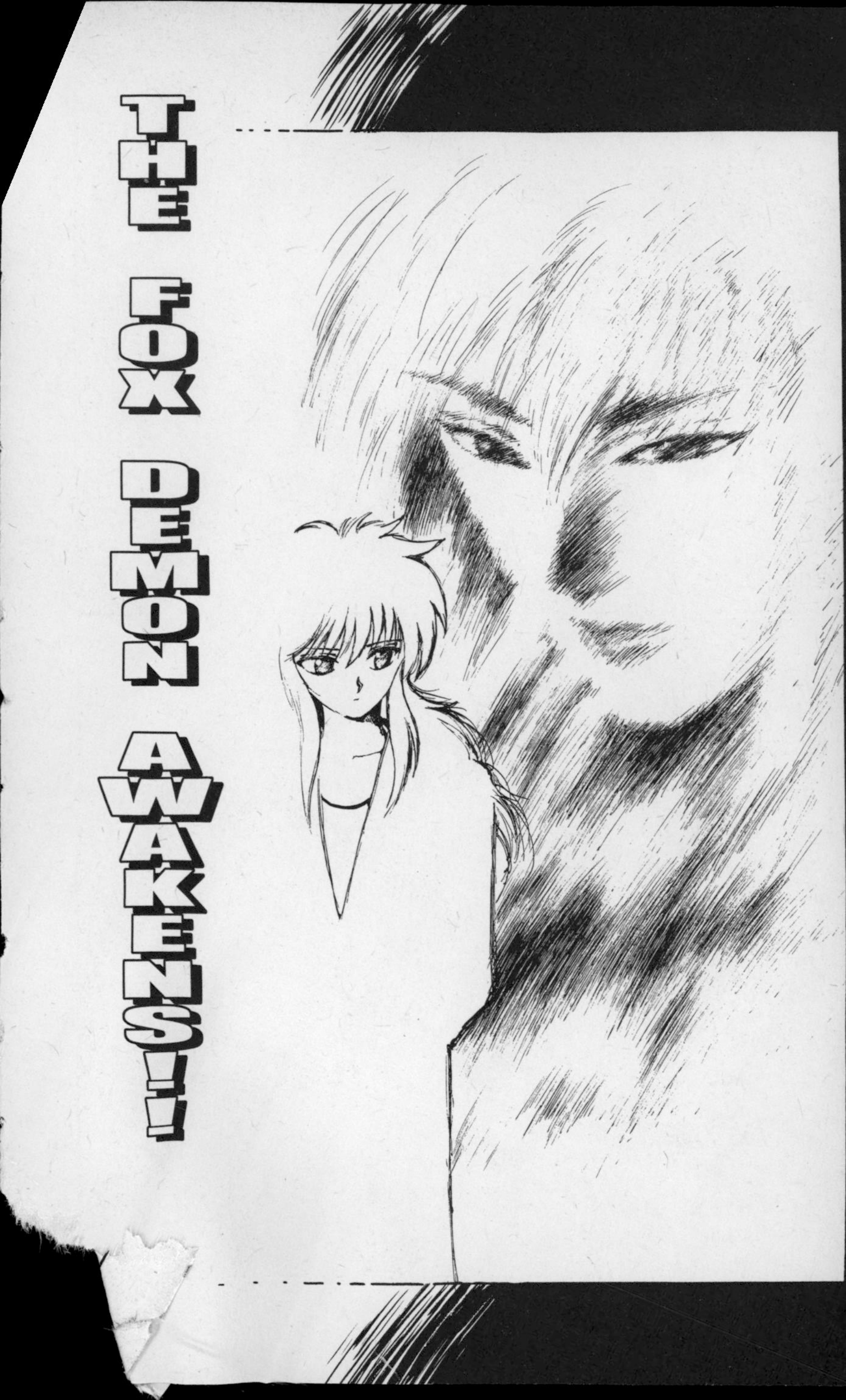

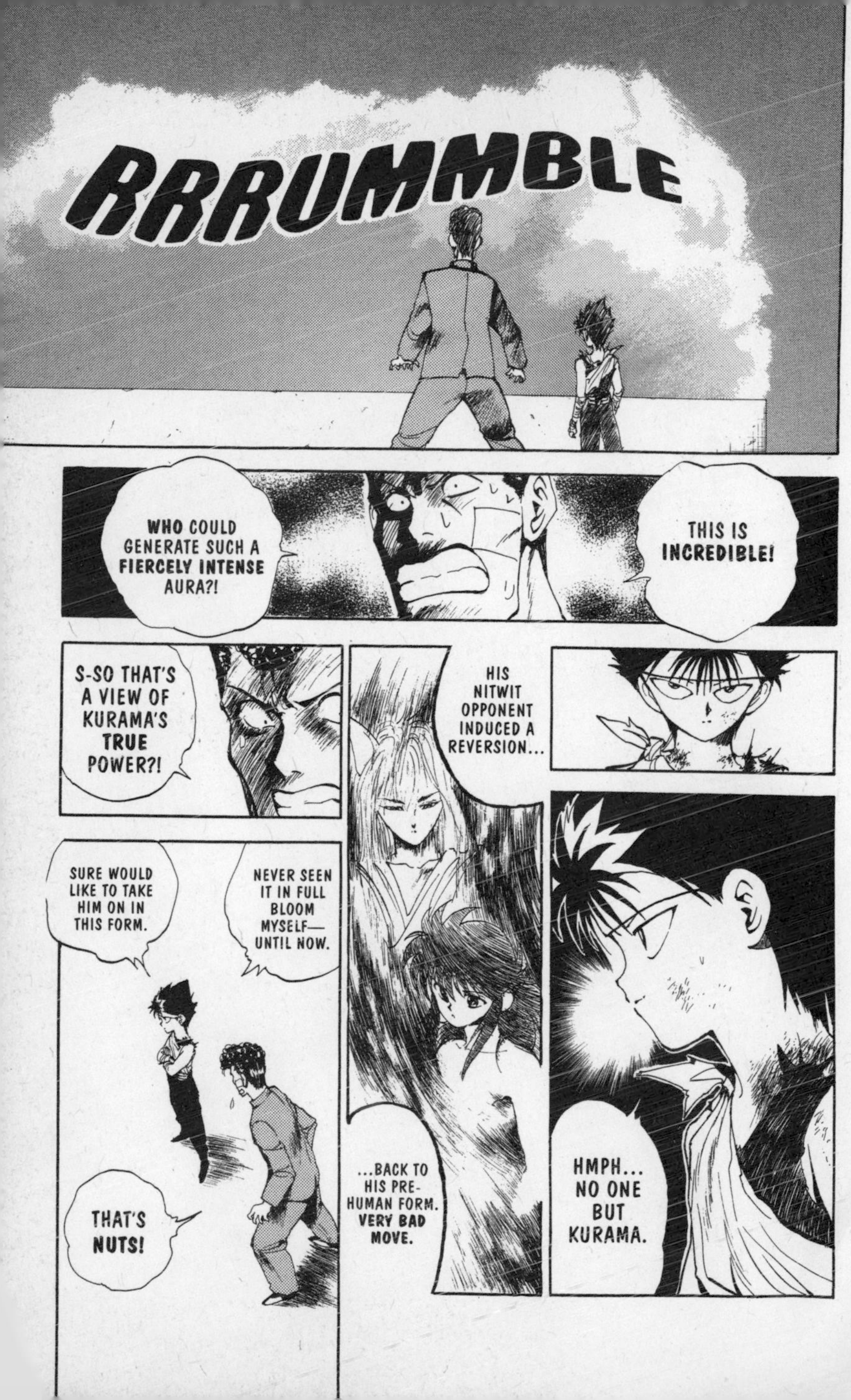
RRRUMMBLE
THIS IS INCREDIBLE!
WHO COULD GENERATE SUCH A FIERCELY INTENSE AURA?!
HMPH... NO ONE BUT KURAMA.
HIS NITWIT OPPONENT INDUCED A REVERSION...
...BACK TO HIS PRE-HUMAN FORM. VERY BAD MOVE.
S-SO THAT'S A VIEW OF KURAMA'S TRUE POWER?!
NEVER SEEN IT IN FULL BLOOM MYSELF— UNTIL NOW.
SURE WOULD LIKE TO TAKE HIM ON IN THIS FORM.
THAT'S NUTS!

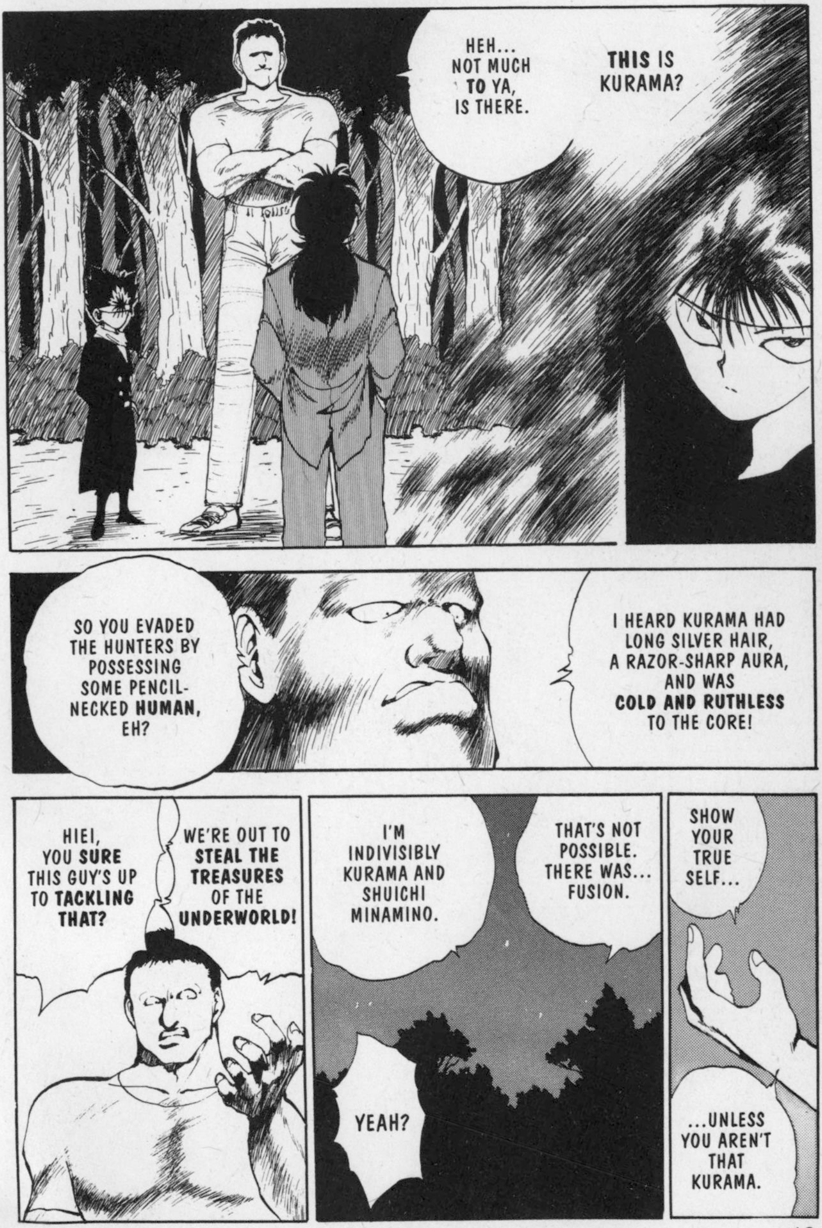
THIS IS KURAMA?
HEH... NOT MUCH TO YA, IS THERE.
I HEARD KURAMA HAD LONG SILVER HAIR, A RAZOR-SHARP AURA, AND WAS COLD AND RUTHLESS TO THE CORE!
SO YOU EVADED THE HUNTERS BY POSSESSING SOME PENCIL-NECKED HUMAN, EH?
SHOW YOUR TRUE SELF...
...UNLESS YOU AREN'T THAT KURAMA.
THAT'S NOT POSSIBLE. THERE WAS... FUSION.
I'M INDIVISIBLY KURAMA AND SHUICHI MINAMINO.
YEAH?
WE'RE OUT TO STEAL THE TREASURES OF THE UNDERWORLD!
HIEI, YOU SURE THIS GUY'S UP TO TACKLING THAT?

READ THIS WAY

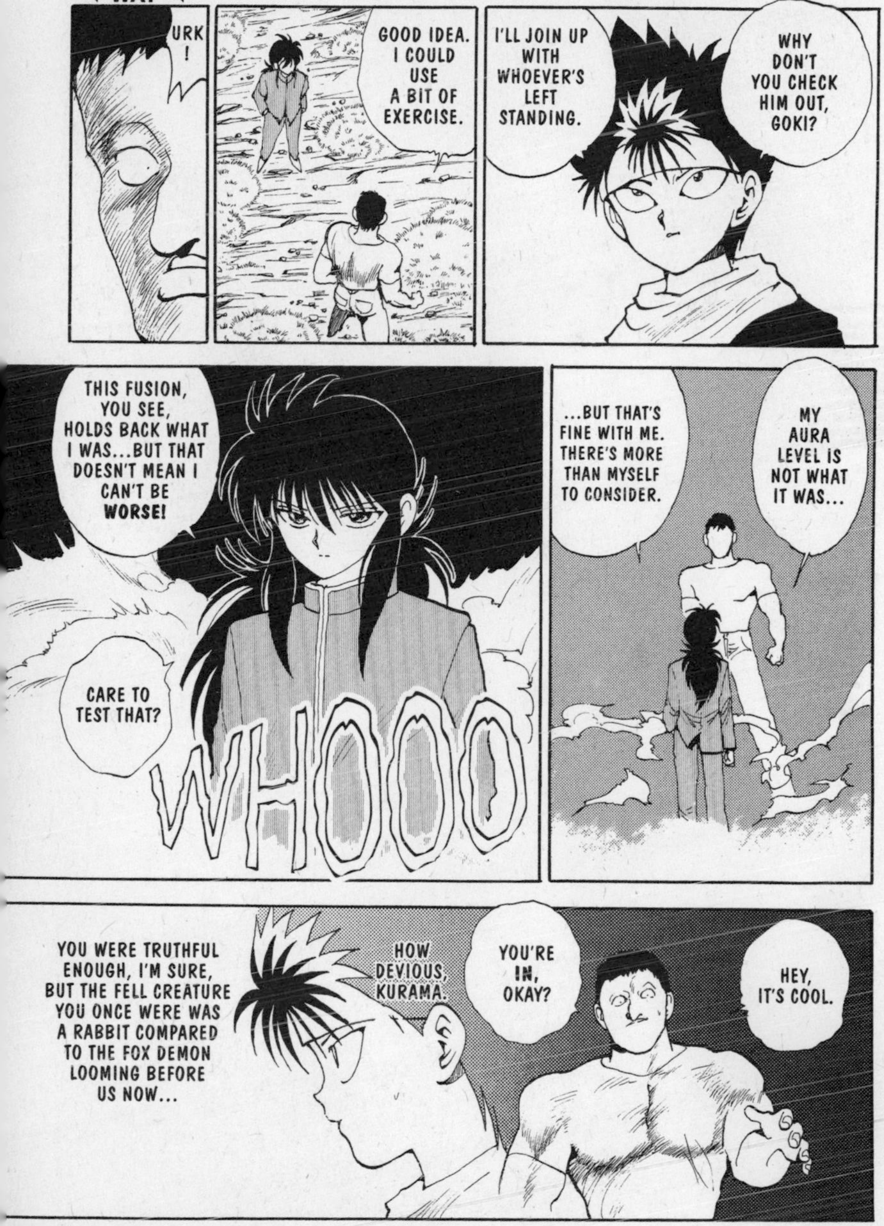

WHY DON'T YOU CHECK HIM OUT, GOKI?
I'LL JOIN UP WITH WHOEVER'S LEFT STANDING.
GOOD IDEA. I COULD USE A BIT OF EXERCISE.
URK!
MY AURA LEVEL IS NOT WHAT IT WAS...
...BUT THAT'S FINE WITH ME. THERE'S MORE THAN MYSELF TO CONSIDER.
THIS FUSION, YOU SEE, HOLDS BACK WHAT I WAS...BUT THAT DOESN'T MEAN I CAN'T BE **WORSE!**
CARE TO TEST THAT?
WHOOO
HEY, IT'S COOL.
YOU'RE **IN**, OKAY?
HOW DEVIOUS, KURAMA.
YOU WERE TRUTHFUL ENOUGH, I'M SURE, BUT THE FELL CREATURE YOU ONCE WERE WAS A RABBIT COMPARED TO THE FOX DEMON LOOMING BEFORE US NOW...

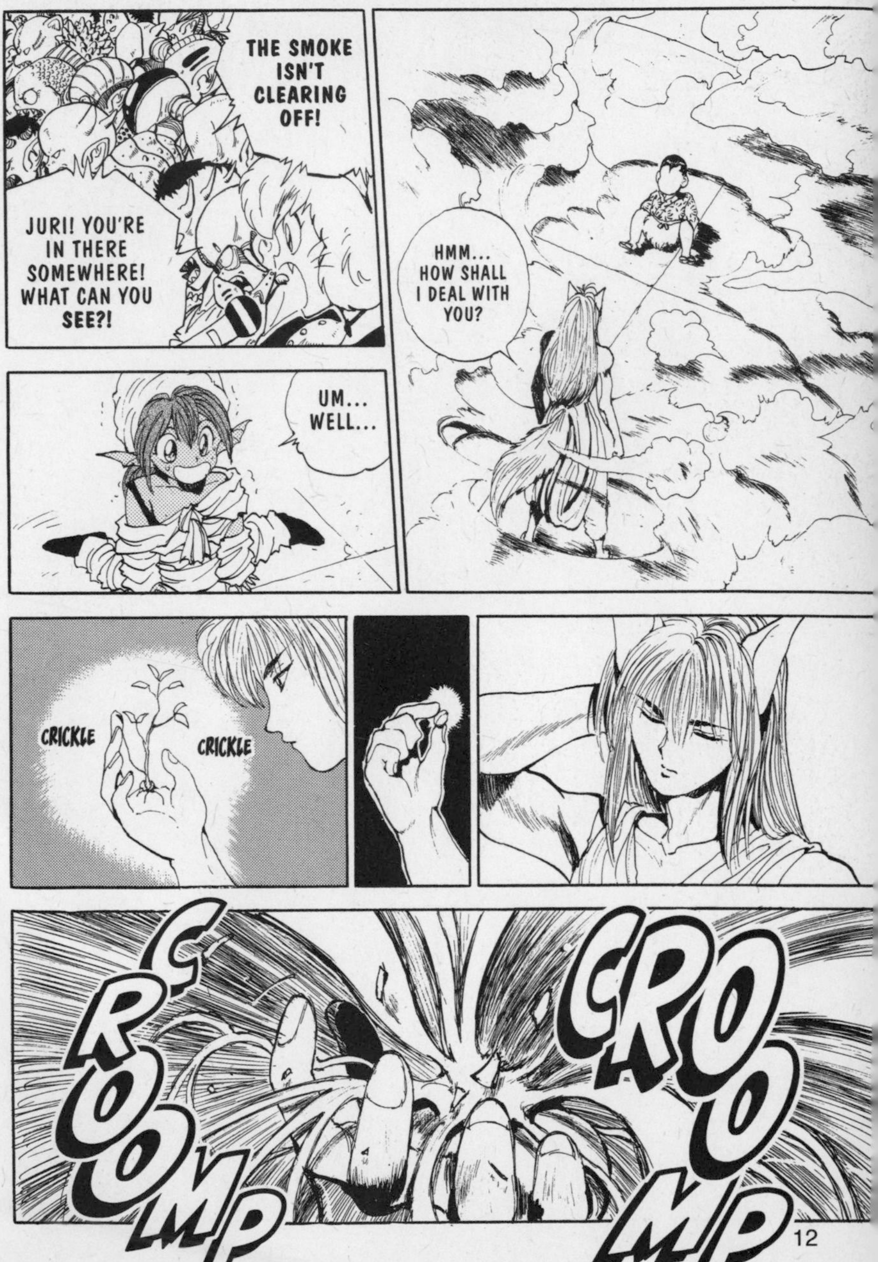
HMM... HOW SHALL I DEAL WITH YOU?
THE SMOKE ISN'T CLEARING OFF!
JURI! YOU'RE IN THERE SOMEWHERE! WHAT CAN YOU SEE?!
UM... WELL...
CRICKLE
CRICKLE
CROOOMP
CROOMP

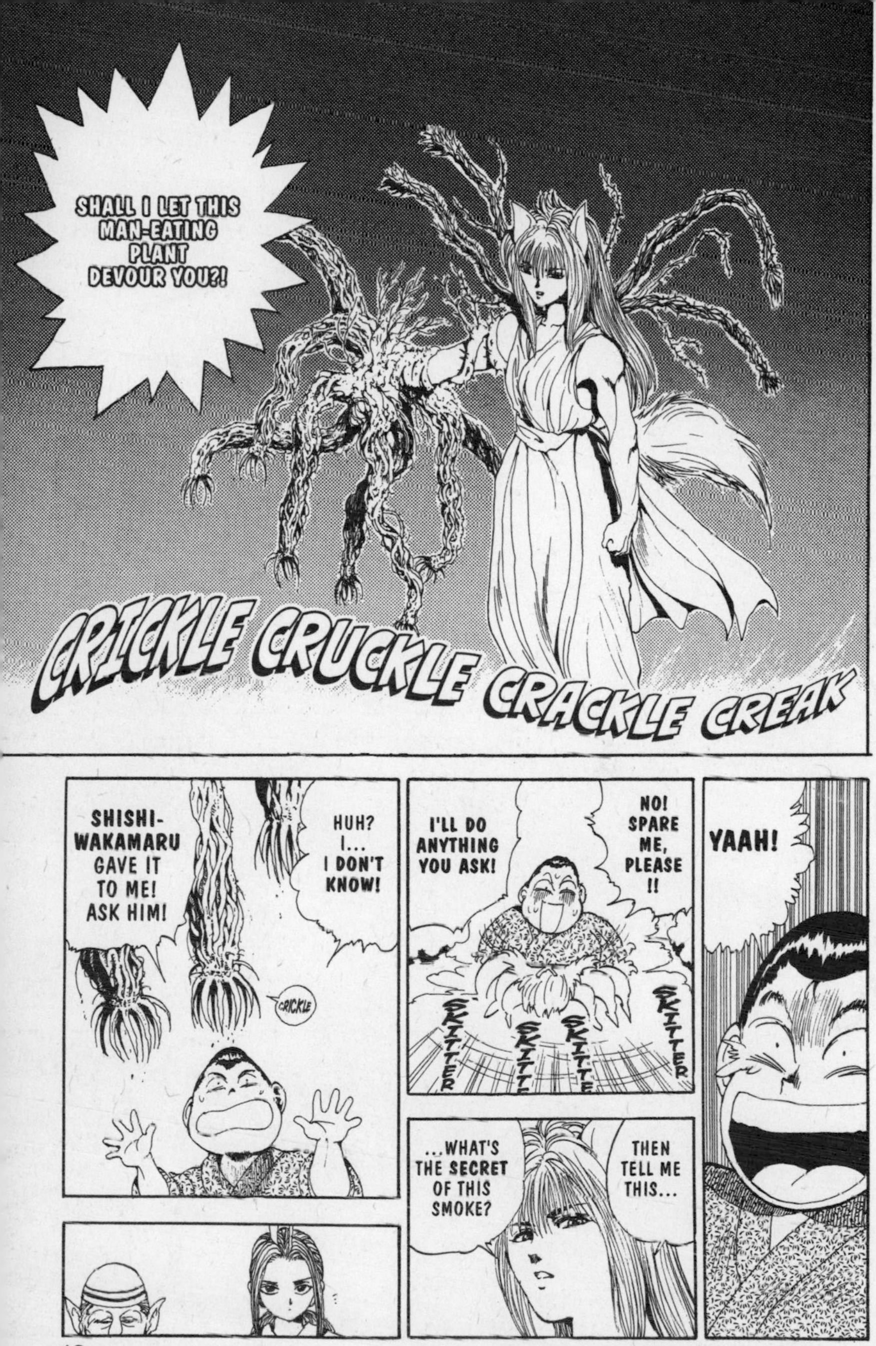
SHALL I LET THIS MAN-EATING PLANT DEVOUR YOU?!
CRICKLE CRUCKLE CRACKLE CREAK
YAAH!
NO! SPARE ME, PLEASE !!
I'LL DO ANYTHING YOU ASK!
SKITTER
SKITTER
SKITTER
SKITTER
THEN TELL ME THIS...
...WHAT'S THE SECRET OF THIS SMOKE?
HUH? I... I DON'T KNOW!
SHISHI-WAKAMARU GAVE IT TO ME! ASK HIM!
CRICKLE

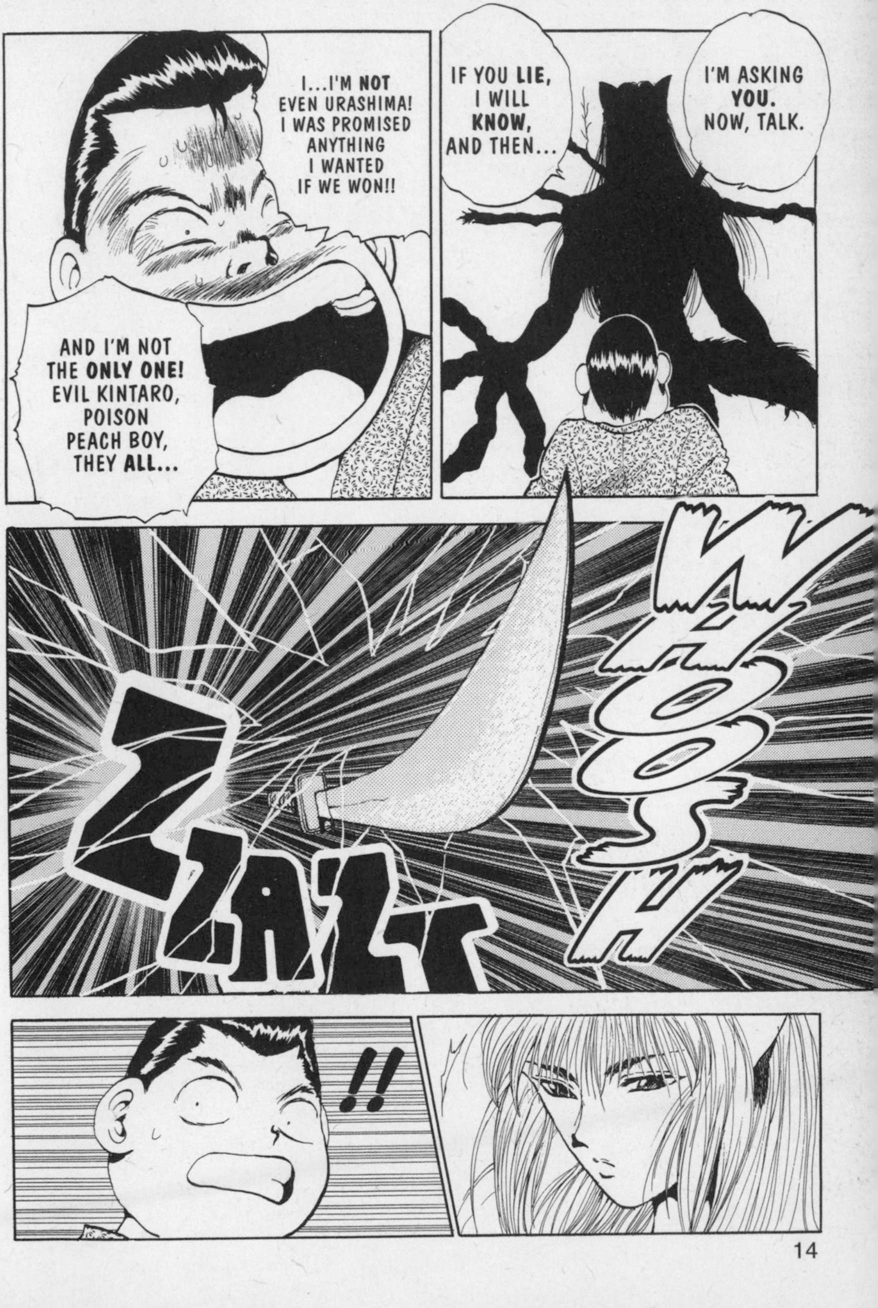
I'M ASKING YOU. NOW, TALK.
IF YOU LIE, I WILL KNOW, AND THEN...
I...I'M NOT EVEN URASHIMA! I WAS PROMISED ANYTHING I WANTED IF WE WON!!
AND I'M NOT THE ONLY ONE! EVIL KINTARO, POISON PEACH BOY, THEY ALL...
WHOOSH
!!

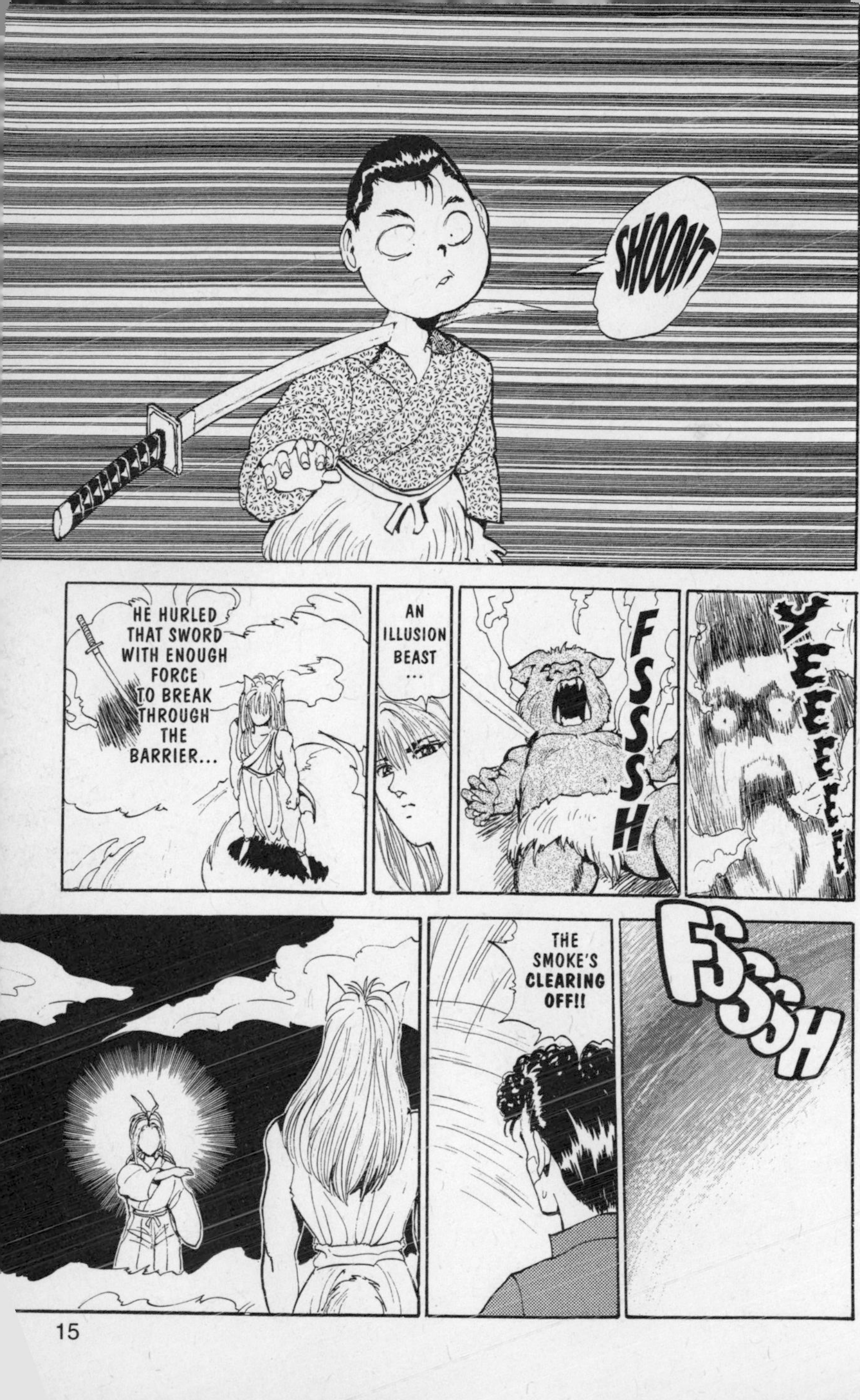
SHOONT
YEEEEEEE
FSSSH
AN ILLUSION BEAST...
HE HURLED THAT SWORD WITH ENOUGH FORCE TO BREAK THROUGH THE BARRIER...
FSSSH
THE SMOKE'S CLEARING OFF!!

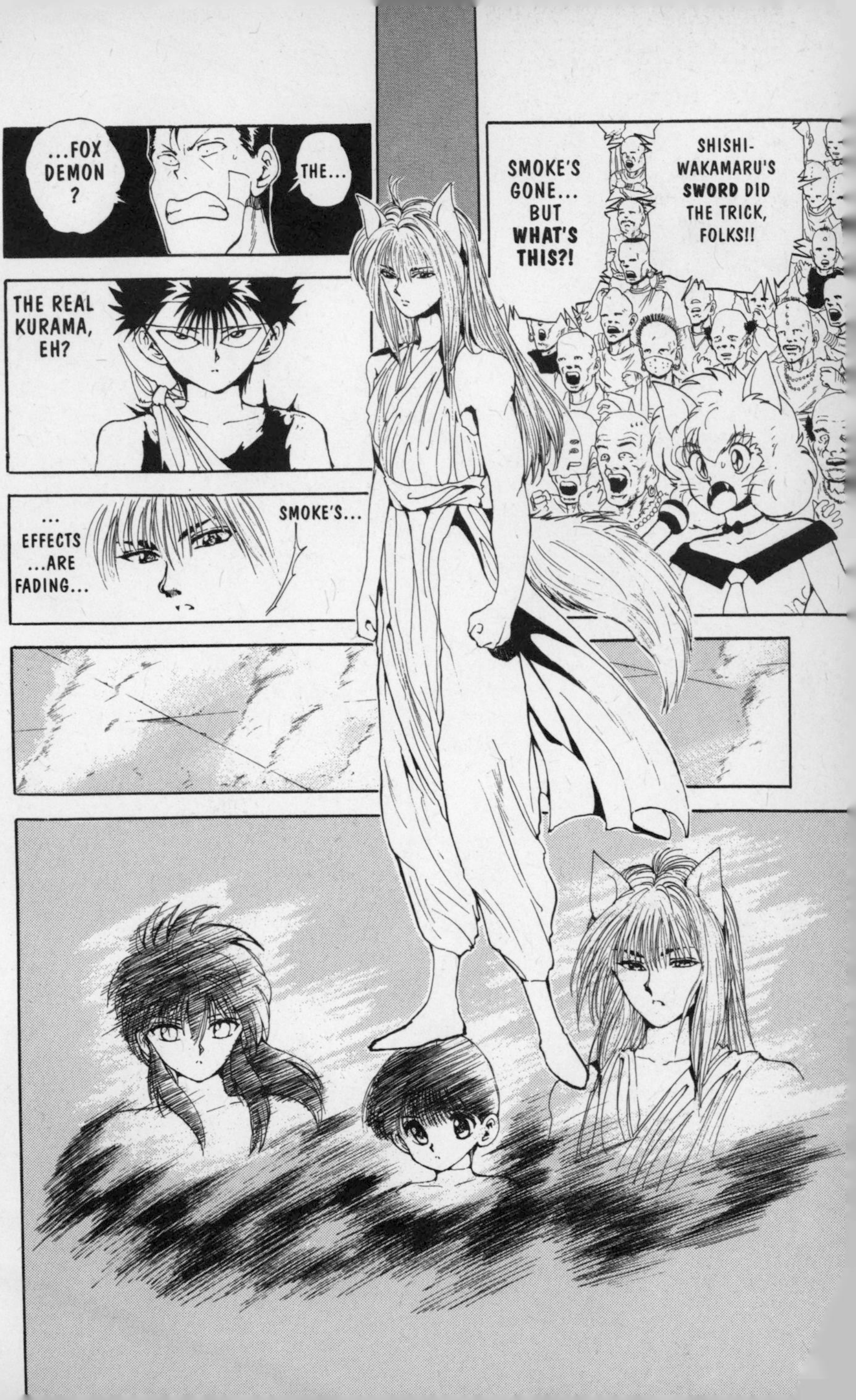
SHISHI-WAKAMARU'S SWORD DID THE TRICK, FOLKS!!
SMOKE'S GONE... BUT WHAT'S THIS?!
THE...
...FOX DEMON ?
THE REAL KURAMA, EH?
SMOKE'S...
... EFFECTS ...ARE FADING...

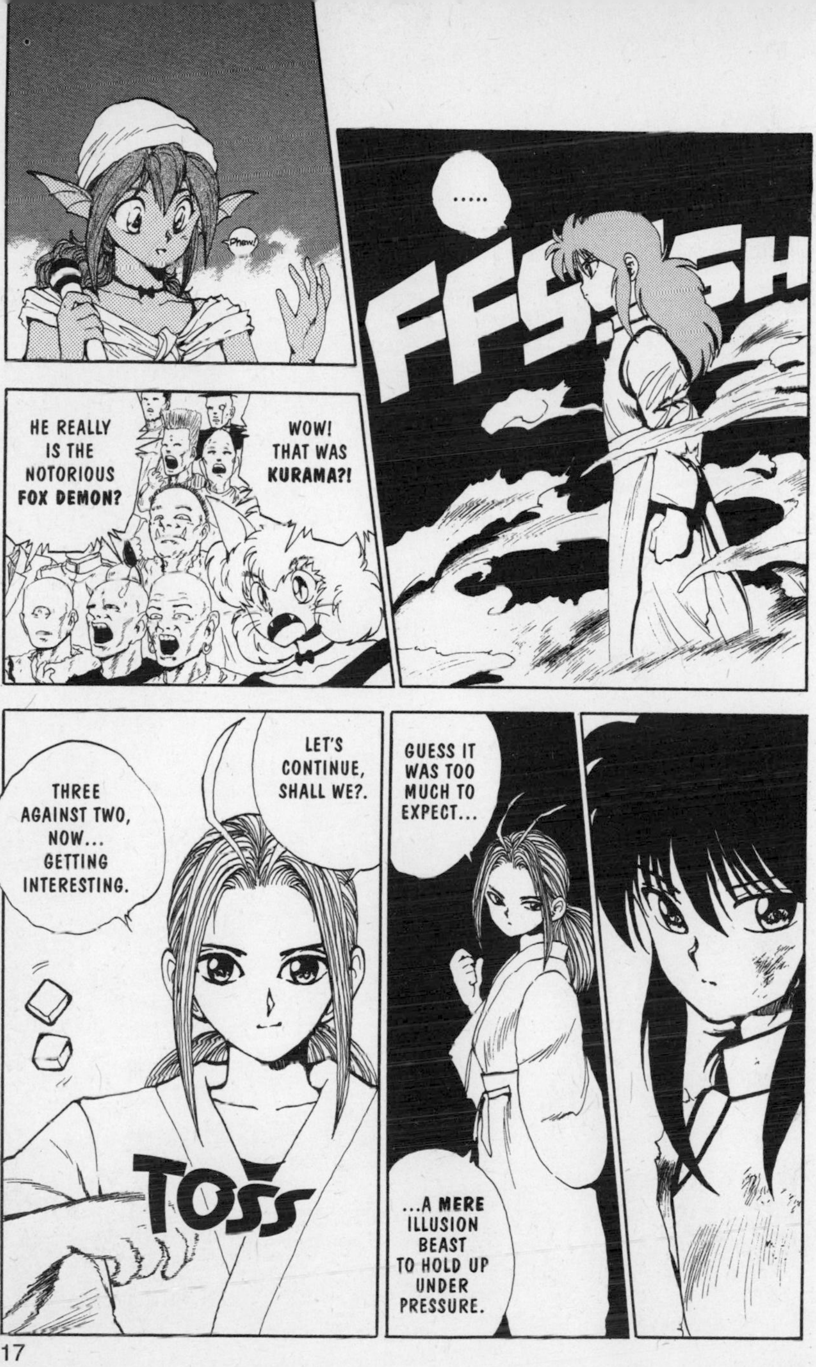
......
FFS SH
Phew!
WOW! THAT WAS KURAMA?!
HE REALLY IS THE NOTORIOUS FOX DEMON?
GUESS IT WAS TOO MUCH TO EXPECT...
...A MERE ILLUSION BEAST TO HOLD UP UNDER PRESSURE.
LET'S CONTINUE, SHALL WE?.
THREE AGAINST TWO, NOW... GETTING INTERESTING.
TOSS

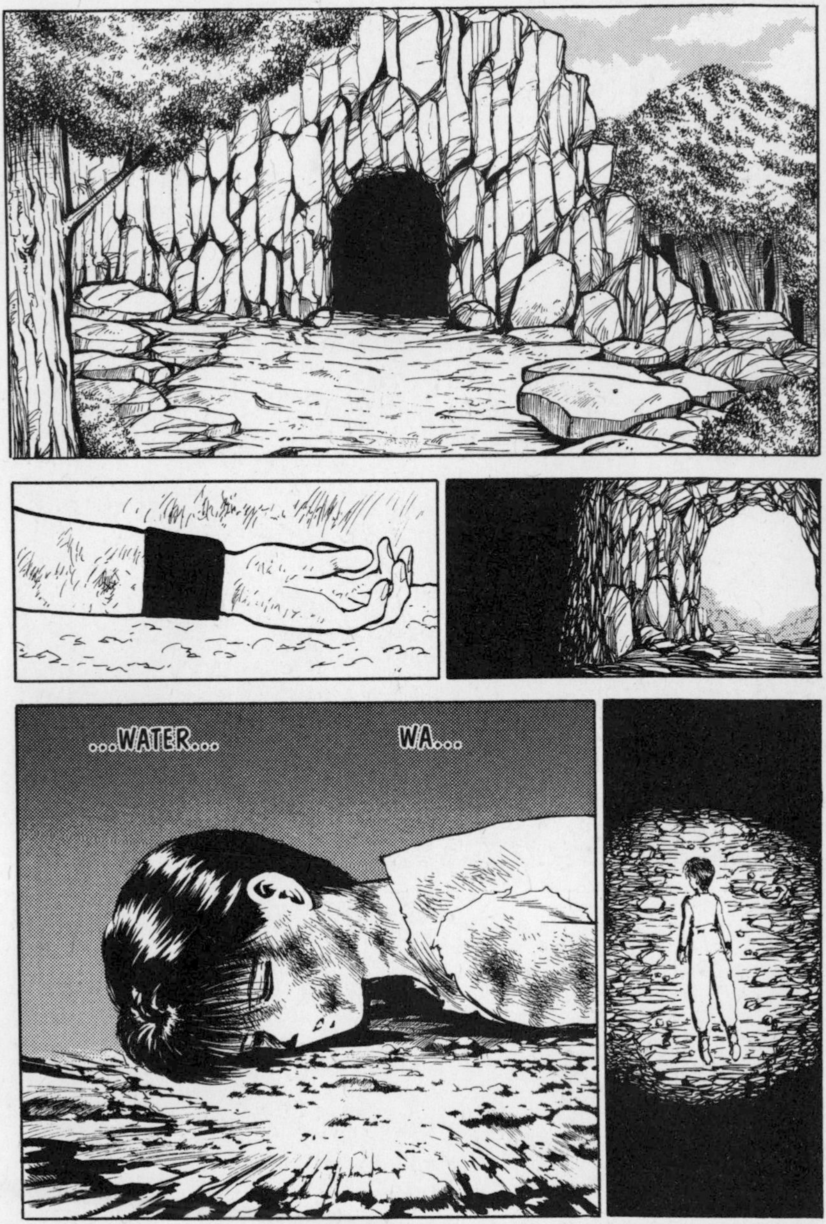
WA...
...WATER...

READ THIS WAY

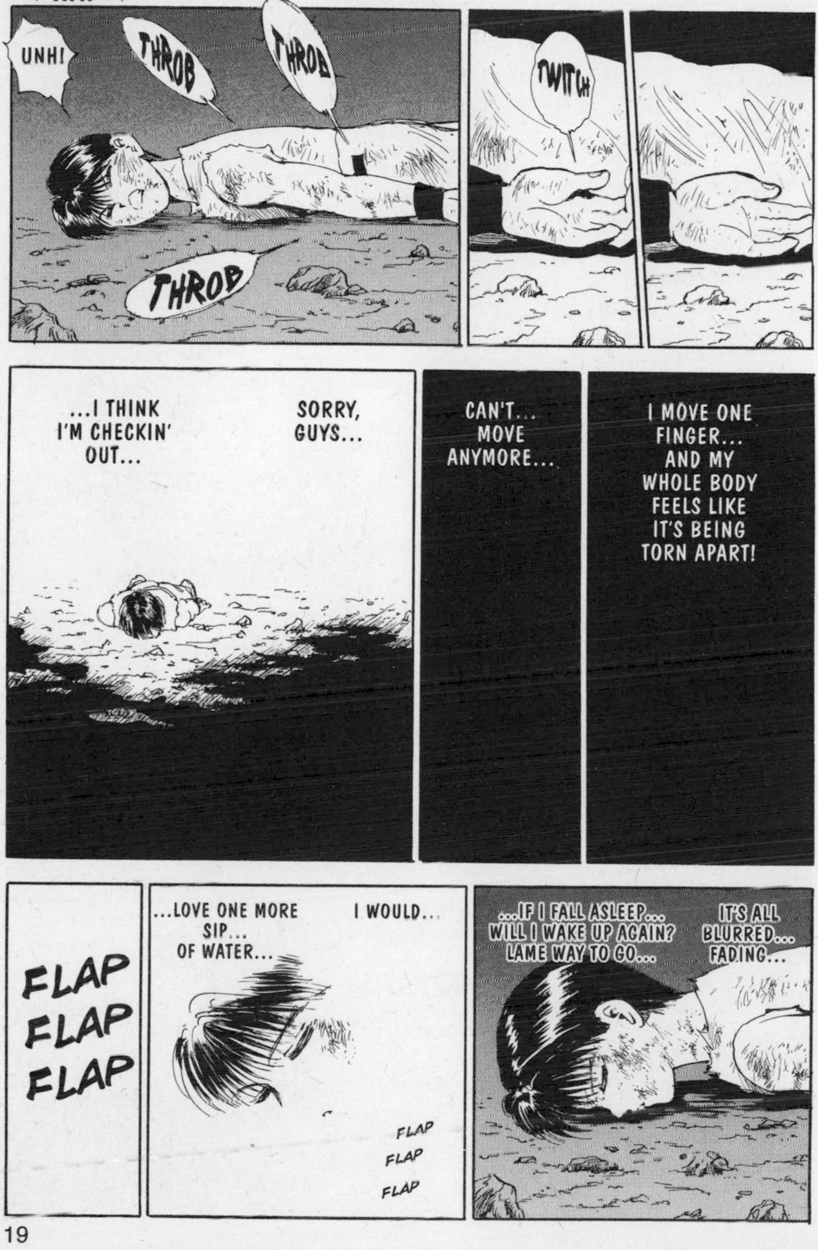

TWITCH
THROB
THROB
UNH!
THROB
I MOVE ONE FINGER... AND MY WHOLE BODY FEELS LIKE IT'S BEING TORN APART!
CAN'T... MOVE ANYMORE...
SORRY, GUYS...
...I THINK I'M CHECKIN' OUT...
IT'S ALL BLURRED... FADING...
...IF I FALL ASLEEP... WILL I WAKE UP AGAIN? LAME WAY TO GO...
I WOULD...
...LOVE ONE MORE SIP... OF WATER...
FLAP FLAP FLAP
FLAP FLAP FLAP

PLIP
PLIP
LICK
HUH? WATER...?
WATER... DELICIOUS! THE MOST DELICIOUS I'VE EVER...
CREAK
P-PU...?
PU

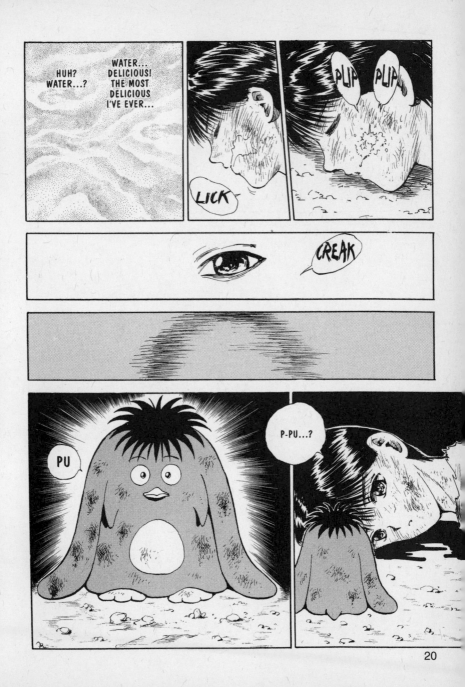

READ THIS WAY

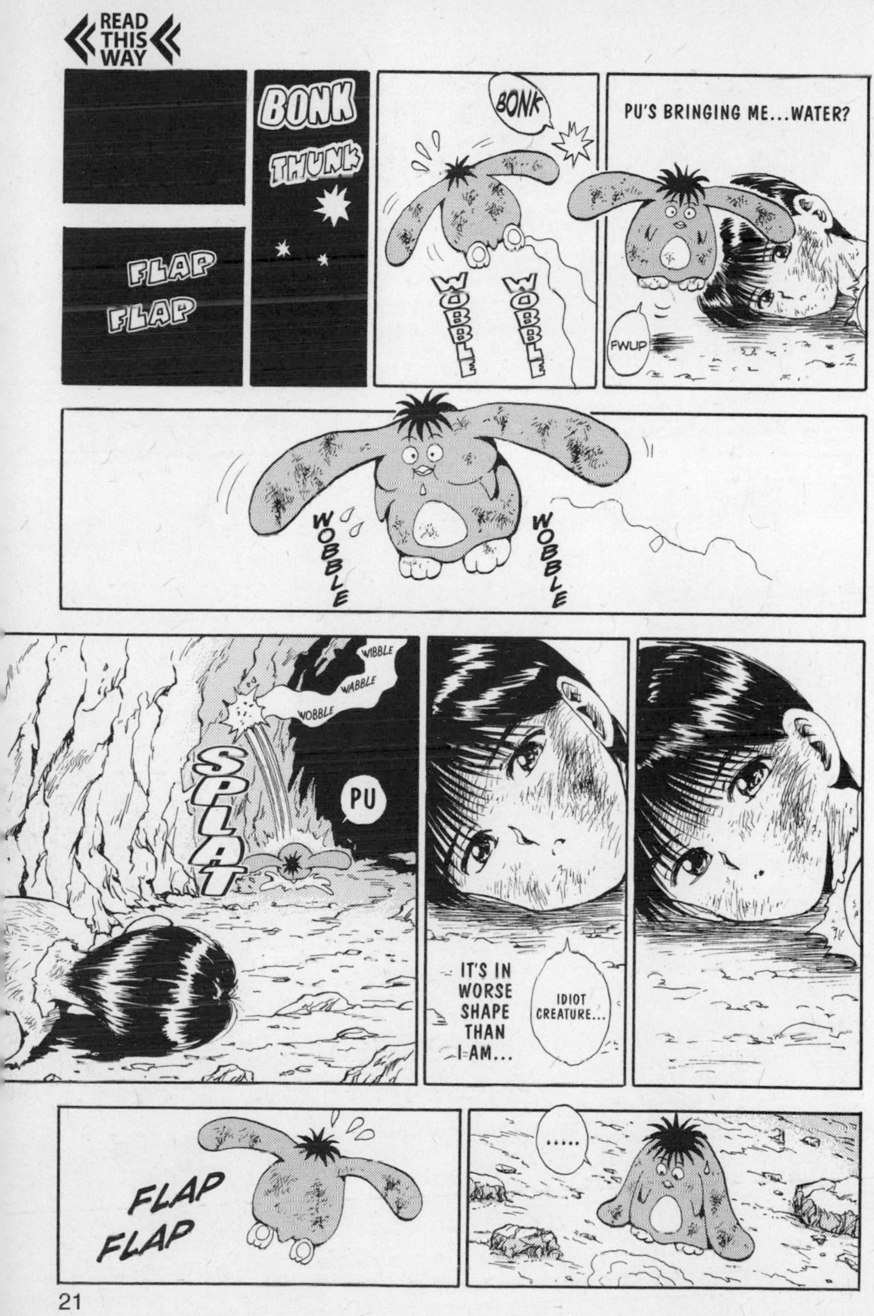
PU'S BRINGING ME...WATER?
FWUP
BONK
WOBBLE
WOBBLE
BONK
THUNK
FLAP
FLAP
WOBBLE
WOBBLE
IDIOT CREATURE...
IT'S IN WORSE SHAPE THAN I AM...
WIBBLE
WABBLE
WOBBLE
SPLAT
PU
......
FLAP
FLAP

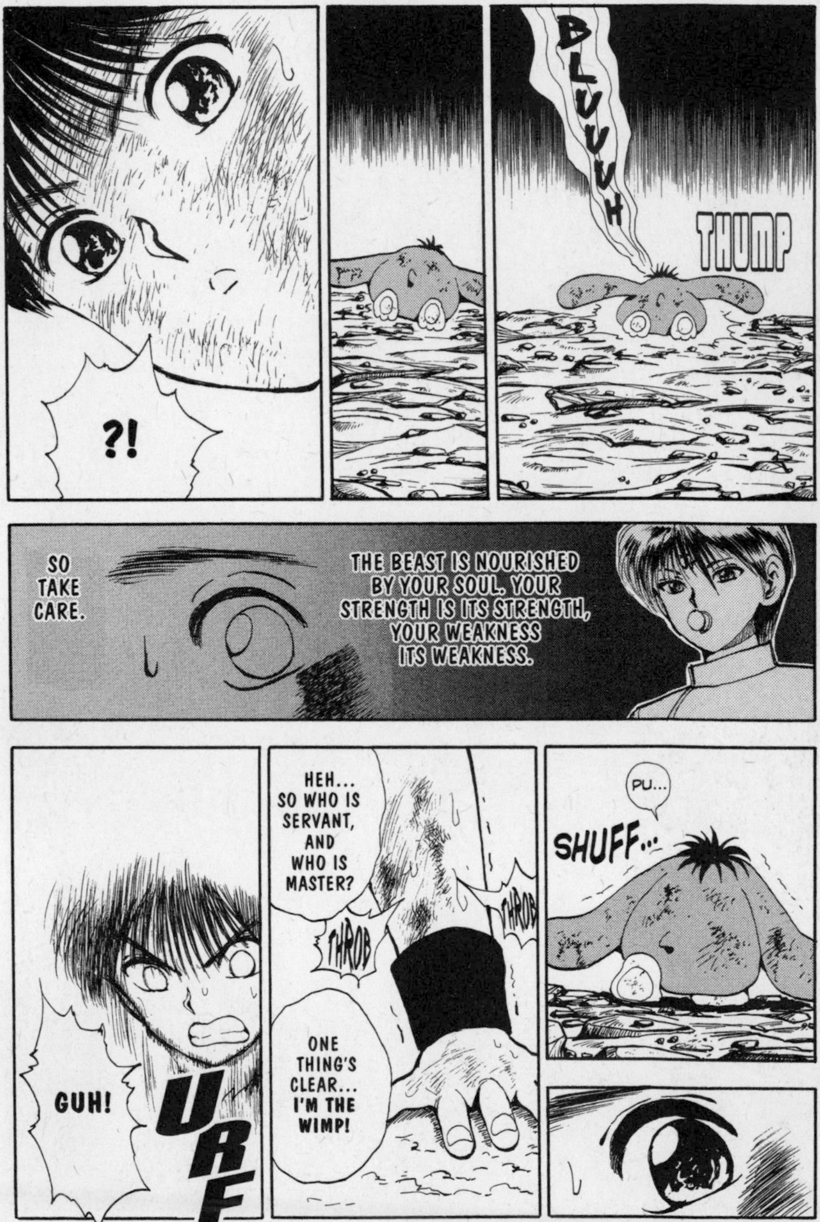
BLUUUH
THUMP
?!
THE BEAST IS NOURISHED BY YOUR SOUL. YOUR STRENGTH IS ITS STRENGTH, YOUR WEAKNESS ITS WEAKNESS.
SO TAKE CARE.
PU...
SHUFF...
HEH... SO WHO IS SERVANT, AND WHO IS MASTER?
THROB
THROB
ONE THING'S CLEAR... I'M THE WIMP!
GUH!
URF

READ THIS WAY

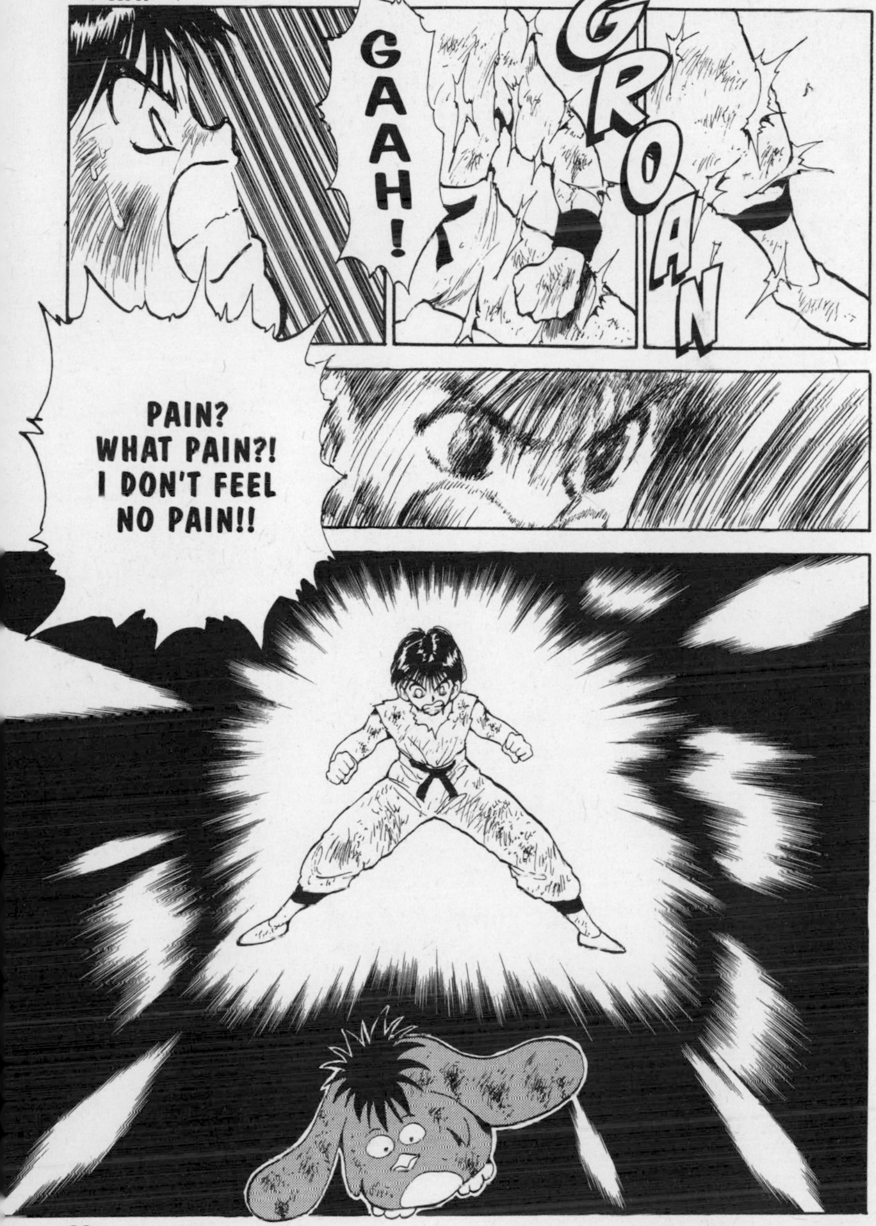

GROAN
GAAH!
PAIN? WHAT PAIN?! I DON'T FEEL NO PAIN!!

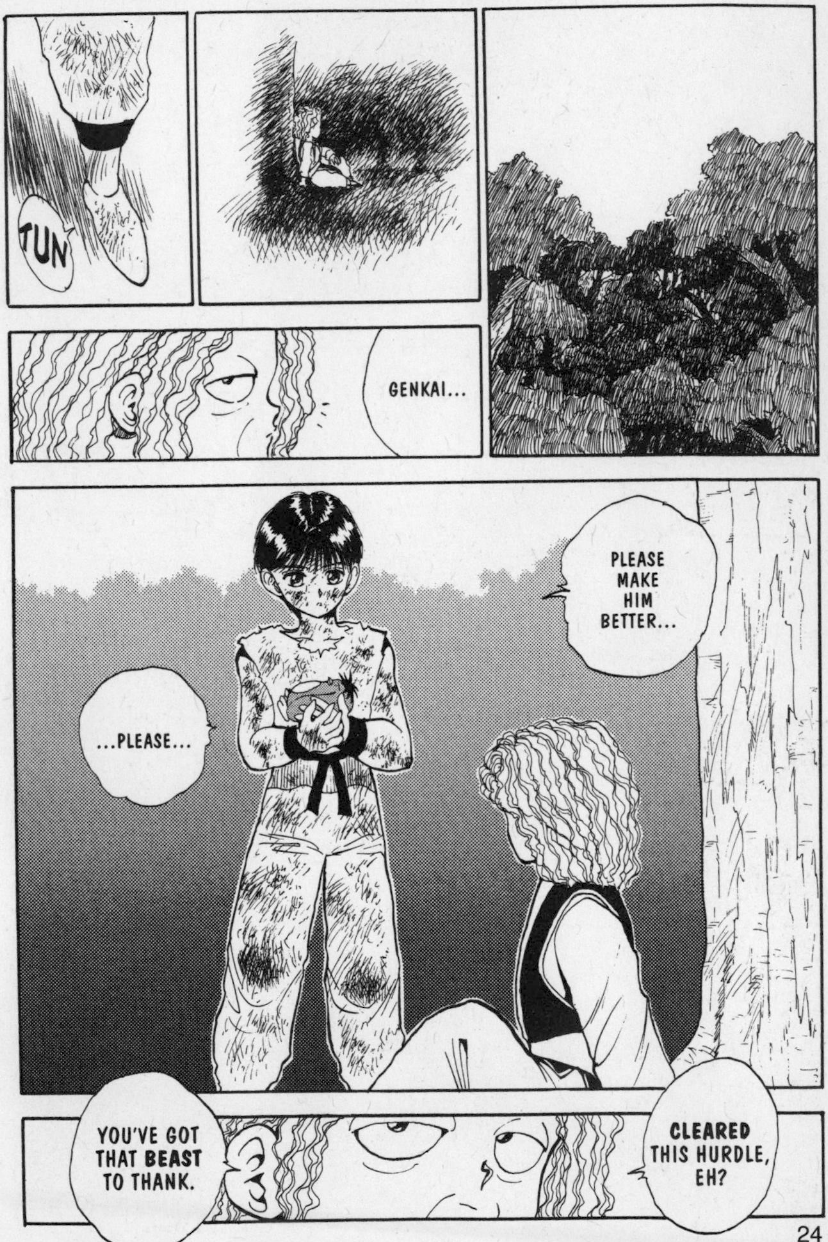
TUN
GENKAI...
PLEASE MAKE HIM BETTER...
...PLEASE...
CLEARED THIS HURDLE, EH?
YOU'VE GOT THAT BEAST TO THANK.

READ THIS WAY

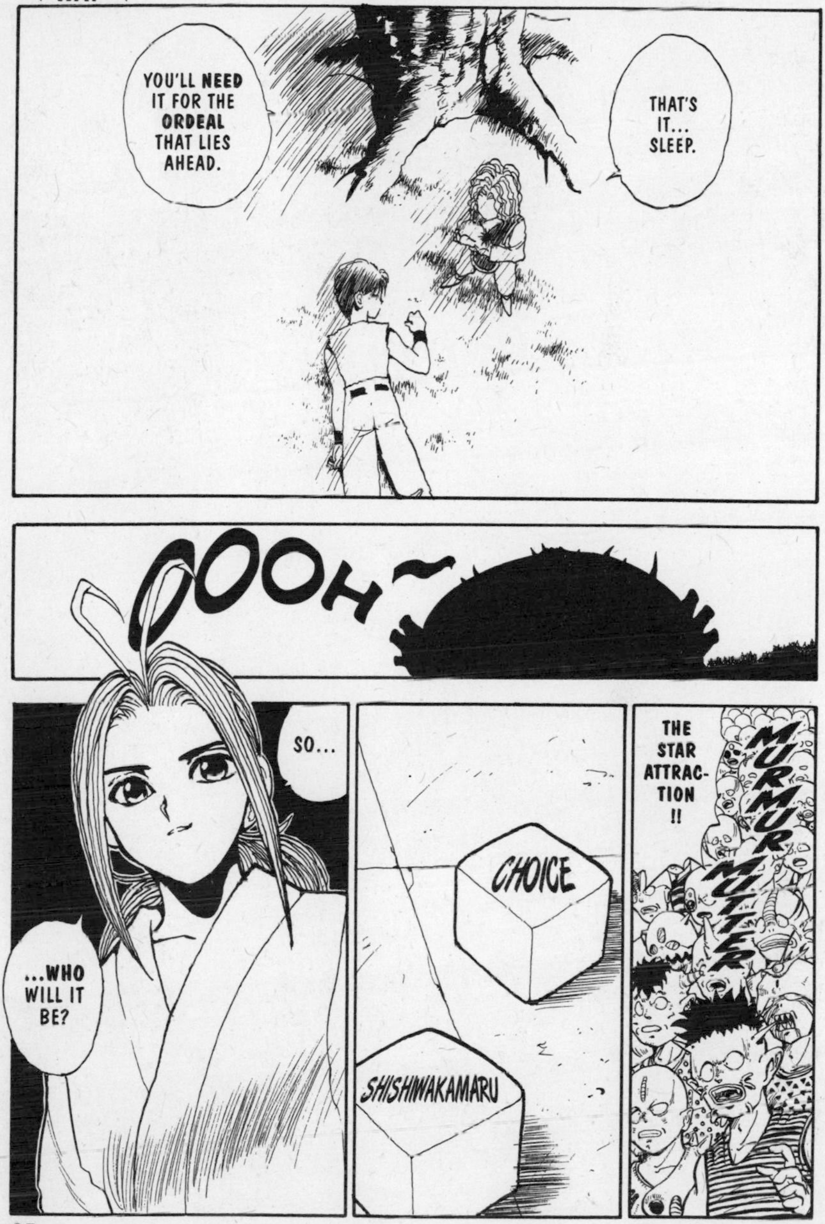
THAT'S IT... SLEEP.
YOU'LL NEED IT FOR THE ORDEAL THAT LIES AHEAD.
OOOH~
THE STAR ATTRACTION!!
MURMUR MUTTER
CHOICE
SHISHWAKAMARU
SO...
...WHO WILL IT BE?

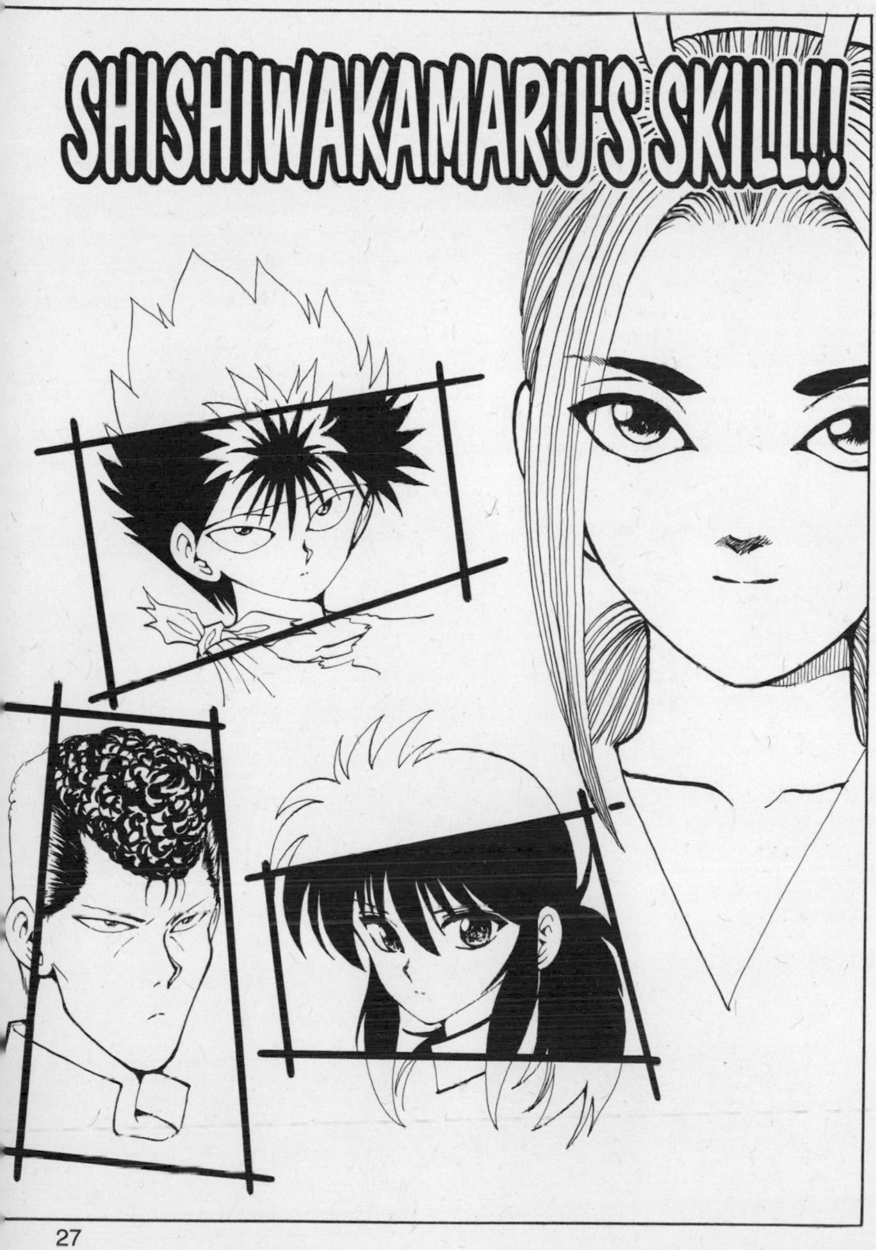
SHISHIWAKAMARU'S SKILL!!

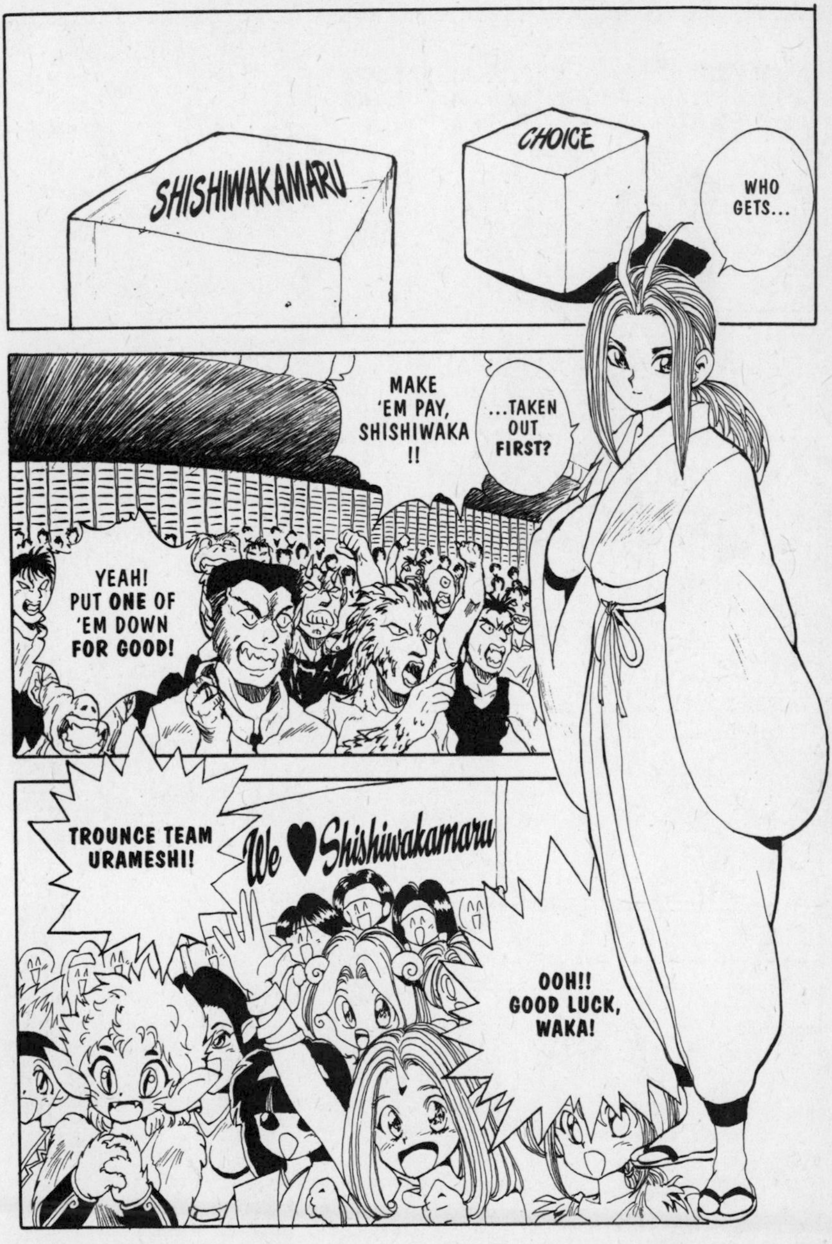
WHO GETS...
CHOICE
SHISHIWAKAMARU
...TAKEN OUT FIRST?
MAKE 'EM PAY, SHISHIWAKA !!
YEAH! PUT ONE OF 'EM DOWN FOR GOOD!
OOH!! GOOD LUCK, WAKA!
We ♥ Shishiwakamaru
TROUNCE TEAM URAMESHI!

READ THIS WAY

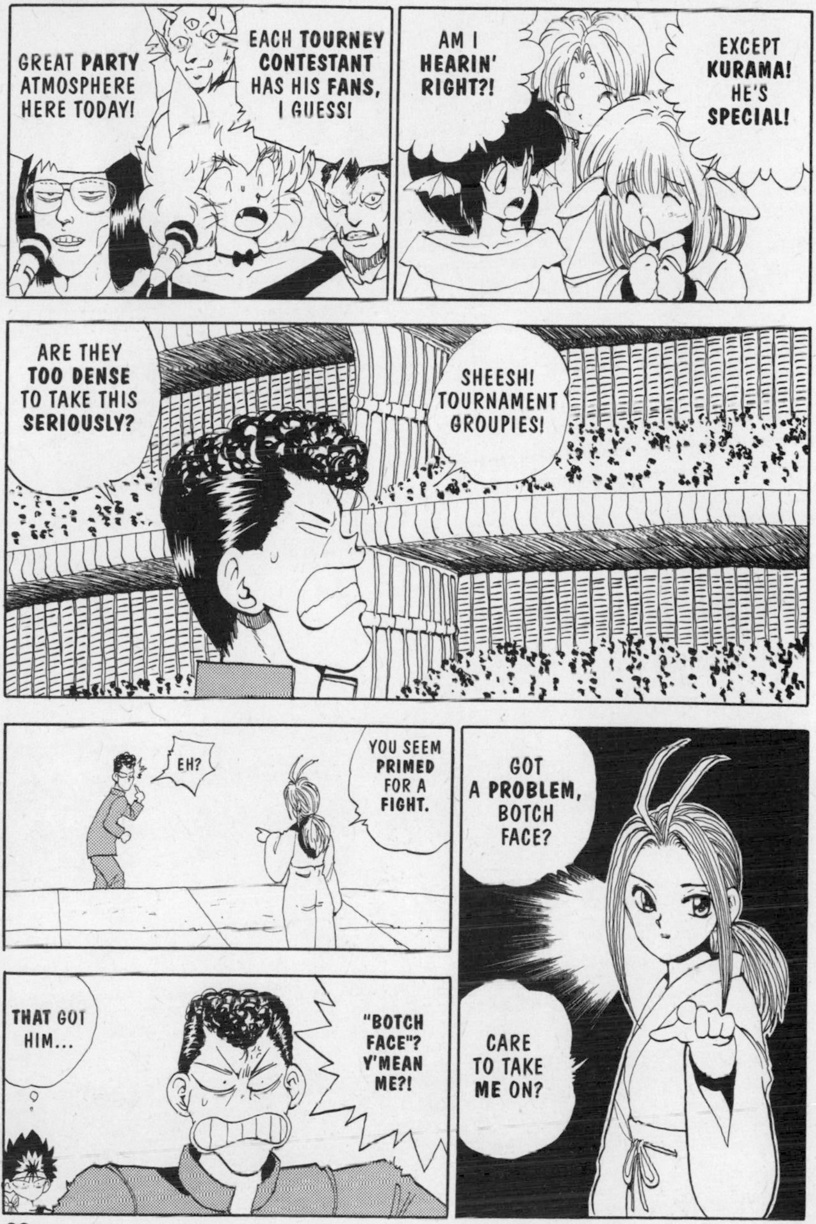
EXCEPT KURAMA! HE'S SPECIAL!
AM I HEARIN' RIGHT?!
EACH TOURNEY CONTESTANT HAS HIS FANS, I GUESS!
GREAT PARTY ATMOSPHERE HERE TODAY!
SHEESH! TOURNAMENT GROUPIES!
ARE THEY TOO DENSE TO TAKE THIS SERIOUSLY?
GOT A PROBLEM, BOTCH FACE?
CARE TO TAKE ME ON?
YOU SEEM PRIMED FOR A FIGHT.
EH?
"BOTCH FACE"? Y'MEAN ME?!
THAT GOT HIM...

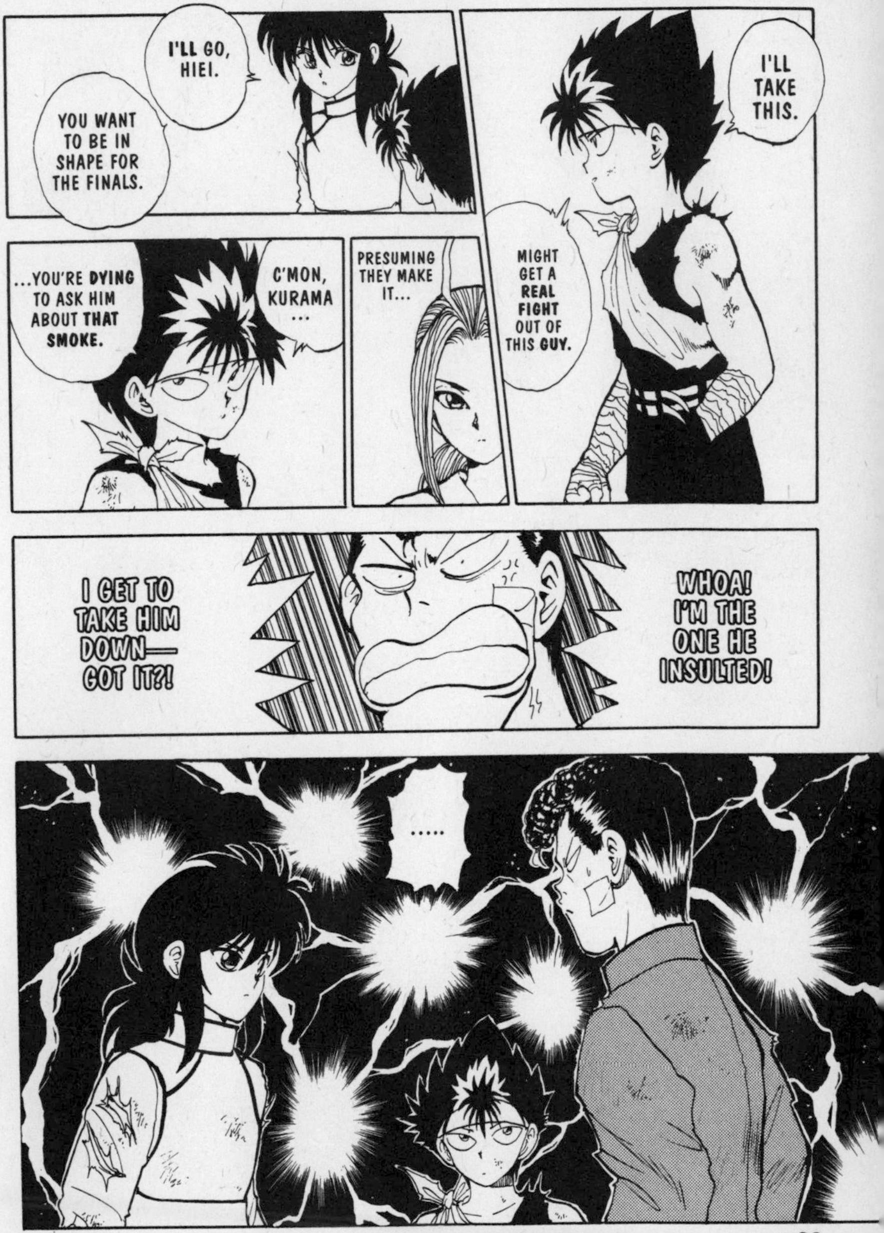
I'LL TAKE THIS.
MIGHT GET A REAL FIGHT OUT OF THIS GUY.
I'LL GO, HIEI.
YOU WANT TO BE IN SHAPE FOR THE FINALS.
PRESUMING THEY MAKE IT...
C'MON, KURAMA...
...YOU'RE DYING TO ASK HIM ABOUT THAT SMOKE.
WHOA! I'M THE ONE HE INSULTED!
I GET TO TAKE HIM DOWN—GOT IT?!
.....

READ THIS WAY

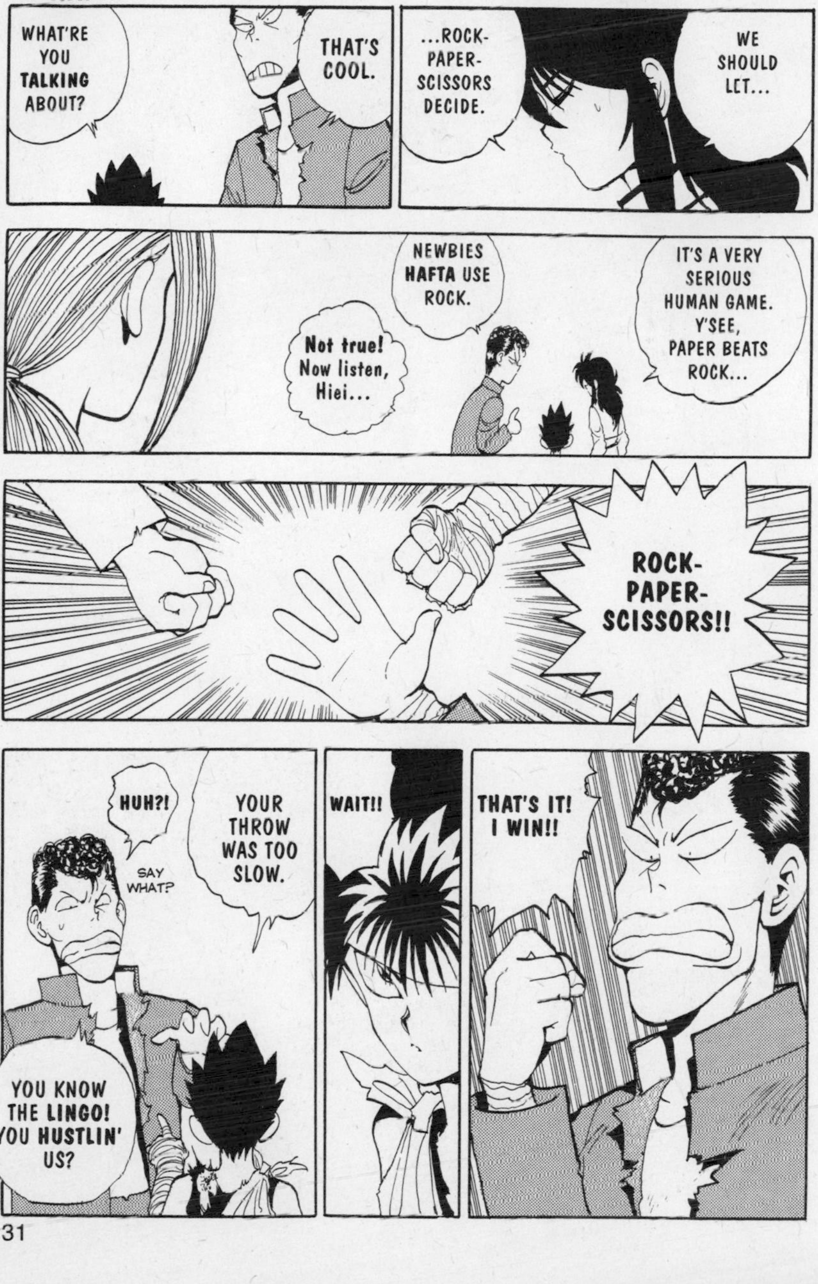

WE SHOULD LET...
...ROCK-PAPER-SCISSORS DECIDE.
THAT'S COOL.
WHAT'RE YOU TALKING ABOUT?
IT'S A VERY SERIOUS HUMAN GAME. Y'SEE, PAPER BEATS ROCK...
NEWBIES HAFTA USE ROCK.
Not true! Now listen, Hiei...
ROCK-PAPER-SCISSORS!!
THAT'S IT! I WIN!!
WAIT!!
YOUR THROW WAS TOO SLOW.
HUH?!
SAY WHAT?
YOU KNOW THE LINGO! YOU HUSTLIN' US?

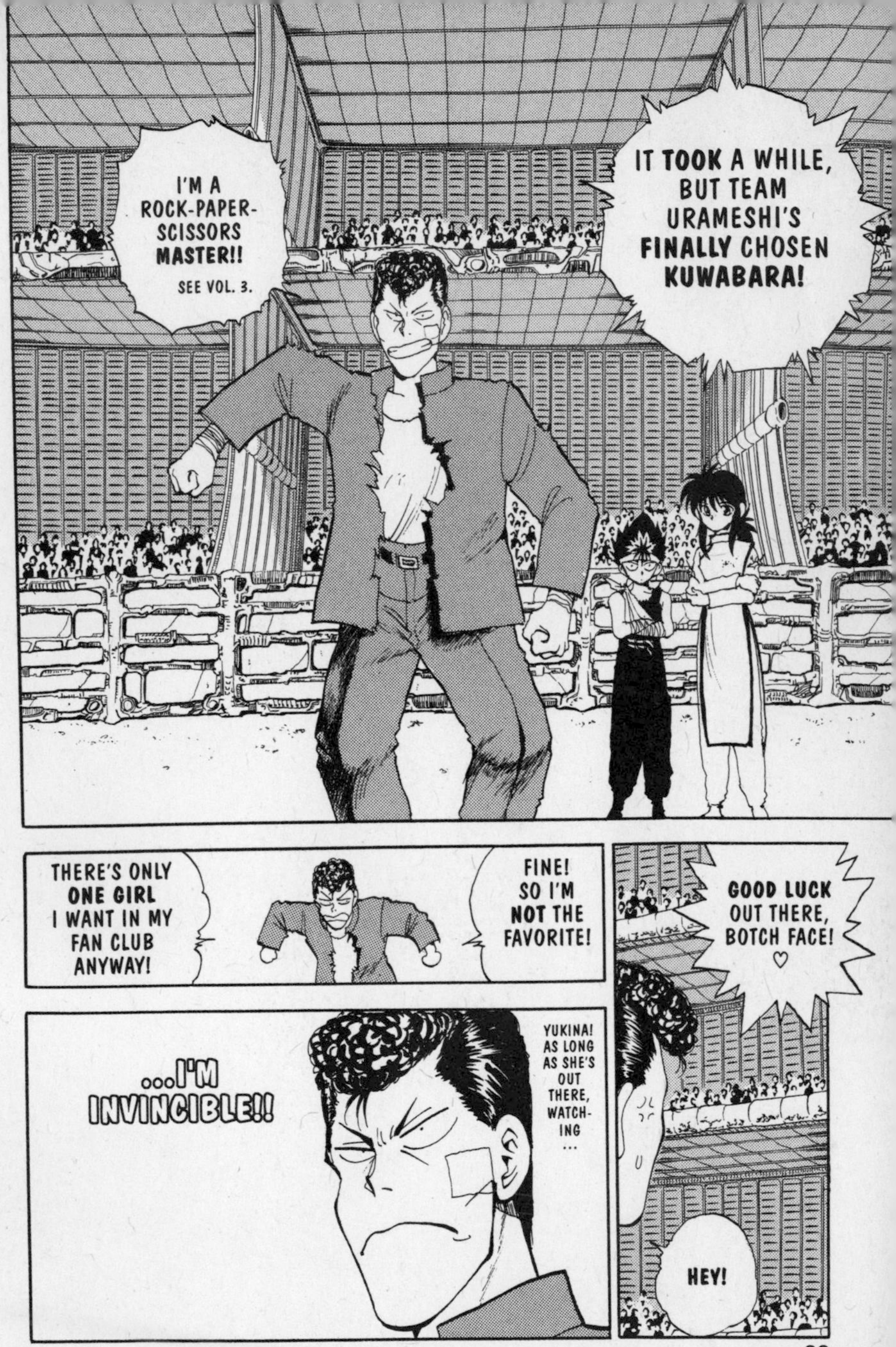
IT TOOK A WHILE, BUT TEAM URAMESHI'S FINALLY CHOSEN KUWABARA!
I'M A ROCK-PAPER-SCISSORS MASTER!!
SEE VOL. 3.
GOOD LUCK OUT THERE, BOTCH FACE! ♡
HEY!
FINE! SO I'M NOT THE FAVORITE!
THERE'S ONLY ONE GIRL I WANT IN MY FAN CLUB ANYWAY!
YUKINA! AS LONG AS SHE'S OUT THERE, WATCHING...
...I'M INVINCIBLE!!

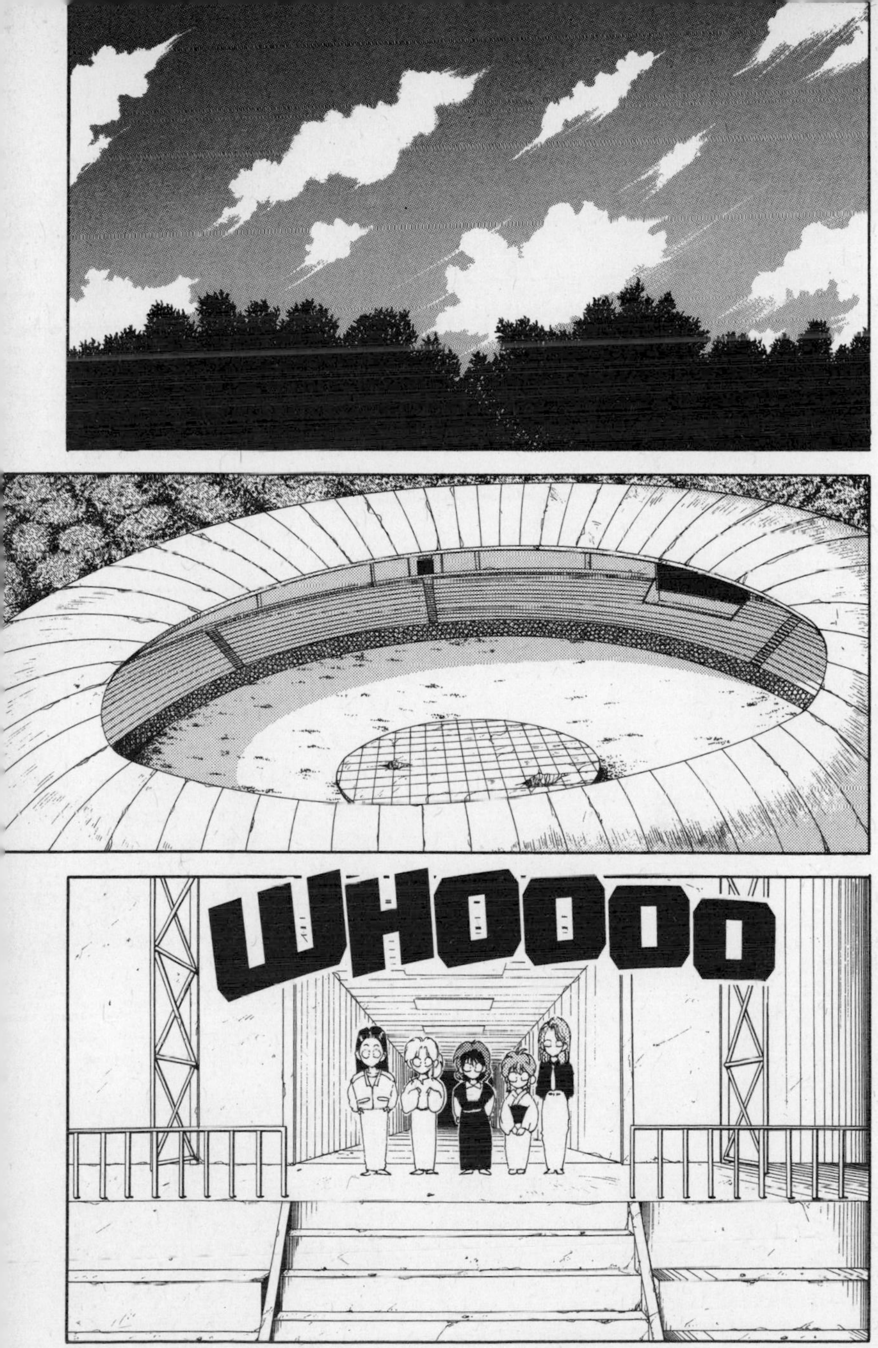
WHOOOO

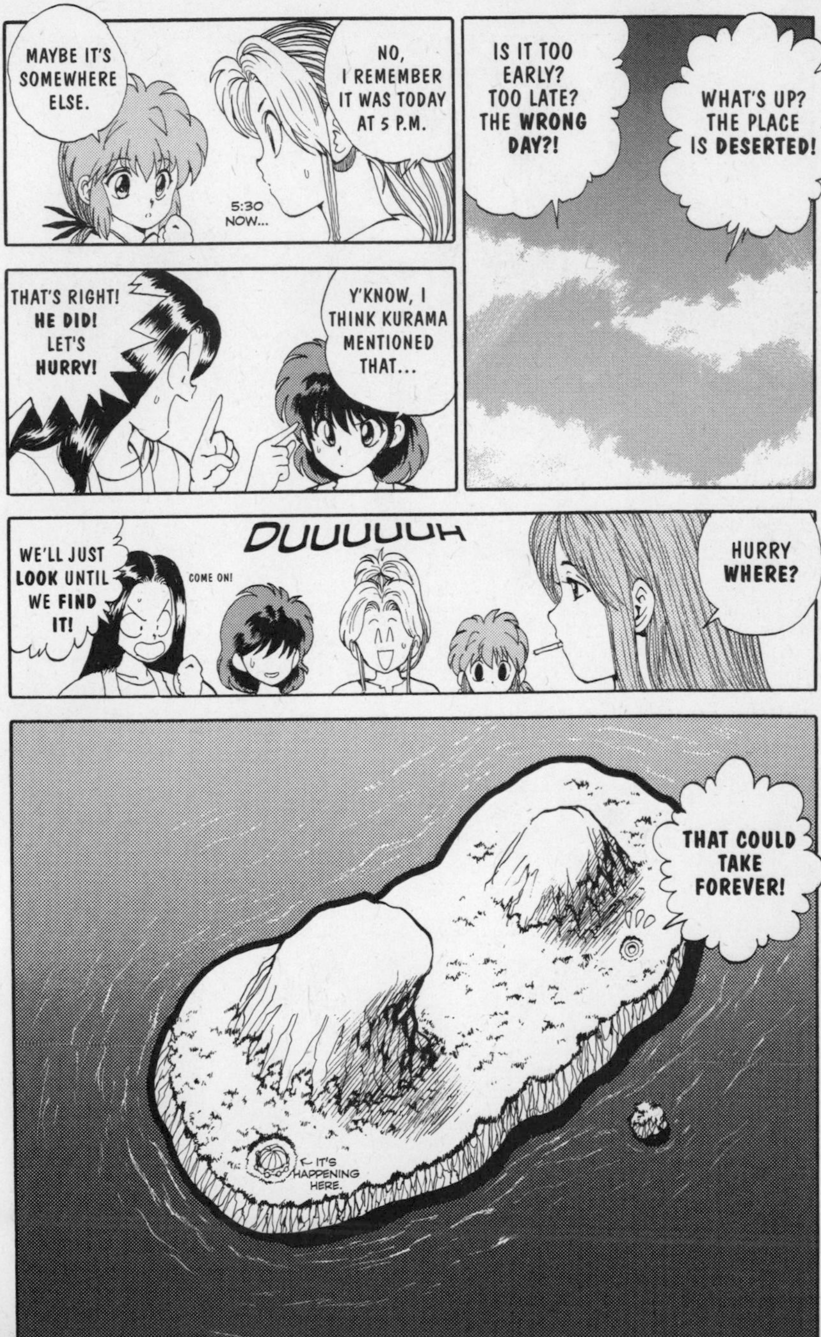
WHAT'S UP? THE PLACE IS DESERTED!
IS IT TOO EARLY? TOO LATE? THE WRONG DAY?!
NO, I REMEMBER IT WAS TODAY AT 5 P.M.
5:30 NOW...
MAYBE IT'S SOMEWHERE ELSE.
Y'KNOW, I THINK KURAMA MENTIONED THAT...
THAT'S RIGHT! HE DID! LET'S HURRY!
HURRY WHERE?
DUUUUUH
COME ON!
WE'LL JUST LOOK UNTIL WE FIND IT!
THAT COULD TAKE FOREVER!
← IT'S HAPPENING HERE.

READ THIS WAY

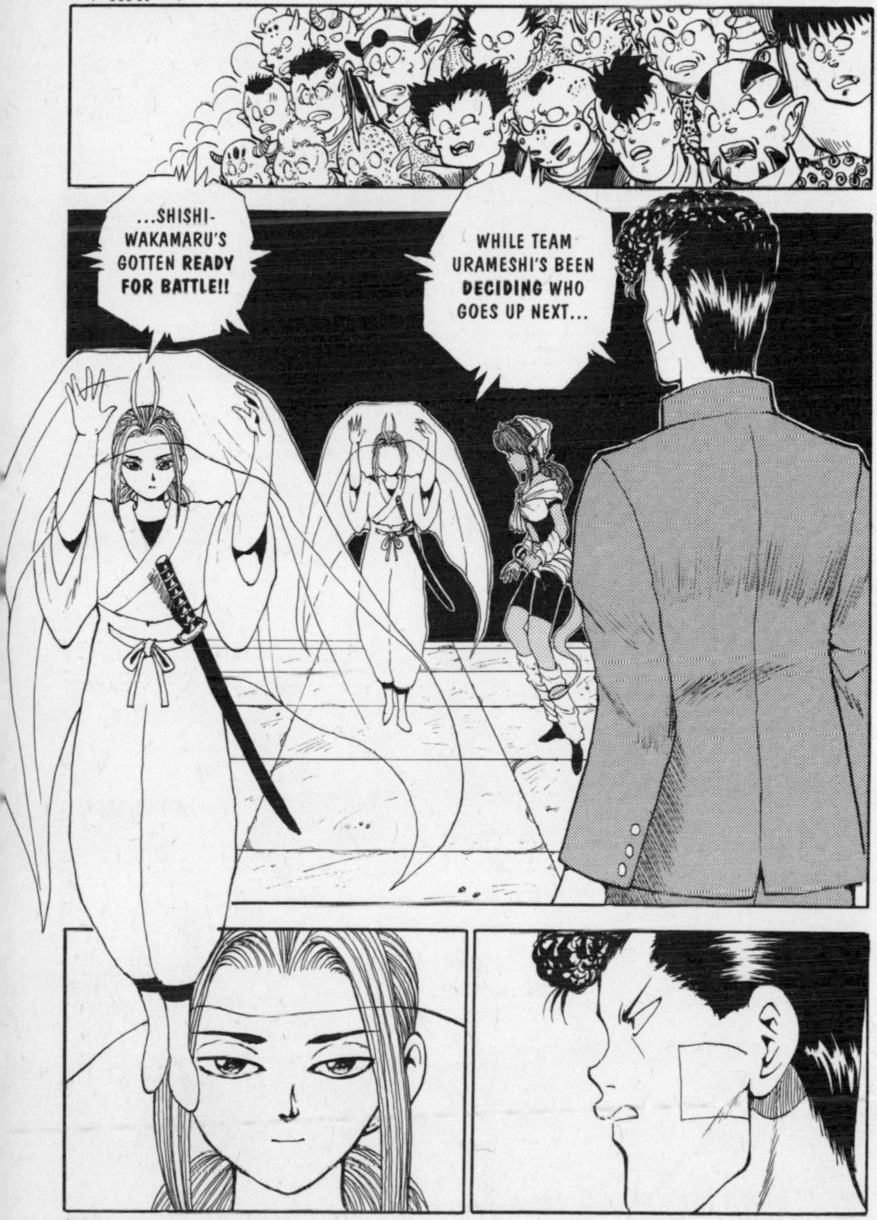
WHILE TEAM URAMESHI'S BEEN DECIDING WHO GOES UP NEXT...
...SHISHI-WAKAMARU'S GOTTEN READY FOR BATTLE!!

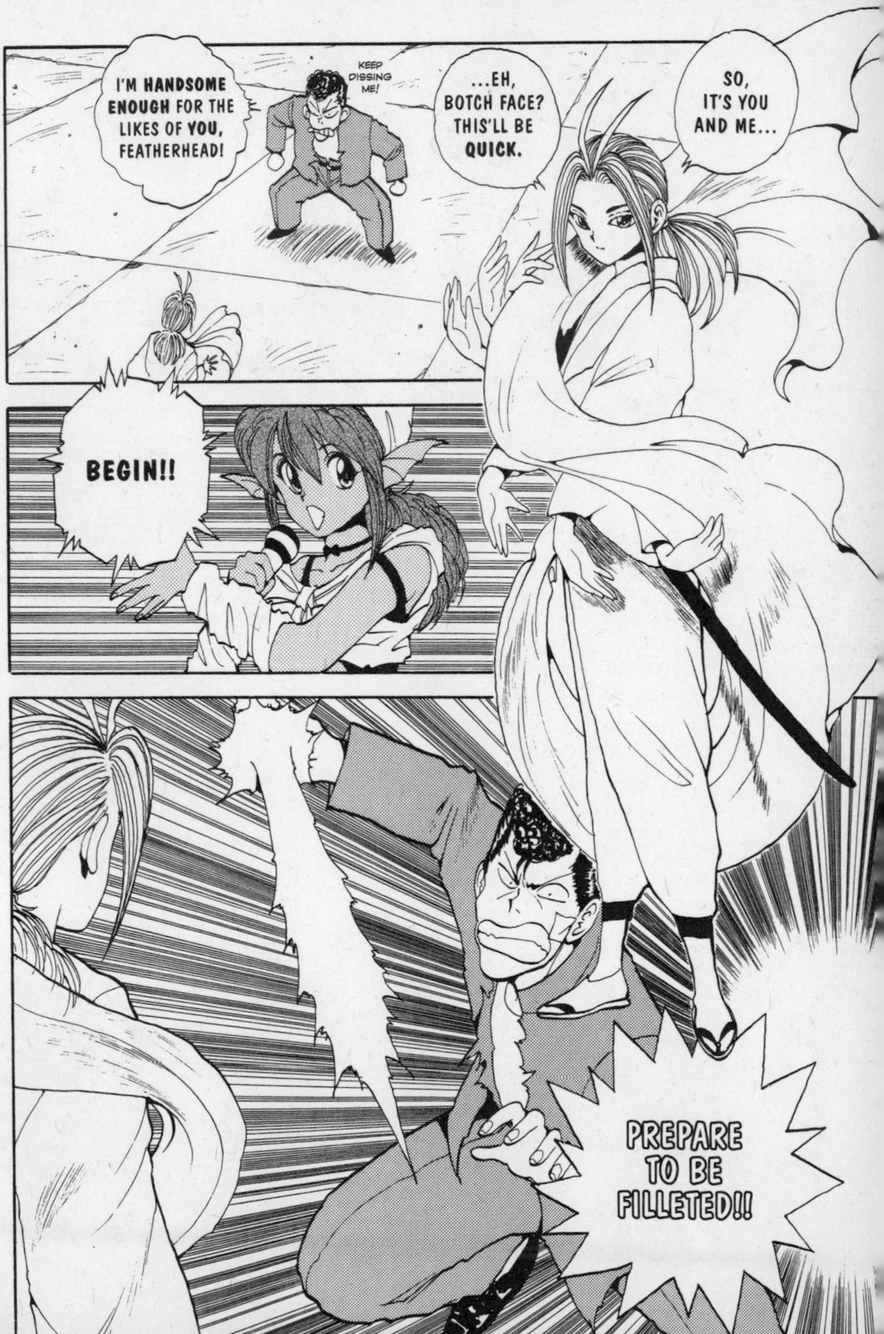
SO, IT'S YOU AND ME...
...EH, BOTCH FACE? THIS'LL BE QUICK.
KEEP DISSING ME!
I'M HANDSOME ENOUGH FOR THE LIKES OF YOU, FEATHERHEAD!
BEGIN!!
PREPARE TO BE FILLETED!!

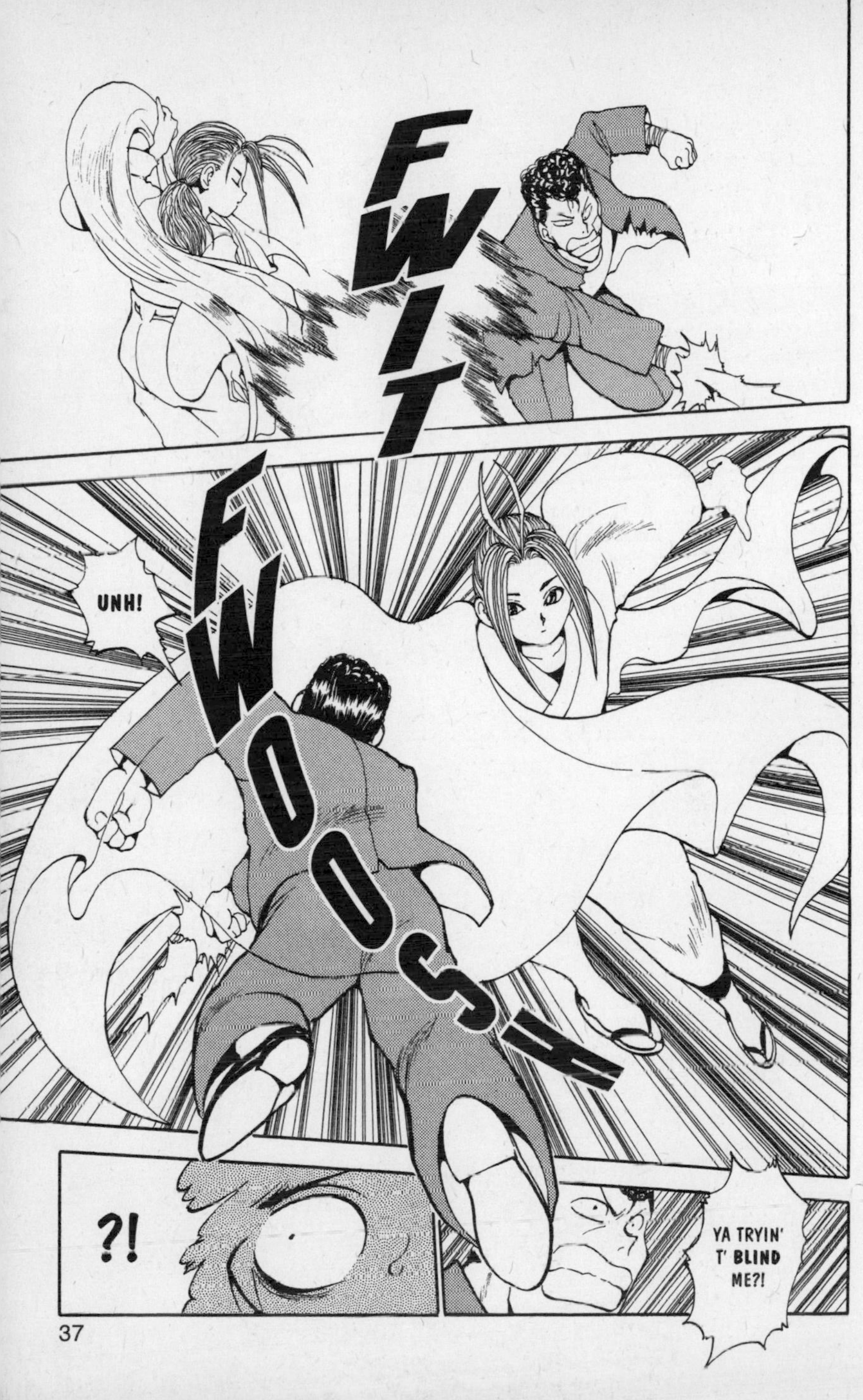
FWIT
UNH!
FWOOSH
YA TRYIN' T' BLIND ME?!
?!

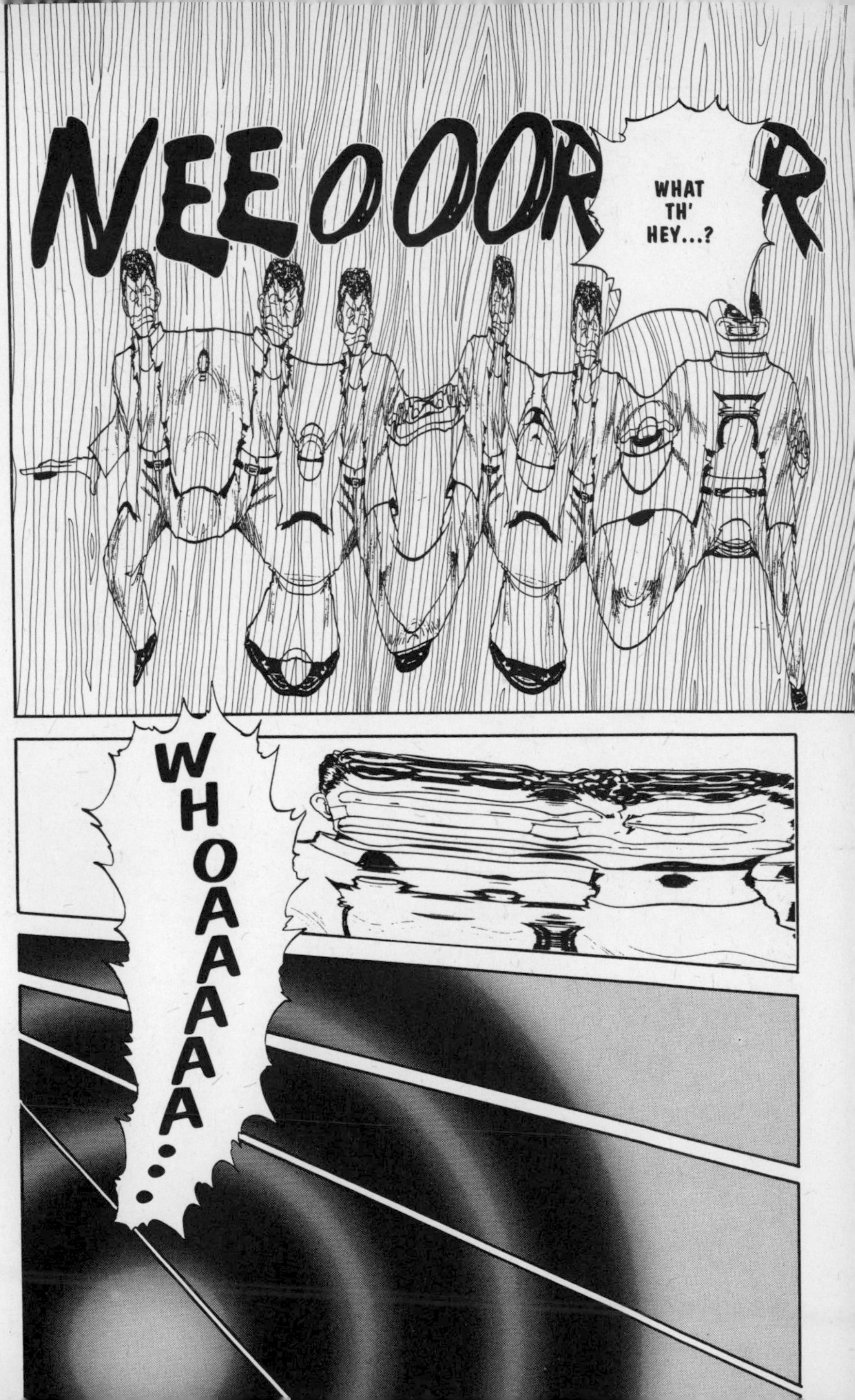
NEEOOOR R
WHAT TH' HEY...?
WHOAAAAAA...

READ THIS WAY

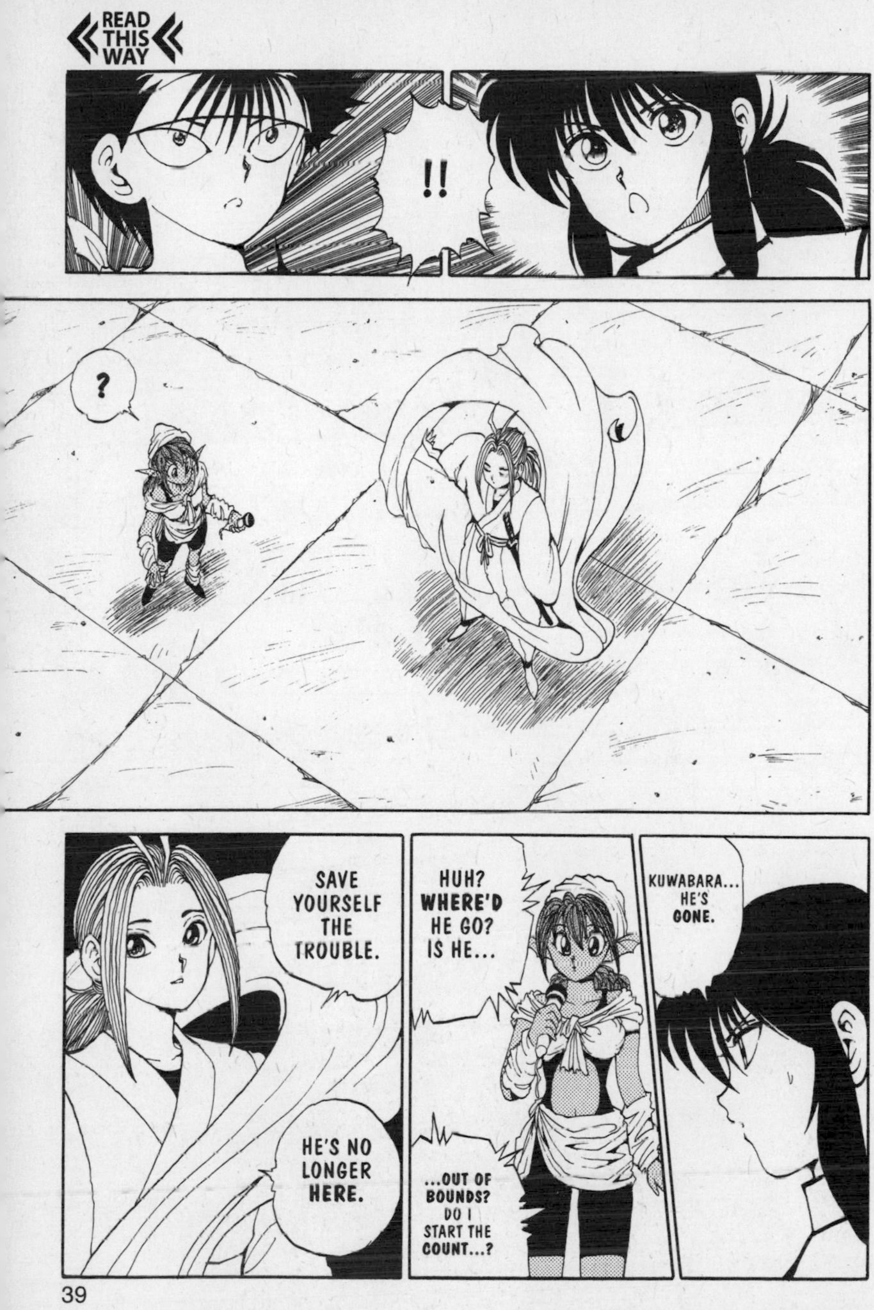
!!
?
KUWABARA... HE'S GONE.
HUH? WHERE'D HE GO? IS HE...
...OUT OF BOUNDS? DO I START THE COUNT...?
SAVE YOURSELF THE TROUBLE.
HE'S NO LONGER HERE.

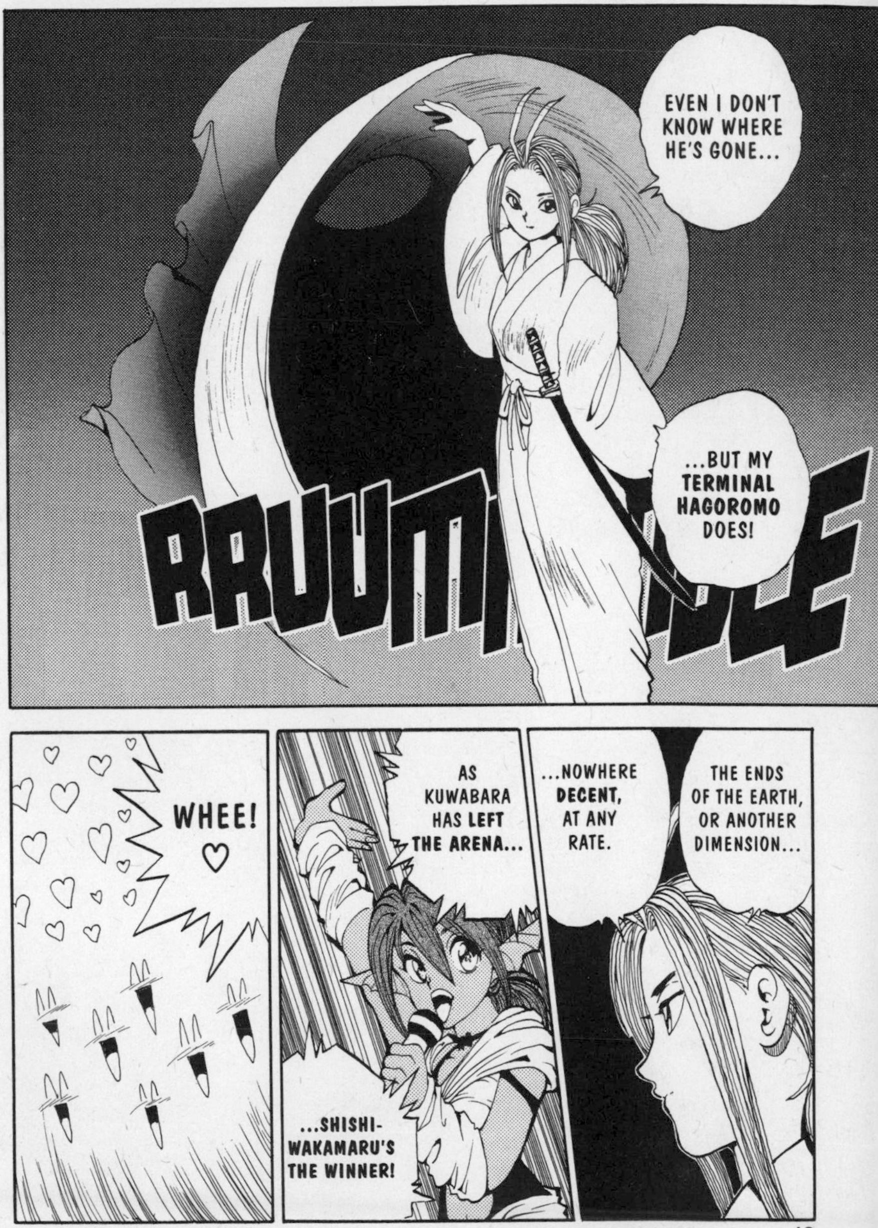
EVEN I DON'T KNOW WHERE HE'S GONE...
...BUT MY **TERMINAL HAGOROMO** DOES!
THE ENDS OF THE EARTH, OR ANOTHER DIMENSION...
...NOWHERE **DECENT,** AT ANY RATE.
AS KUWABARA HAS **LEFT THE ARENA...**
...SHISHI-WAKAMARU'S THE WINNER!
WHEE! ♥

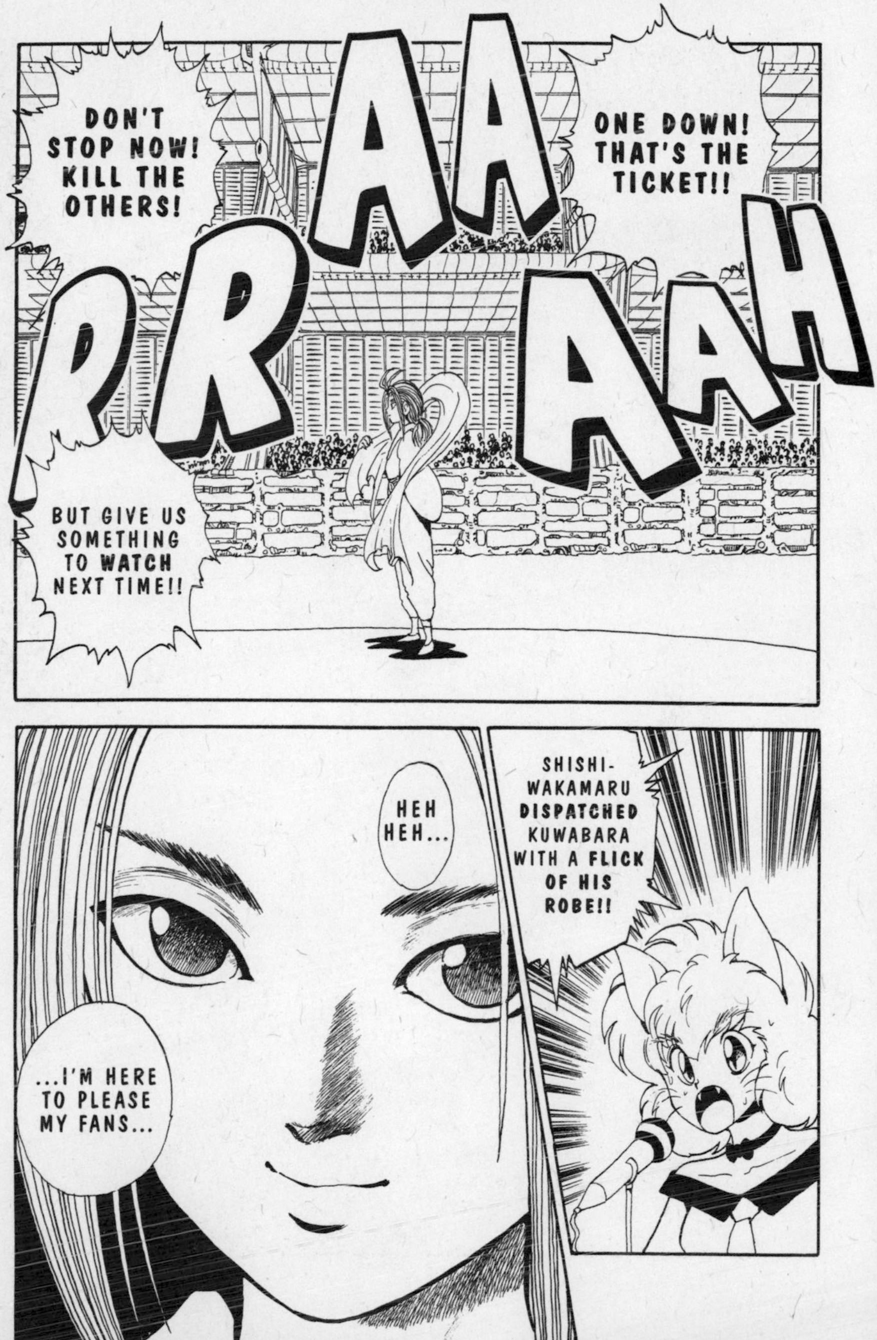
ONE DOWN! THAT'S THE TICKET!!
DON'T STOP NOW! KILL THE OTHERS!
PRAAAAH
BUT GIVE US SOMETHING TO WATCH NEXT TIME!!
SHISHI-WAKAMARU DISPATCHED KUWABARA WITH A FLICK OF HIS ROBE!!
HEH HEH...
...I'M HERE TO PLEASE MY FANS...

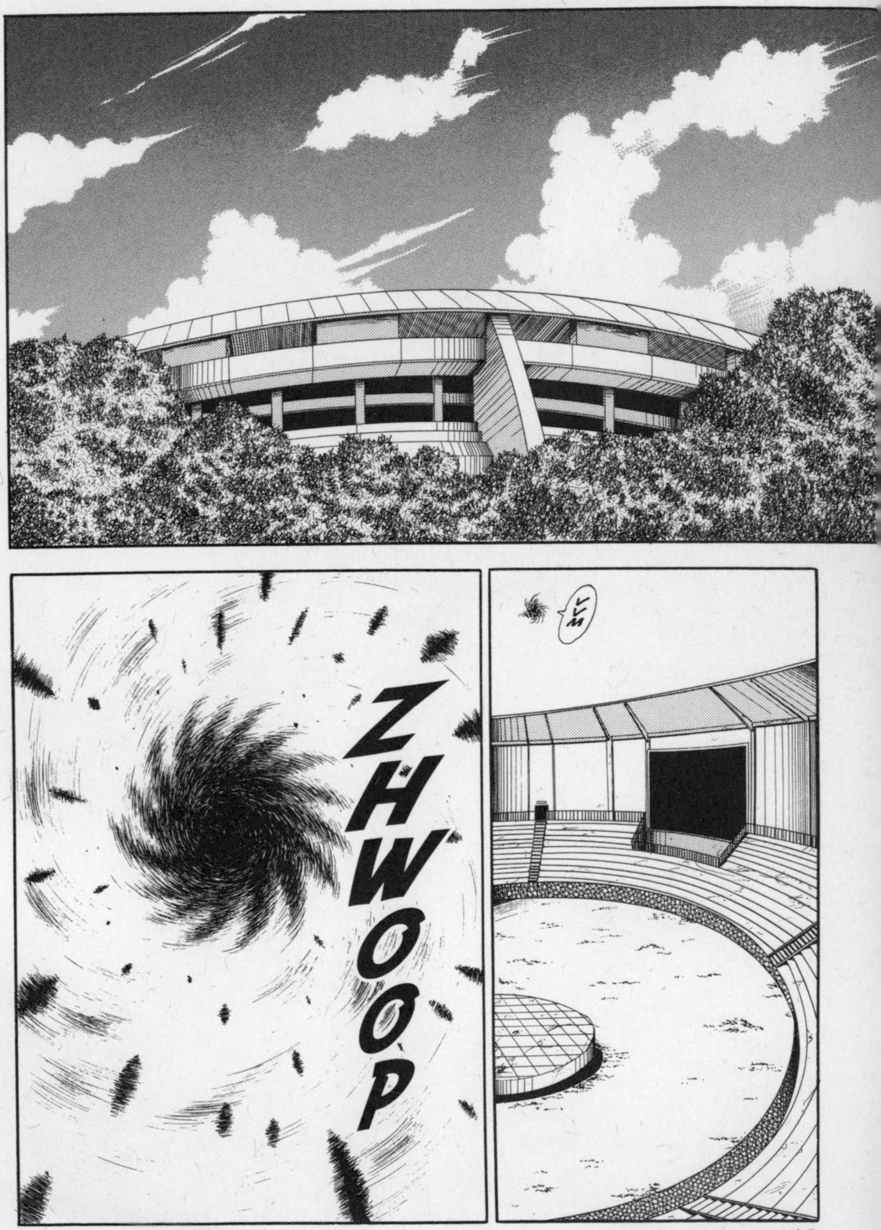
ZHWOOP

READ THIS WAY

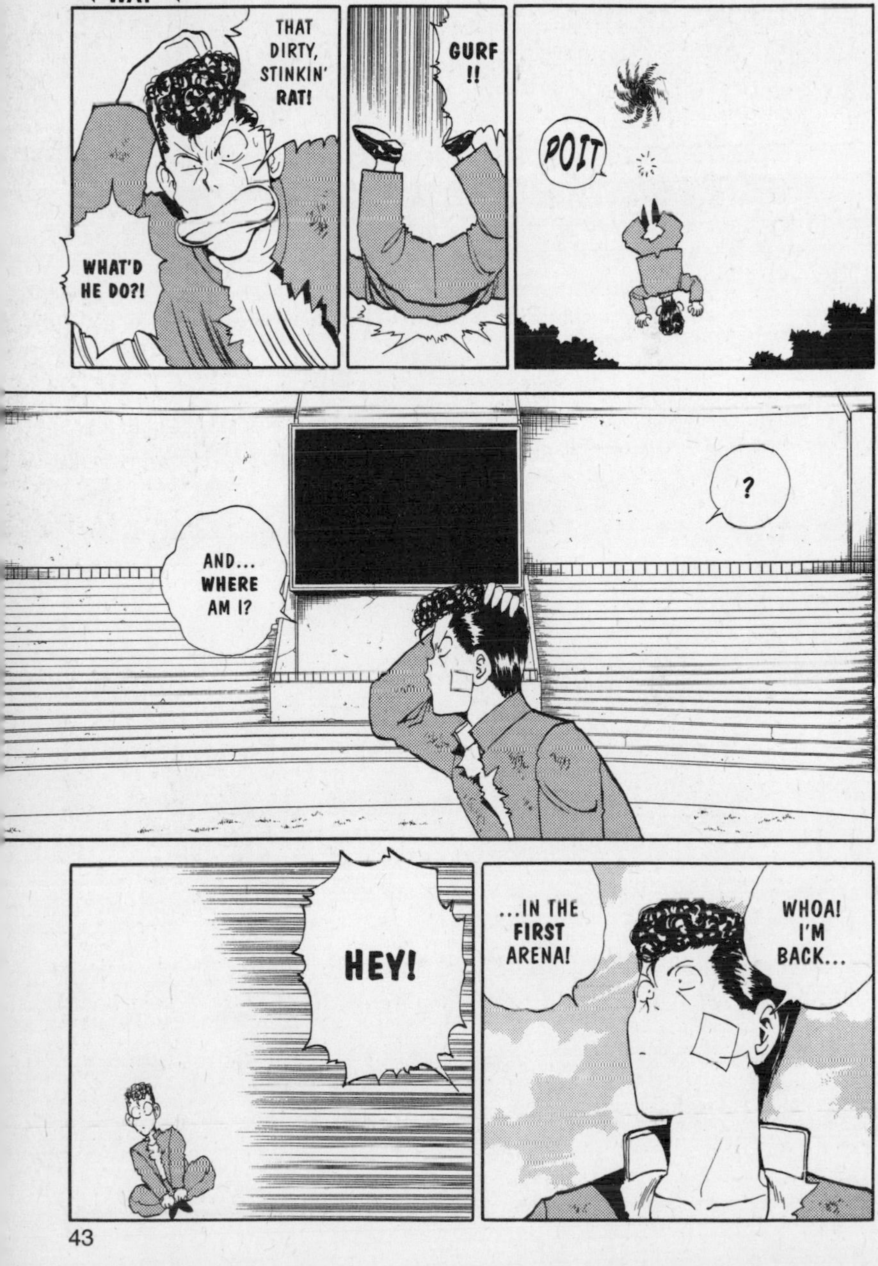
POIT
GURF !!
THAT DIRTY, STINKIN' RAT!
WHAT'D HE DO?!
?
AND... WHERE AM I?
WHOA! I'M BACK...
...IN THE FIRST ARENA!
HEY!

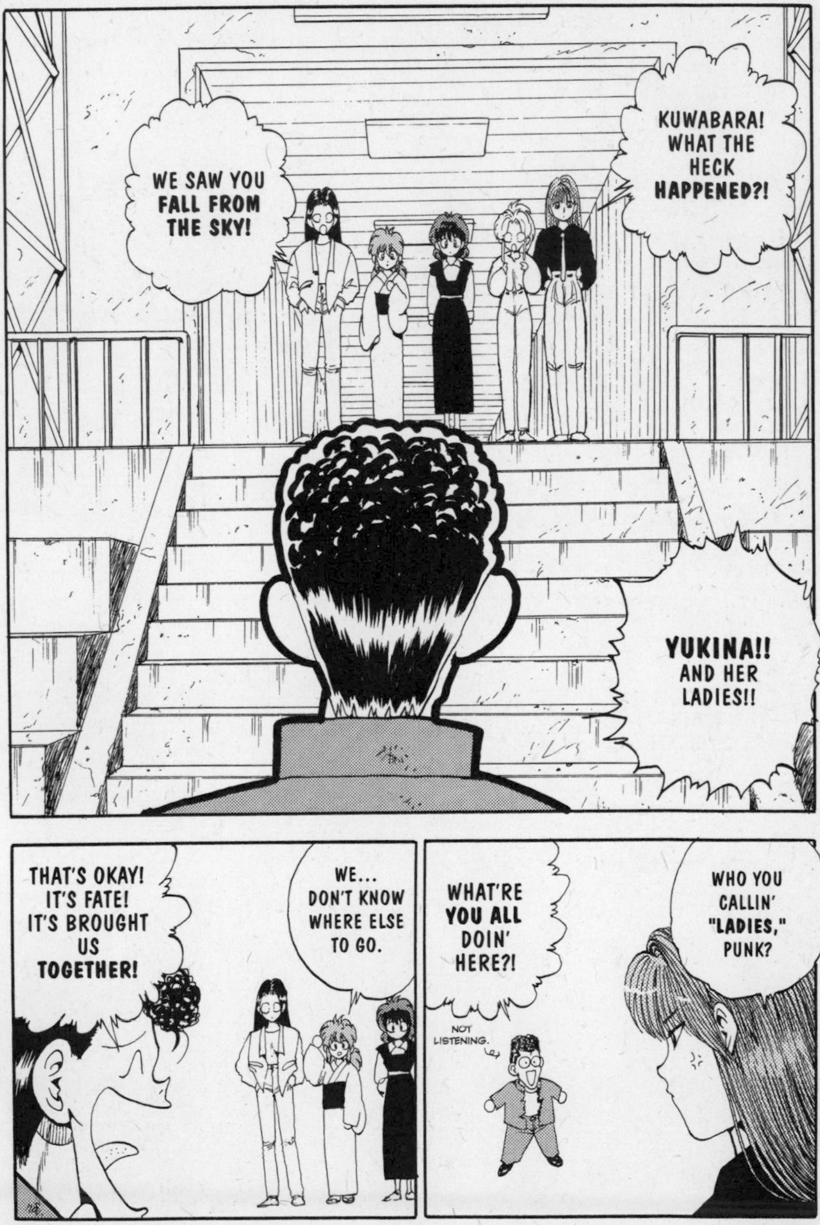
KUWABARA! WHAT THE HECK HAPPENED?!
WE SAW YOU FALL FROM THE SKY!
YUKINA!! AND HER LADIES!!
WHO YOU CALLIN' "LADIES," PUNK?
WHAT'RE YOU ALL DOIN' HERE?!
NOT LISTENING.
WE... DON'T KNOW WHERE ELSE TO GO.
THAT'S OKAY! IT'S FATE! IT'S BROUGHT US TOGETHER!

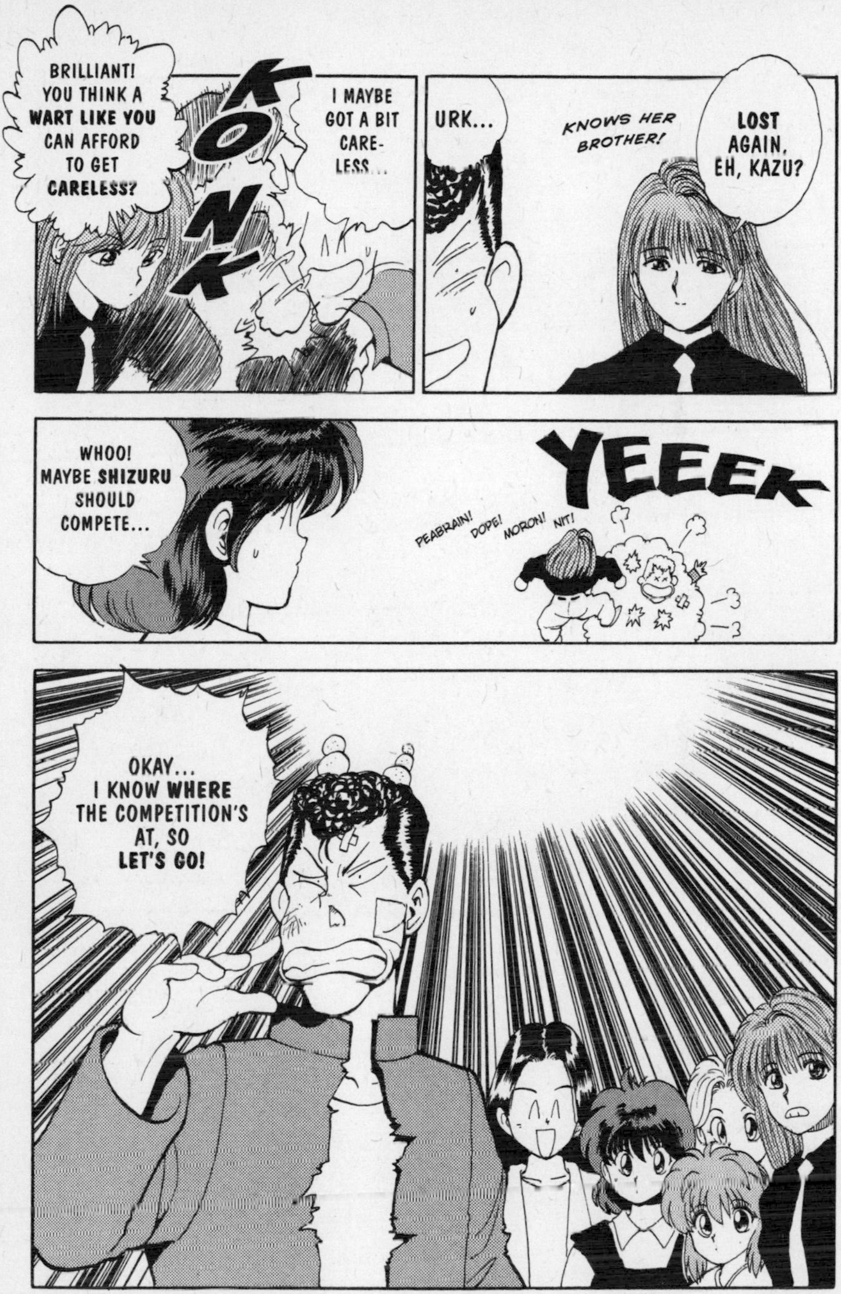
LOST AGAIN, EH, KAZU?
KNOWS HER BROTHER!
URK...
I MAYBE GOT A BIT CARE-LESS...
KONK
BRILLIANT! YOU THINK A WART LIKE YOU CAN AFFORD TO GET CARELESS?
YEEEK
NIT! MORON! DOPE! PEABRAIN!
WHOO! MAYBE SHIZURU SHOULD COMPETE...
OKAY... I KNOW WHERE THE COMPETITION'S AT, SO LET'S GO!

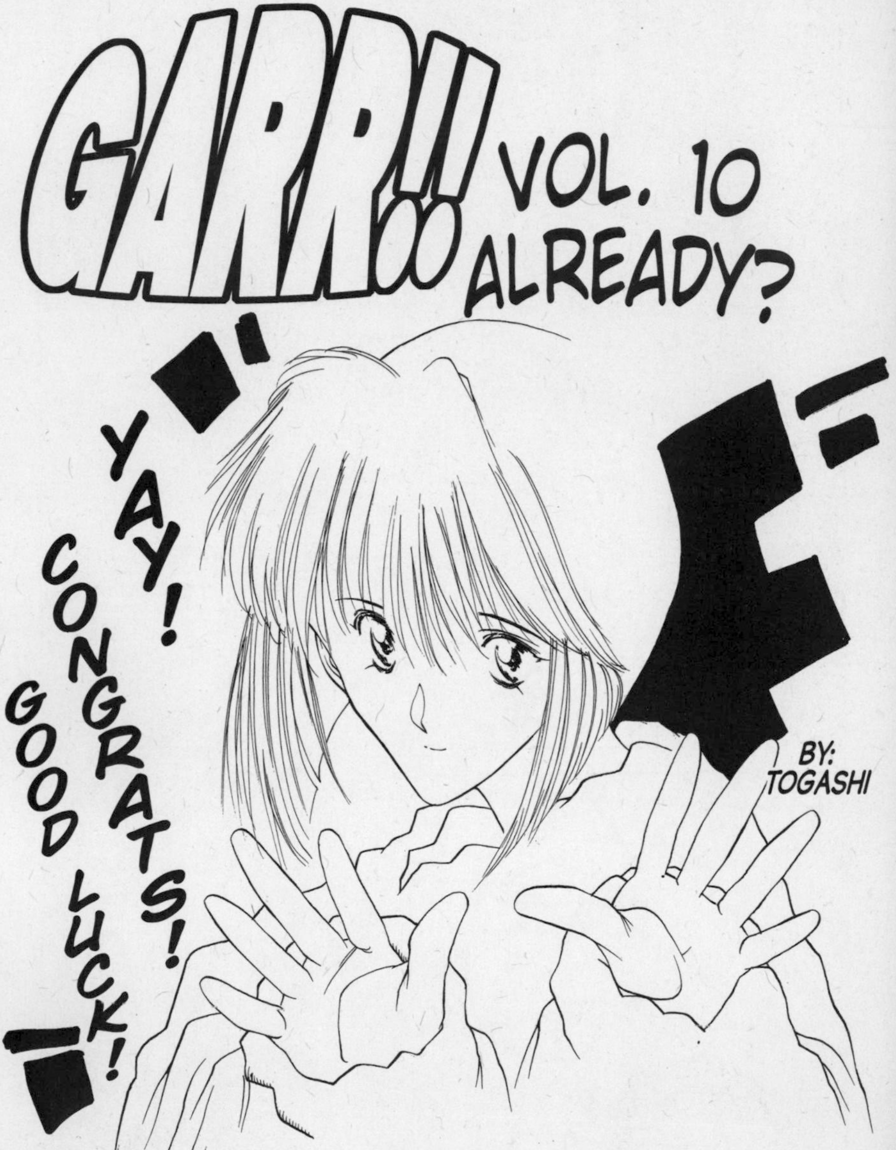
GARR!! VOL. 10 ALREADY?
YAY! CONGRATS! GOOD LUCK!
BY: TOGASHI

IDENTITY REVEALED!!

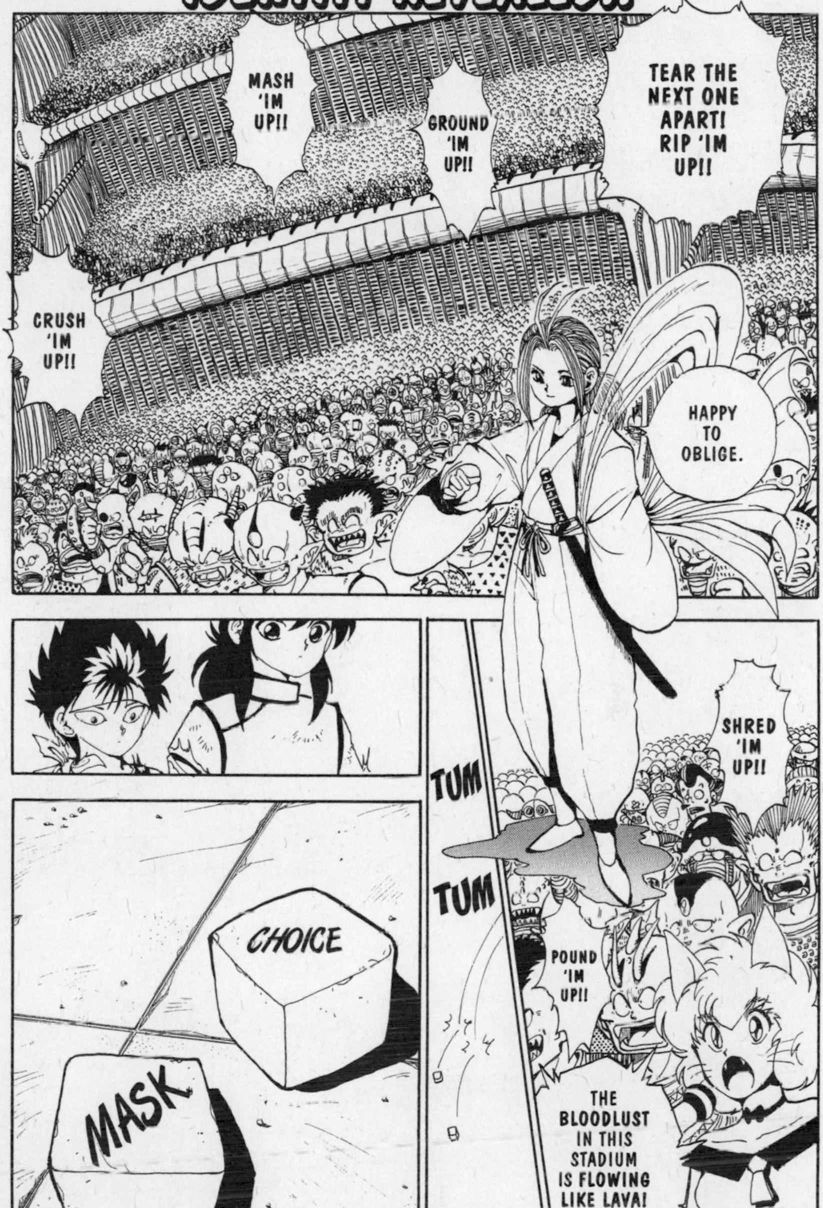

TEAR THE NEXT ONE APART! RIP 'IM UP!!
HAPPY TO OBLIGE.
GROUND 'IM UP!!
MASH 'IM UP!!
CRUSH 'IM UP!!
SHRED 'IM UP!!
TUM
TUM
POUND 'IM UP!!
THE BLOODLUST IN THIS STADIUM IS FLOWING LIKE LAVA!
CHOICE
MASK

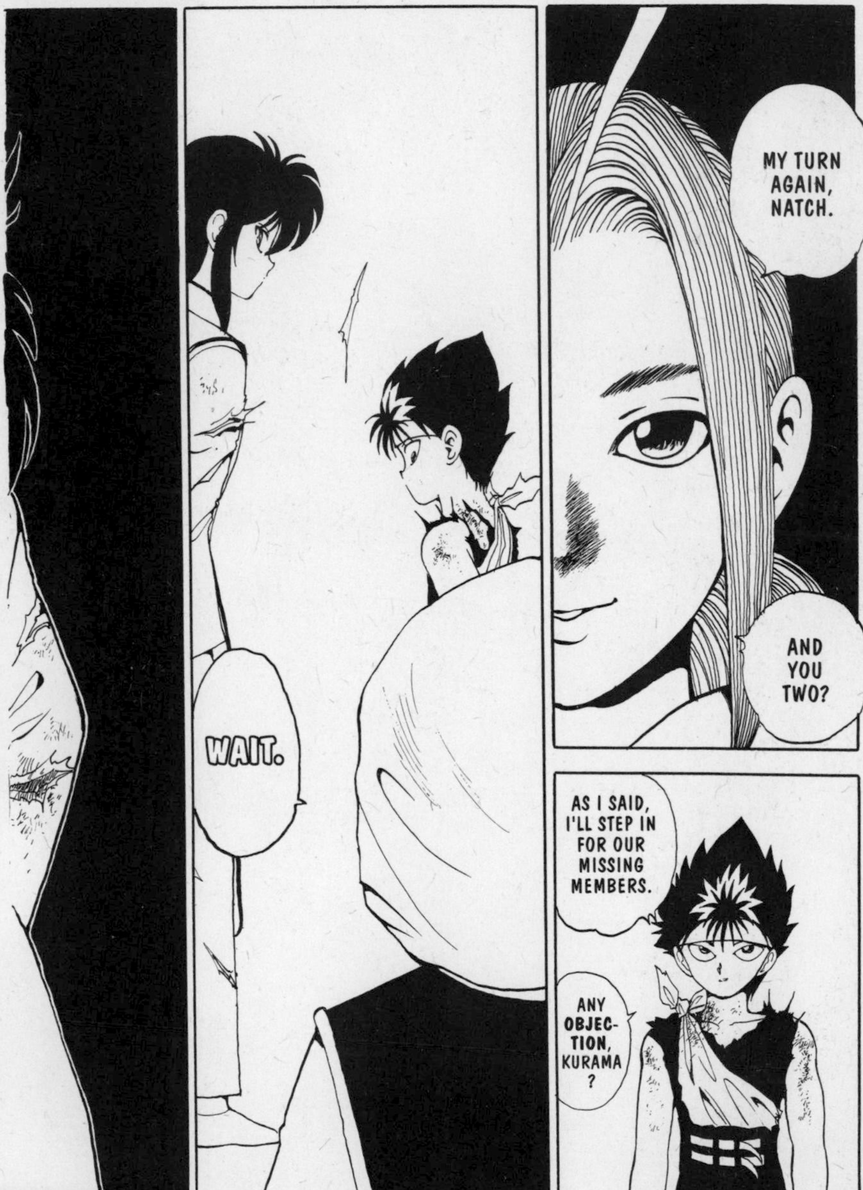
MY TURN AGAIN, NATCH.
AND YOU TWO?
AS I SAID, I'LL STEP IN FOR OUR MISSING MEMBERS.
ANY OBJECTION, KURAMA?
WAIT.

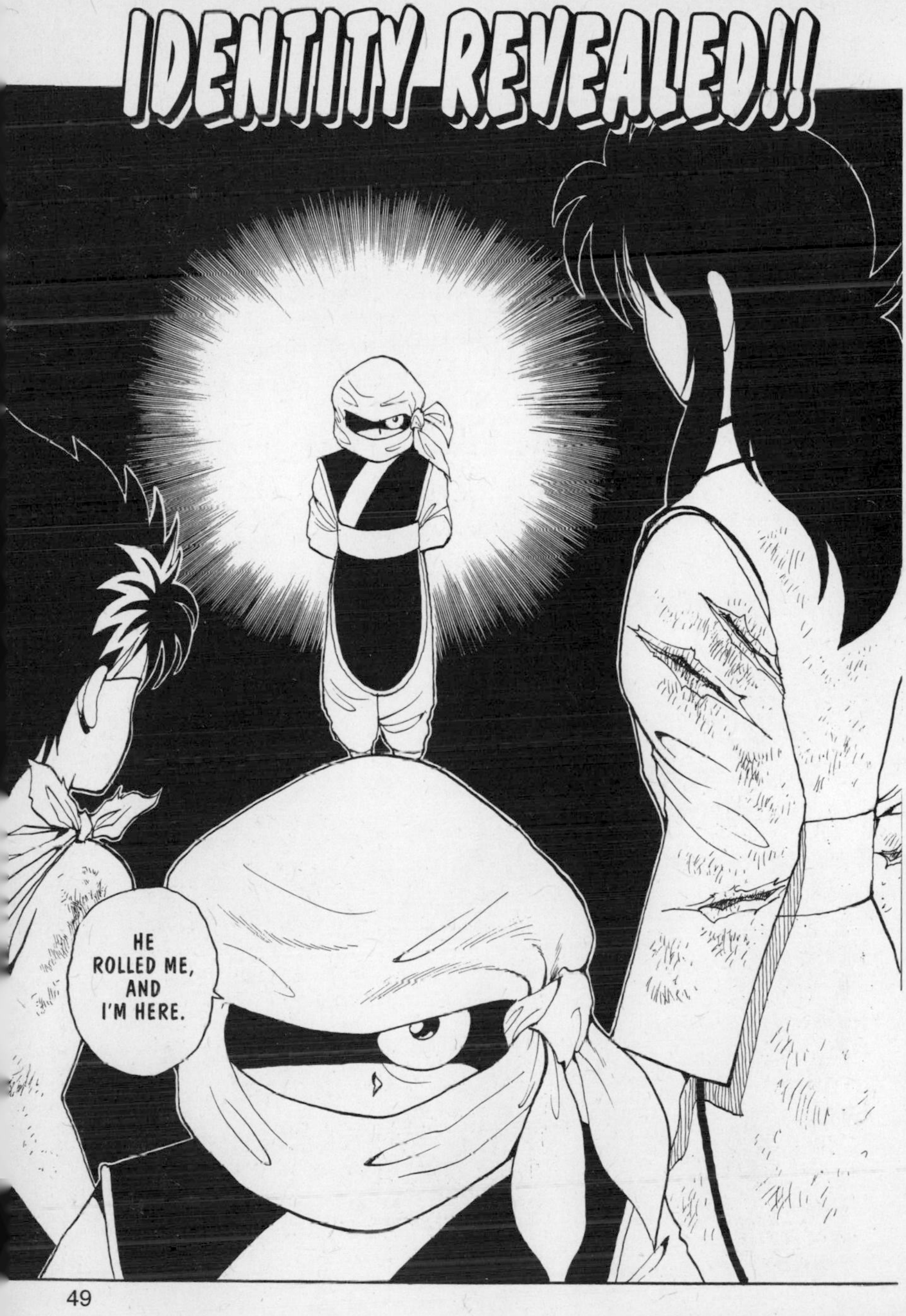
IDENTITY REVEALED!!
HE ROLLED ME, AND I'M HERE.

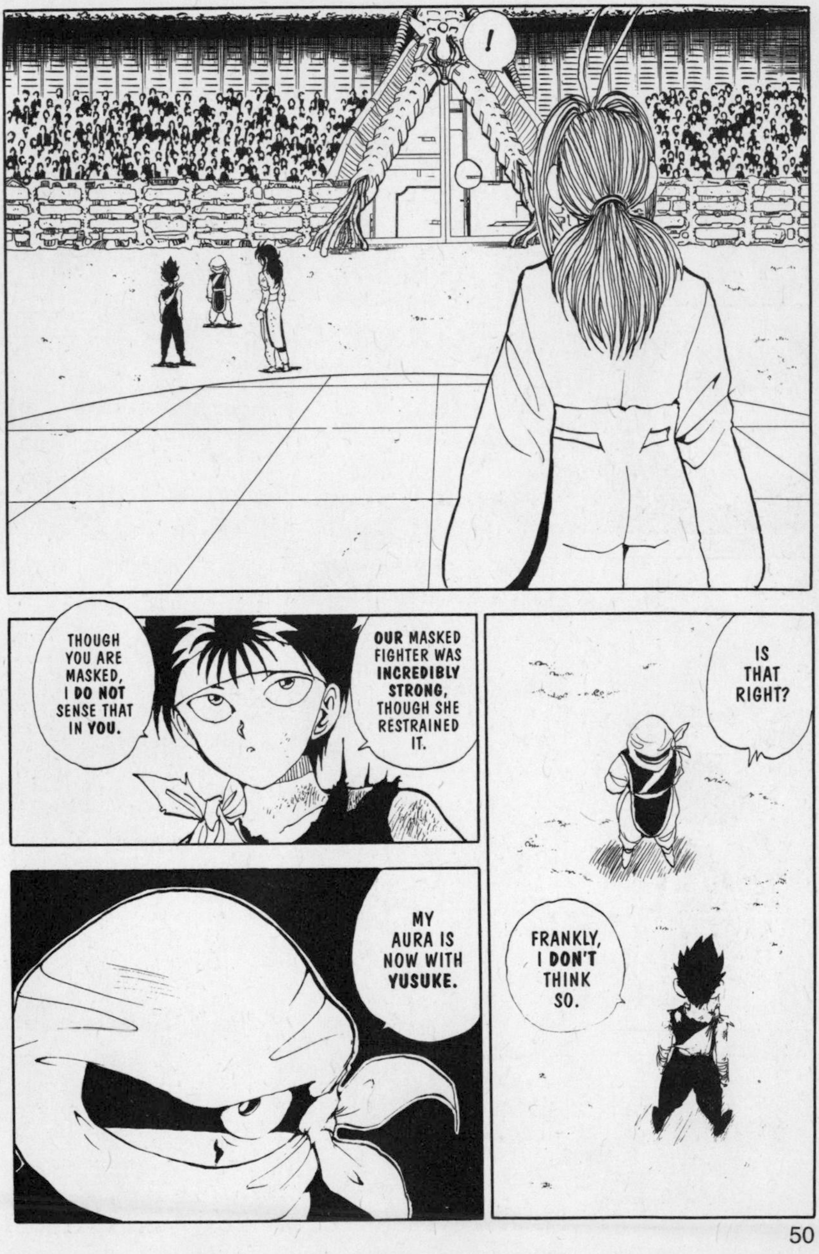
!
IS THAT RIGHT?
FRANKLY, I DON'T THINK SO.
OUR MASKED FIGHTER WAS INCREDIBLY STRONG, THOUGH SHE RESTRAINED IT.
THOUGH YOU ARE MASKED, I DO NOT SENSE THAT IN YOU.
MY AURA IS NOW WITH YUSUKE.

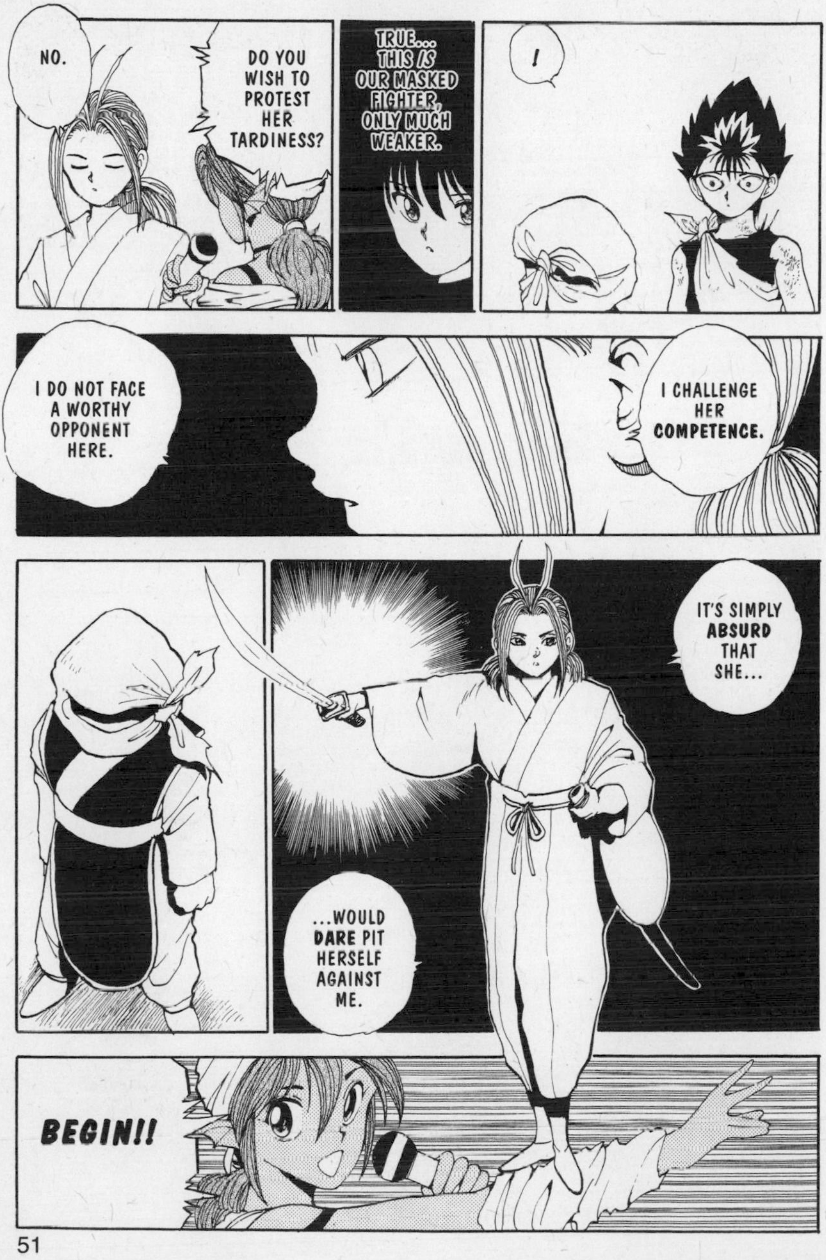
!
TRUE... THIS *IS* OUR MASKED FIGHTER, ONLY MUCH WEAKER.
DO YOU WISH TO PROTEST HER TARDINESS?
NO.
I CHALLENGE HER **COMPETENCE.**
I DO NOT FACE A WORTHY OPPONENT HERE.
IT'S SIMPLY **ABSURD** THAT SHE...
...WOULD **DARE** PIT HERSELF AGAINST ME.
BEGIN!!

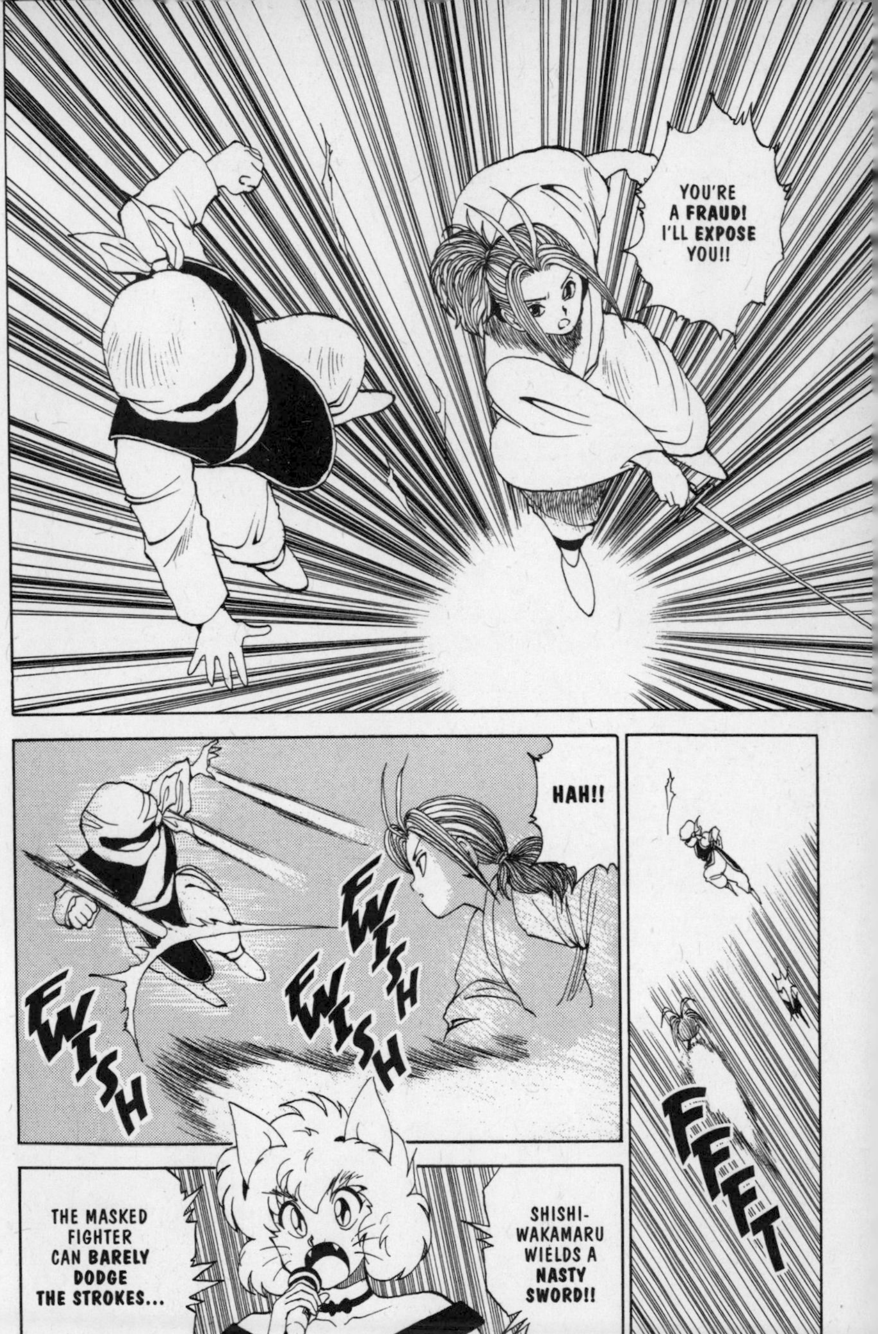
YOU'RE A FRAUD! I'LL EXPOSE YOU!!
FFFFT
HAH!!
FWISH
FWISH
FWISH
SHISHI-WAKAMARU WIELDS A NASTY SWORD!!
THE MASKED FIGHTER CAN BARELY DODGE THE STROKES...

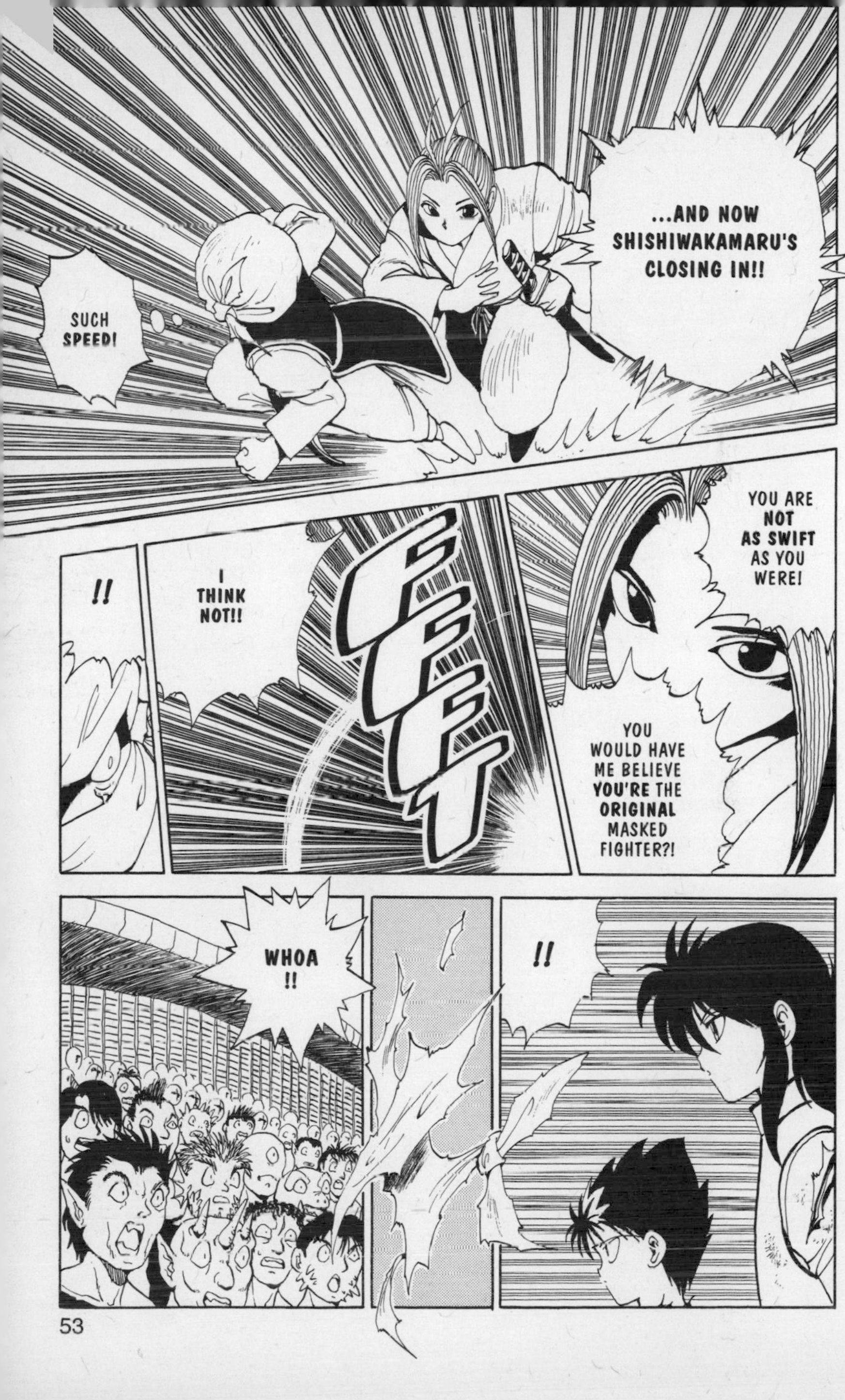
...AND NOW SHISHIWAKAMARU'S CLOSING IN!!
SUCH SPEED!
YOU ARE NOT AS SWIFT AS YOU WERE!
YOU WOULD HAVE ME BELIEVE YOU'RE THE ORIGINAL MASKED FIGHTER?!
I THINK NOT!!
!!
!!
WHOA !!

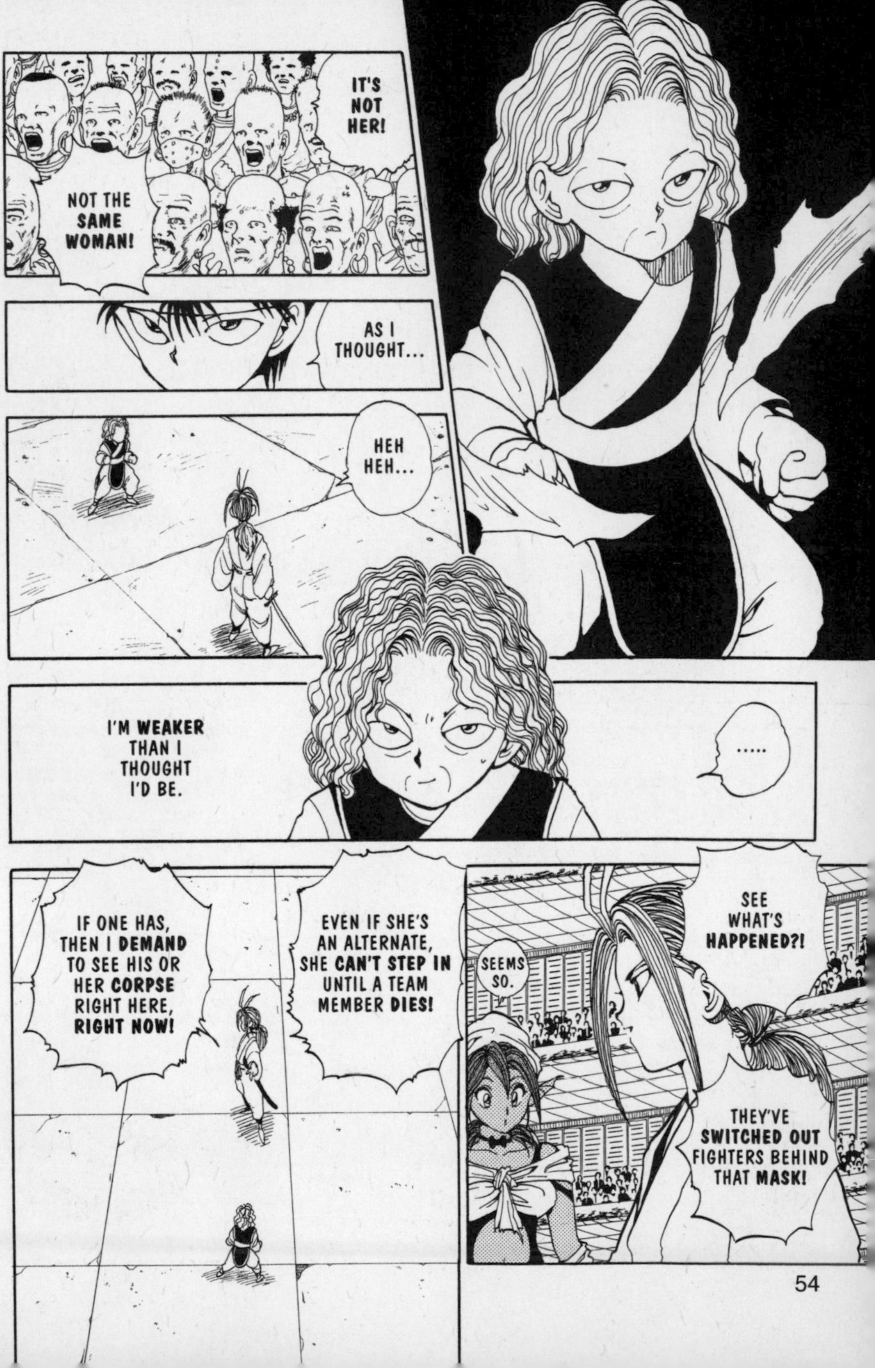
IT'S NOT HER!
NOT THE SAME WOMAN!
AS I THOUGHT...
HEH HEH...
.....
I'M WEAKER THAN I THOUGHT I'D BE.
SEE WHAT'S HAPPENED?!
SEEMS SO.
THEY'VE SWITCHED OUT FIGHTERS BEHIND THAT MASK!
EVEN IF SHE'S AN ALTERNATE, SHE CAN'T STEP IN UNTIL A TEAM MEMBER DIES!
IF ONE HAS, THEN I DEMAND TO SEE HIS OR HER CORPSE RIGHT HERE, RIGHT NOW!

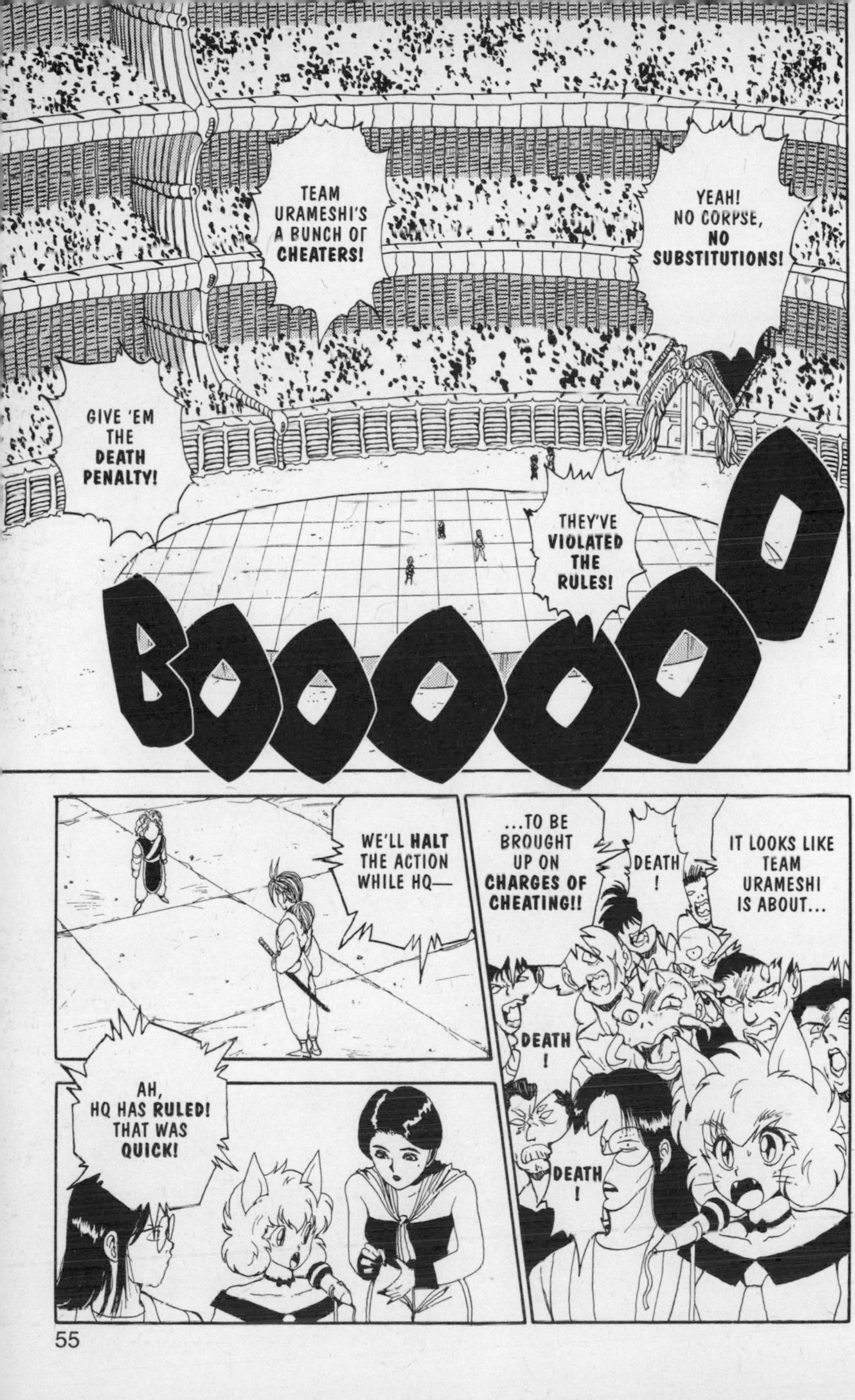
YEAH! NO CORPSE, NO SUBSTITUTIONS!
TEAM URAMESHI'S A BUNCH OF CHEATERS!
THEY'VE VIOLATED THE RULES!
GIVE 'EM THE DEATH PENALTY!
BOOOOOOO
IT LOOKS LIKE TEAM URAMESHI IS ABOUT...
DEATH!
...TO BE BROUGHT UP ON CHARGES OF CHEATING!!
DEATH!
DEATH!
WE'LL HALT THE ACTION WHILE HQ—
AH, HQ HAS RULED! THAT WAS QUICK!

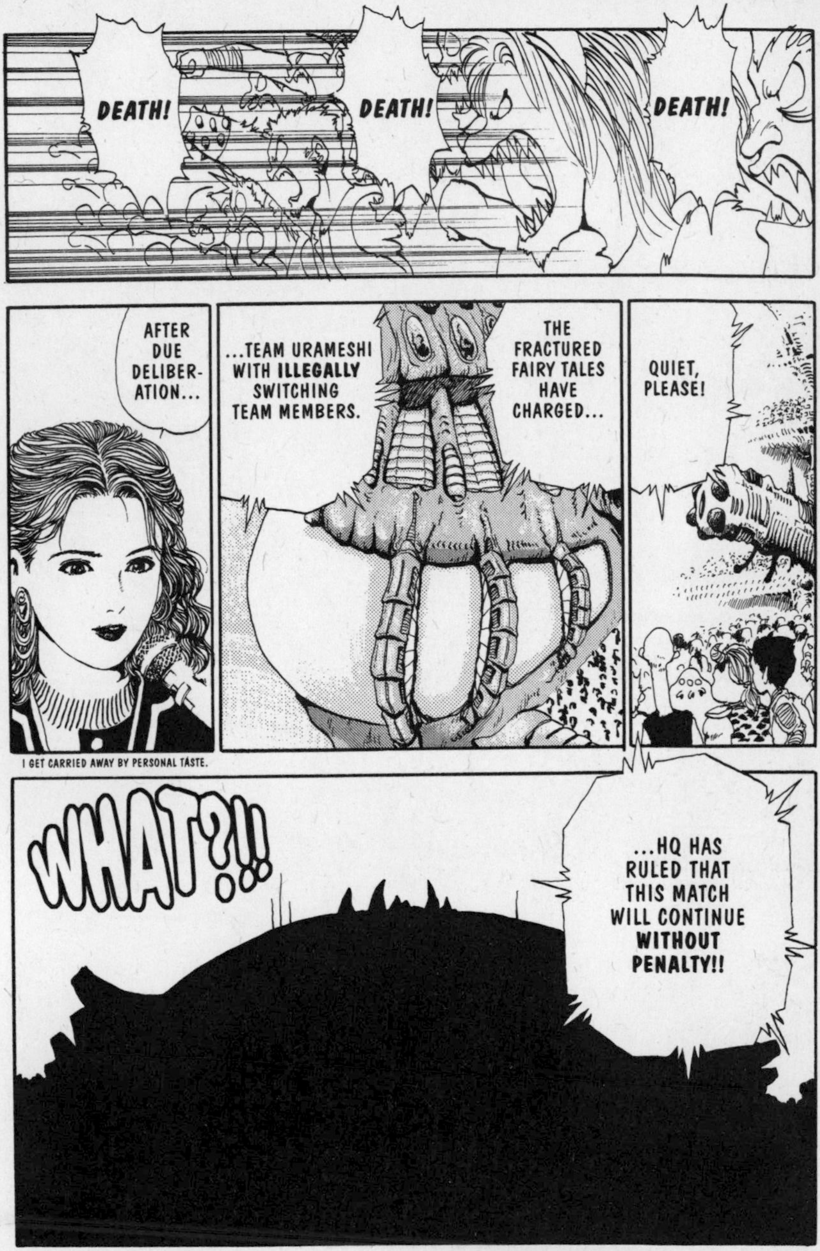
DEATH!
DEATH!
DEATH!
QUIET, PLEASE!
THE FRACTURED FAIRY TALES HAVE CHARGED...
...TEAM URAMESHI WITH **ILLEGALLY** SWITCHING TEAM MEMBERS.
AFTER DUE DELIBER-ATION...
I GET CARRIED AWAY BY PERSONAL TASTE.
...HQ HAS RULED THAT THIS MATCH WILL CONTINUE **WITHOUT PENALTY!!**
WHAT?!!

READ THIS WAY

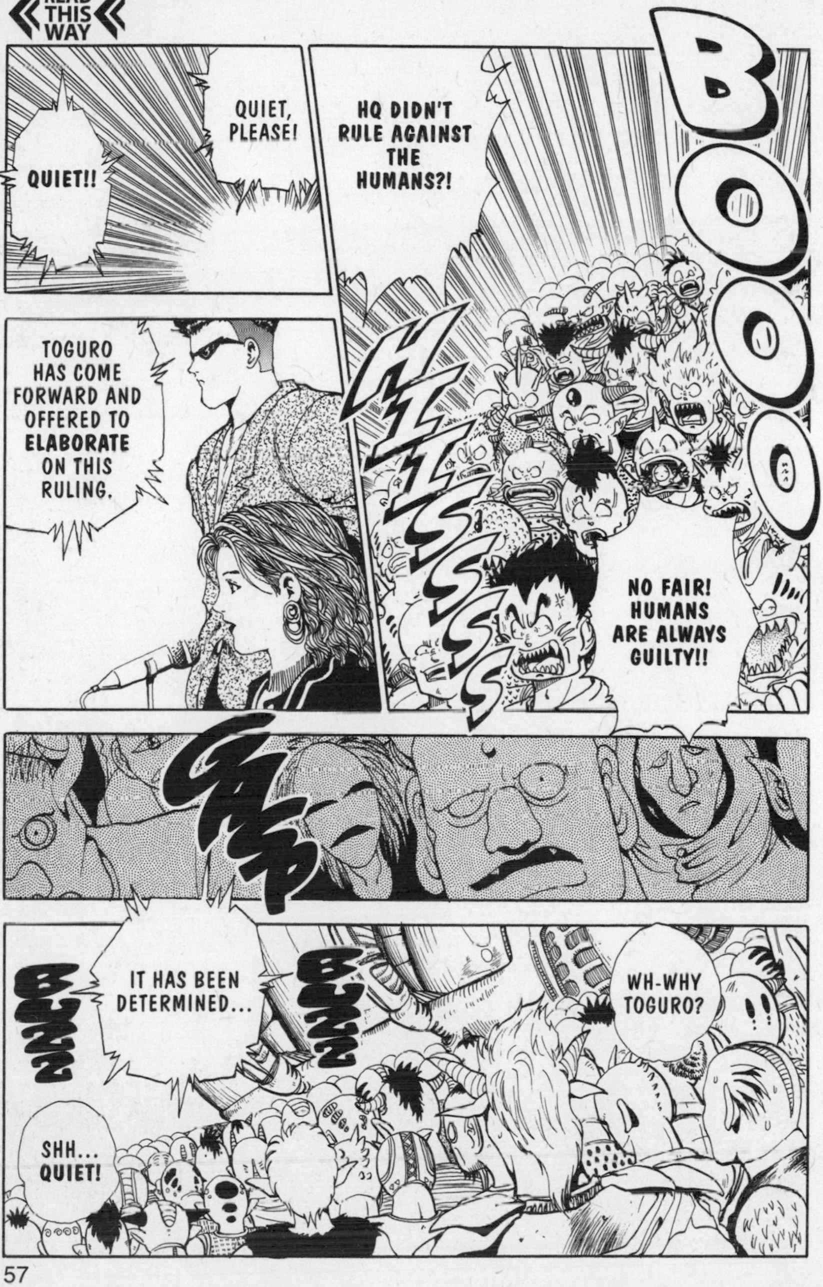

HQ DIDN'T RULE AGAINST THE HUMANS?!
BOOOOO
HISSSS
NO FAIR! HUMANS ARE ALWAYS GUILTY!!
QUIET, PLEASE!
QUIET!!
TOGURO HAS COME FORWARD AND OFFERED TO ELABORATE ON THIS RULING.
GASP
WH-WHY TOGURO?
BUZZZZ
IT HAS BEEN DETERMINED...
BUZZZZ
SHH... QUIET!

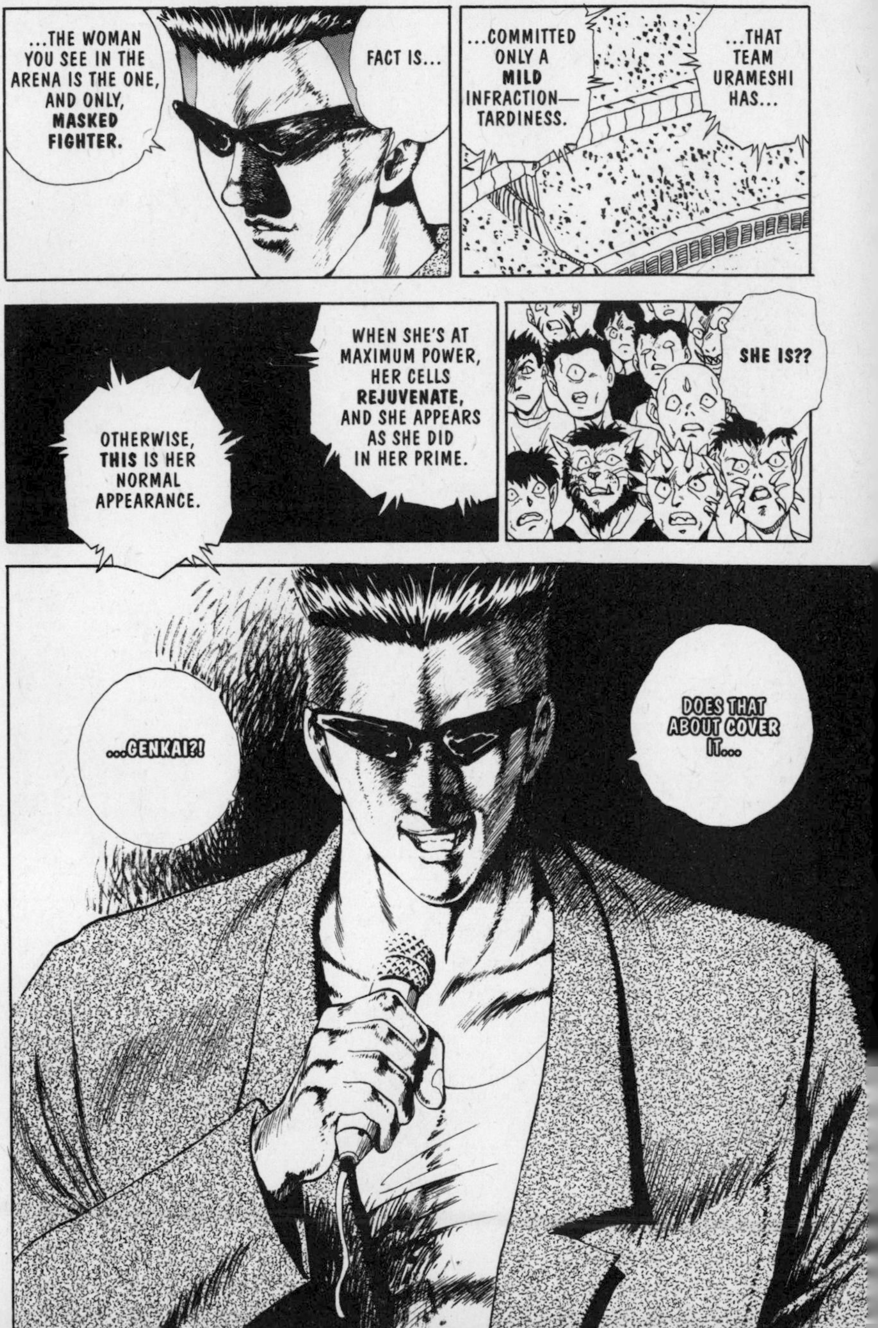
...THAT TEAM URAMESHI HAS...
...COMMITTED ONLY A MILD INFRACTION—TARDINESS.
FACT IS...
...THE WOMAN YOU SEE IN THE ARENA IS THE ONE, AND ONLY, MASKED FIGHTER.
SHE IS??
WHEN SHE'S AT MAXIMUM POWER, HER CELLS REJUVENATE, AND SHE APPEARS AS SHE DID IN HER PRIME.
OTHERWISE, THIS IS HER NORMAL APPEARANCE.
DOES THAT ABOUT COVER IT...
...GENKAI?!

READ THIS WAY

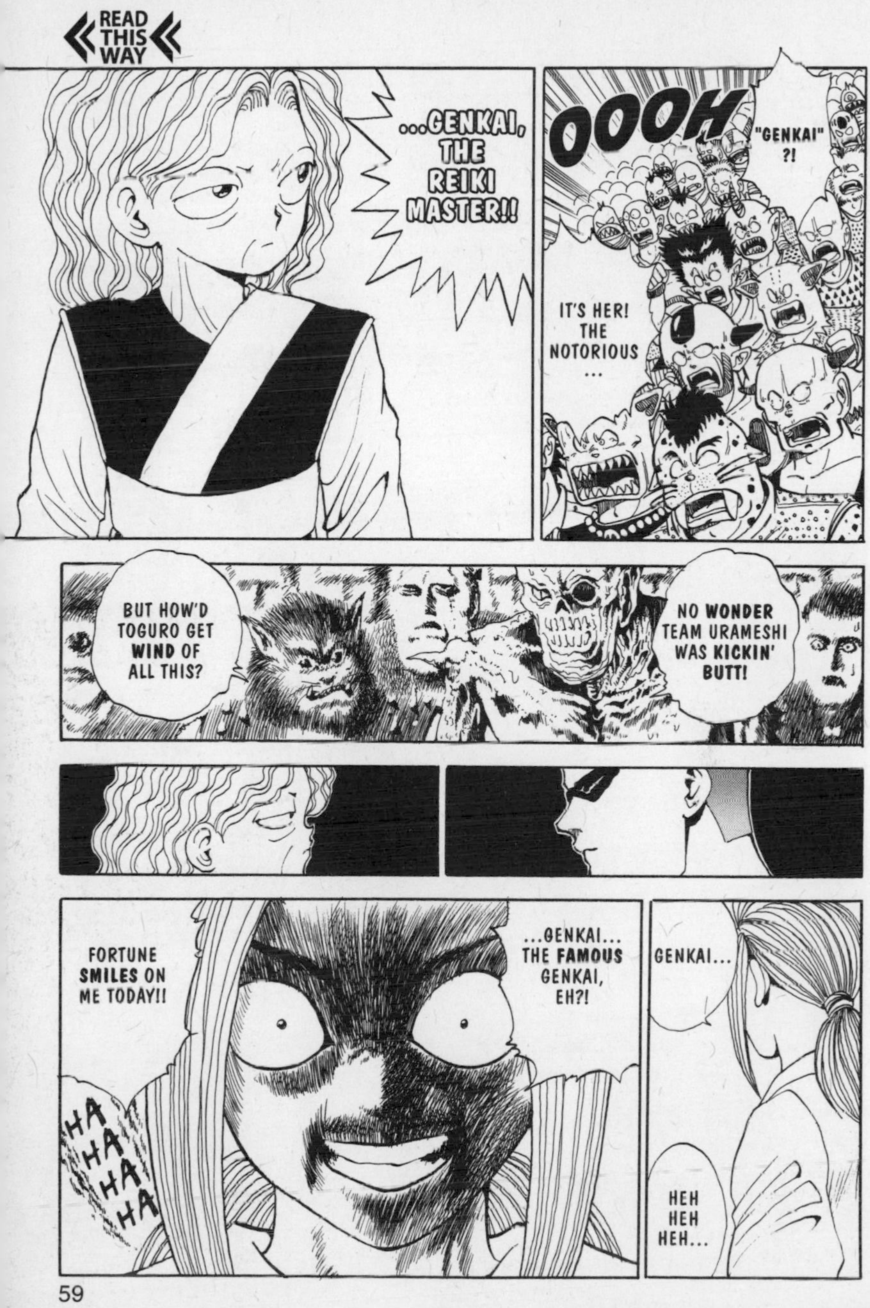
OOOH
"GENKAI" ?!
IT'S HER! THE NOTORIOUS ...
...GENKAI, THE REIKI MASTER!!
NO WONDER TEAM URAMESHI WAS KICKIN' BUTT!
BUT HOW'D TOGURO GET WIND OF ALL THIS?
GENKAI...
HEH HEH HEH...
...GENKAI... THE FAMOUS GENKAI, EH?!
FORTUNE SMILES ON ME TODAY!!
HA HA HA HA

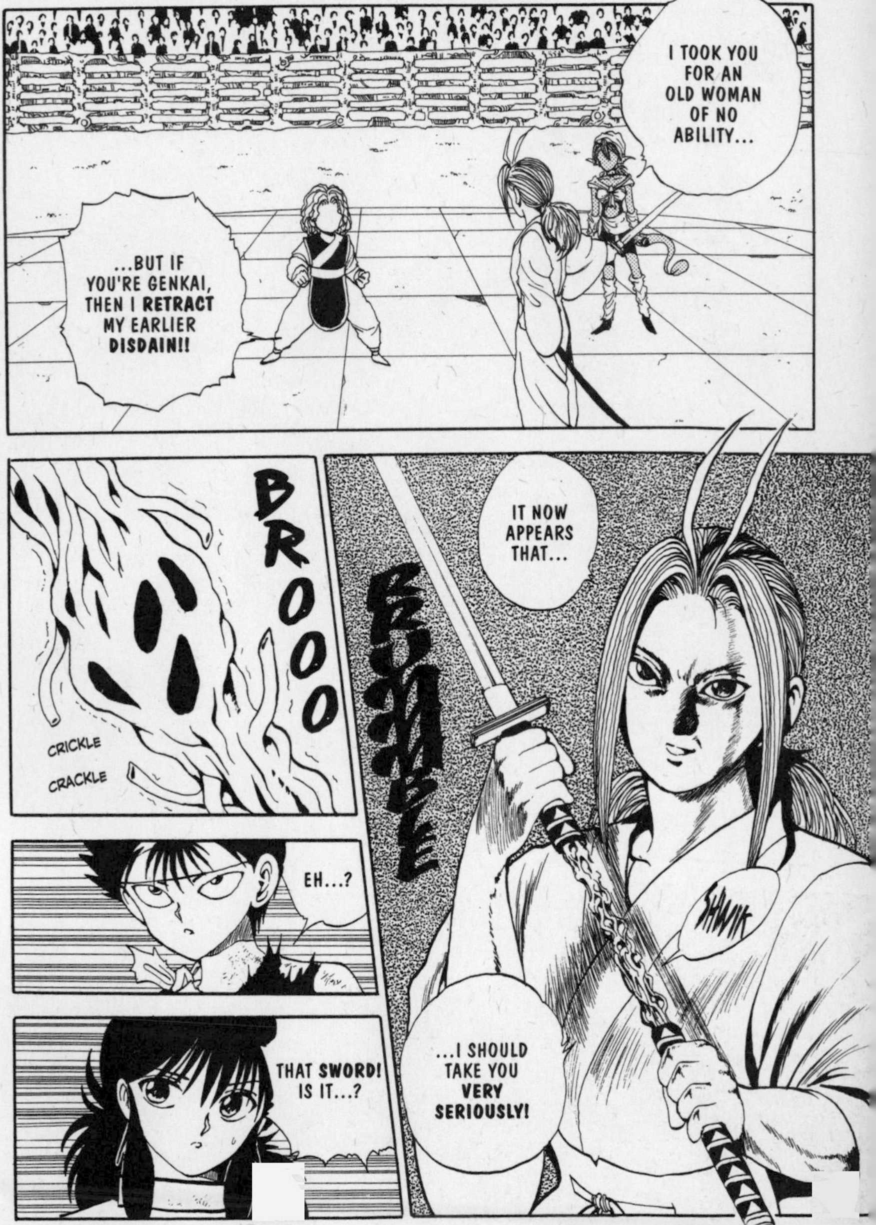
I TOOK YOU FOR AN OLD WOMAN OF NO ABILITY...
...BUT IF YOU'RE GENKAI, THEN I RETRACT MY EARLIER DISDAIN!!
IT NOW APPEARS THAT...
SHWIK
...I SHOULD TAKE YOU VERY SERIOUSLY!
BROOOO
CRICKLE
CRACKLE
EH...?
THAT SWORD! IS IT...?

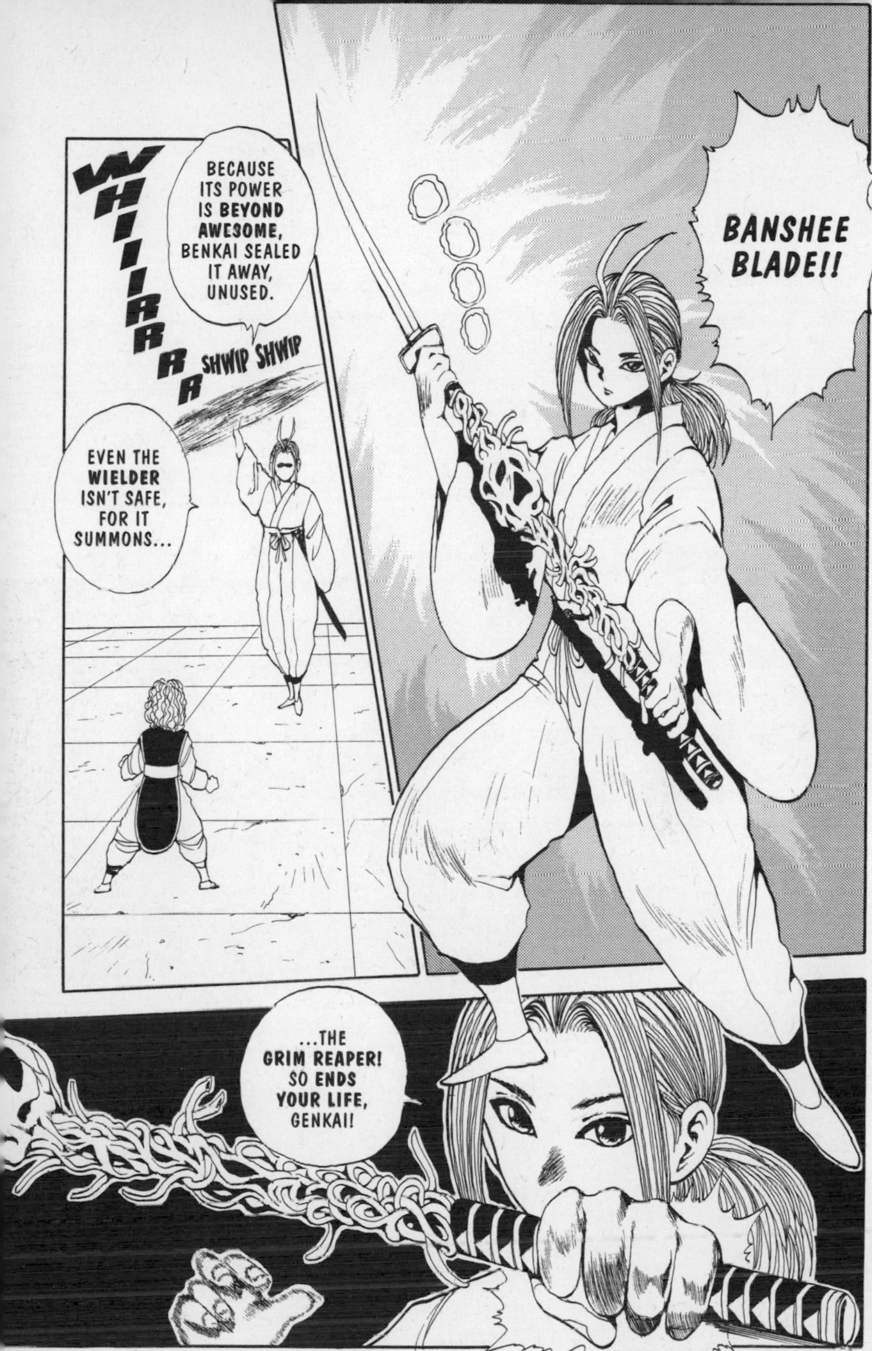
BANSHEE BLADE!!
WHIRRRR
BECAUSE ITS POWER IS BEYOND AWESOME, BENKAI SEALED IT AWAY, UNUSED.
SHWIP SHWIP
EVEN THE WIELDER ISN'T SAFE, FOR IT SUMMONS...
...THE GRIM REAPER! SO ENDS YOUR LIFE, GENKAI!

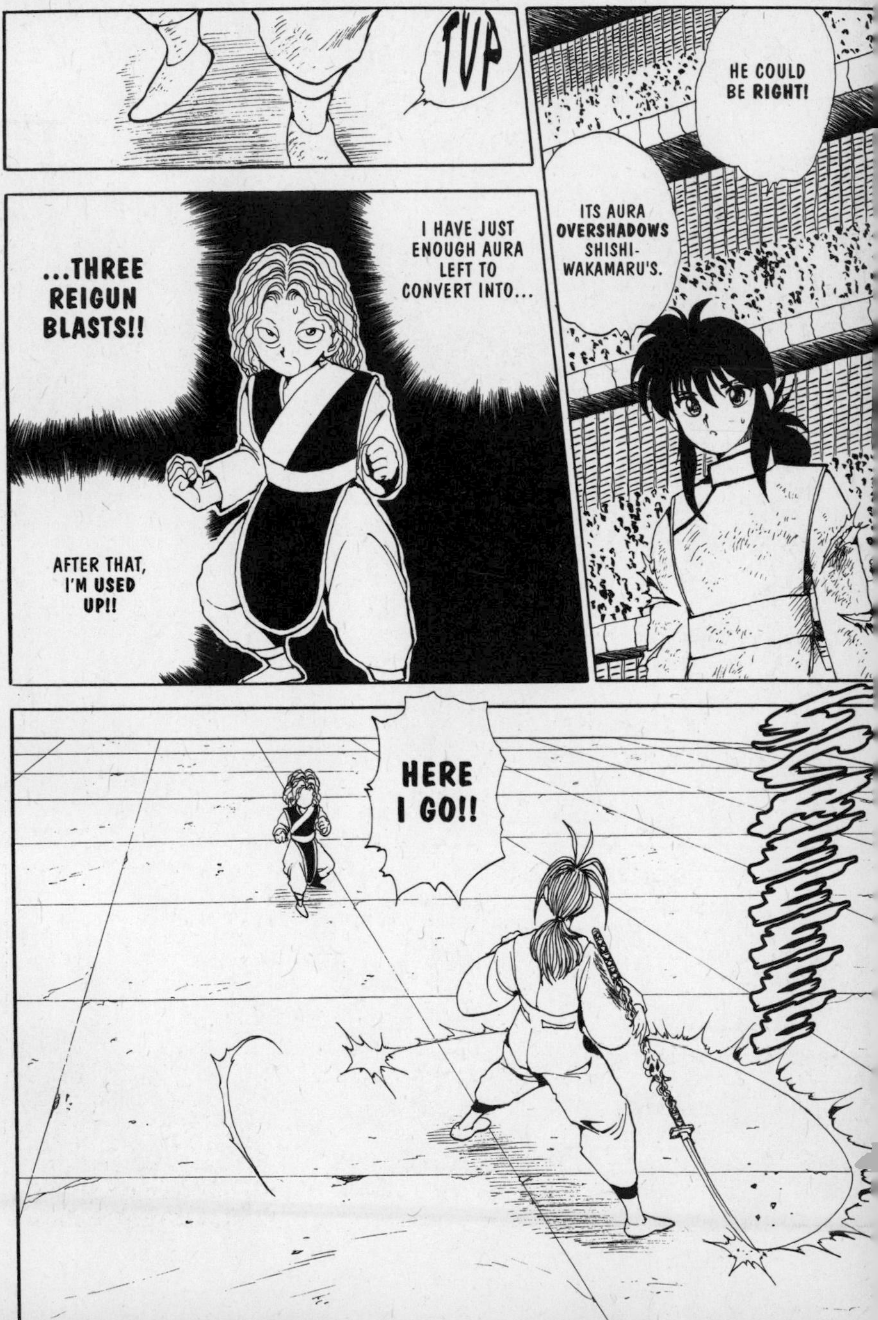
HE COULD BE RIGHT!
ITS AURA OVERSHADOWS SHISHI-WAKAMARU'S.
TUP
I HAVE JUST ENOUGH AURA LEFT TO CONVERT INTO...
...THREE REIGUN BLASTS!!
AFTER THAT, I'M USED UP!!
HERE I GO!!

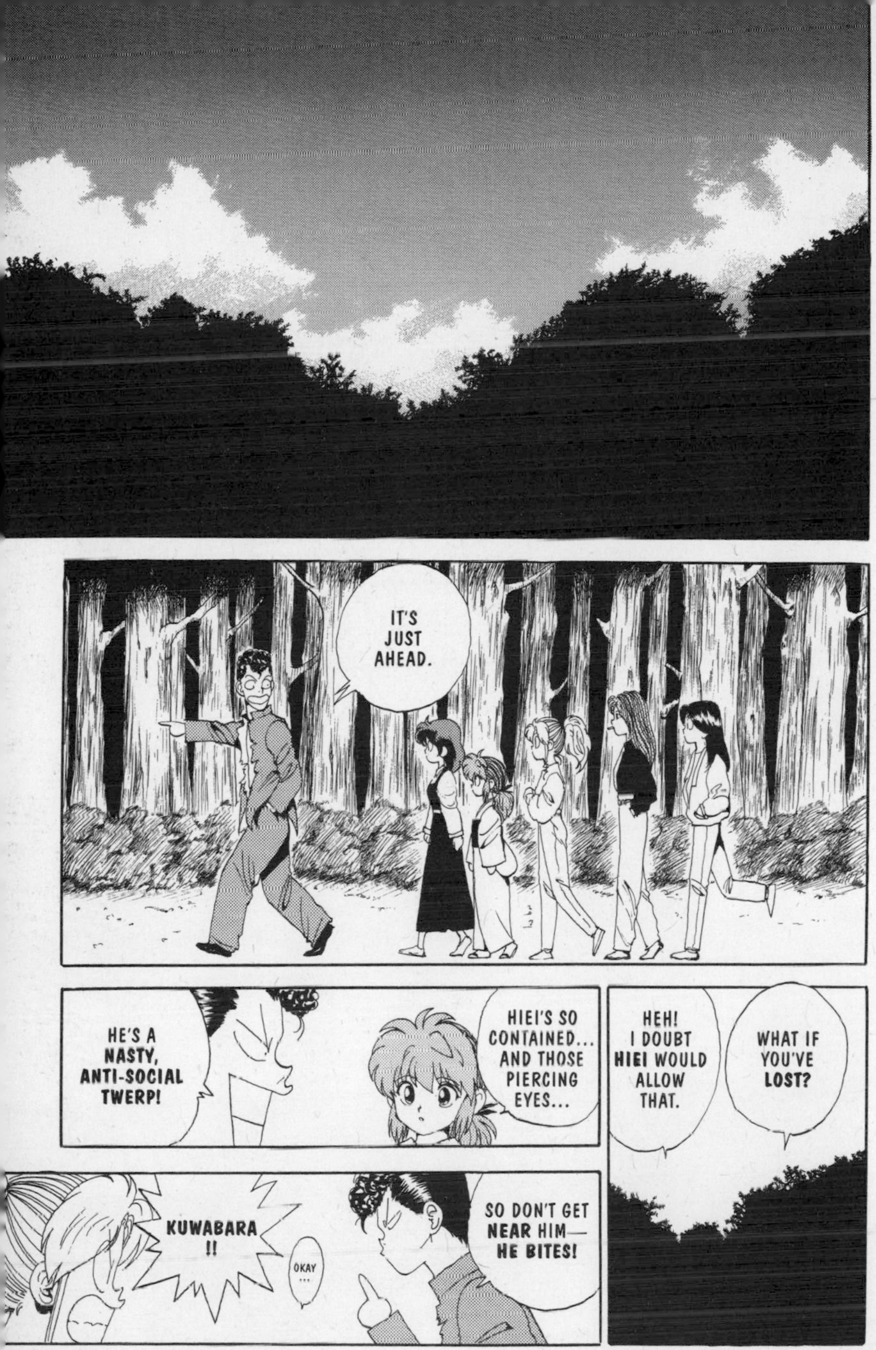
IT'S JUST AHEAD.
WHAT IF YOU'VE LOST?
HEH! I DOUBT HIEI WOULD ALLOW THAT.
HIEI'S SO CONTAINED... AND THOSE PIERCING EYES...
HE'S A NASTY, ANTI-SOCIAL TWERP!
SO DON'T GET NEAR HIM— HE BITES!
OKAY ...
KUWABARA !!

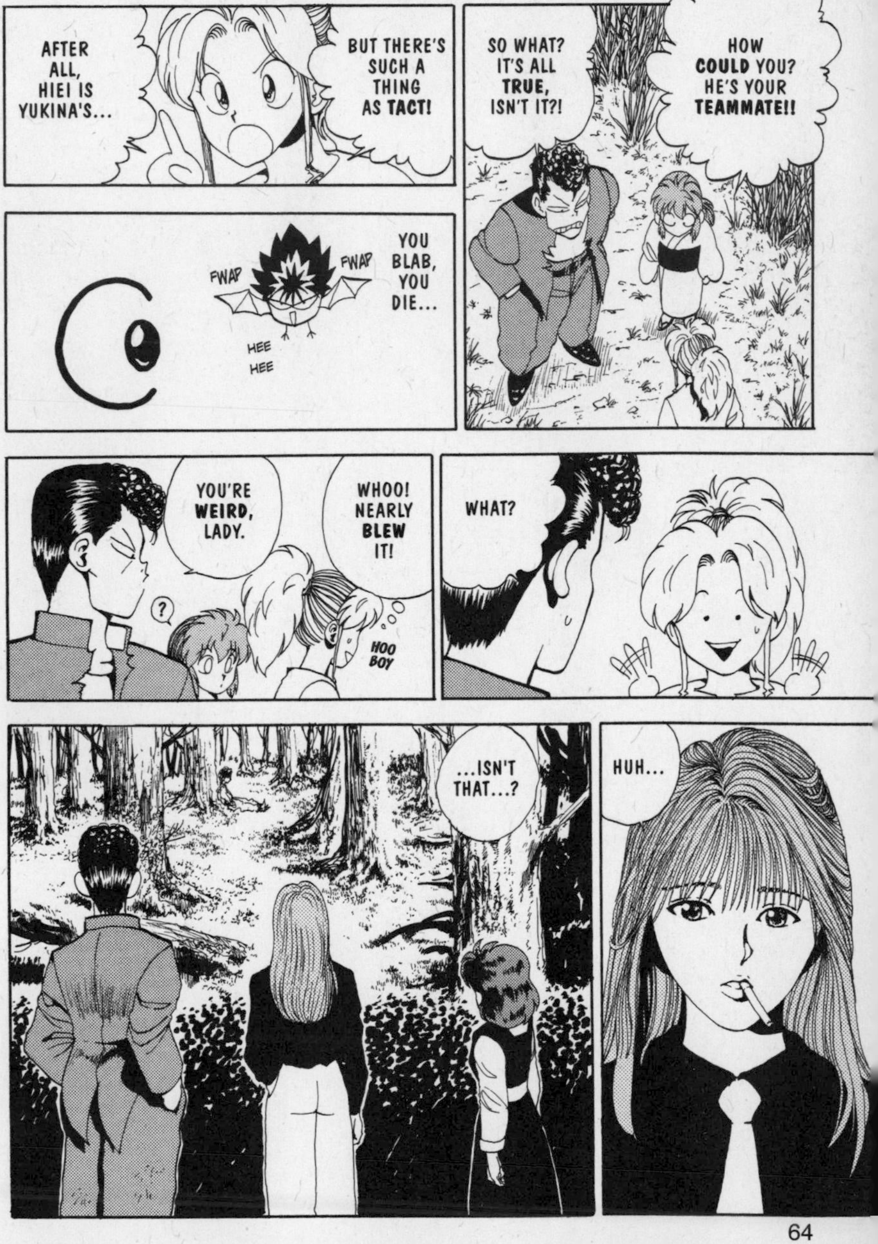

HOW COULD YOU? HE'S YOUR TEAMMATE!!
SO WHAT? IT'S ALL TRUE, ISN'T IT?!
BUT THERE'S SUCH A THING AS TACT!
AFTER ALL, HIEI IS YUKINA'S...
YOU BLAB, YOU DIE...
FWAP
FWAP
HEE HEE
WHAT?
WHOO! NEARLY BLEW IT!
HOO BOY
YOU'RE WEIRD, LADY.
?
HUH...
...ISN'T THAT...?

READ THIS WAY

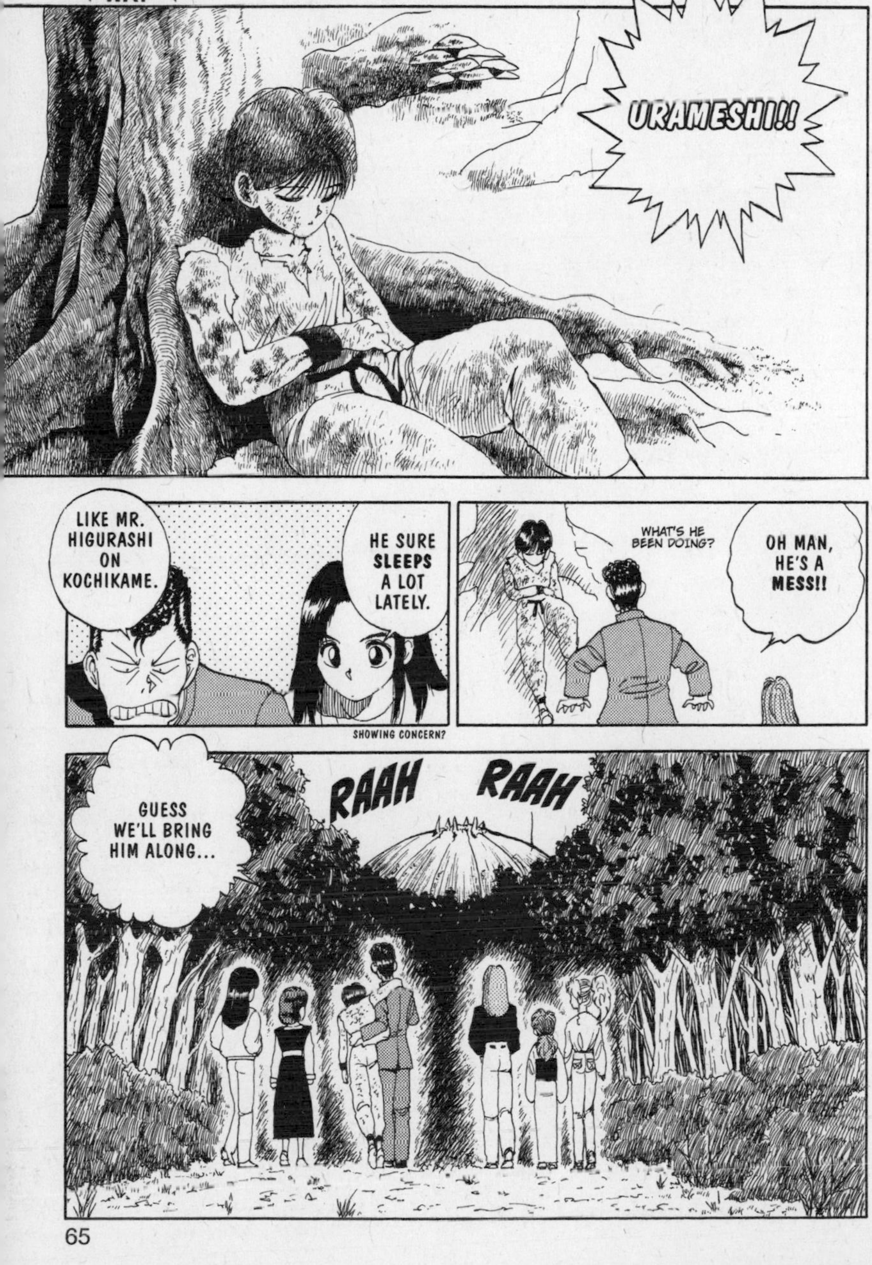
URAMESHI!!
OH MAN, HE'S A MESS!!
WHAT'S HE BEEN DOING?
HE SURE SLEEPS A LOT LATELY.
LIKE MR. HIGURASHI ON KOCHIKAME.
SHOWING CONCERN?
RAAH
RAAH
GUESS WE'LL BRING HIM ALONG...

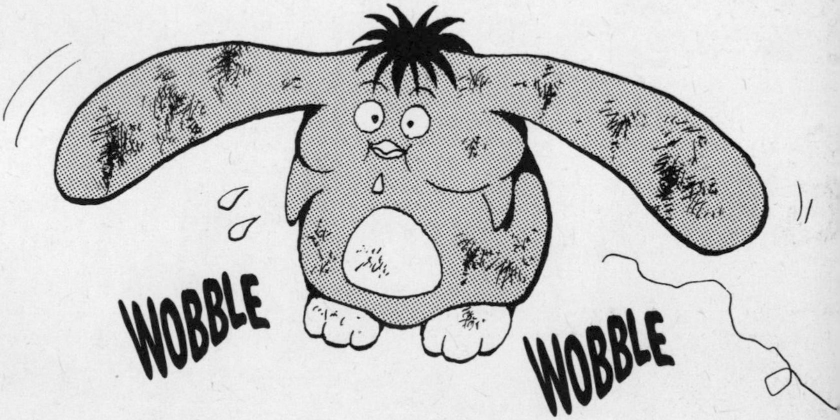
WOBBLE
WOBBLE

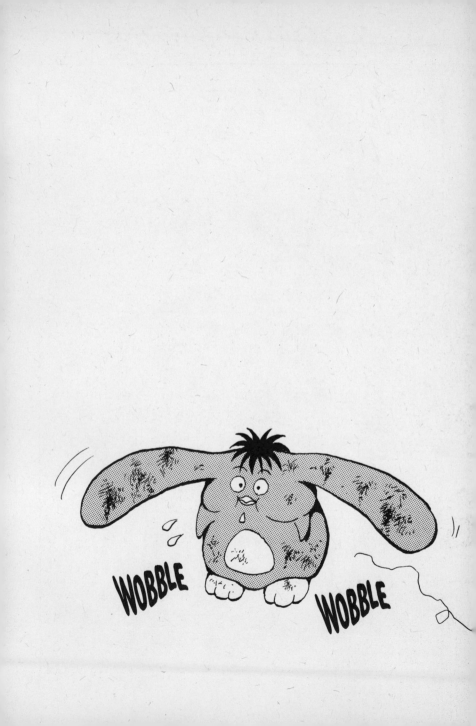

CALLS OF THE DEAD!!

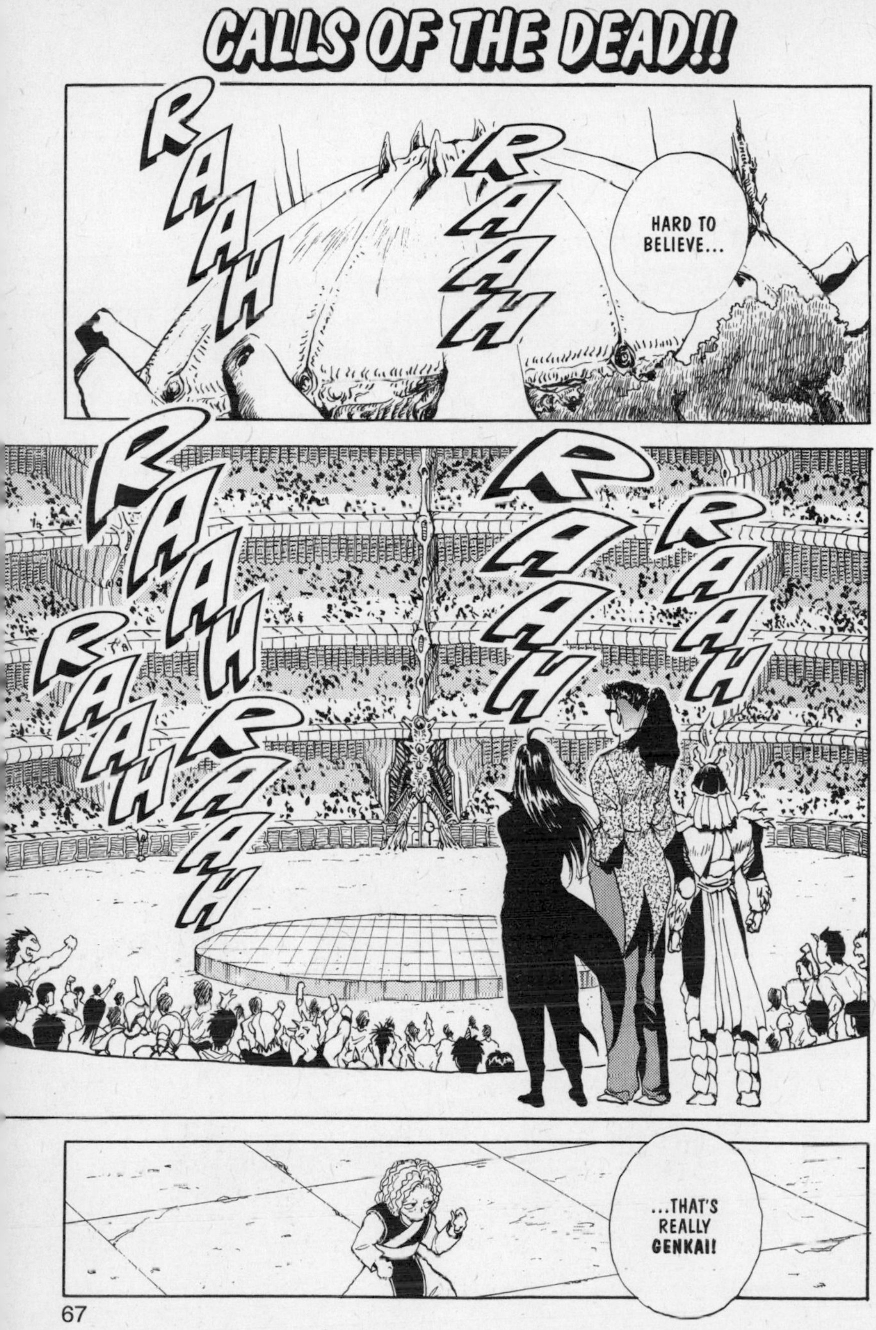
HARD TO BELIEVE...
...THAT'S REALLY GENKAI!

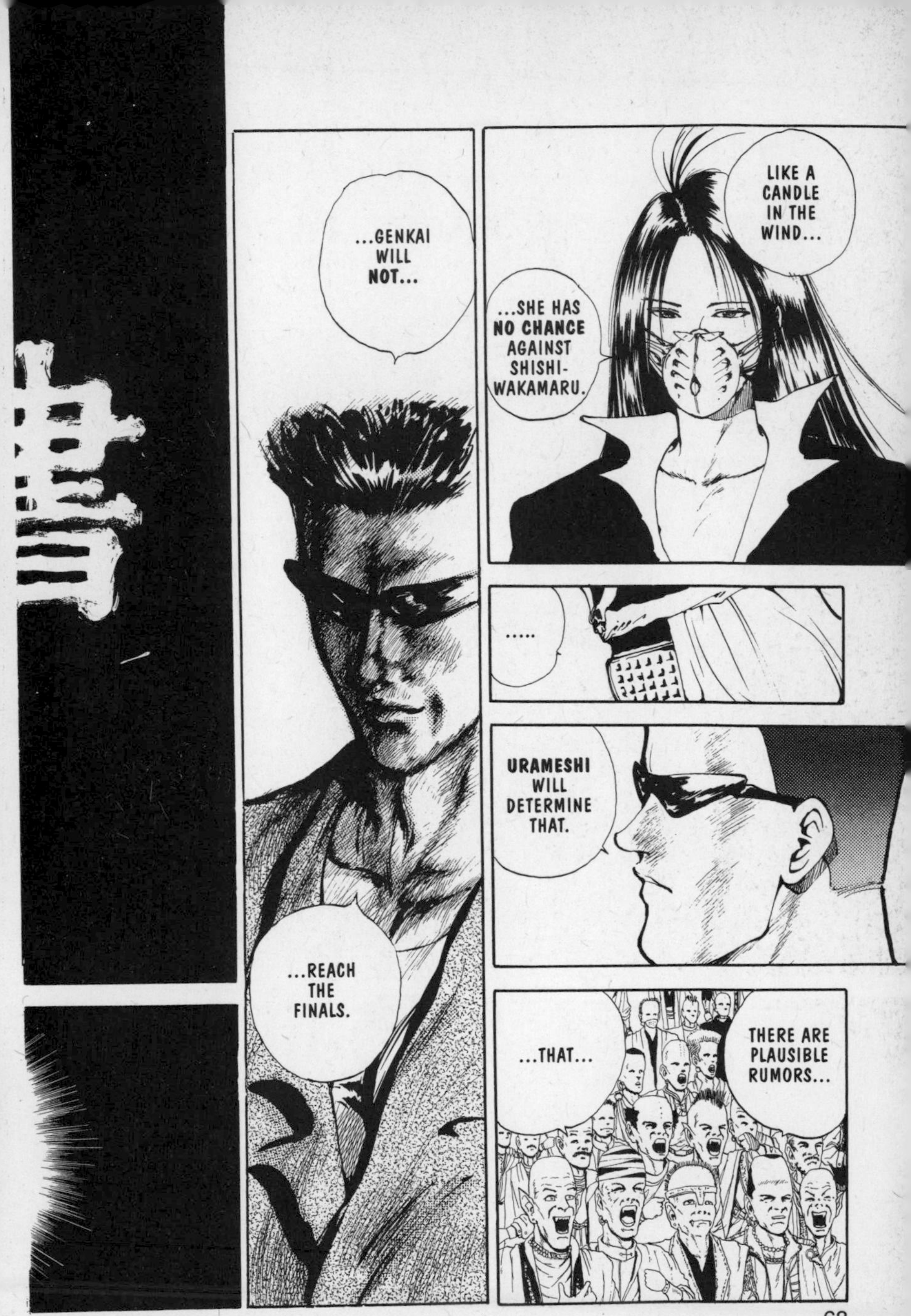
LIKE A CANDLE IN THE WIND...
...SHE HAS NO CHANCE AGAINST SHISHI-WAKAMARU.
.....
URAMESHI WILL DETERMINE THAT.
THERE ARE PLAUSIBLE RUMORS...
...THAT...
...GENKAI WILL NOT...
...REACH THE FINALS.

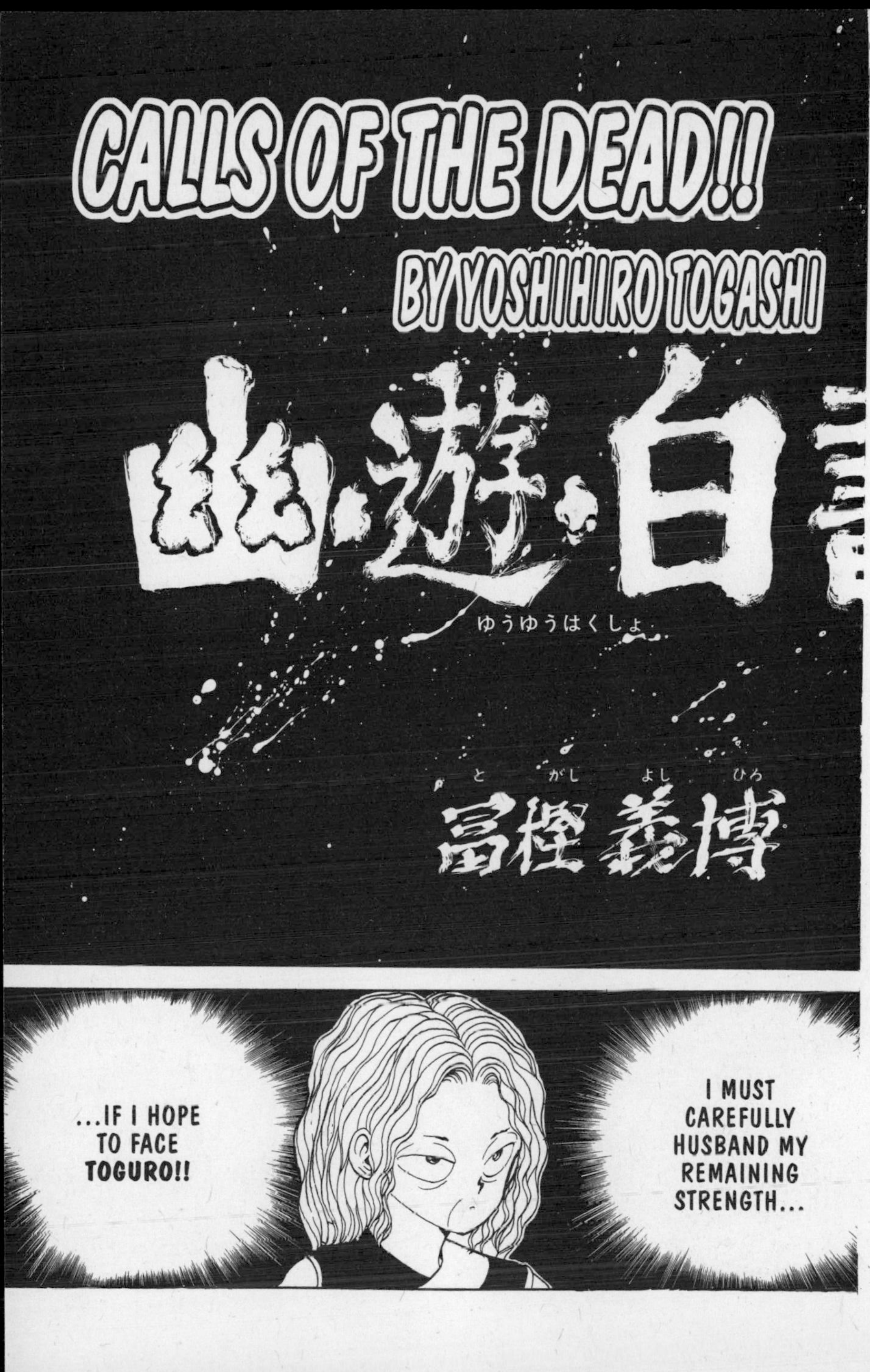
CALLS OF THE DEAD!!
BY YOSHIHIRO TOGASHI
幽遊白
ゆうゆうはくしょ
冨樫義博
とがし よしひろ
I MUST CAREFULLY HUSBAND MY REMAINING STRENGTH...
...IF I HOPE TO FACE TOGURO!!

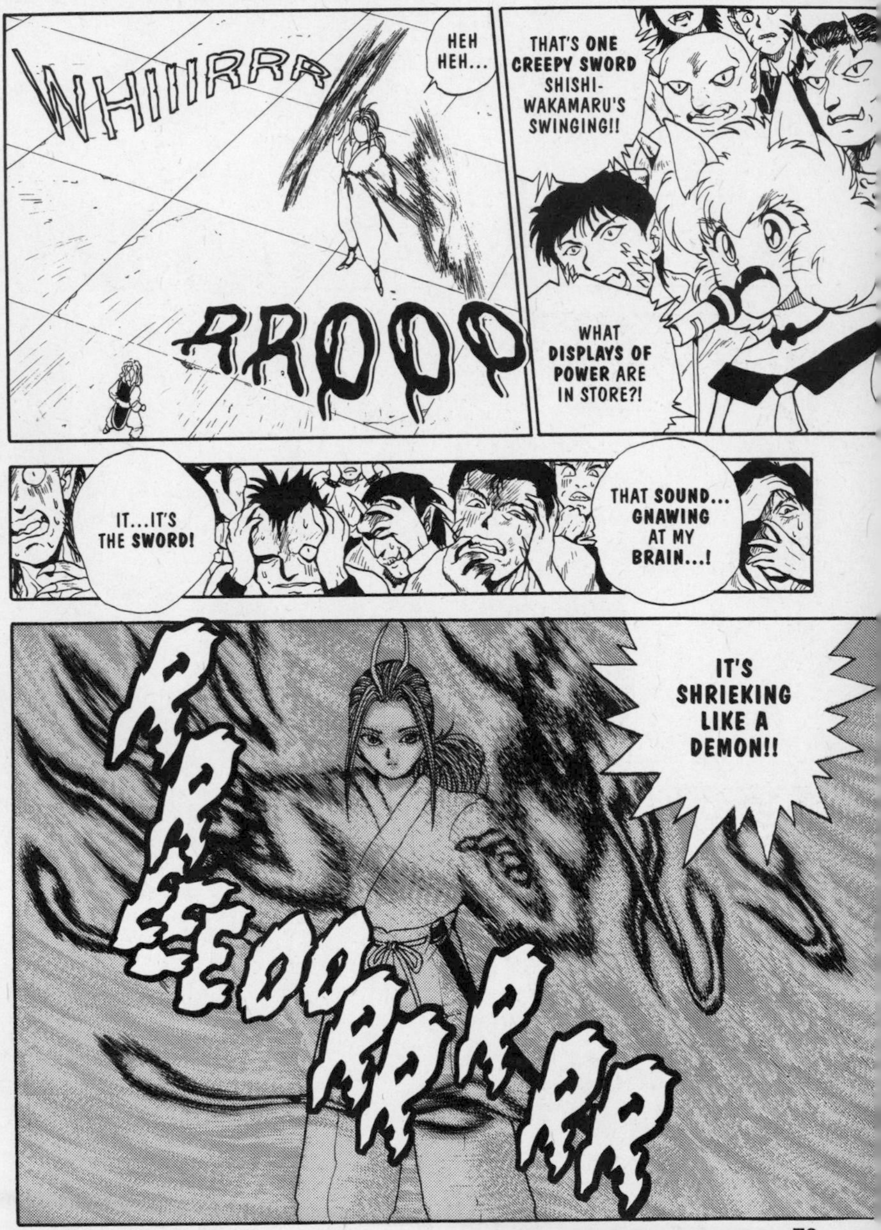
THAT'S ONE CREEPY SWORD SHISHI-WAKAMARU'S SWINGING!!
WHAT DISPLAYS OF POWER ARE IN STORE?!
HEH HEH...
WHIIIRRR
RROOOO
THAT SOUND... GNAWING AT MY BRAIN...!
IT...IT'S THE SWORD!
IT'S SHRIEKING LIKE A DEMON!!
RREEOORRRRR

READ THIS WAY

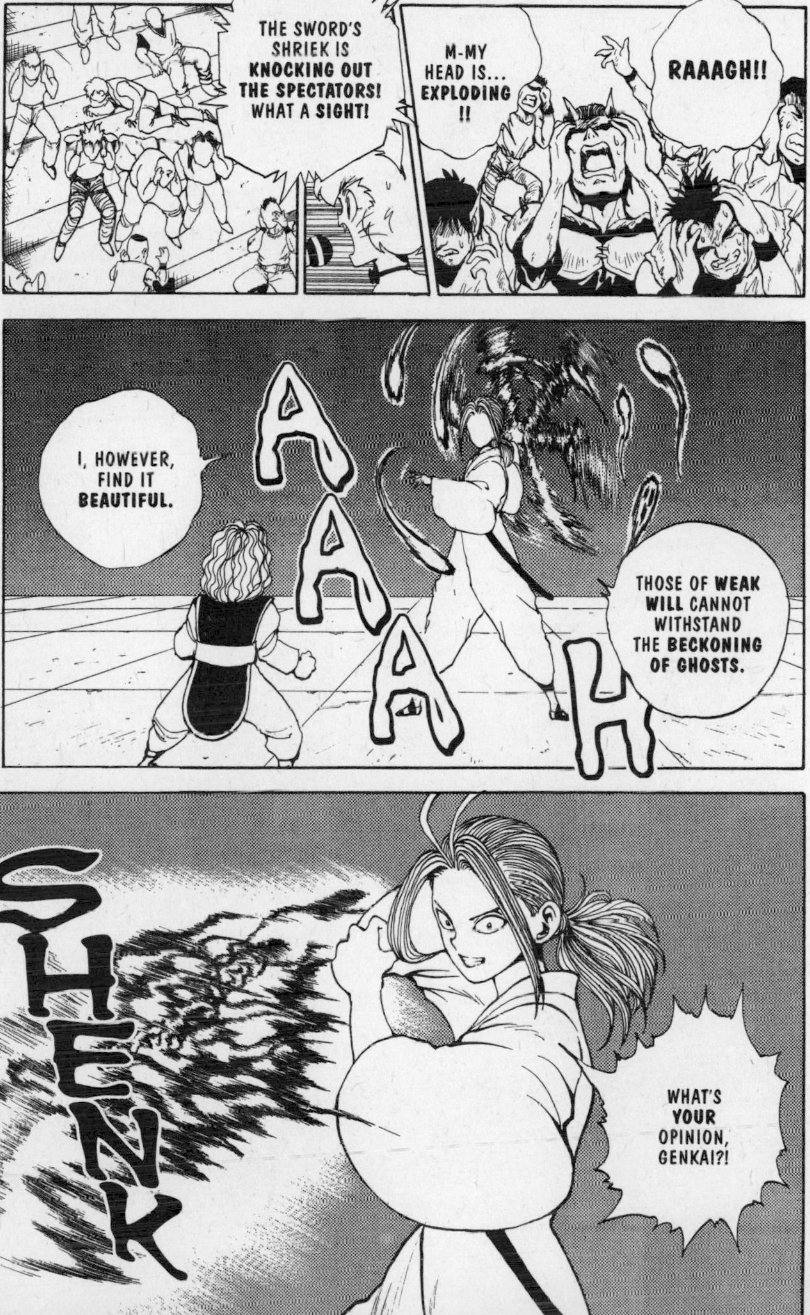

RAAAGH!!
M-MY HEAD IS... EXPLODING !!
THE SWORD'S SHRIEK IS KNOCKING OUT THE SPECTATORS! WHAT A SIGHT!
AAAH
I, HOWEVER, FIND IT BEAUTIFUL.
THOSE OF WEAK WILL CANNOT WITHSTAND THE BECKONING OF GHOSTS.
WHAT'S YOUR OPINION, GENKAI?!
SHENK

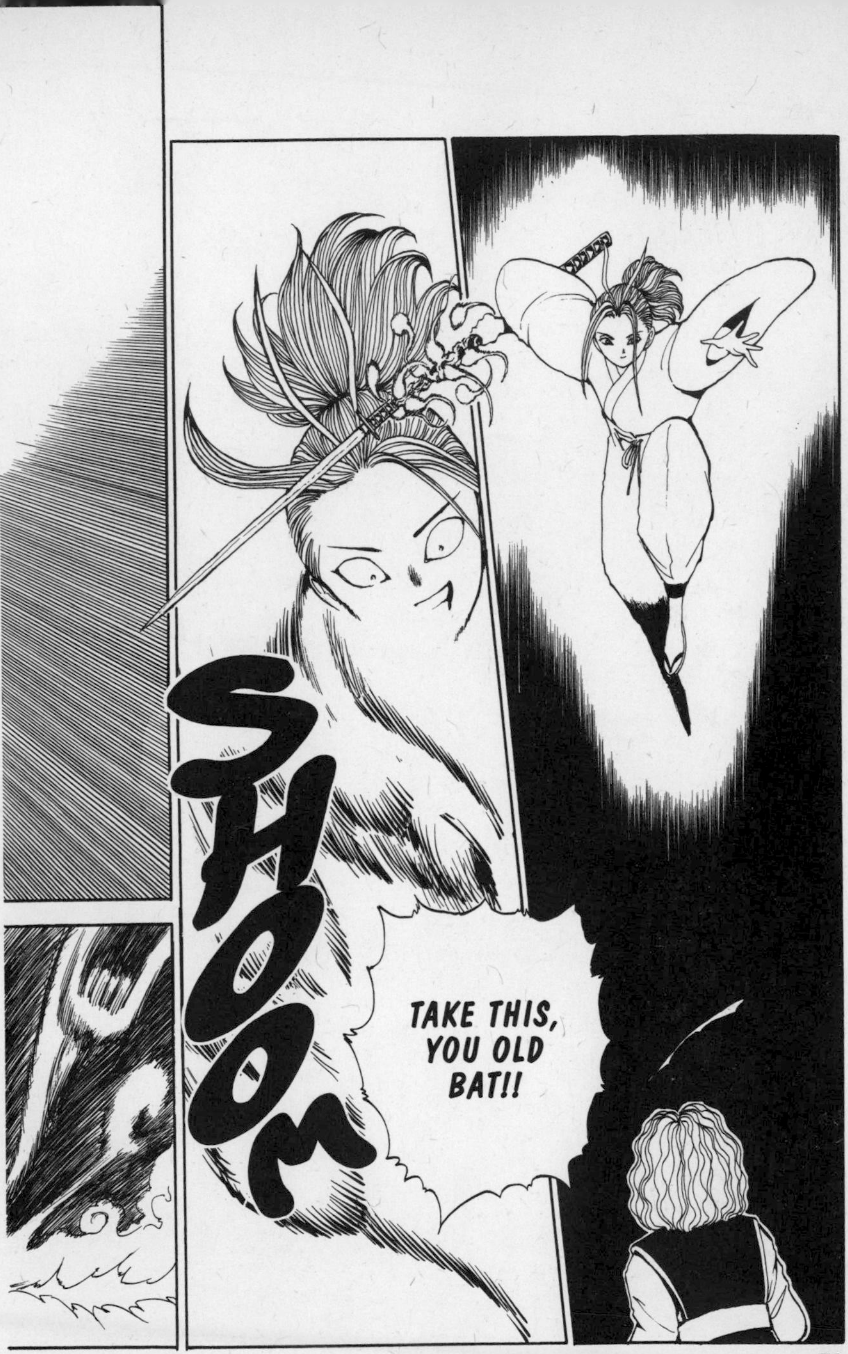
SHOOM
TAKE THIS, YOU OLD BAT!!

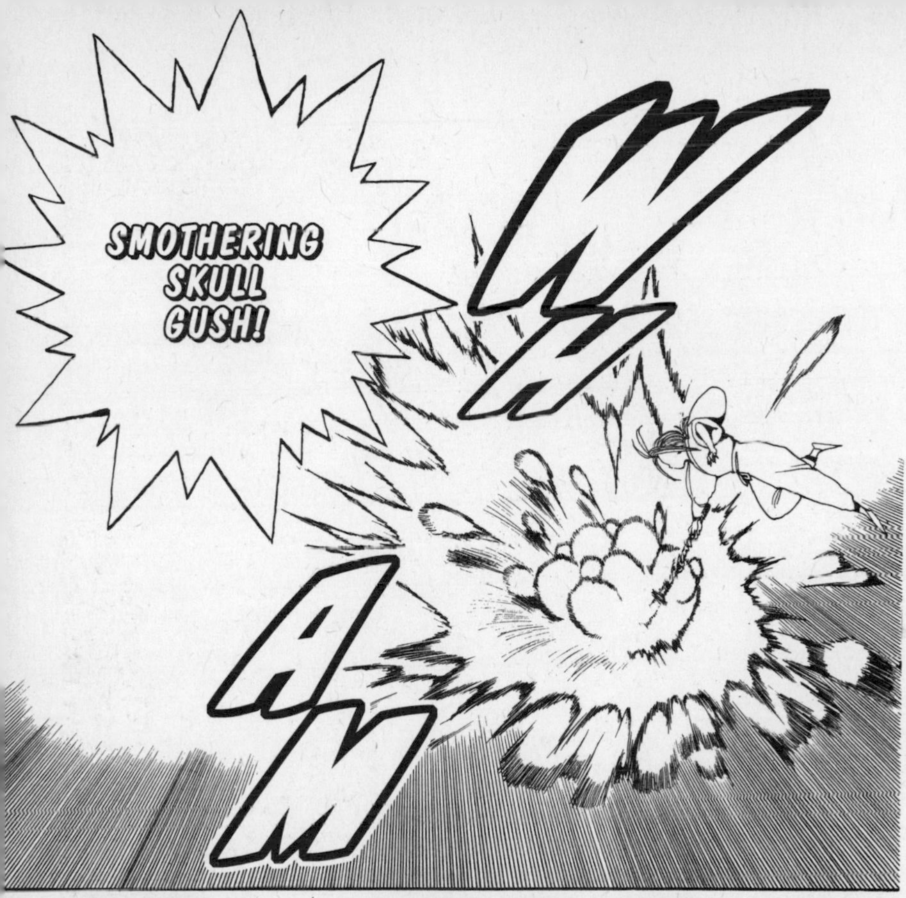
SMOTHERING SKULL GUSH!
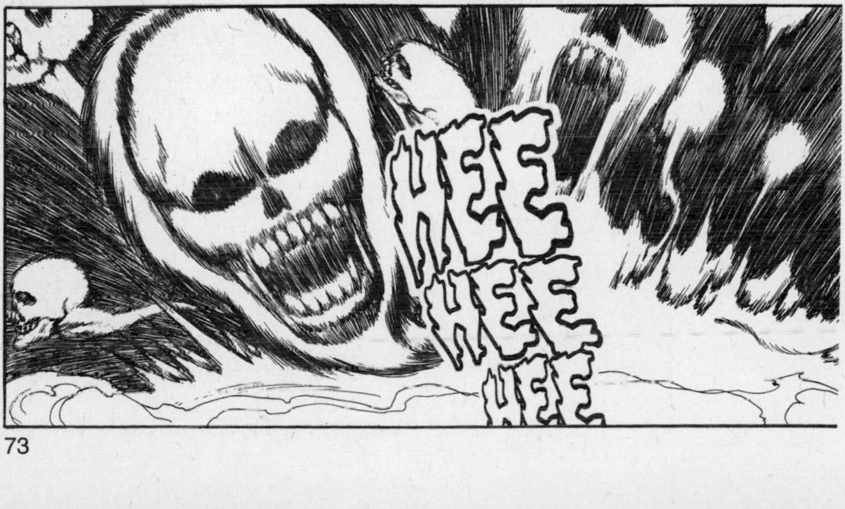
HEE HEE HEE

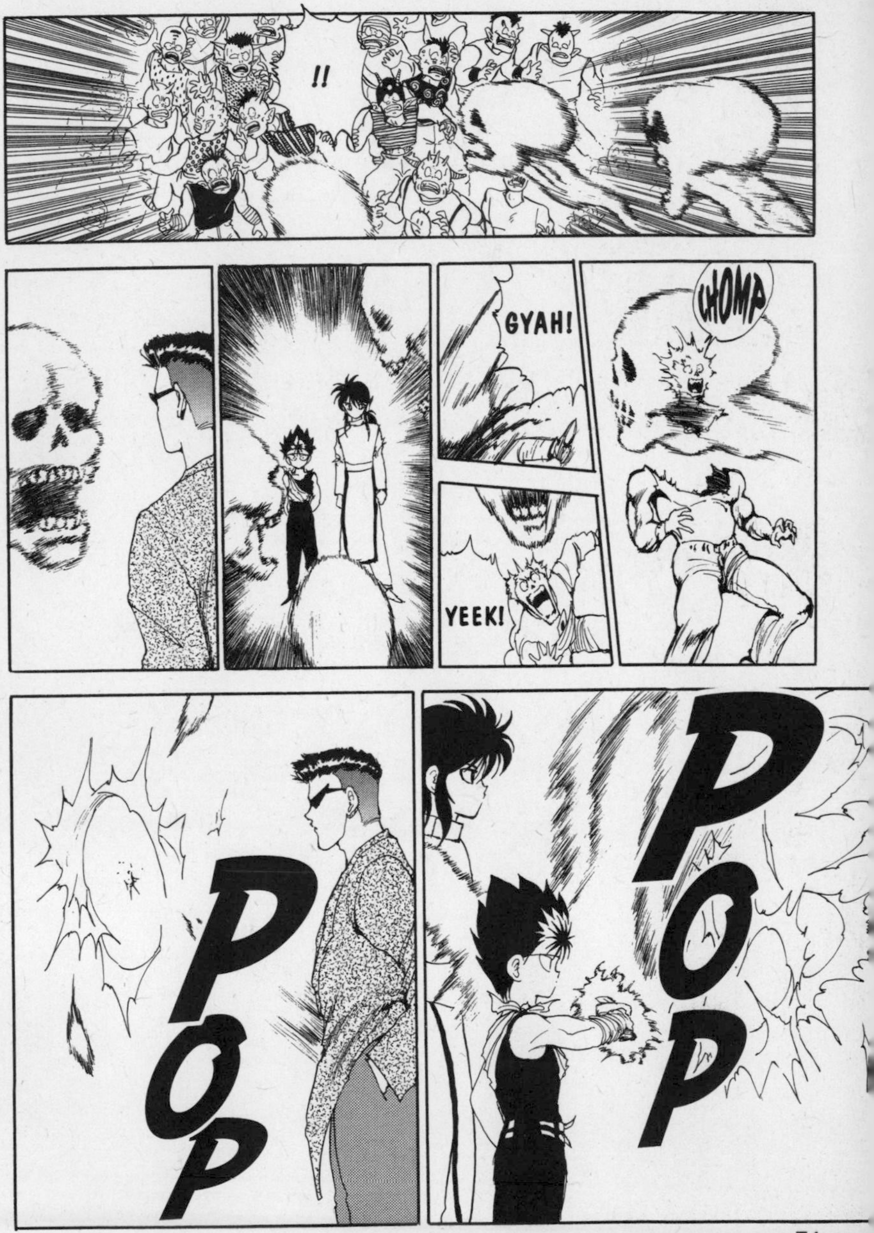
!!
CHOMP
GYAH!
YEEK!
POP
POP

READ THIS WAY

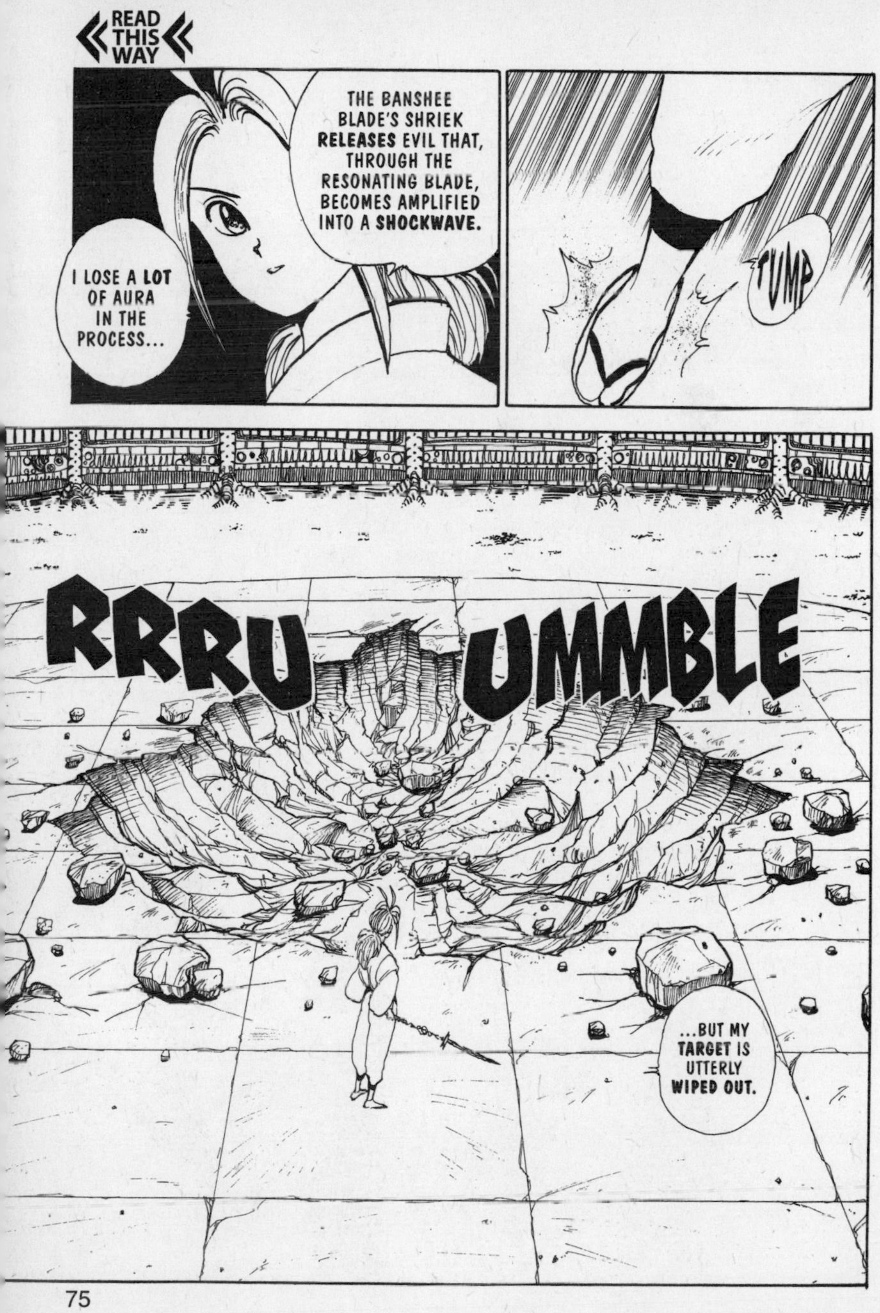
TUMP
THE BANSHEE BLADE'S SHRIEK RELEASES EVIL THAT, THROUGH THE RESONATING BLADE, BECOMES AMPLIFIED INTO A SHOCKWAVE.
I LOSE A LOT OF AURA IN THE PROCESS...
RRRUUMMBLE
...BUT MY TARGET IS UTTERLY WIPED OUT.

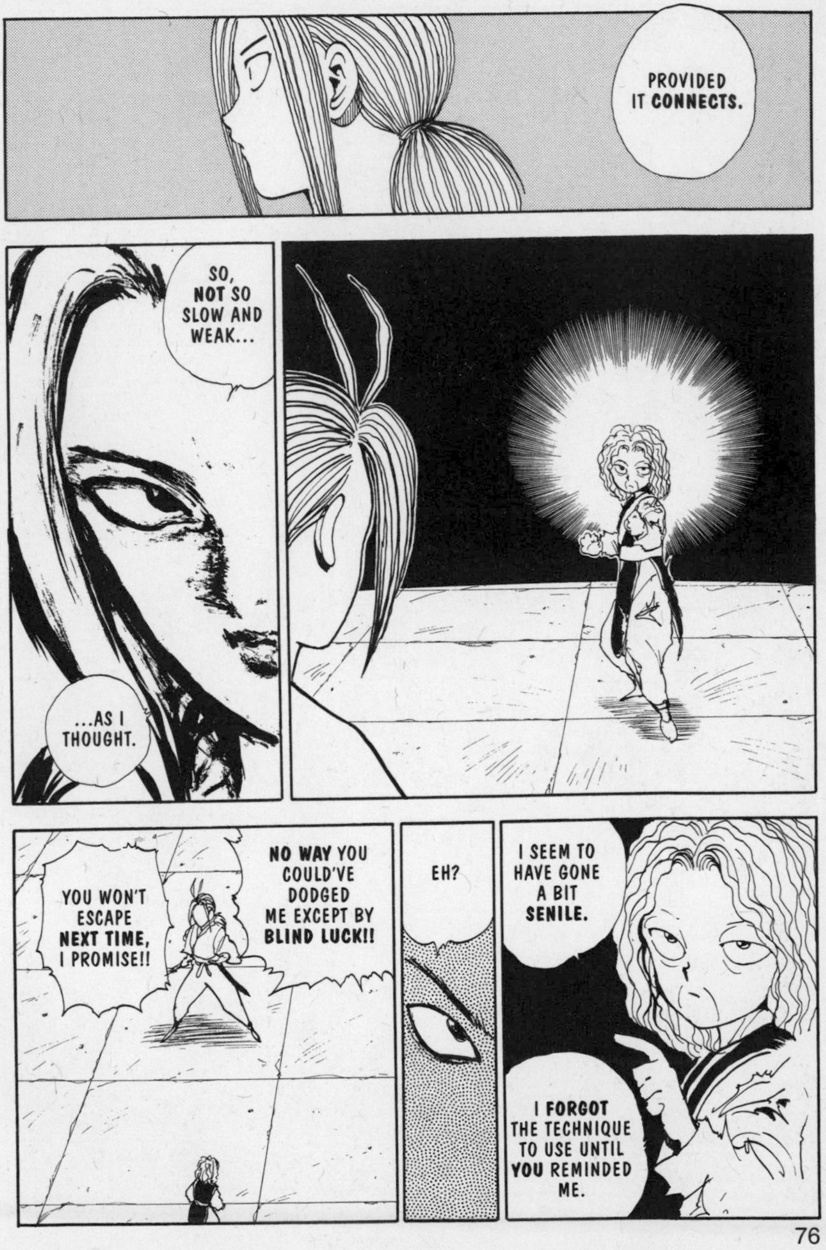
PROVIDED IT CONNECTS.
SO, NOT SO SLOW AND WEAK...
...AS I THOUGHT.
I SEEM TO HAVE GONE A BIT SENILE.
I FORGOT THE TECHNIQUE TO USE UNTIL YOU REMINDED ME.
EH?
NO WAY YOU COULD'VE DODGED ME EXCEPT BY BLIND LUCK!!
YOU WON'T ESCAPE NEXT TIME, I PROMISE!!

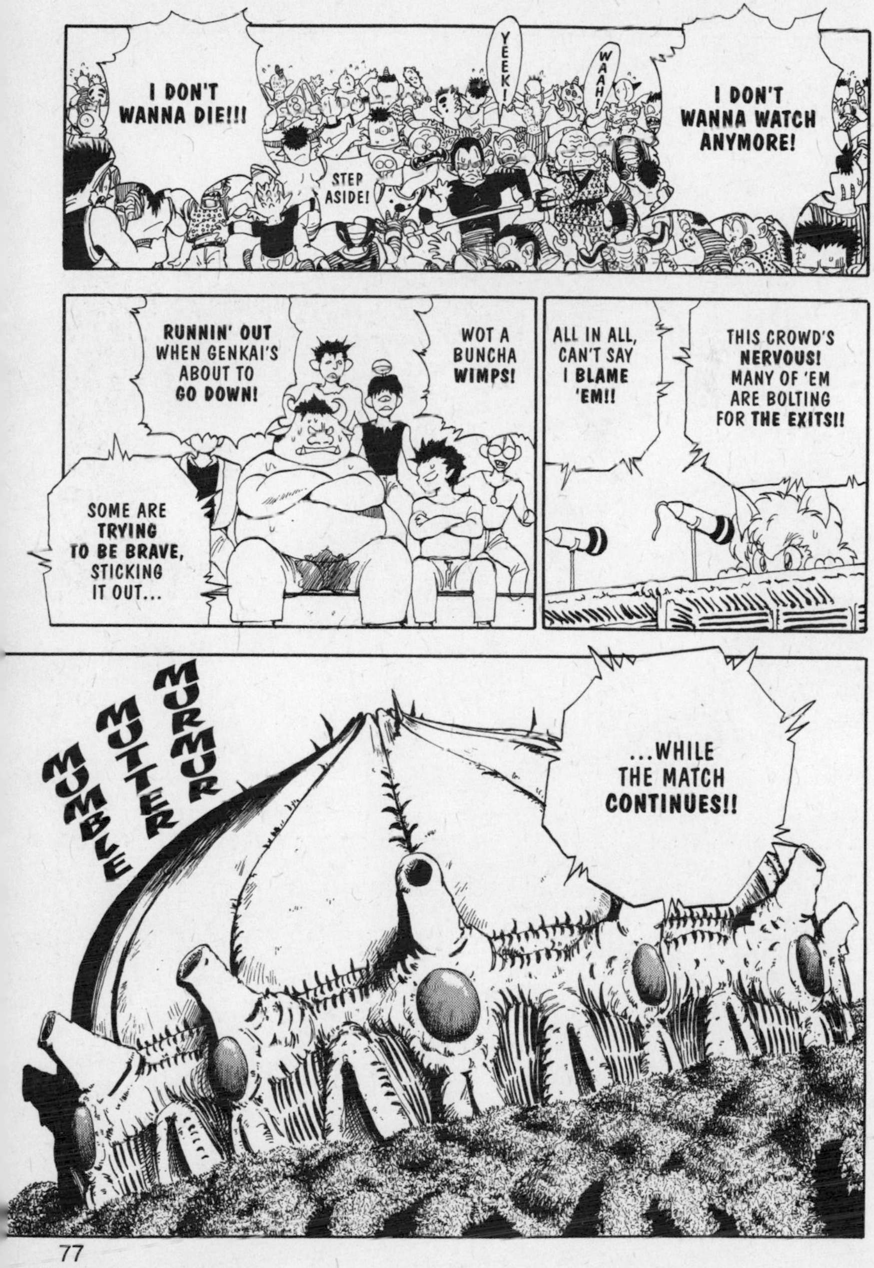
I DON'T WANNA WATCH ANYMORE!
WAAH!
YEEK!
STEP ASIDE!
I DON'T WANNA DIE!!!
THIS CROWD'S NERVOUS! MANY OF 'EM ARE BOLTING FOR THE EXITS!!
ALL IN ALL, CAN'T SAY I BLAME 'EM!!
WOT A BUNCHA WIMPS!
RUNNIN' OUT WHEN GENKAI'S ABOUT TO GO DOWN!
SOME ARE TRYING TO BE BRAVE, STICKING IT OUT...
...WHILE THE MATCH CONTINUES!!
MURMUR
MUTTER
MUMBLE

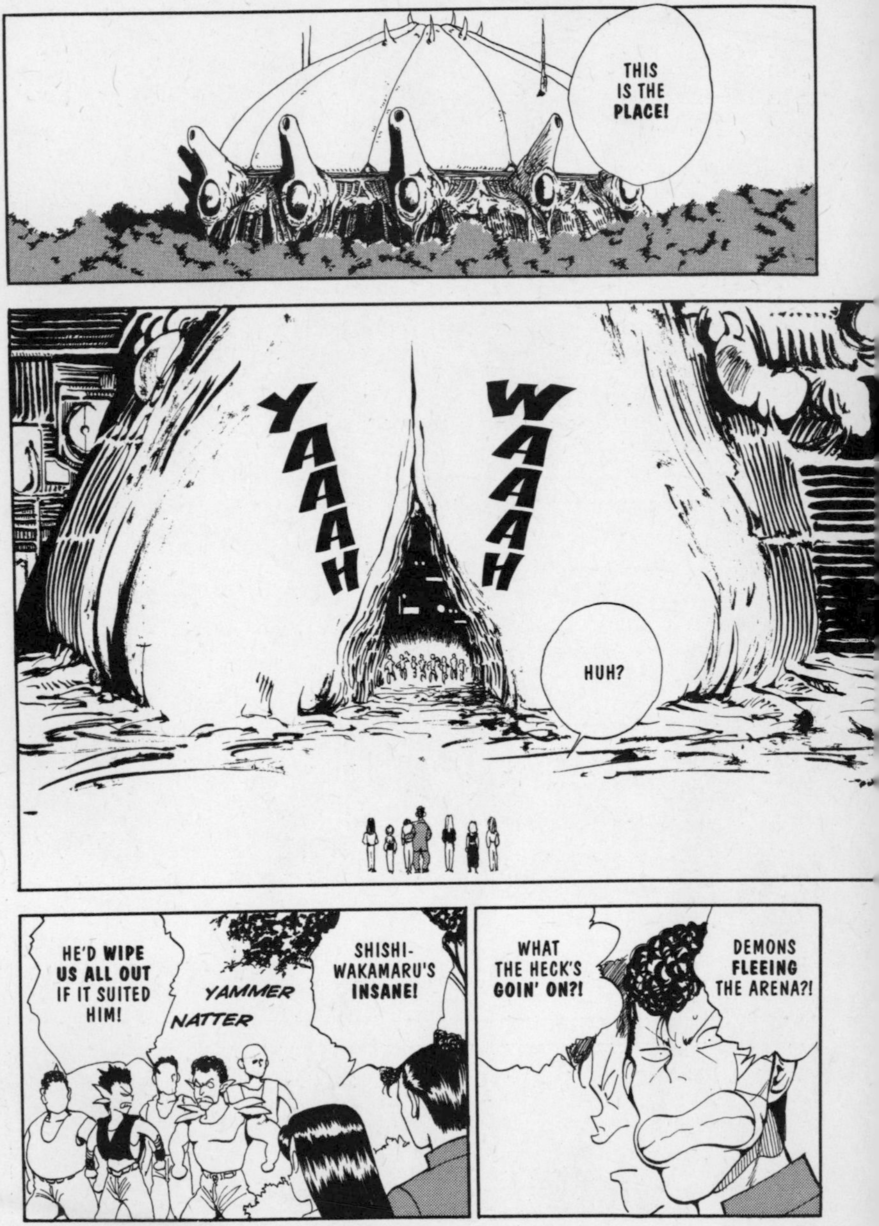
THIS IS THE PLACE!
WAAAAH
YAAAAH
HUH?
DEMONS FLEEING THE ARENA?!
WHAT THE HECK'S GOIN' ON?!
SHISHI-WAKAMARU'S INSANE!
YAMMER
NATTER
HE'D WIPE US ALL OUT IF IT SUITED HIM!

READ THIS WAY

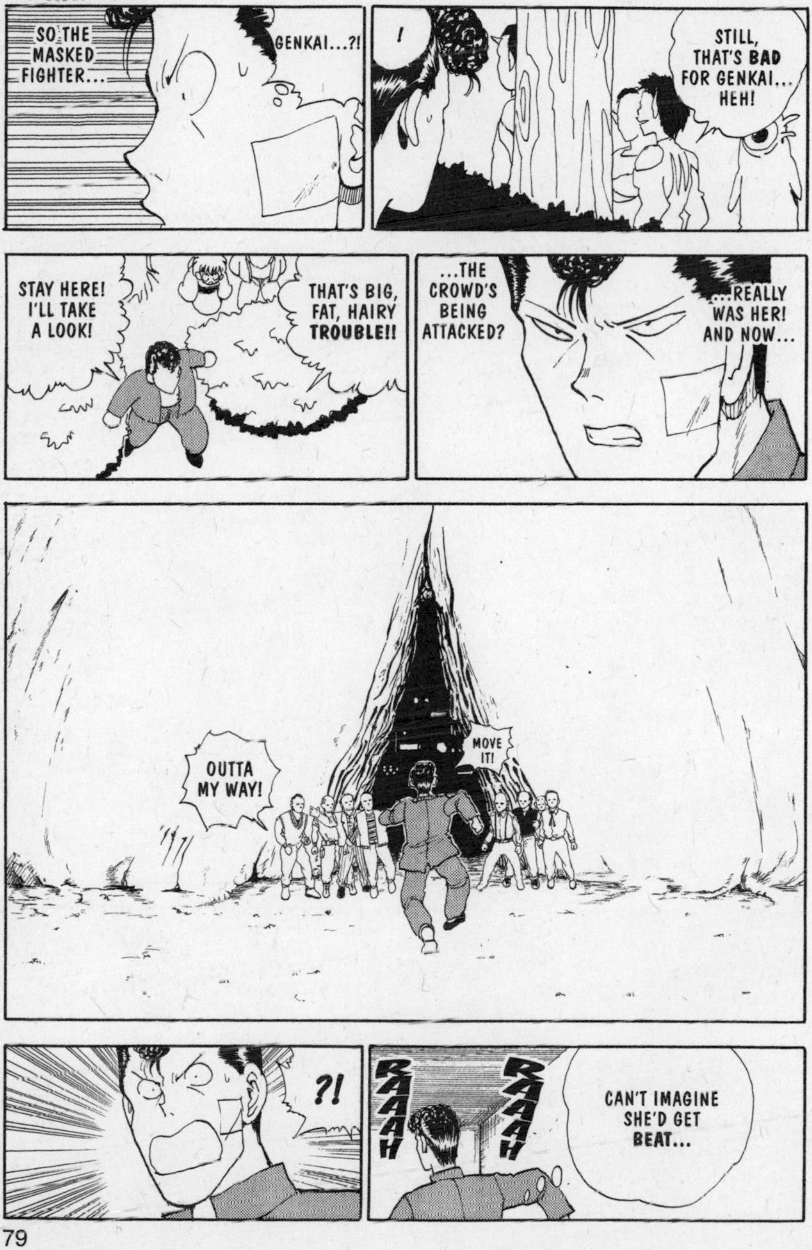
STILL, THAT'S BAD FOR GENKAI... HEH!
!
GENKAI...?!
SO THE MASKED FIGHTER...
...REALLY WAS HER! AND NOW...
...THE CROWD'S BEING ATTACKED?
THAT'S BIG, FAT, HAIRY TROUBLE!!
STAY HERE! I'LL TAKE A LOOK!
MOVE IT!
OUTTA MY WAY!
CAN'T IMAGINE SHE'D GET BEAT...
RAAAH
RAAAH
?!

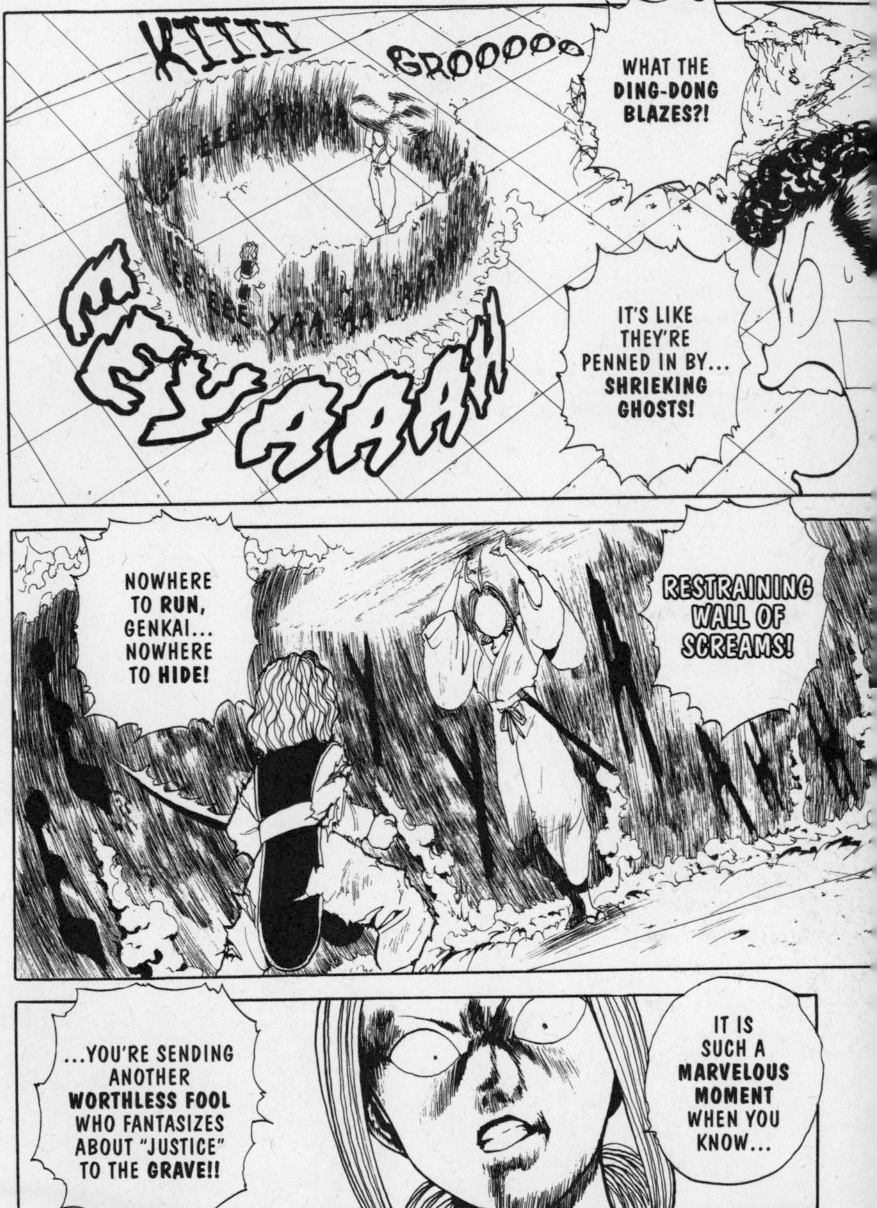
WHAT THE DING-DONG BLAZES?!
IT'S LIKE THEY'RE PENNED IN BY... SHRIEKING GHOSTS!
GROOOOO
KIIII
KYAAAH
RESTRAINING WALL OF SCREAMS!
NOWHERE TO RUN, GENKAI... NOWHERE TO HIDE!
IT IS SUCH A MARVELOUS MOMENT WHEN YOU KNOW...
...YOU'RE SENDING ANOTHER WORTHLESS FOOL WHO FANTASIZES ABOUT "JUSTICE" TO THE GRAVE!!

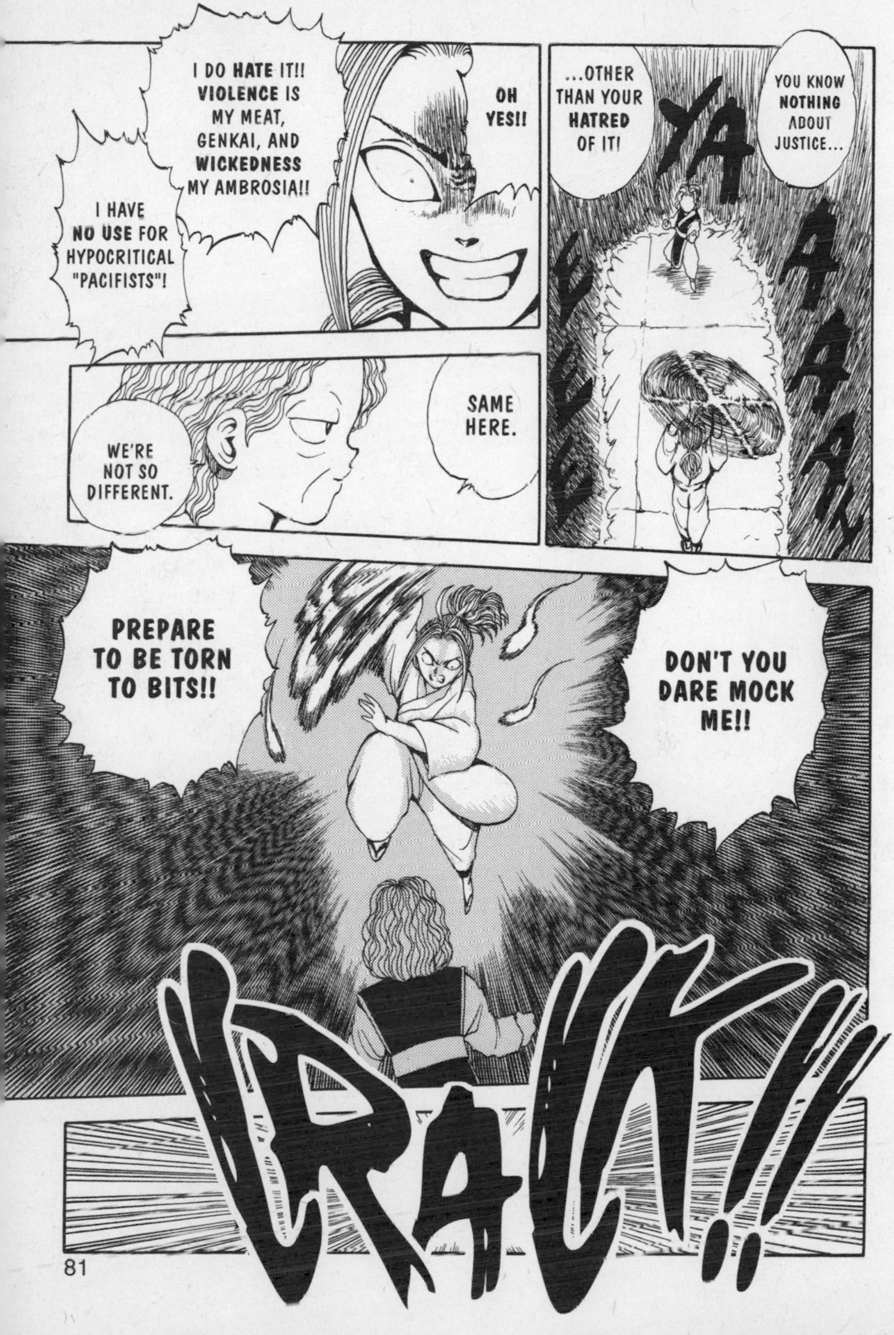
YOU KNOW NOTHING ABOUT JUSTICE...
...OTHER THAN YOUR HATRED OF IT!
OH YES!!
I DO HATE IT!! VIOLENCE IS MY MEAT, GENKAI, AND WICKEDNESS MY AMBROSIA!!
I HAVE NO USE FOR HYPOCRITICAL "PACIFISTS"!
SAME HERE.
WE'RE NOT SO DIFFERENT.
DON'T YOU DARE MOCK ME!!
PREPARE TO BE TORN TO BITS!!

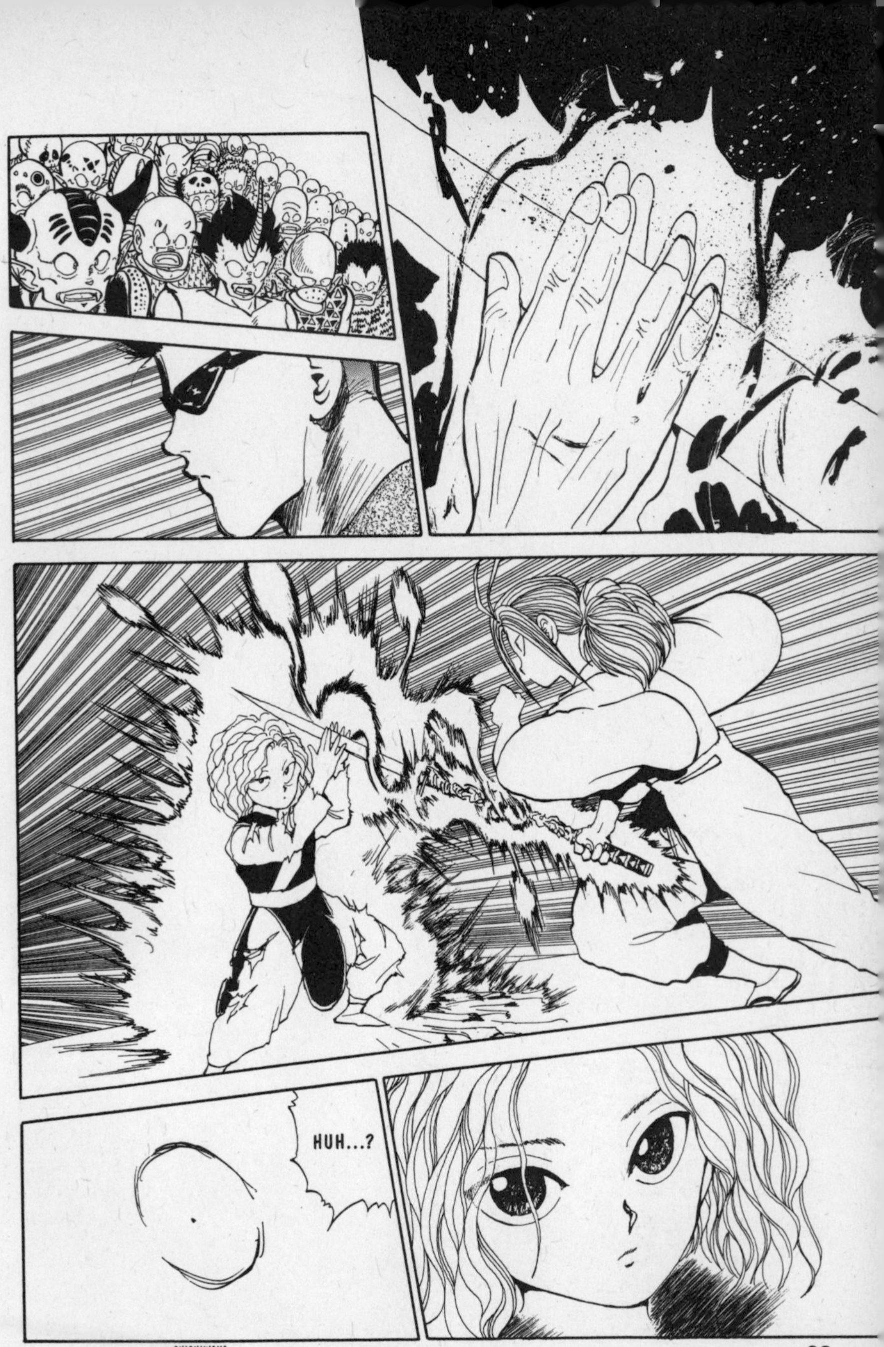
HUH...?

SHISHIWAKA

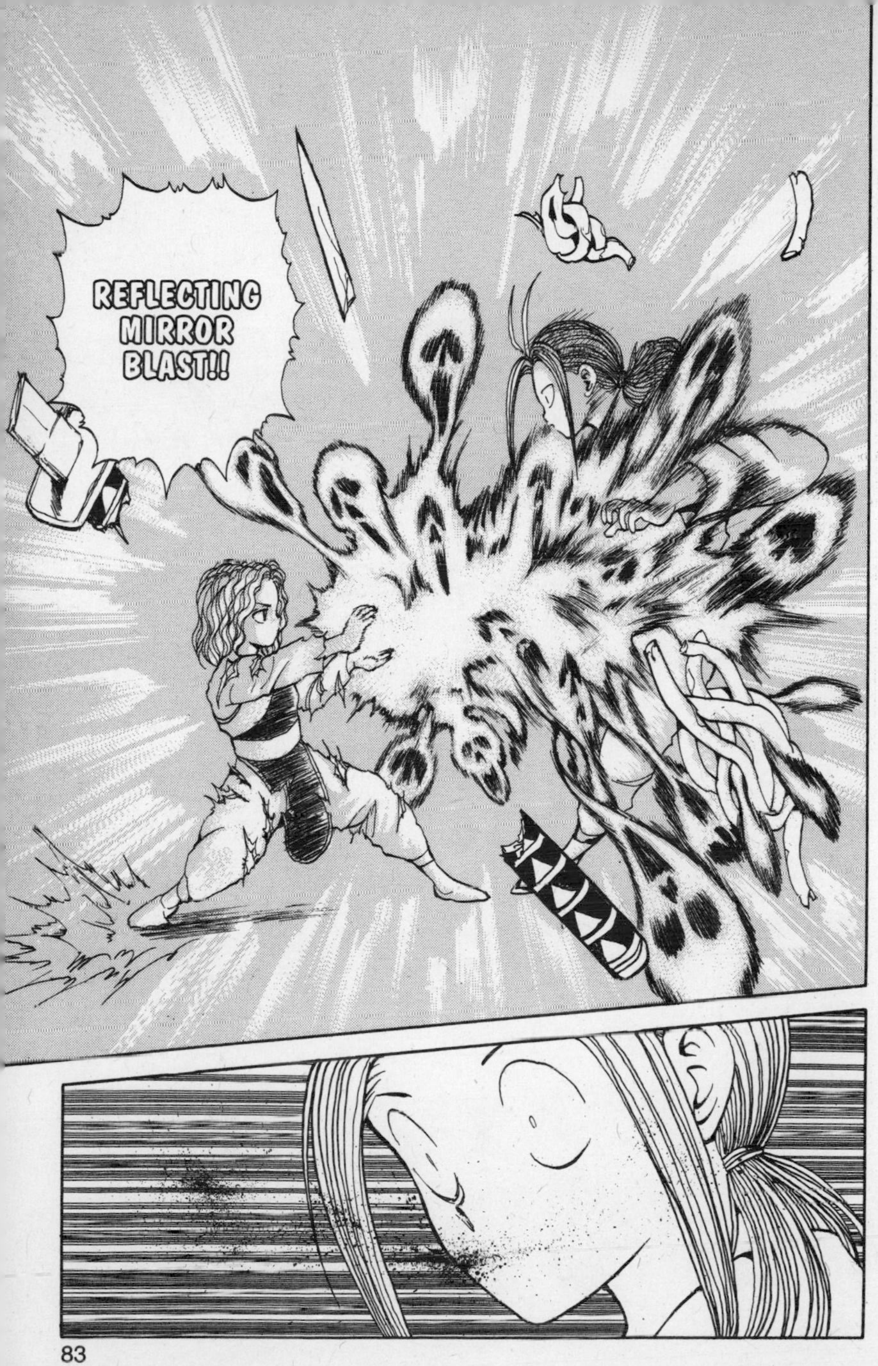
REFLECTING MIRROR BLAST!!

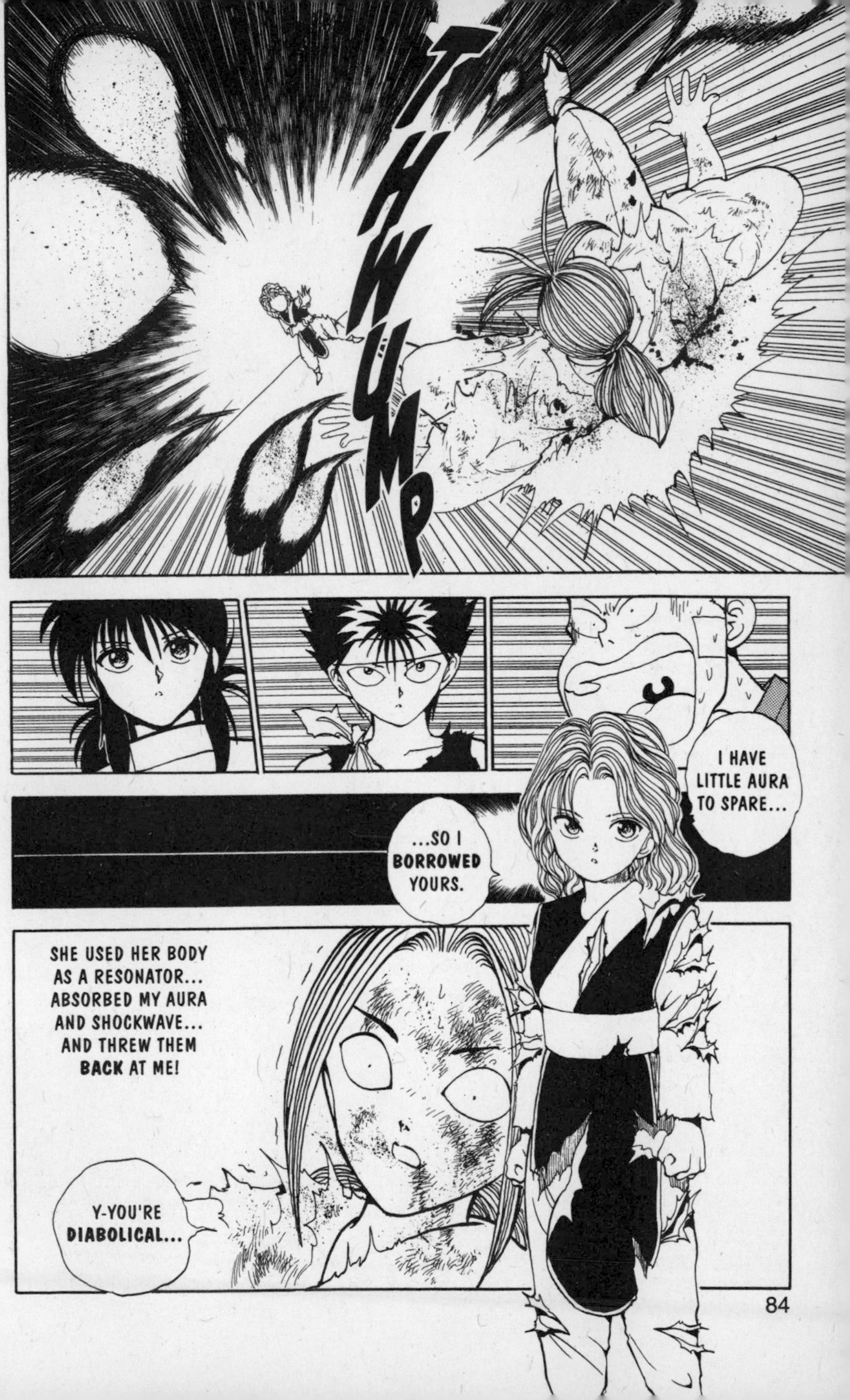
THWUMP
I HAVE LITTLE AURA TO SPARE...
...SO I BORROWED YOURS.
SHE USED HER BODY AS A RESONATOR... ABSORBED MY AURA AND SHOCKWAVE... AND THREW THEM BACK AT ME!
Y-YOU'RE DIABOLICAL...

READ THIS WAY

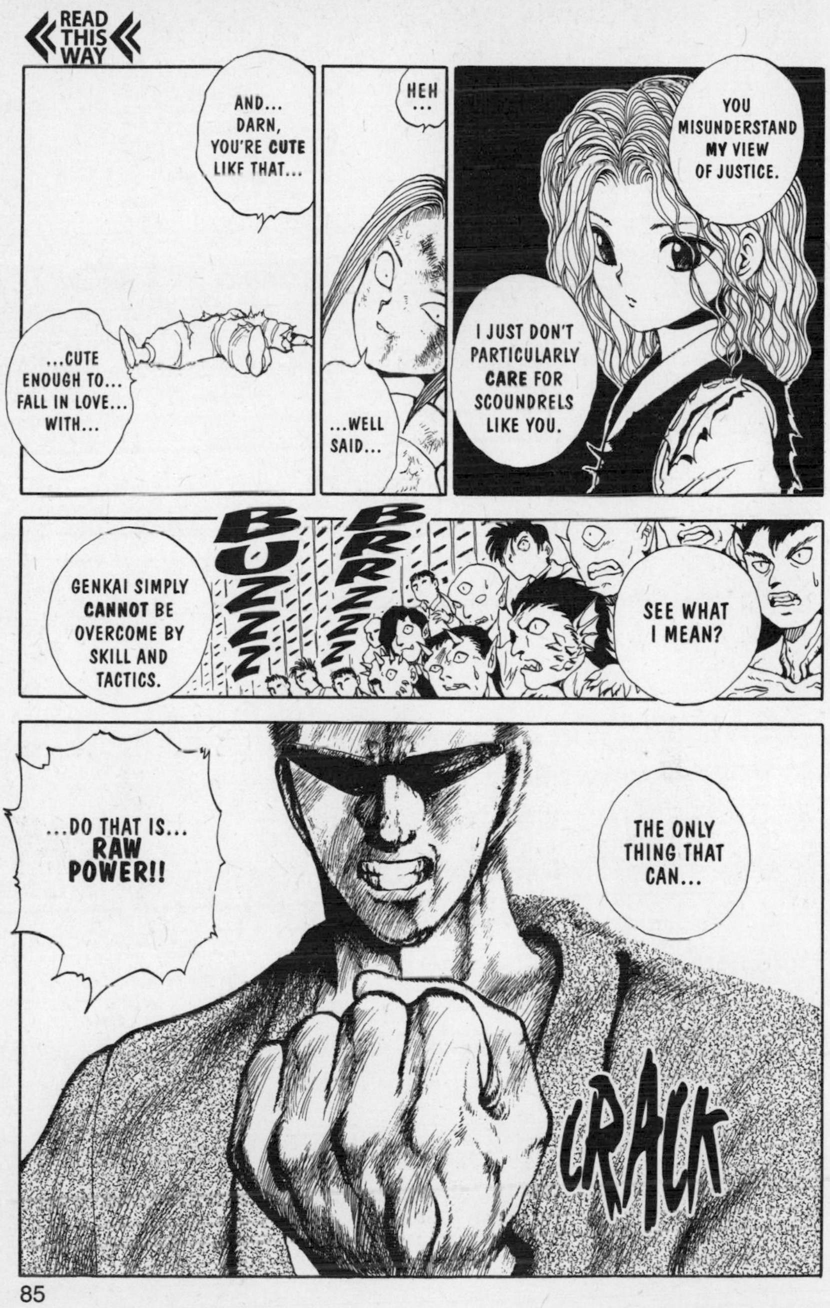
YOU MISUNDERSTAND MY VIEW OF JUSTICE.
I JUST DON'T PARTICULARLY CARE FOR SCOUNDRELS LIKE YOU.
HEH...
...WELL SAID...
AND... DARN, YOU'RE CUTE LIKE THAT...
...CUTE ENOUGH TO... FALL IN LOVE... WITH...
SEE WHAT I MEAN?
BRRZZZZ
BUZZZZ
GENKAI SIMPLY CANNOT BE OVERCOME BY SKILL AND TACTICS.
THE ONLY THING THAT CAN...
...DO THAT IS... RAW POWER!!
CRACK

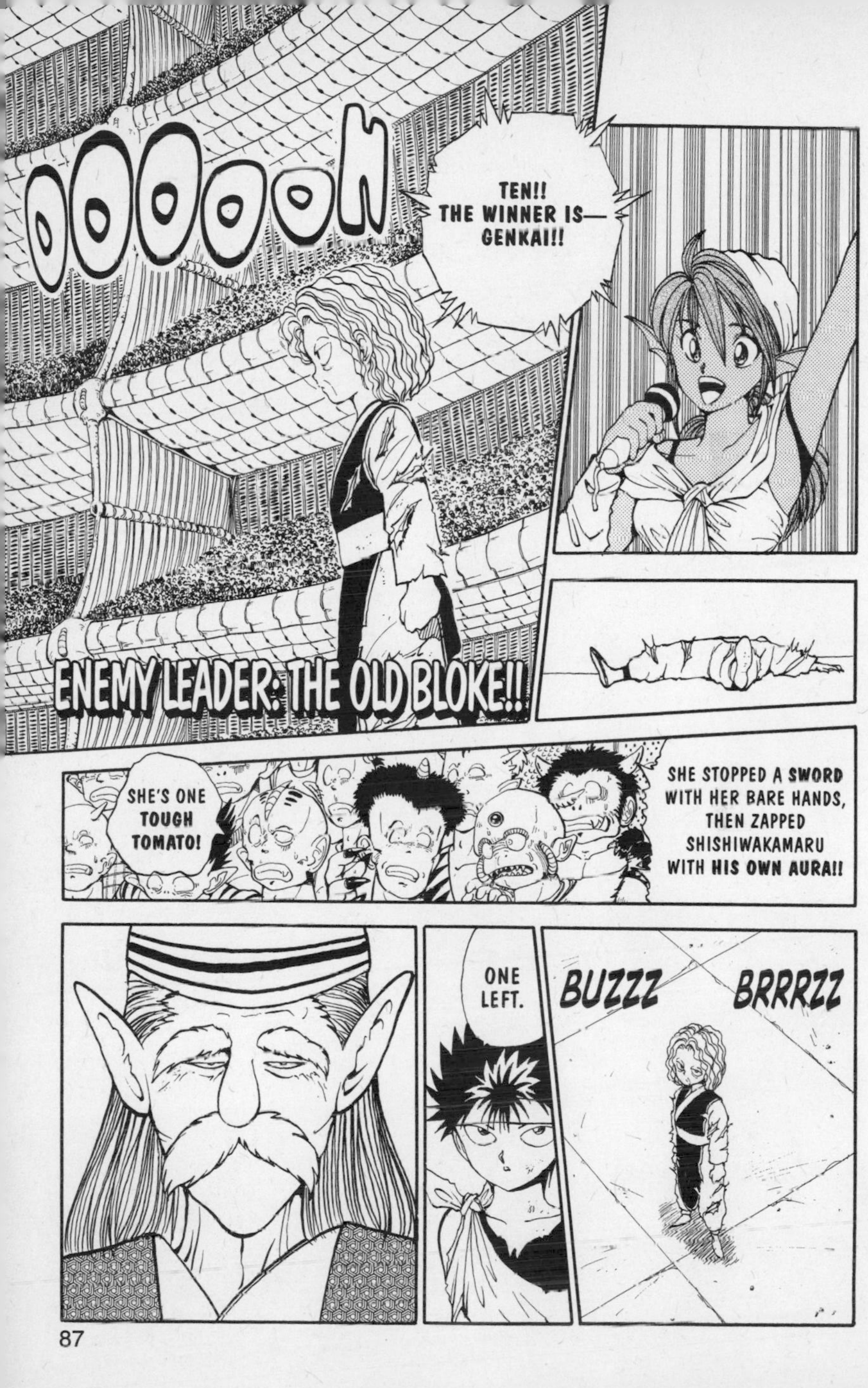
TEN!! THE WINNER IS— GENKAI!!
OOOOOH
ENEMY LEADER: THE OLD BLOKE!!
SHE STOPPED A SWORD WITH HER BARE HANDS, THEN ZAPPED SHISHIWAKAMARU WITH HIS OWN AURA!!
SHE'S ONE TOUGH TOMATO!
BUZZZ
BRRRZZ
ONE LEFT.

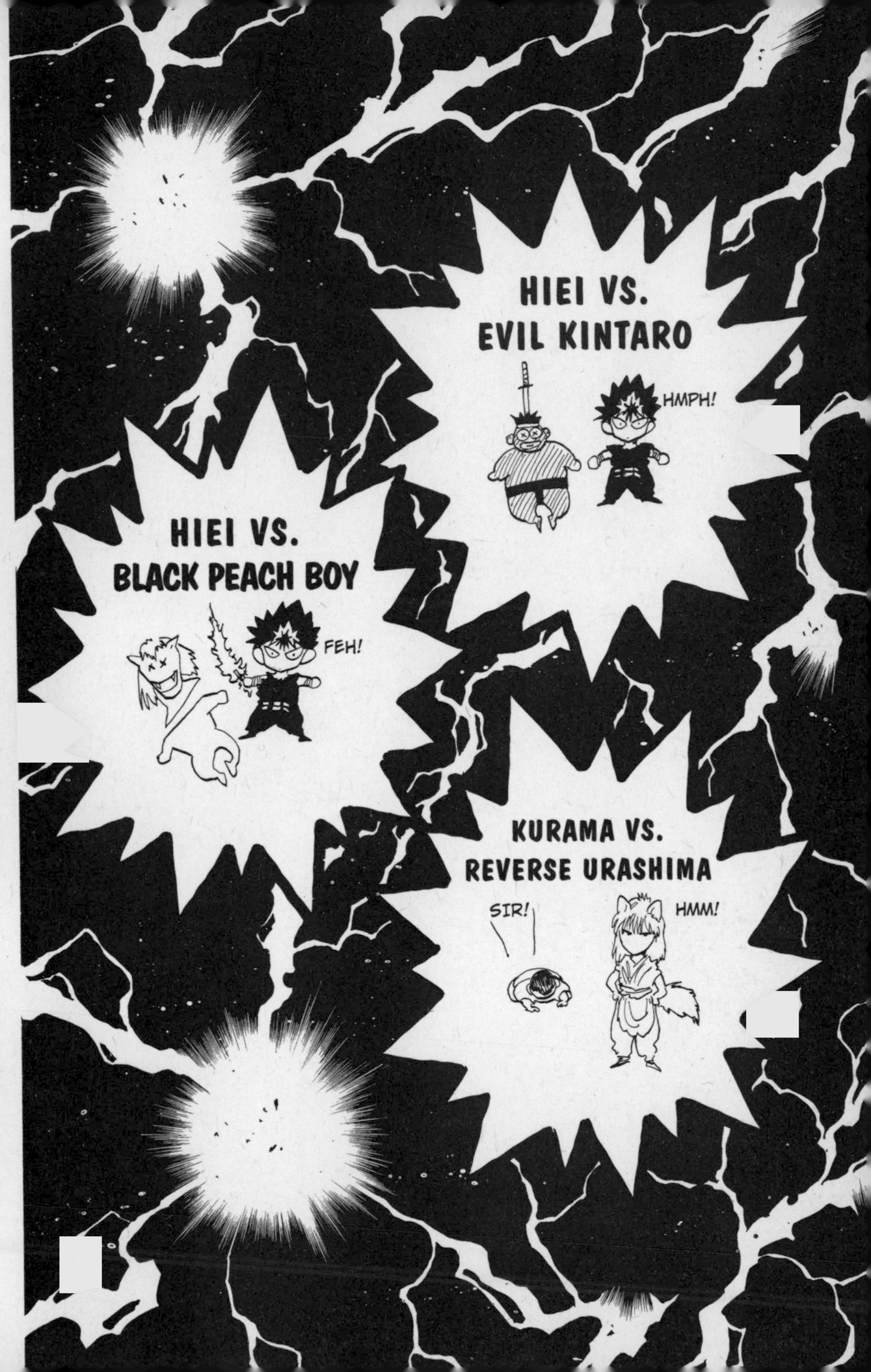
HIEI VS.
EVIL KINTARO
HMPH!
HIEI VS.
BLACK PEACH BOY
FEH!
KURAMA VS.
REVERSE URASHIMA
HMM!
SIR!

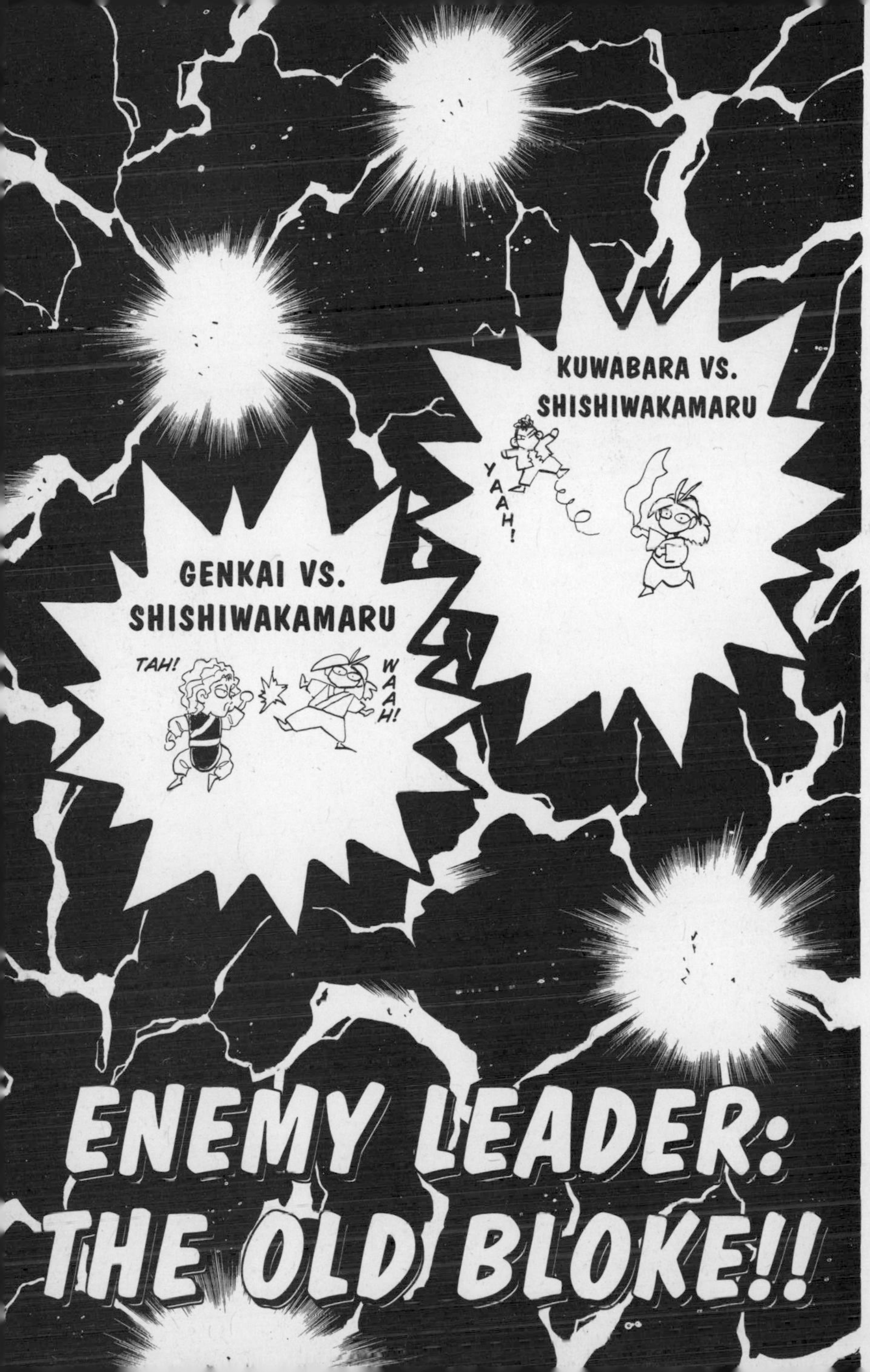
KUWABARA VS. SHISHIWAKAMARU
YAAAH!
GENKAI VS. SHISHIWAKAMARU
WAAAH!
TAH!
ENEMY LEADER: THE OLD BLOKE!!

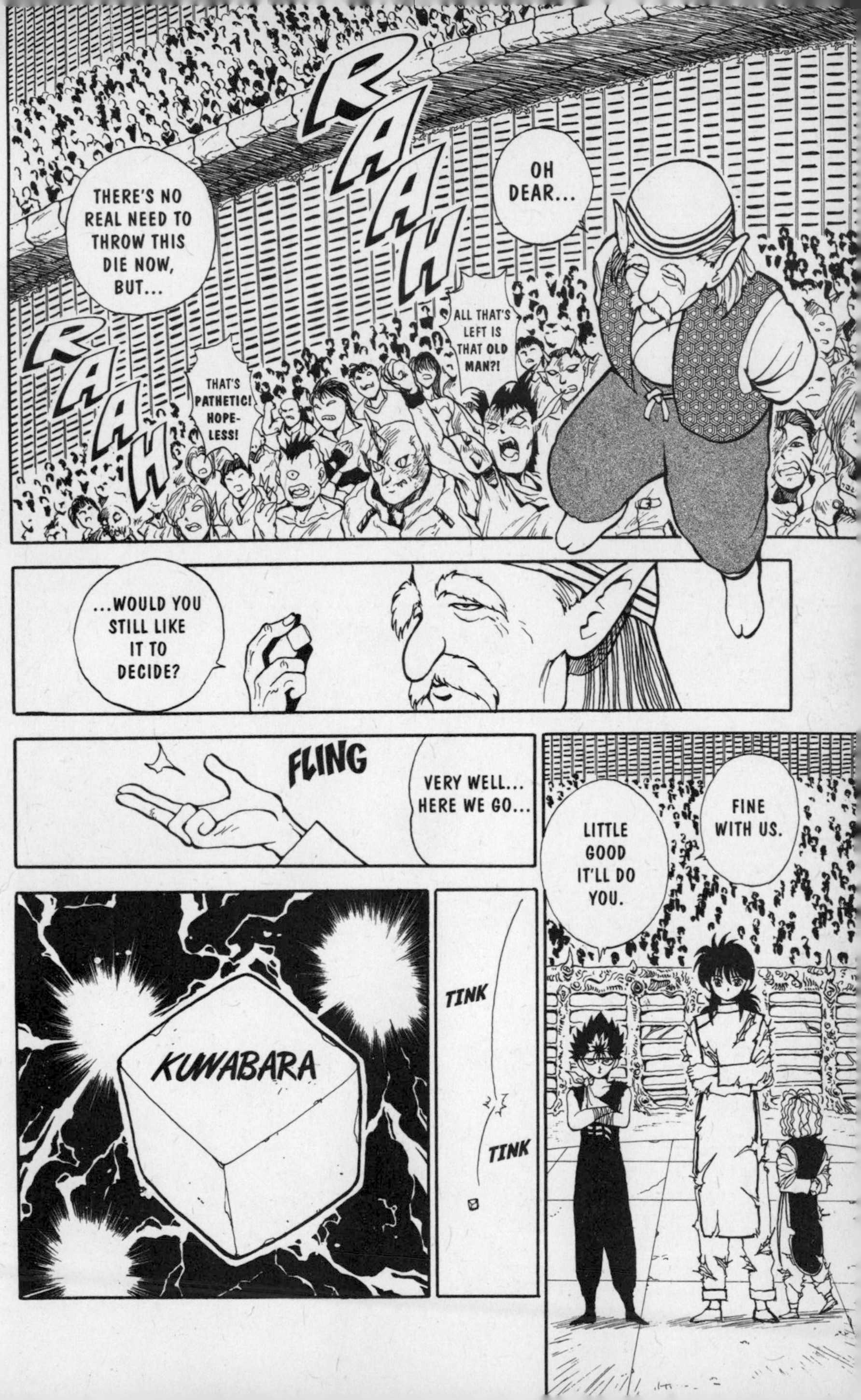
RAAAH
OH DEAR...
THERE'S NO REAL NEED TO THROW THIS DIE NOW, BUT...
ALL THAT'S LEFT IS THAT OLD MAN?!
THAT'S PATHETIC! HOPE-LESS!
RAAAH
...WOULD YOU STILL LIKE IT TO DECIDE?
FINE WITH US.
LITTLE GOOD IT'LL DO YOU.
VERY WELL... HERE WE GO...
FLING
TINK
TINK
KUWABARA

READ THIS WAY

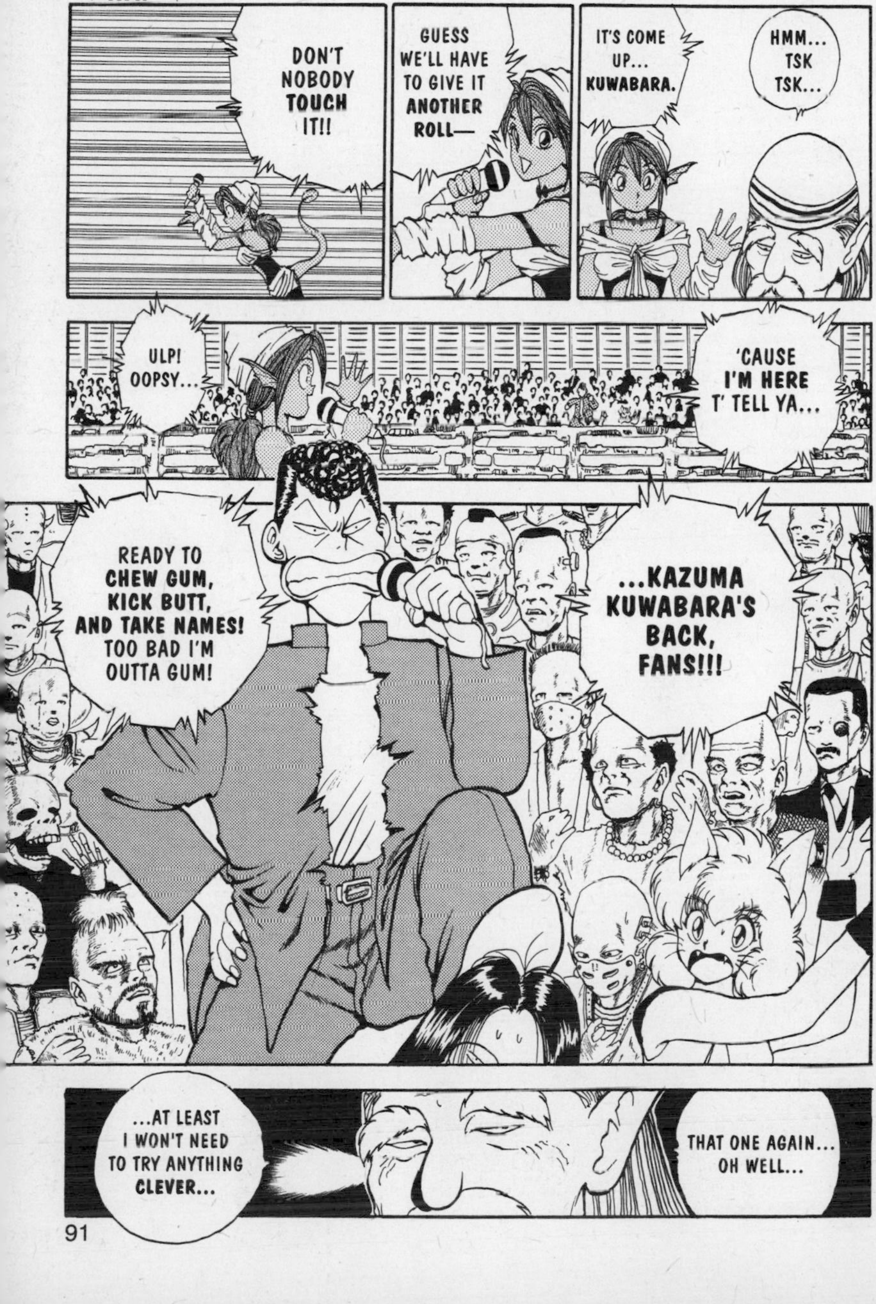
HMM... TSK TSK...
IT'S COME UP... KUWABARA.
GUESS WE'LL HAVE TO GIVE IT ANOTHER ROLL—
DON'T NOBODY TOUCH IT!!
ULP! OOPSY...
'CAUSE I'M HERE T' TELL YA...
...KAZUMA KUWABARA'S BACK, FANS!!!
READY TO CHEW GUM, KICK BUTT, AND TAKE NAMES! TOO BAD I'M OUTTA GUM!
THAT ONE AGAIN... OH WELL...
...AT LEAST I WON'T NEED TO TRY ANYTHING CLEVER...

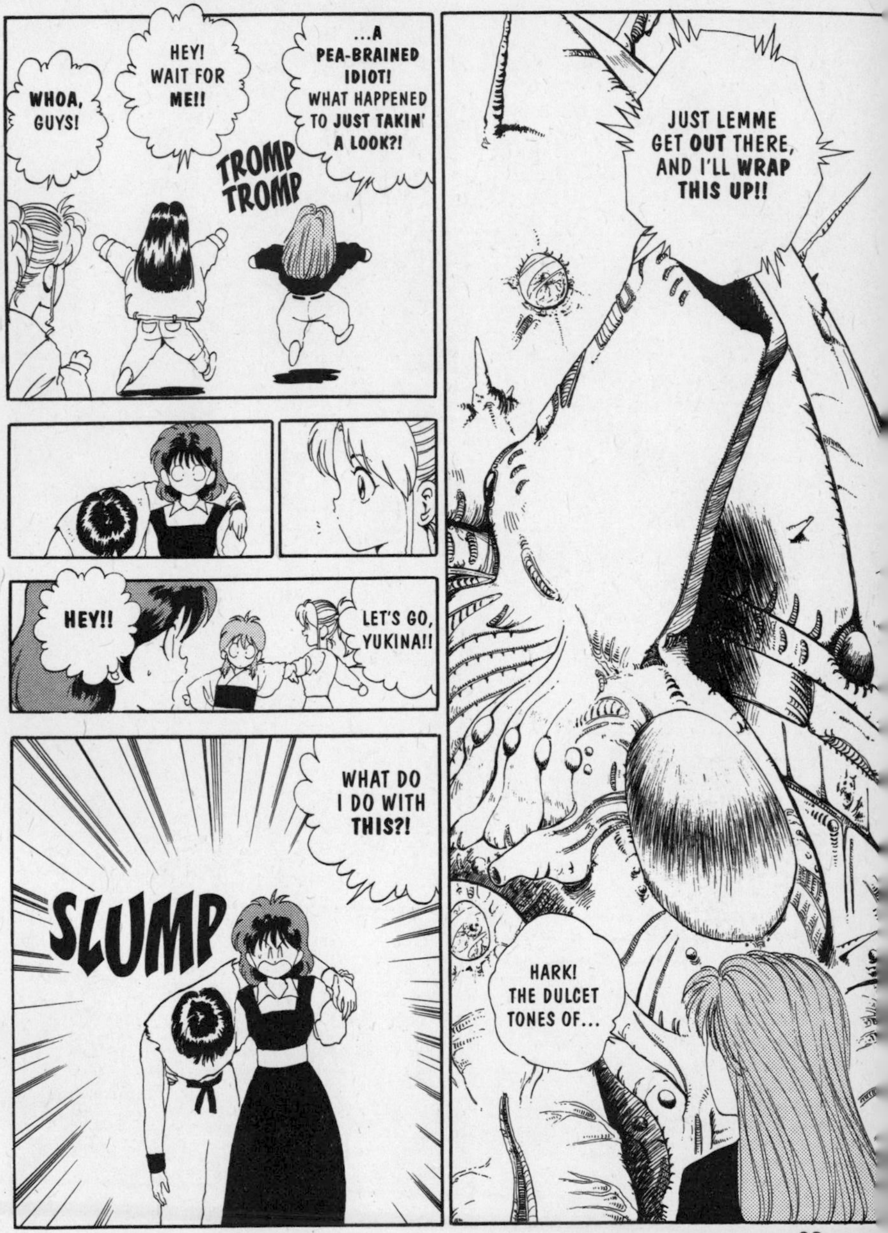
JUST LEMME GET OUT THERE, AND I'LL WRAP THIS UP!!
HARK! THE DULCET TONES OF...
...A PEA-BRAINED IDIOT! WHAT HAPPENED TO JUST TAKIN' A LOOK?!
TROMP TROMP
HEY! WAIT FOR ME!!
WHOA, GUYS!
LET'S GO, YUKINA!!
HEY!!
WHAT DO I DO WITH THIS?!
SLUMP

READ THIS WAY

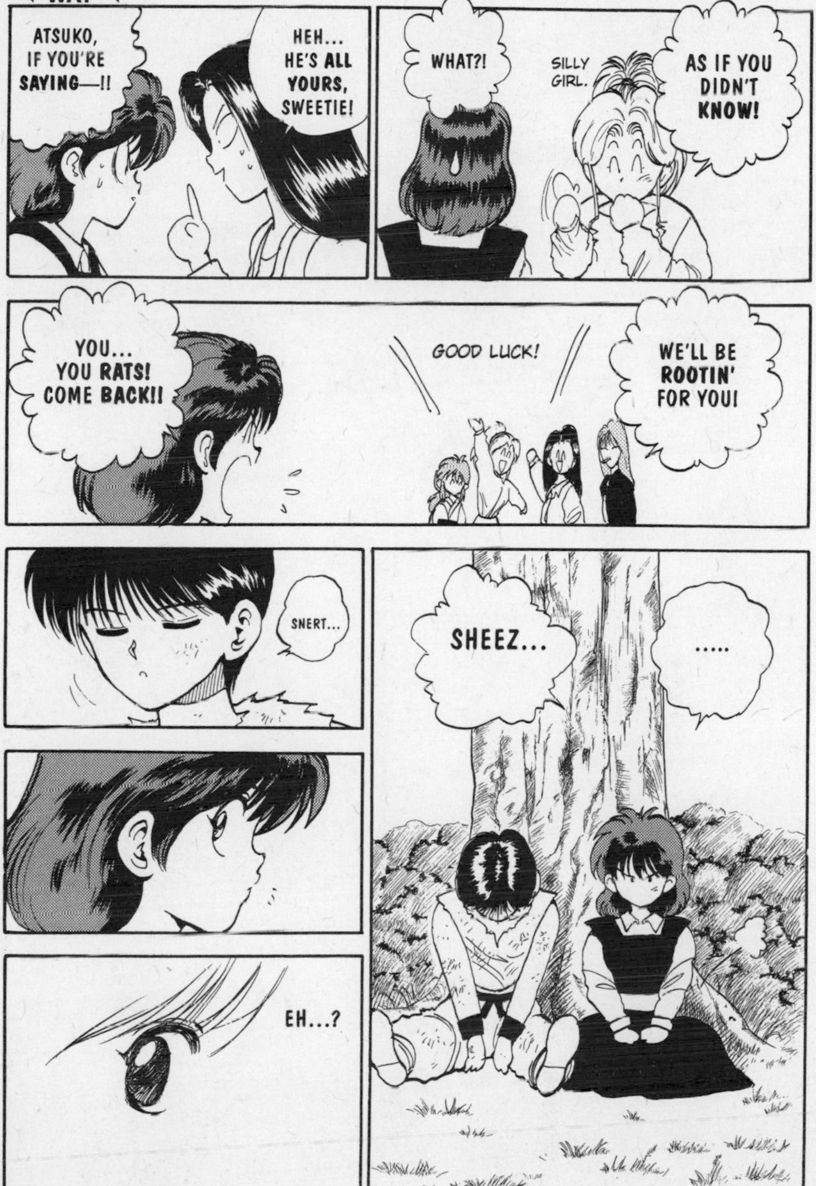
AS IF YOU DIDN'T KNOW!
SILLY GIRL.
WHAT?!
HEH... HE'S ALL YOURS, SWEETIE!
ATSUKO, IF YOU'RE SAYING—!!
WE'LL BE ROOTIN' FOR YOU!
GOOD LUCK!
YOU... YOU RATS! COME BACK!!
.....
SHEEZ...
SNERT...
EH...?

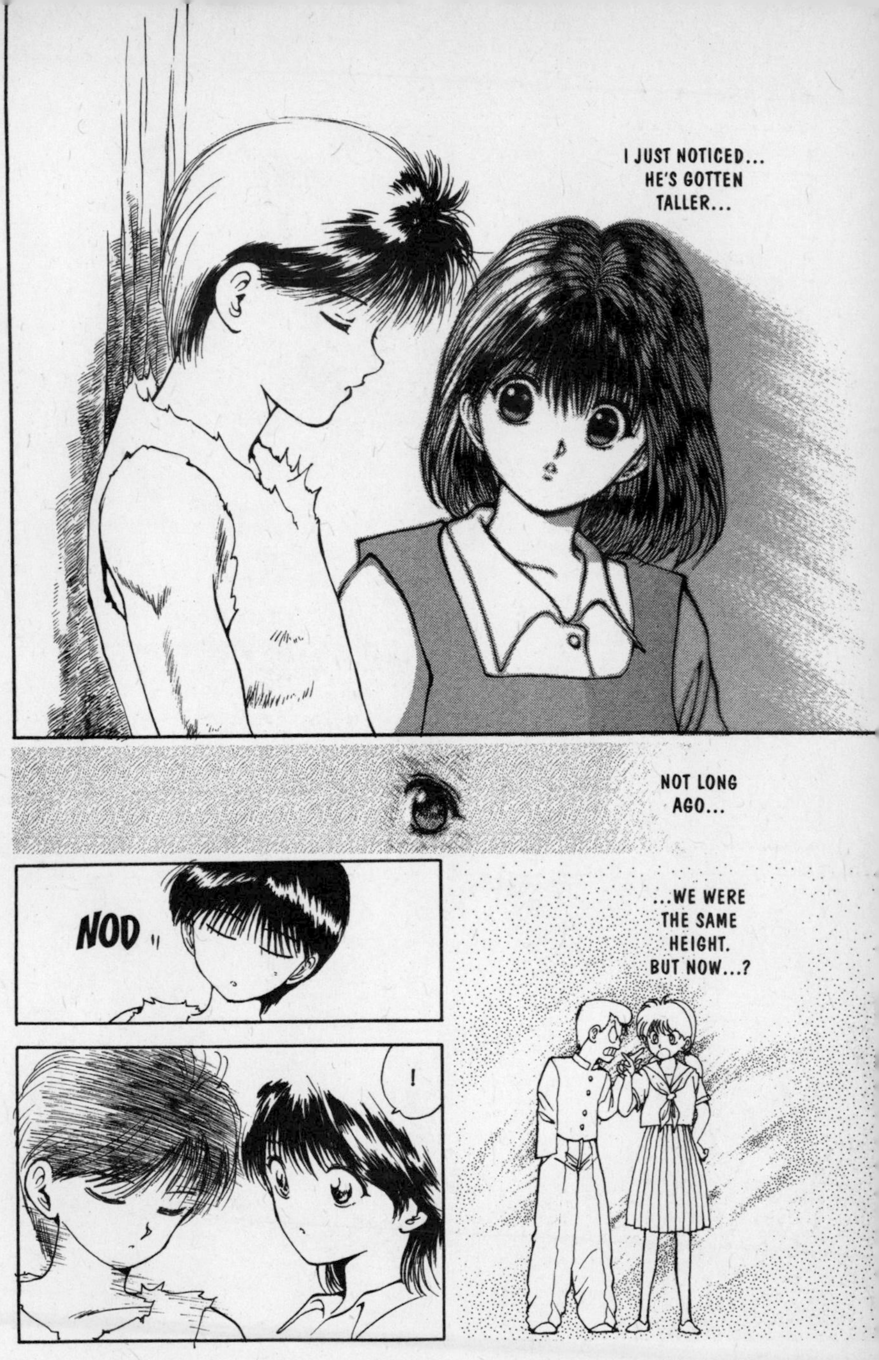
I JUST NOTICED... HE'S GOTTEN TALLER...
NOT LONG AGO...
...WE WERE THE SAME HEIGHT. BUT NOW...?
NOD
!

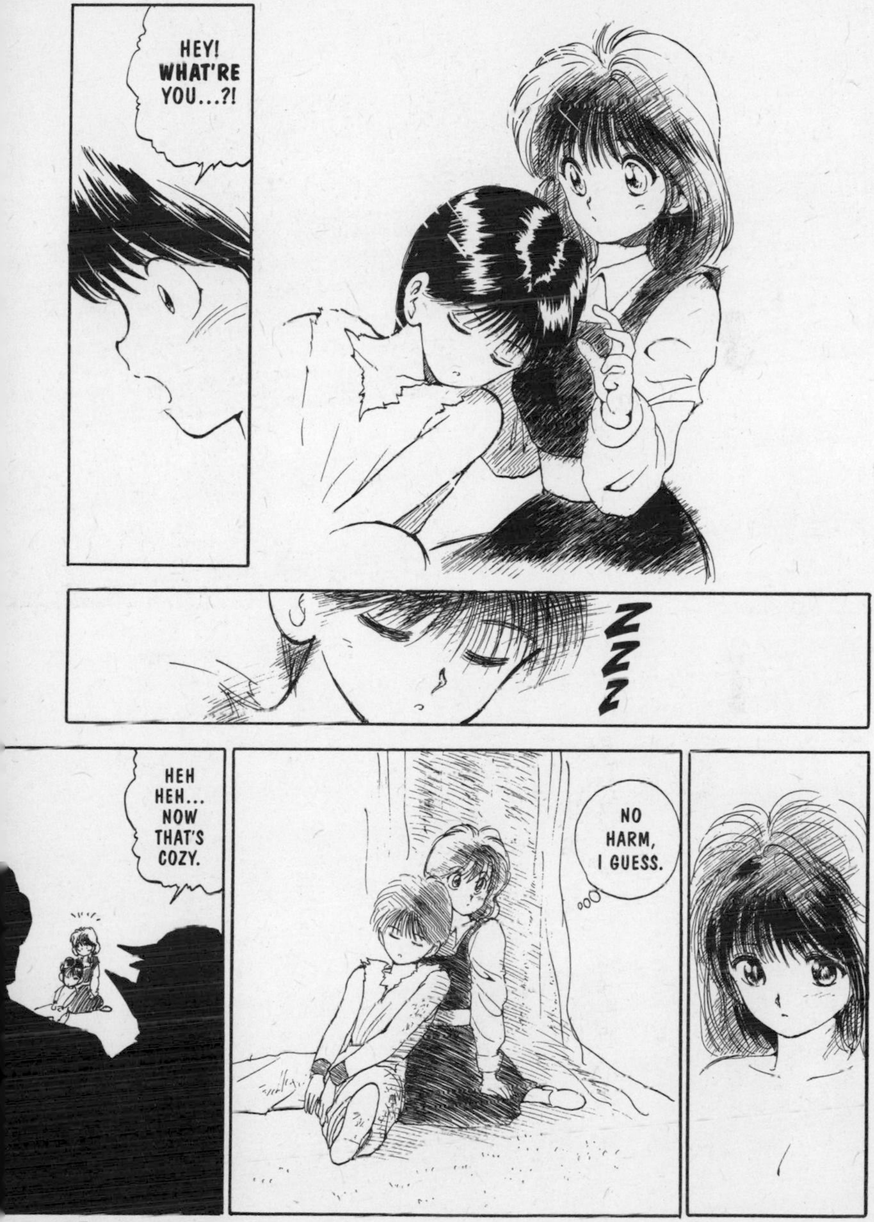
HEY! WHAT'RE YOU...?!
ZZZ
NO HARM, I GUESS.
HEH HEH... NOW THAT'S COZY.

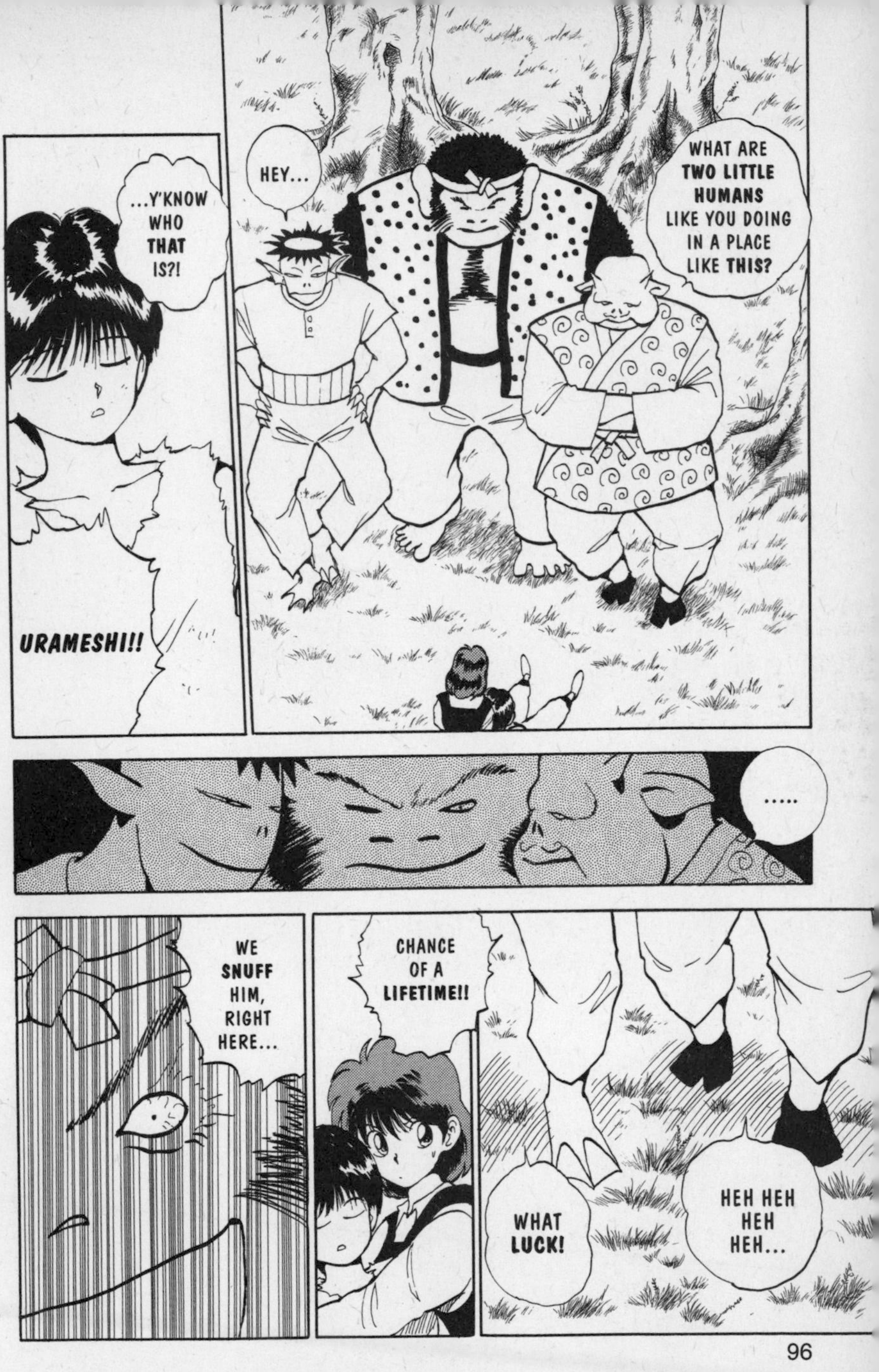

WHAT ARE TWO LITTLE HUMANS LIKE YOU DOING IN A PLACE LIKE THIS?
HEY...
...Y'KNOW WHO THAT IS?!
URAMESHI!!
.....
HEH HEH HEH HEH...
WHAT LUCK!
CHANCE OF A LIFETIME!!
WE SNUFF HIM, RIGHT HERE...

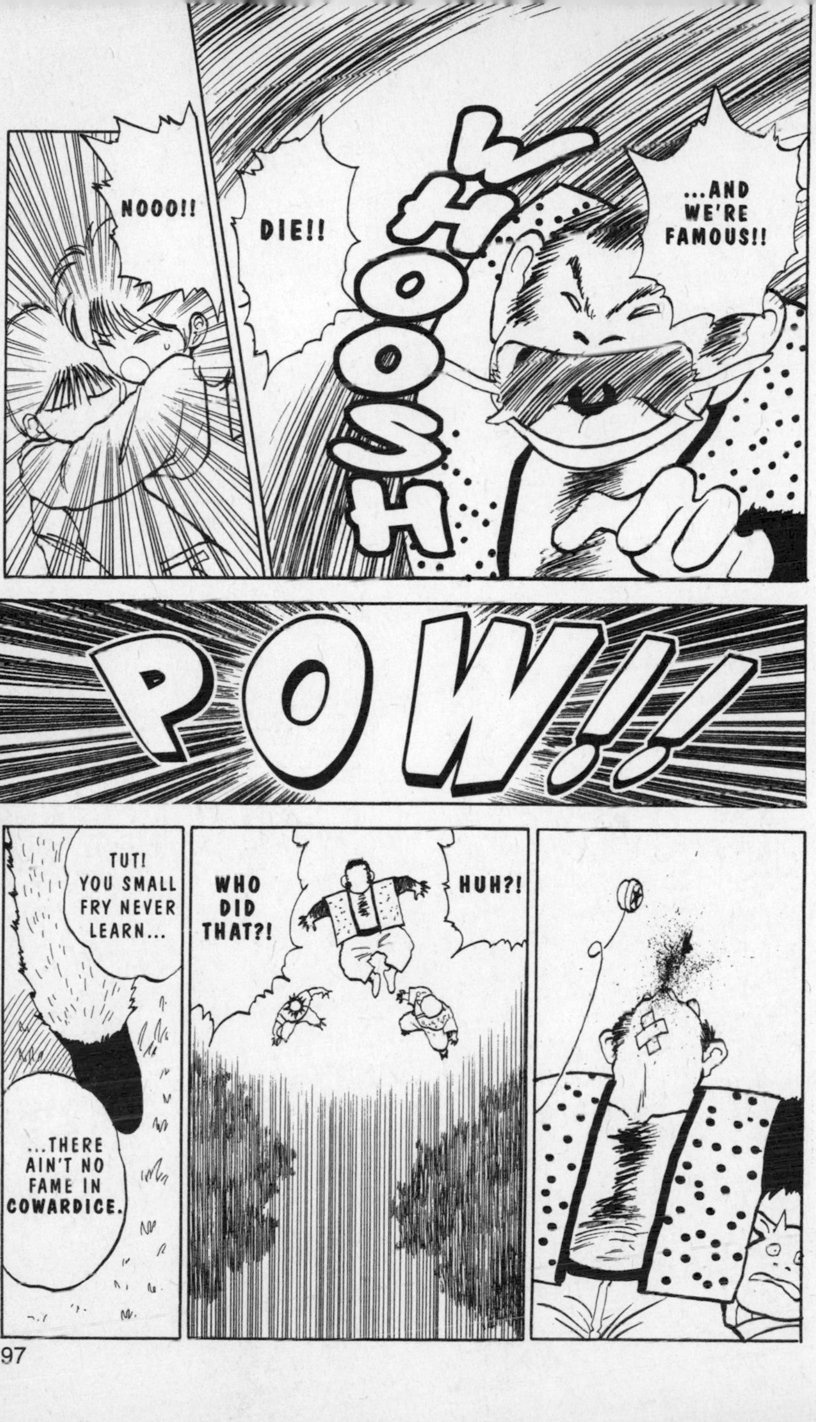
...AND WE'RE FAMOUS!!
WHOOSH
DIE!!
NOOO!!
POW!!
HUH?!
WHO DID THAT?!
TUT! YOU SMALL FRY NEVER LEARN...
...THERE AIN'T NO FAME IN COWARDICE.

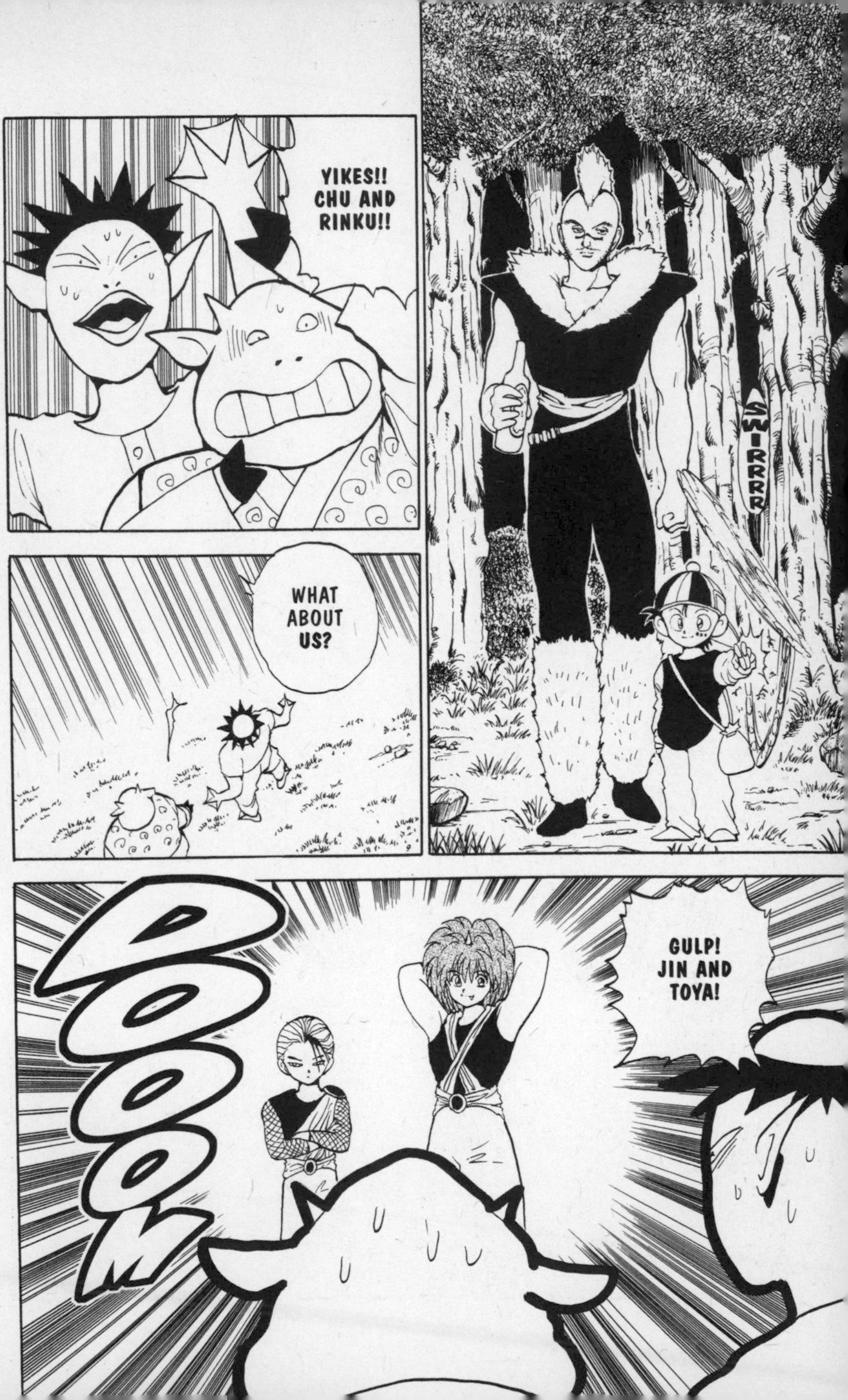
SWIRRR
YIKES!! CHU AND RINKU!!
WHAT ABOUT US?
GULP! JIN AND TOYA!
DOOOOM

READ THIS WAY

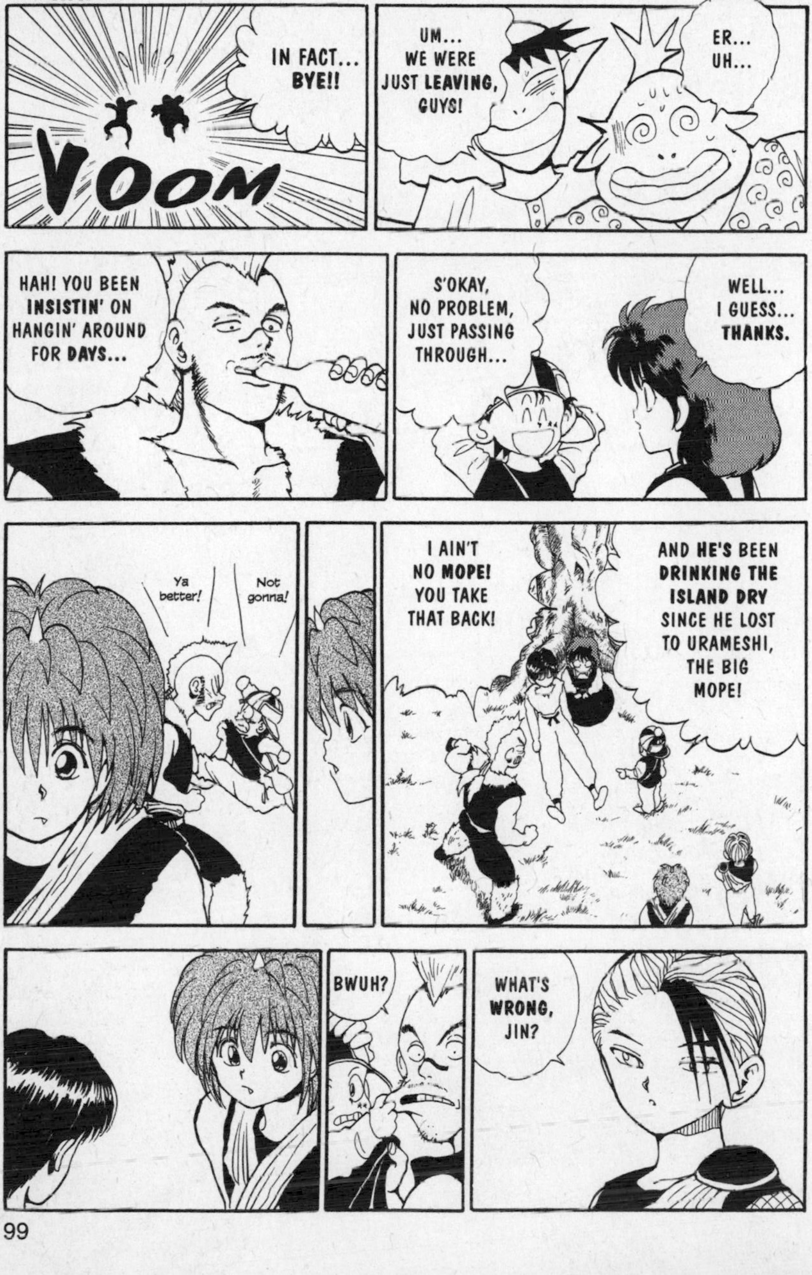
ER... UH...
UM... WE WERE JUST LEAVING, GUYS!
IN FACT... BYE!!
VOOM
WELL... I GUESS... THANKS.
S'OKAY, NO PROBLEM, JUST PASSING THROUGH...
HAH! YOU BEEN INSISTIN' ON HANGIN' AROUND FOR DAYS...
AND HE'S BEEN DRINKING THE ISLAND DRY SINCE HE LOST TO URAMESHI, THE BIG MOPE!
I AIN'T NO MOPE! YOU TAKE THAT BACK!
Not gonna!
Ya better!
WHAT'S WRONG, JIN?
BWUH?

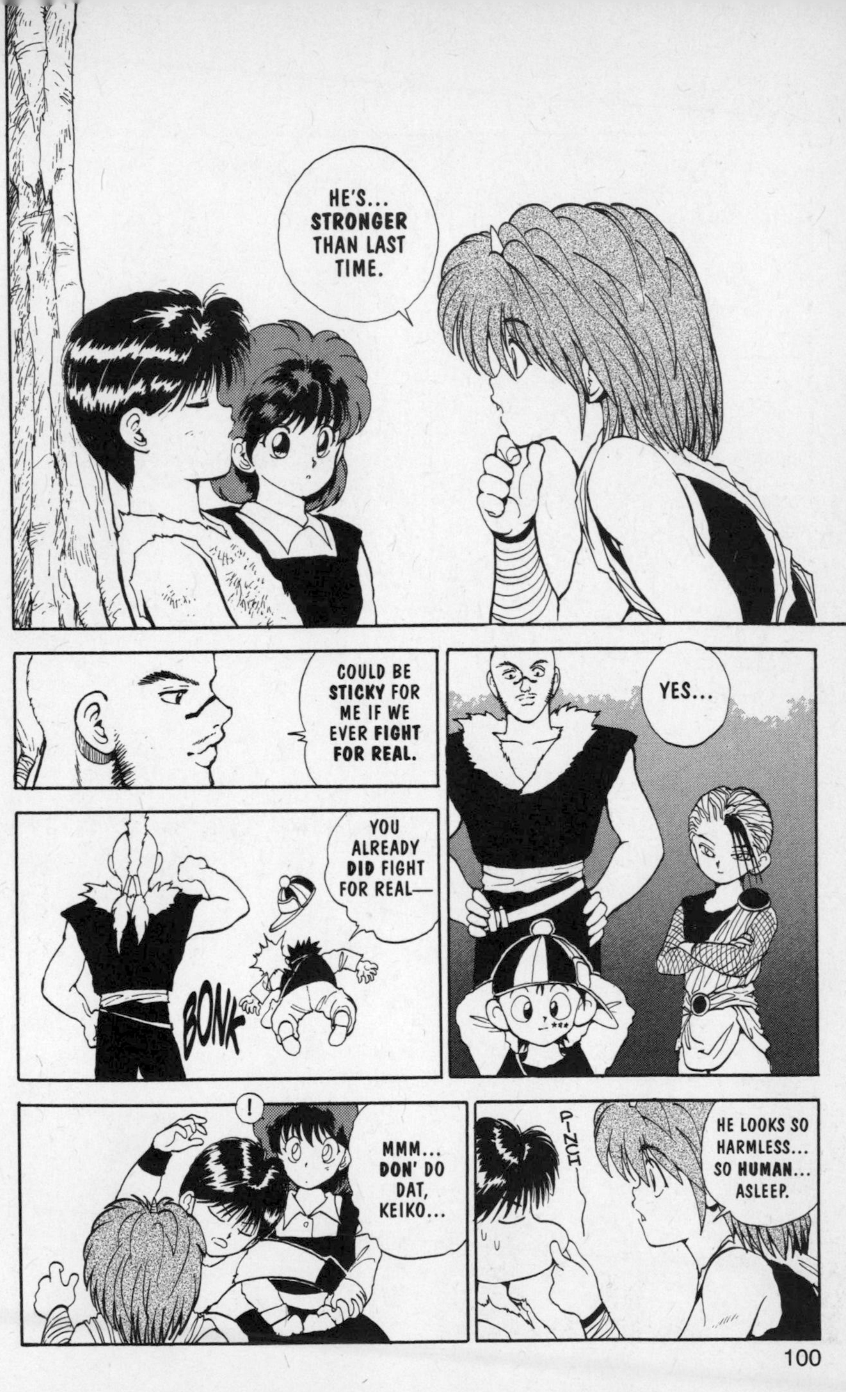
HE'S... STRONGER THAN LAST TIME.
YES...
COULD BE STICKY FOR ME IF WE EVER FIGHT FOR REAL.
YOU ALREADY DID FIGHT FOR REAL—
BONK
HE LOOKS SO HARMLESS... SO HUMAN... ASLEEP.
PINCH
!
MMM... DON' DO DAT, KEIKO...

READ THIS WAY

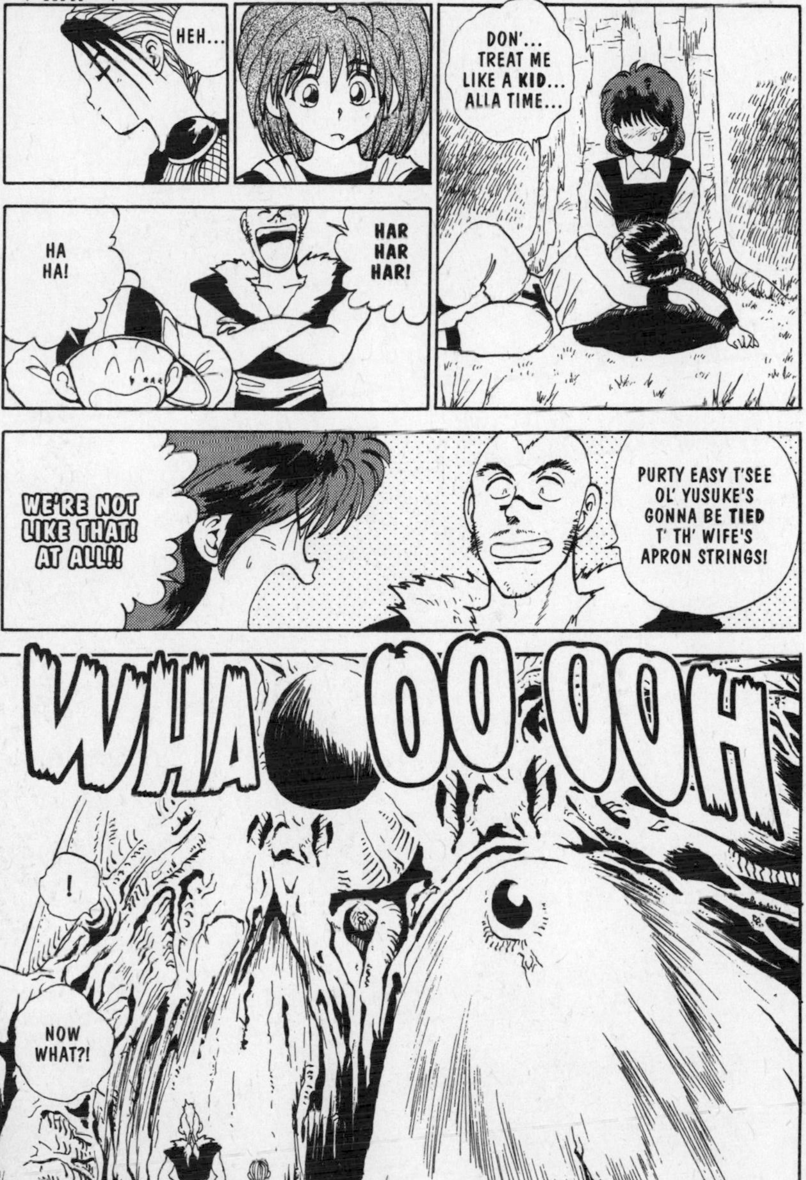
DON'... TREAT ME LIKE A KID... ALLA TIME...
HEH...
HAR HAR HAR!
HA HA!
PURTY EASY T'SEE OL' YUSUKE'S GONNA BE TIED T' TH' WIFE'S APRON STRINGS!
WE'RE NOT LIKE THAT! AT ALL!!
WHAOOOOOH
!
NOW WHAT?!

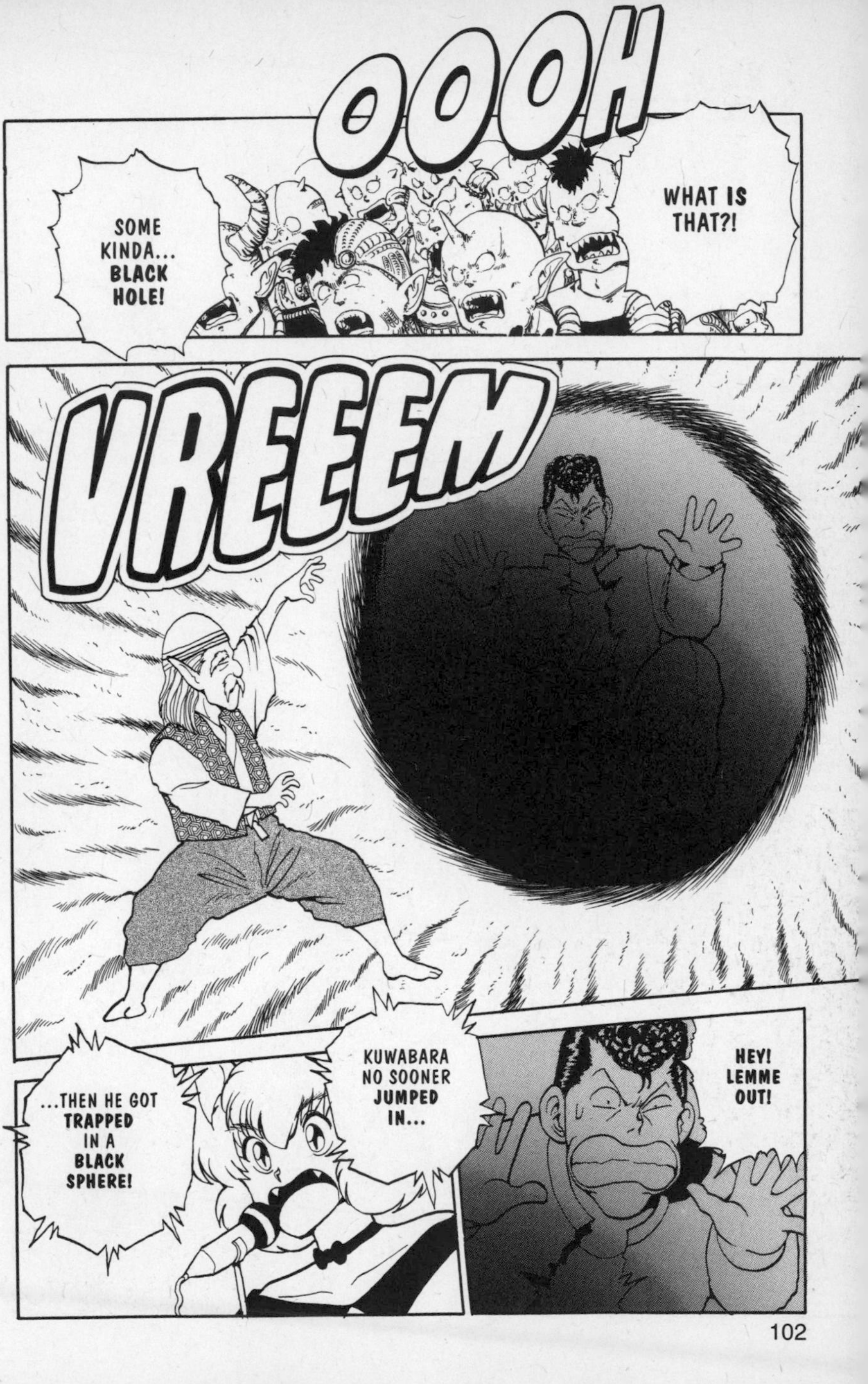
OOOH
WHAT IS THAT?!
SOME KINDA... BLACK HOLE!
VREEEM
HEY! LEMME OUT!
KUWABARA NO SOONER JUMPED IN...
...THEN HE GOT TRAPPED IN A BLACK SPHERE!

READ THIS WAY

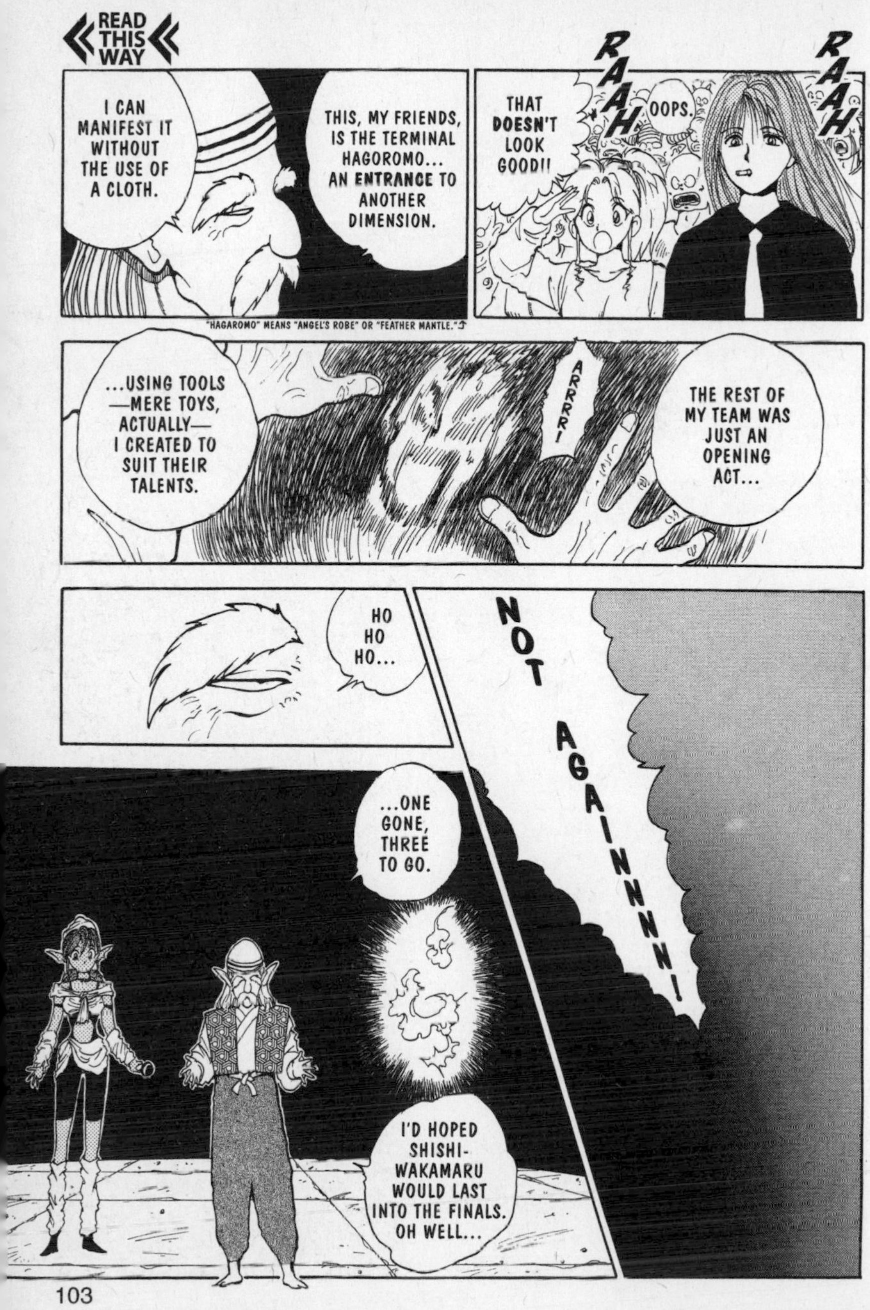
RAAH
OOPS.
THAT DOESN'T LOOK GOOD!!
RAAH
THIS, MY FRIENDS, IS THE TERMINAL HAGOROMO... AN ENTRANCE TO ANOTHER DIMENSION.
I CAN MANIFEST IT WITHOUT THE USE OF A CLOTH.
"HAGAROMO" MEANS "ANGEL'S ROBE" OR "FEATHER MANTLE."
THE REST OF MY TEAM WAS JUST AN OPENING ACT...
ARRRR!
...USING TOOLS —MERE TOYS, ACTUALLY— I CREATED TO SUIT THEIR TALENTS.
NOT AGAINNNN!
HO HO HO...
...ONE GONE, THREE TO GO.
I'D HOPED SHISHI-WAKAMARU WOULD LAST INTO THE FINALS. OH WELL...

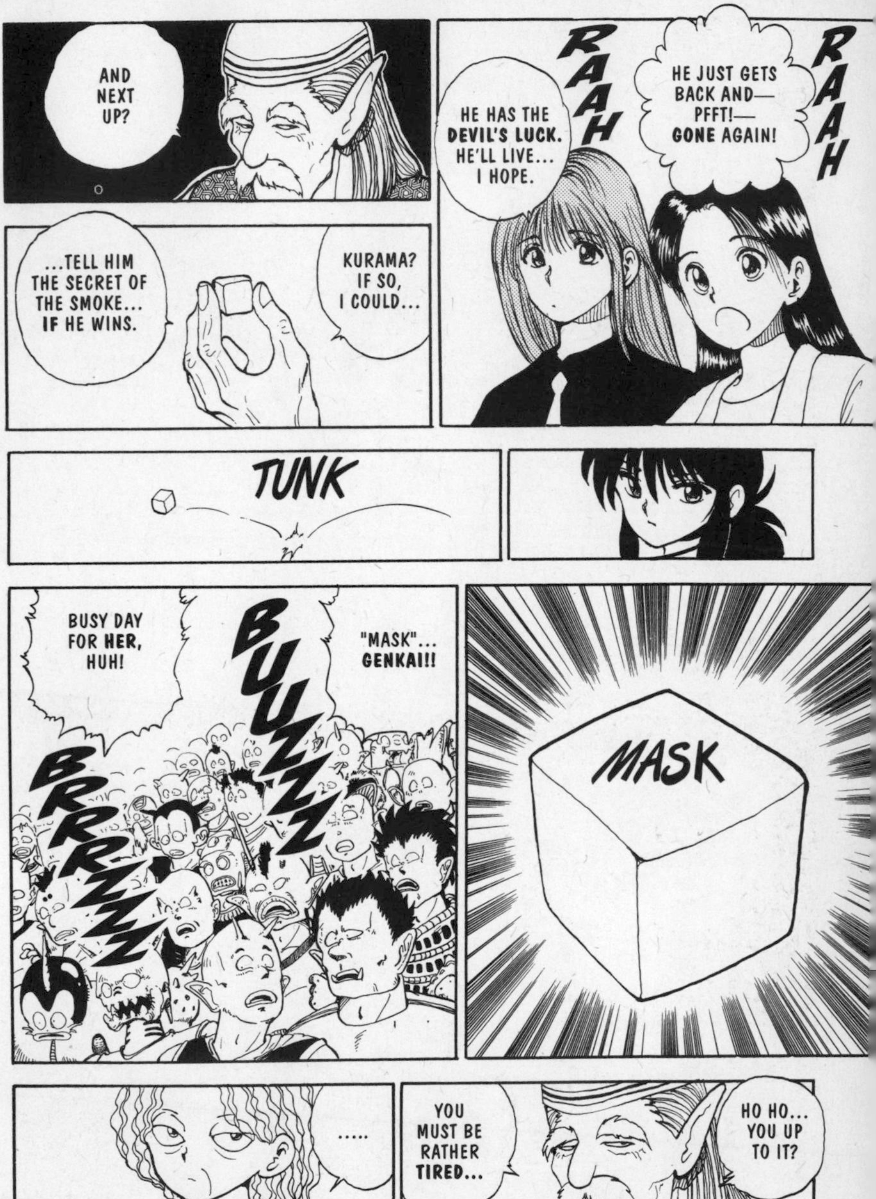
RAAH
HE JUST GETS BACK AND— PFFT!— GONE AGAIN!
RAAH
HE HAS THE DEVIL'S LUCK. HE'LL LIVE... I HOPE.
AND NEXT UP?
KURAMA? IF SO, I COULD...
...TELL HIM THE SECRET OF THE SMOKE... IF HE WINS.
TUNK
MASK
"MASK"... GENKAI!!
BUUZZZ
BUSY DAY FOR HER, HUH!
BRRRZZZ
HO HO... YOU UP TO IT?
YOU MUST BE RATHER TIRED...
.....

READ THIS WAY

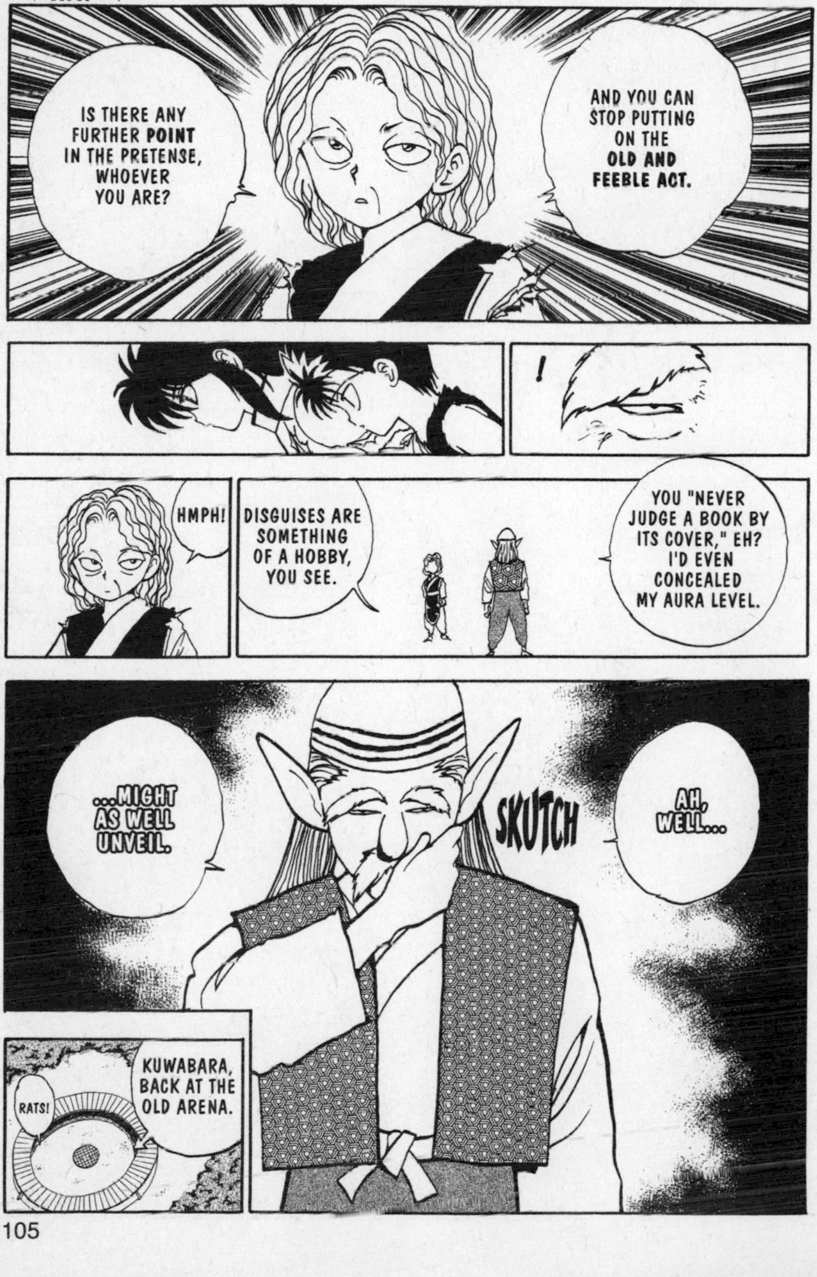
IS THERE ANY FURTHER POINT IN THE PRETENSE, WHOEVER YOU ARE?
AND YOU CAN STOP PUTTING ON THE OLD AND FEEBLE ACT.
!
YOU "NEVER JUDGE A BOOK BY ITS COVER," EH? I'D EVEN CONCEALED MY AURA LEVEL.
DISGUISES ARE SOMETHING OF A HOBBY, YOU SEE.
HMPH!
AH, WELL...
SKUTCH
...MIGHT AS WELL UNVEIL.
KUWABARA, BACK AT THE OLD ARENA.
RATS!

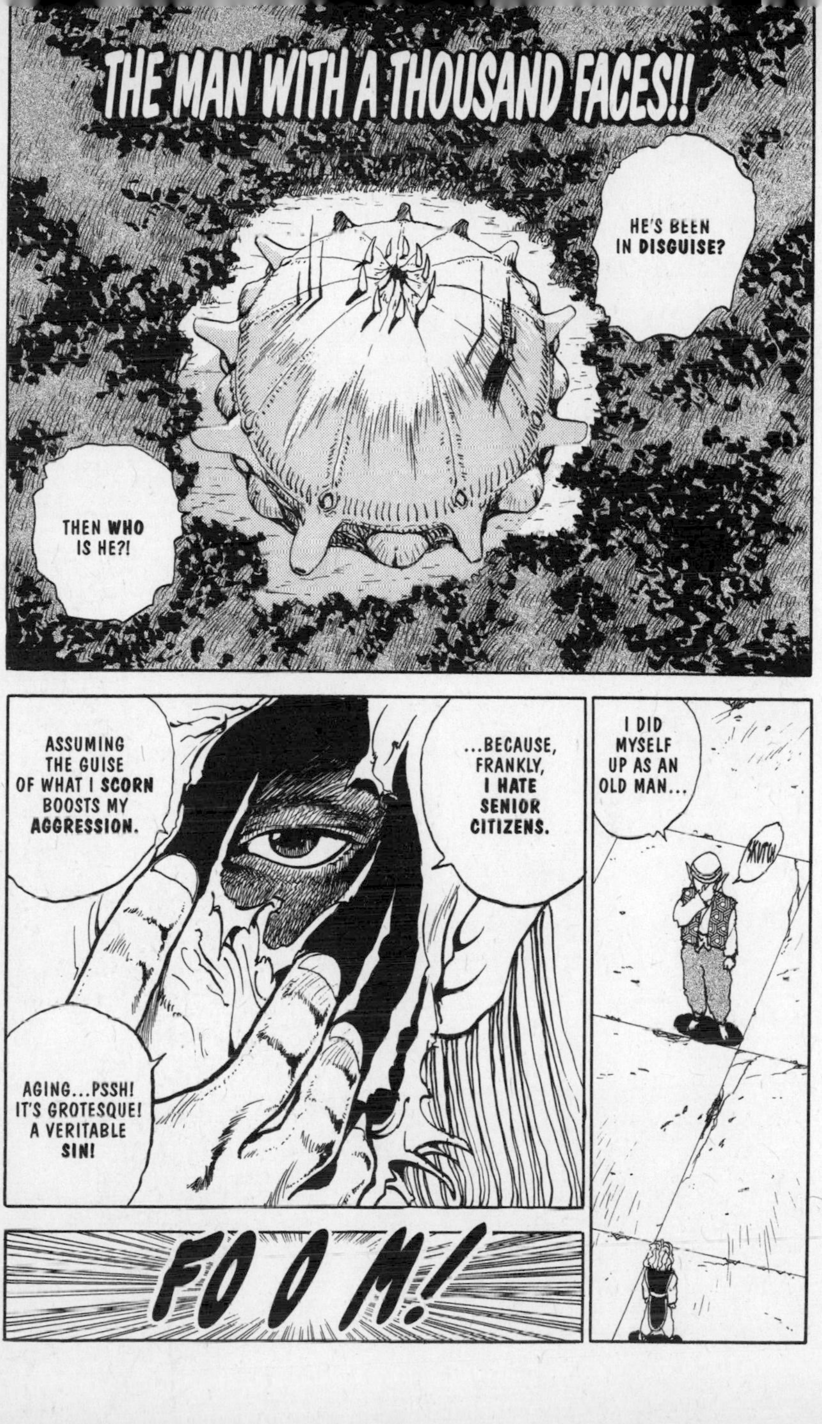
THE MAN WITH A THOUSAND FACES!!
HE'S BEEN IN DISGUISE?
THEN WHO IS HE?!
I DID MYSELF UP AS AN OLD MAN...
...BECAUSE, FRANKLY, I HATE SENIOR CITIZENS.
ASSUMING THE GUISE OF WHAT I SCORN BOOSTS MY AGGRESSION.
AGING...PSSH! IT'S GROTESQUE! A VERITABLE SIN!
FOOM!

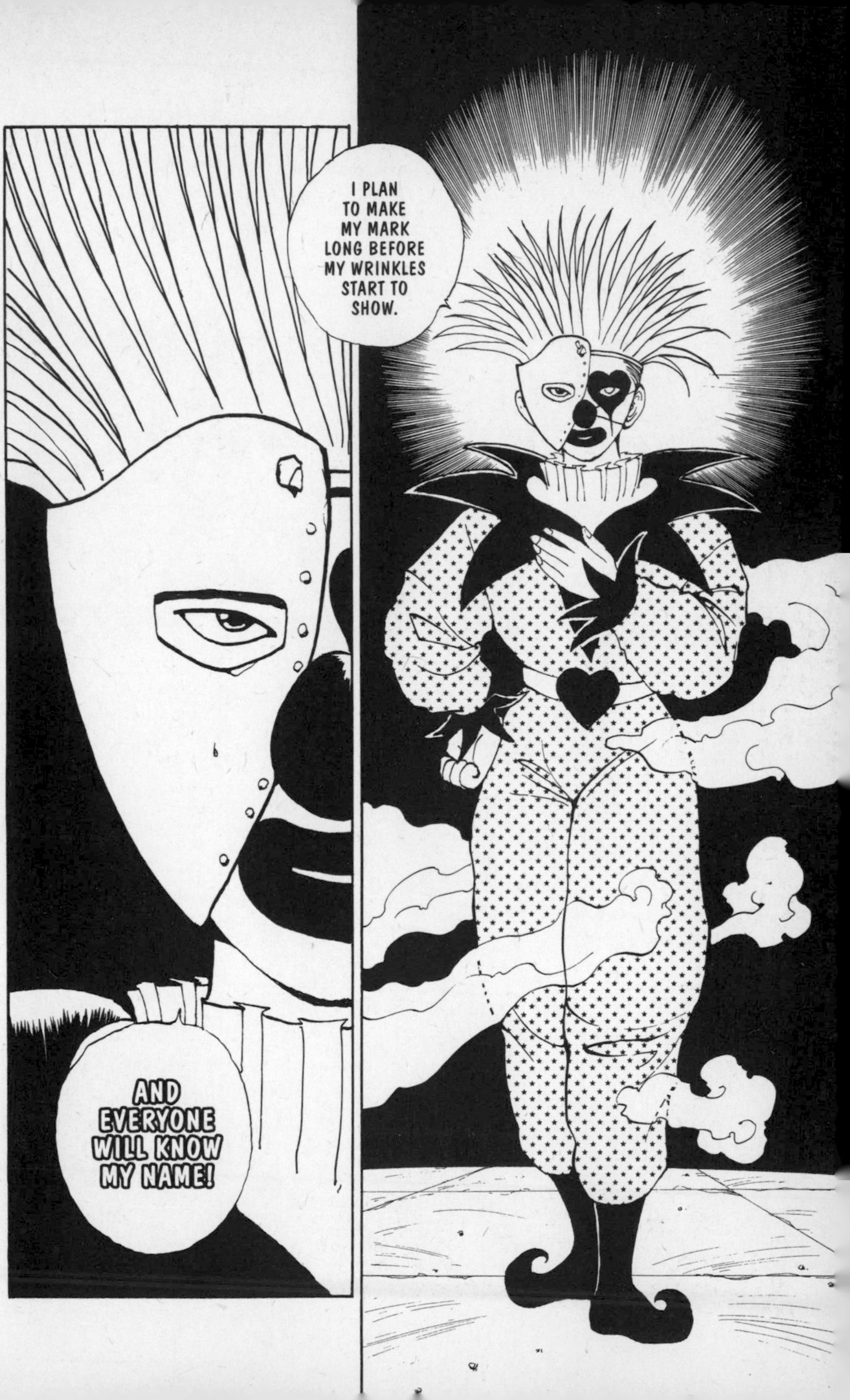
I PLAN TO MAKE MY MARK LONG BEFORE MY WRINKLES START TO SHOW.
AND EVERYONE WILL KNOW MY NAME!

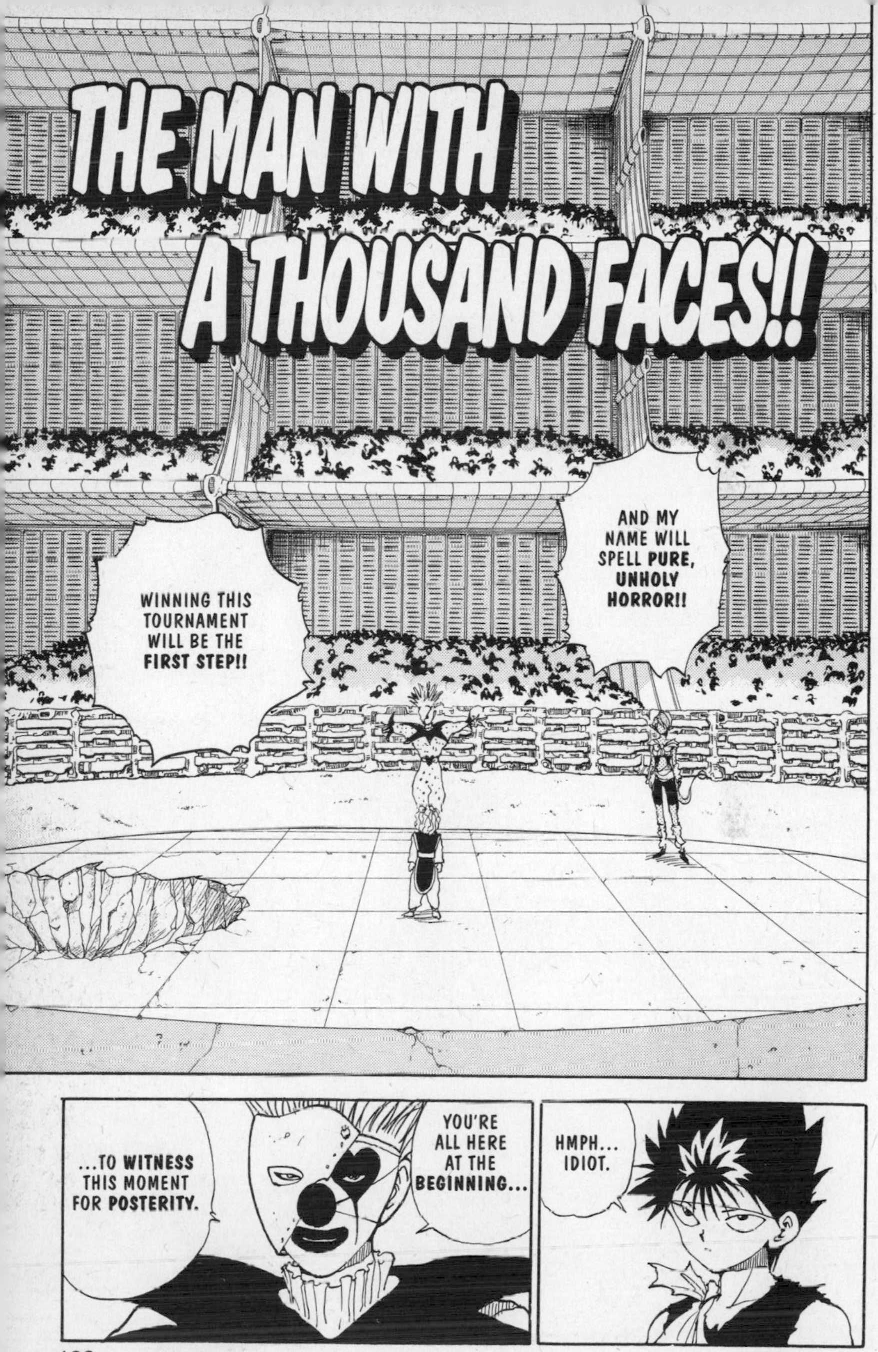
THE MAN WITH A THOUSAND FACES!!
AND MY NAME WILL SPELL PURE, UNHOLY HORROR!!
WINNING THIS TOURNAMENT WILL BE THE FIRST STEP!!
HMPH... IDIOT.
YOU'RE ALL HERE AT THE BEGINNING...
...TO WITNESS THIS MOMENT FOR POSTERITY.

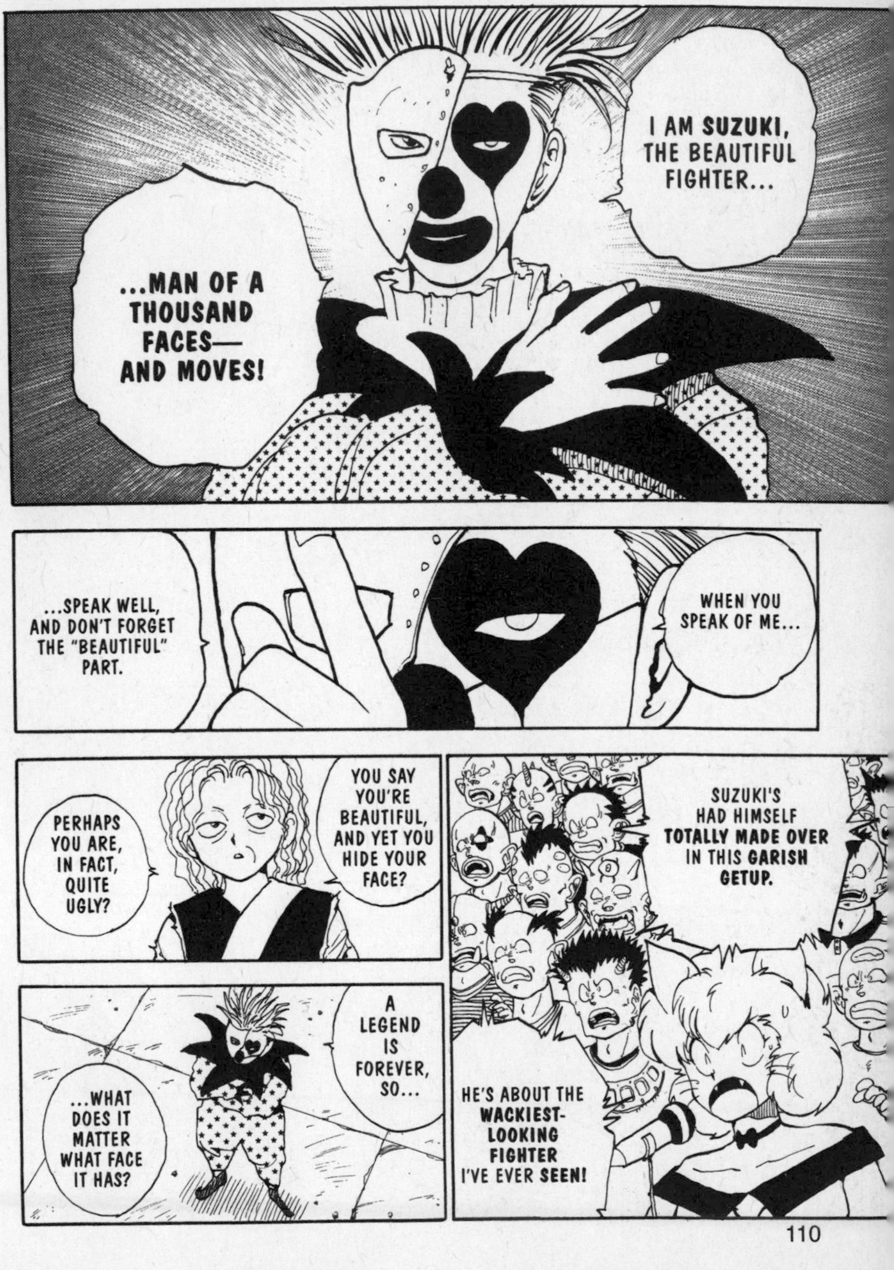
I AM SUZUKI, THE BEAUTIFUL FIGHTER...
...MAN OF A THOUSAND FACES—AND MOVES!
WHEN YOU SPEAK OF ME...
...SPEAK WELL, AND DON'T FORGET THE "BEAUTIFUL" PART.
SUZUKI'S HAD HIMSELF TOTALLY MADE OVER IN THIS GARISH GETUP.
HE'S ABOUT THE WACKIEST-LOOKING FIGHTER I'VE EVER SEEN!
YOU SAY YOU'RE BEAUTIFUL, AND YET YOU HIDE YOUR FACE?
PERHAPS YOU ARE, IN FACT, QUITE UGLY?
A LEGEND IS FOREVER, SO...
...WHAT DOES IT MATTER WHAT FACE IT HAS?

READ THIS WAY

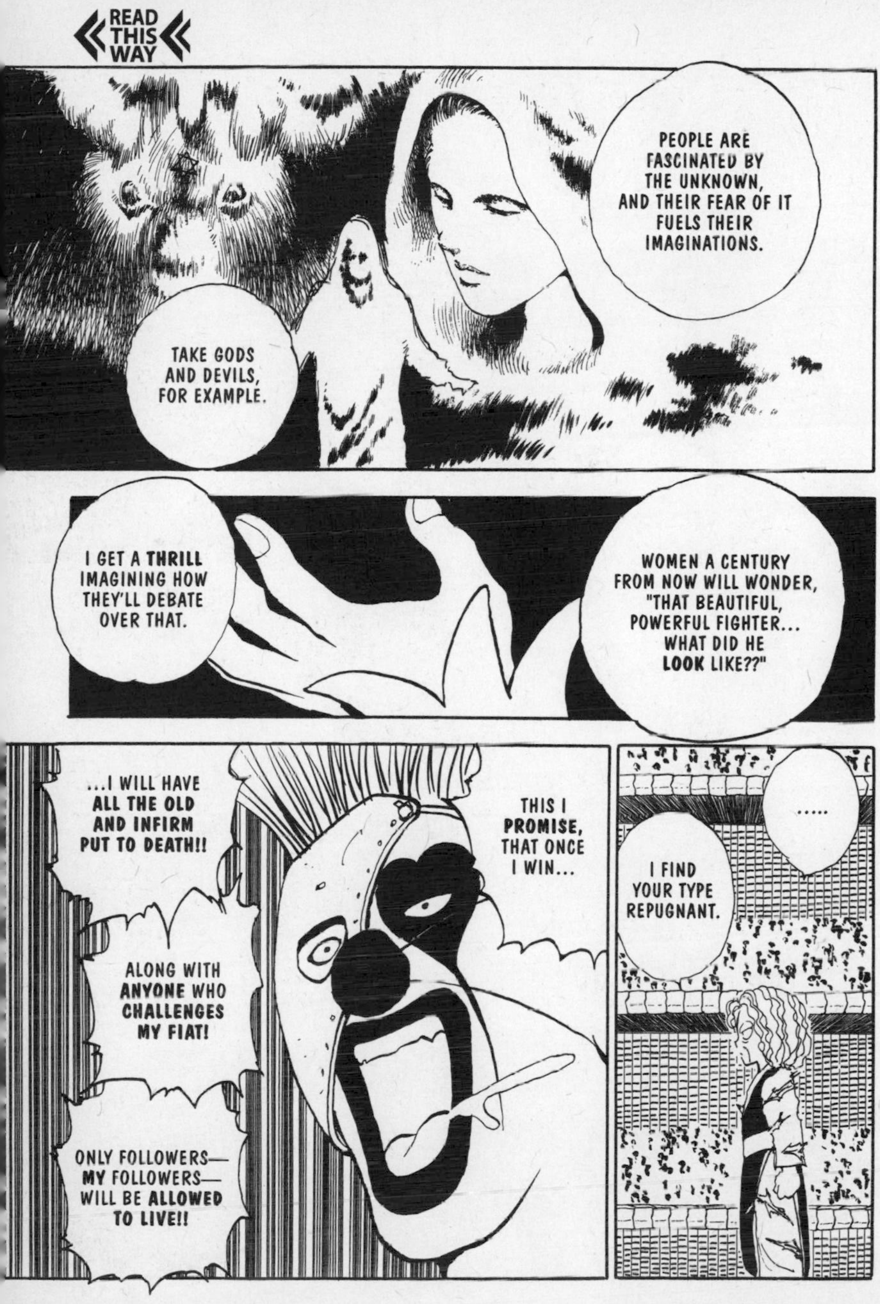

PEOPLE ARE FASCINATED BY THE UNKNOWN, AND THEIR FEAR OF IT FUELS THEIR IMAGINATIONS.
TAKE GODS AND DEVILS, FOR EXAMPLE.
WOMEN A CENTURY FROM NOW WILL WONDER, "THAT BEAUTIFUL, POWERFUL FIGHTER... WHAT DID HE LOOK LIKE??"
I GET A THRILL IMAGINING HOW THEY'LL DEBATE OVER THAT.
.....
I FIND YOUR TYPE REPUGNANT.
THIS I PROMISE, THAT ONCE I WIN...
...I WILL HAVE ALL THE OLD AND INFIRM PUT TO DEATH!!
ALONG WITH ANYONE WHO CHALLENGES MY FIAT!
ONLY FOLLOWERS— MY FOLLOWERS— WILL BE ALLOWED TO LIVE!!

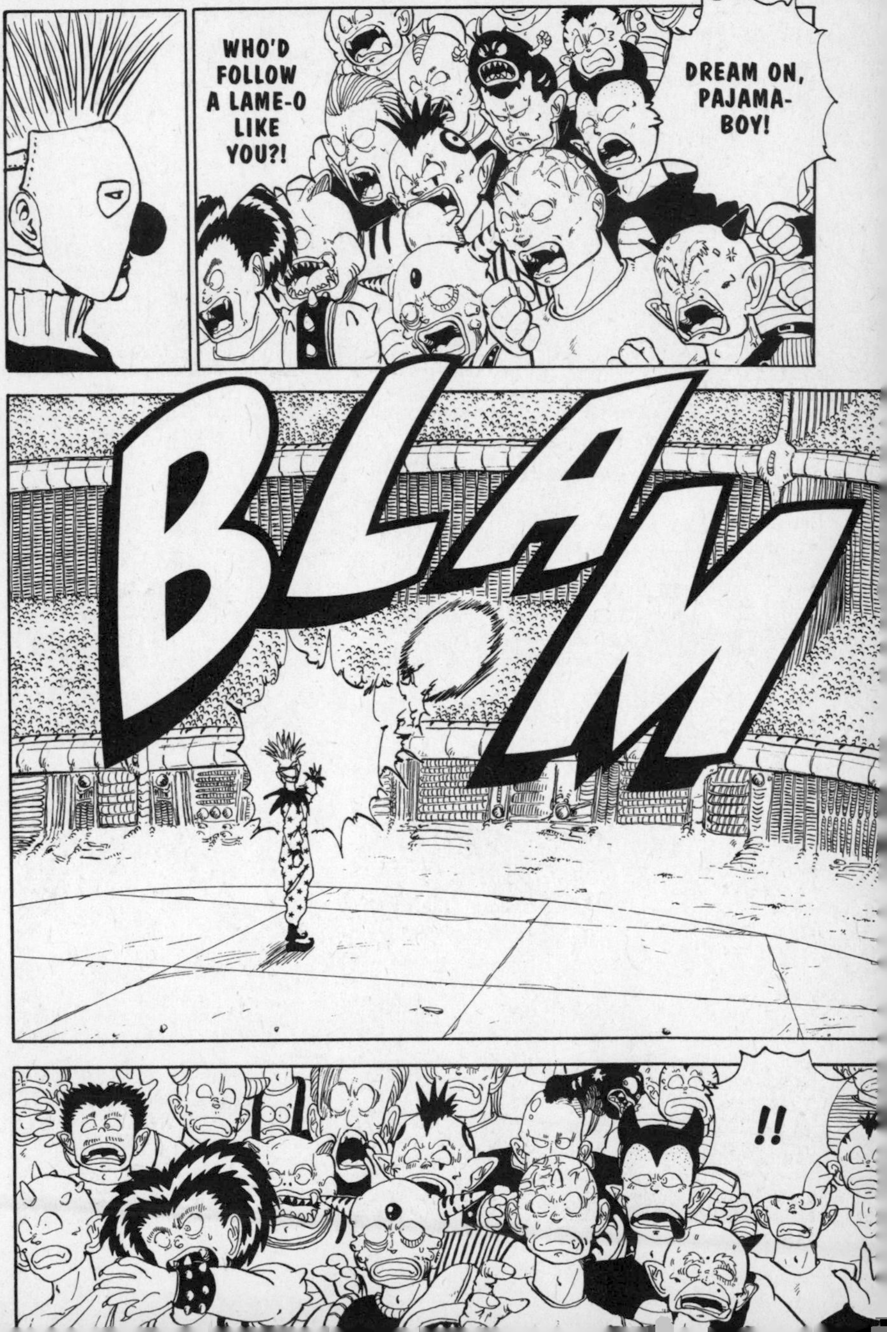
DREAM ON, PAJAMA-BOY!
WHO'D FOLLOW A LAME-O LIKE YOU?!
BLAM
!!

READ THIS WAY

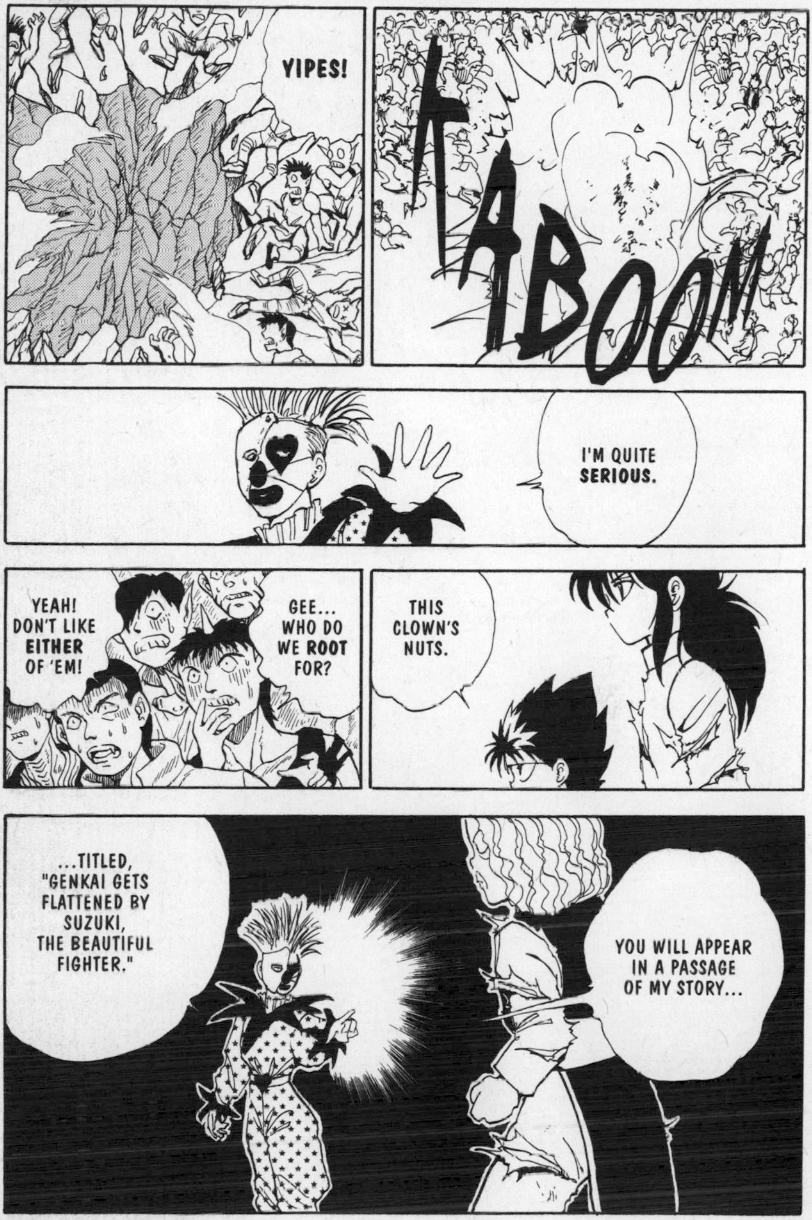
KABOOM
YIPES!
I'M QUITE SERIOUS.
THIS CLOWN'S NUTS.
GEE... WHO DO WE ROOT FOR?
YEAH! DON'T LIKE EITHER OF 'EM!
YOU WILL APPEAR IN A PASSAGE OF MY STORY...
...TITLED, "GENKAI GETS FLATTENED BY SUZUKI, THE BEAUTIFUL FIGHTER."

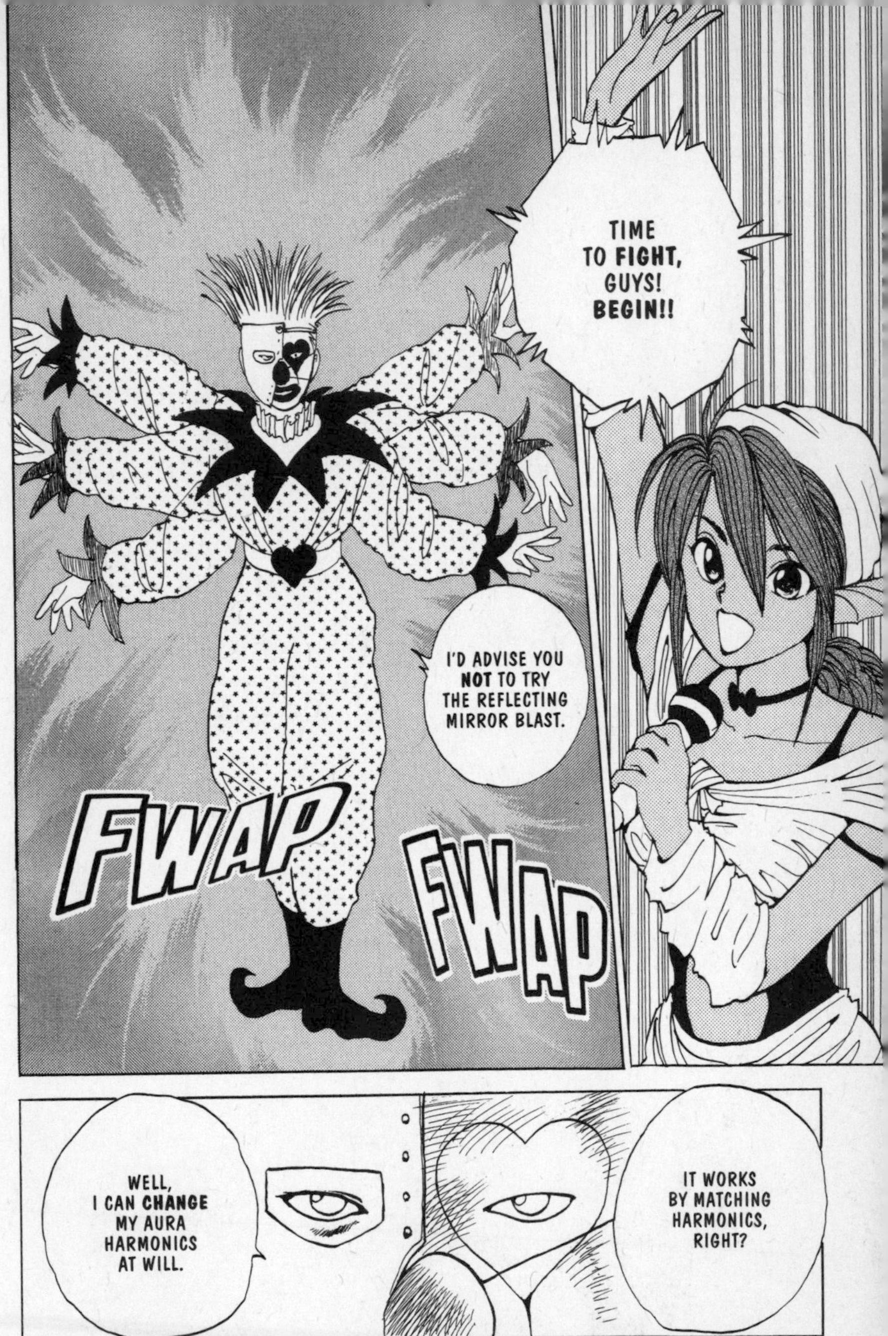
TIME TO FIGHT, GUYS! BEGIN!!
I'D ADVISE YOU NOT TO TRY THE REFLECTING MIRROR BLAST.
FWAP
FWAP
IT WORKS BY MATCHING HARMONICS, RIGHT?
WELL, I CAN CHANGE MY AURA HARMONICS AT WILL.

READ THIS WAY

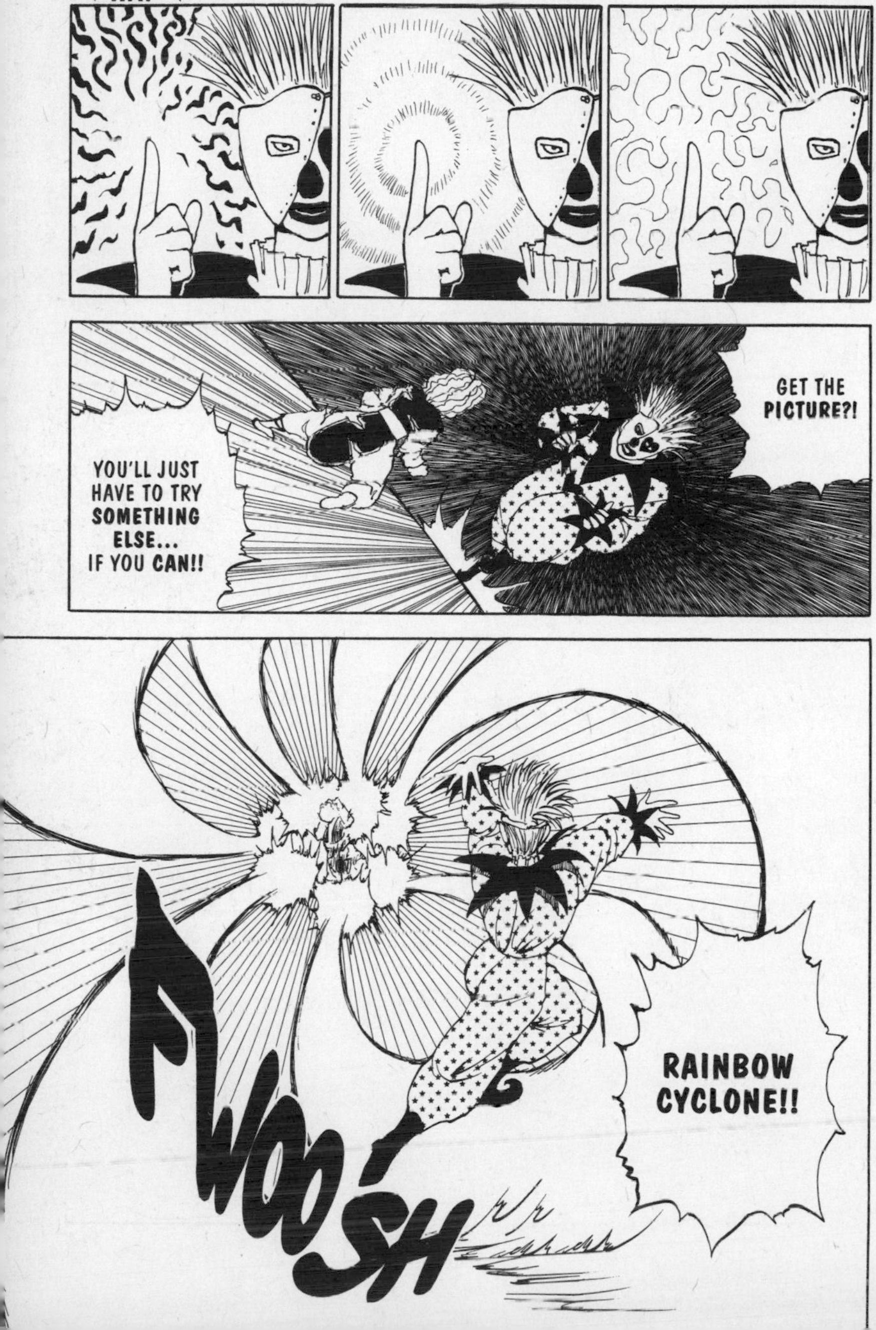
GET THE PICTURE?!
YOU'LL JUST HAVE TO TRY SOMETHING ELSE... IF YOU CAN!!
RAINBOW CYCLONE!!
FWOOSH

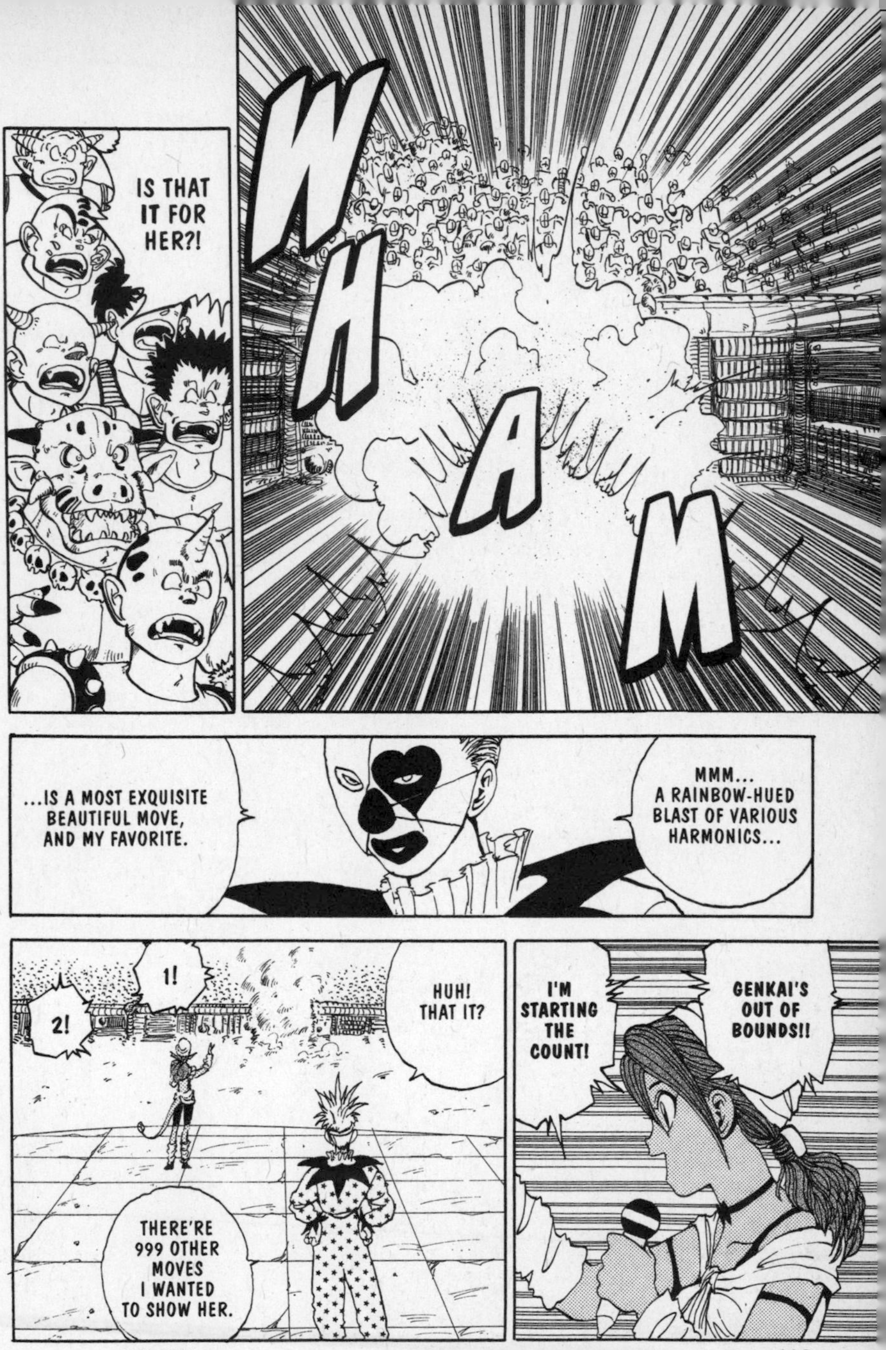
WHAM
IS THAT IT FOR HER?!
MMM... A RAINBOW-HUED BLAST OF VARIOUS HARMONICS...
...IS A MOST EXQUISITE BEAUTIFUL MOVE, AND MY FAVORITE.
GENKAI'S OUT OF BOUNDS!!
I'M STARTING THE COUNT!
HUH! THAT IT?
1!
2!
THERE'RE 999 OTHER MOVES I WANTED TO SHOW HER.

YEAH, RIGHT.

READ THIS WAY

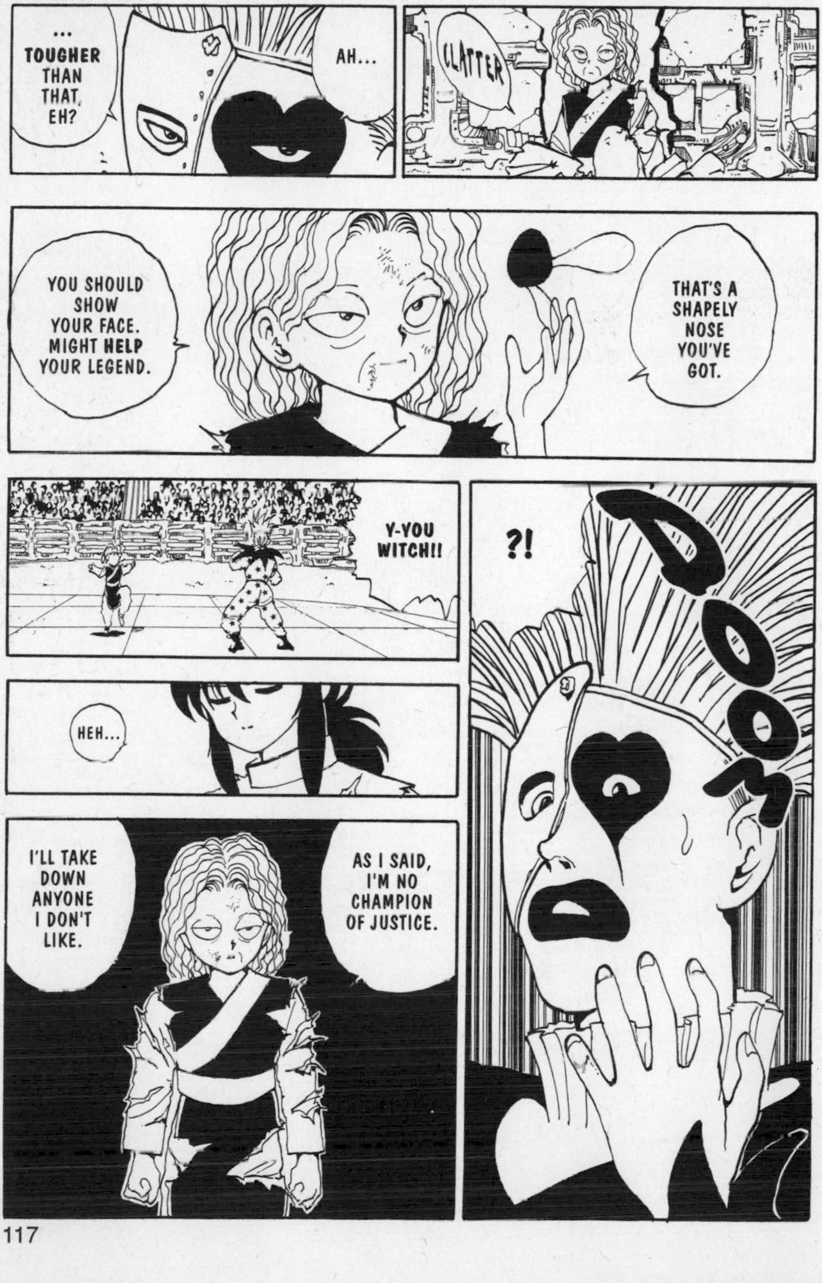
CLATTER
AH...
... TOUGHER THAN THAT, EH?
THAT'S A SHAPELY NOSE YOU'VE GOT.
YOU SHOULD SHOW YOUR FACE. MIGHT HELP YOUR LEGEND.
?!
DOOOM
Y-YOU WITCH!!
HEH...
AS I SAID, I'M NO CHAMPION OF JUSTICE.
I'LL TAKE DOWN ANYONE I DON'T LIKE.

... TOUGHER THAN THAT, EH?

AH...

CLATTER

YOU SHOULD SHOW YOUR FACE. MIGHT **HELP** YOUR LEGEND.

THAT'S A SHAPELY NOSE YOU'VE GOT.

Y-YOU WITCH!!

?!

HEH...

I'LL TAKE DOWN ANYONE I DON'T LIKE.

AS I SAID, I'M NO CHAMPION OF JUSTICE.

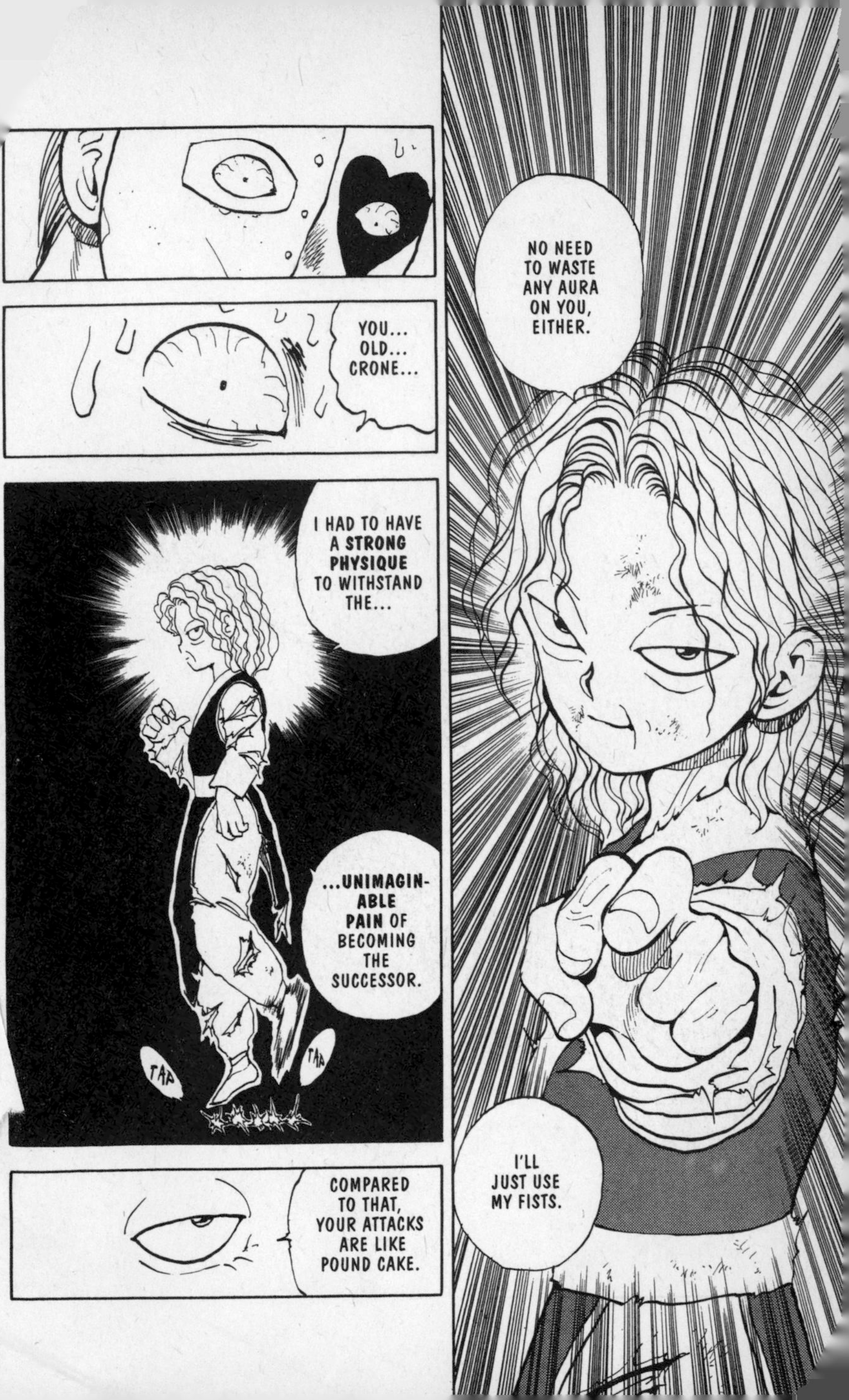
NO NEED TO WASTE ANY AURA ON YOU, EITHER.
I'LL JUST USE MY FISTS.
YOU... OLD... CRONE...
I HAD TO HAVE A STRONG PHYSIQUE TO WITHSTAND THE...
...UNIMAGIN-ABLE PAIN OF BECOMING THE SUCCESSOR.
TAP
TAP
COMPARED TO THAT, YOUR ATTACKS ARE LIKE POUND CAKE.

READ THIS WAY

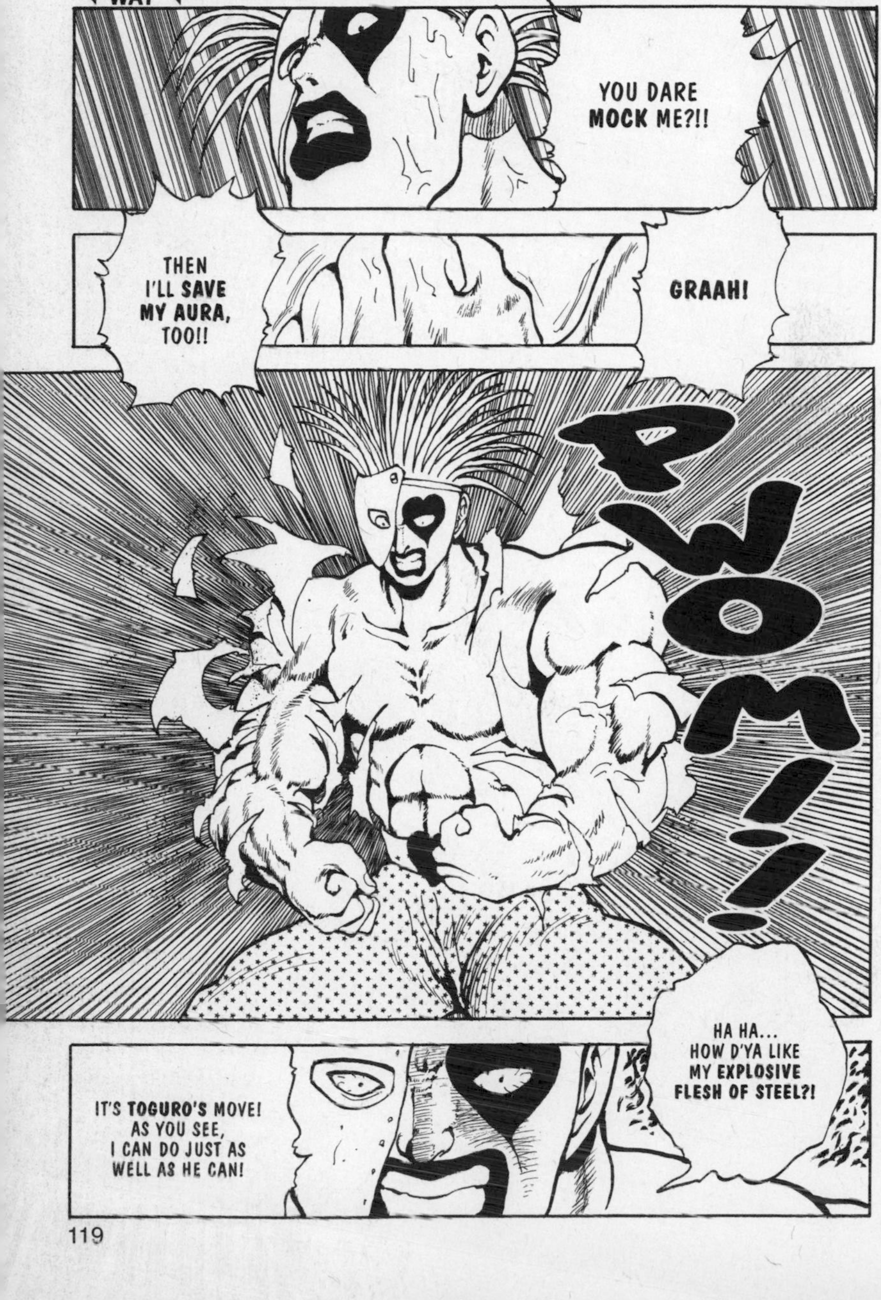

YOU DARE MOCK ME?!!
GRAAH!
THEN I'LL SAVE MY AURA, TOO!!
HA HA... HOW D'YA LIKE MY EXPLOSIVE FLESH OF STEEL?!
IT'S TOGURO'S MOVE! AS YOU SEE, I CAN DO JUST AS WELL AS HE CAN!

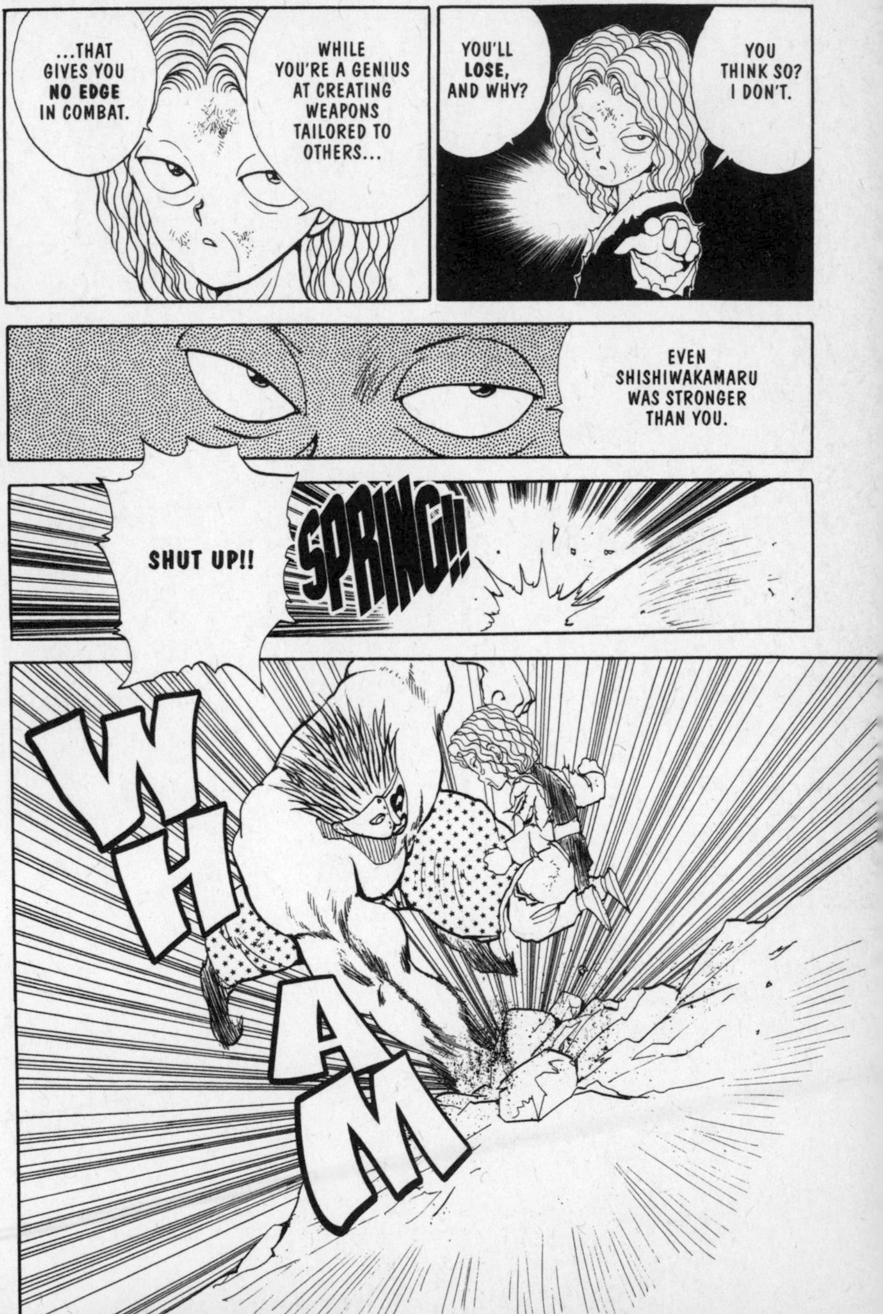
YOU THINK SO? I DON'T.
YOU'LL LOSE, AND WHY?
WHILE YOU'RE A GENIUS AT CREATING WEAPONS TAILORED TO OTHERS...
...THAT GIVES YOU NO EDGE IN COMBAT.
EVEN SHISHIWAKAMARU WAS STRONGER THAN YOU.
SPRING!!
SHUT UP!!
WHAM

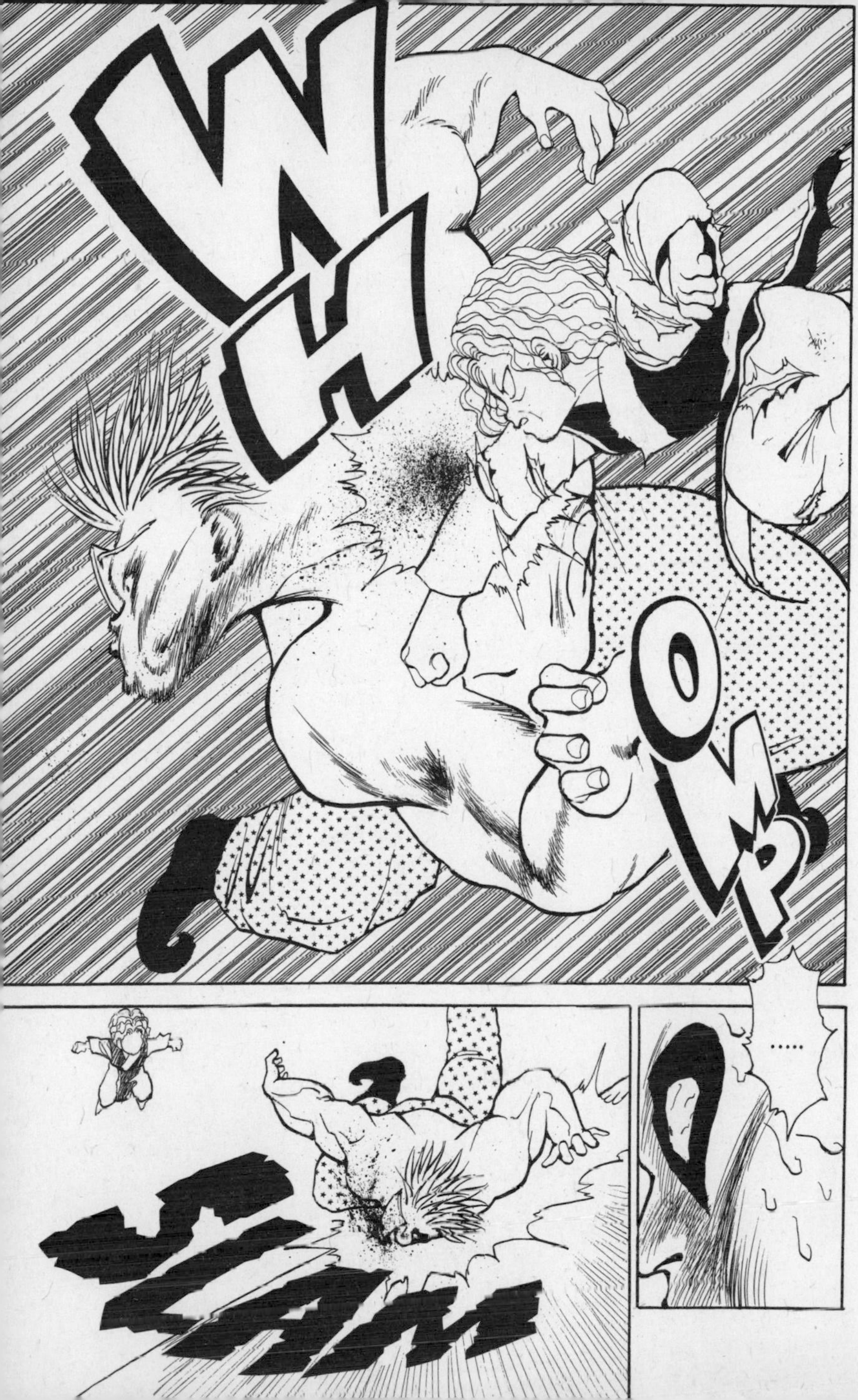
WHOMP
.....
SLAM

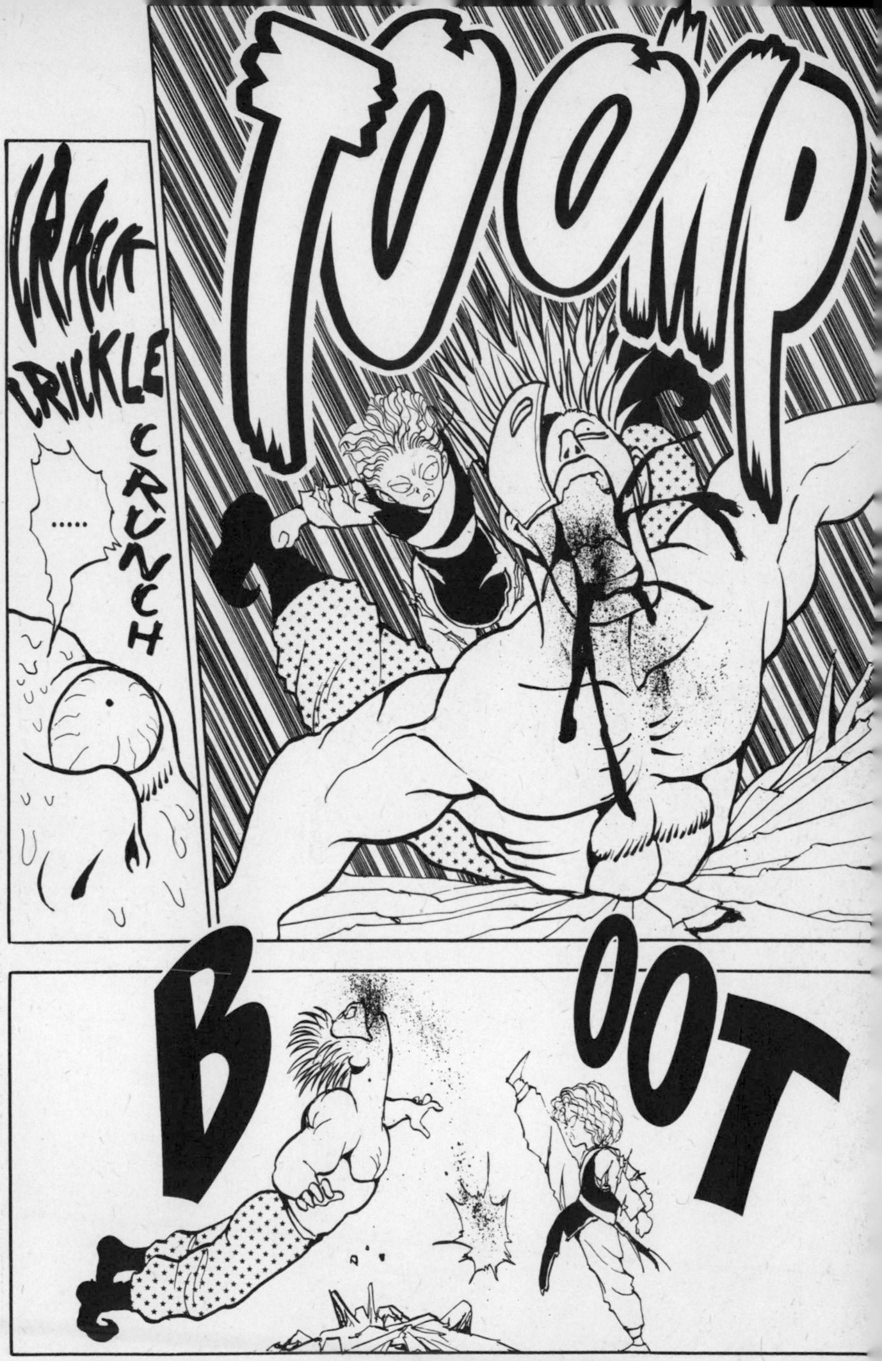

TOOMP
CRACK
CRICKLE
CRUNCH
.....
BOOT

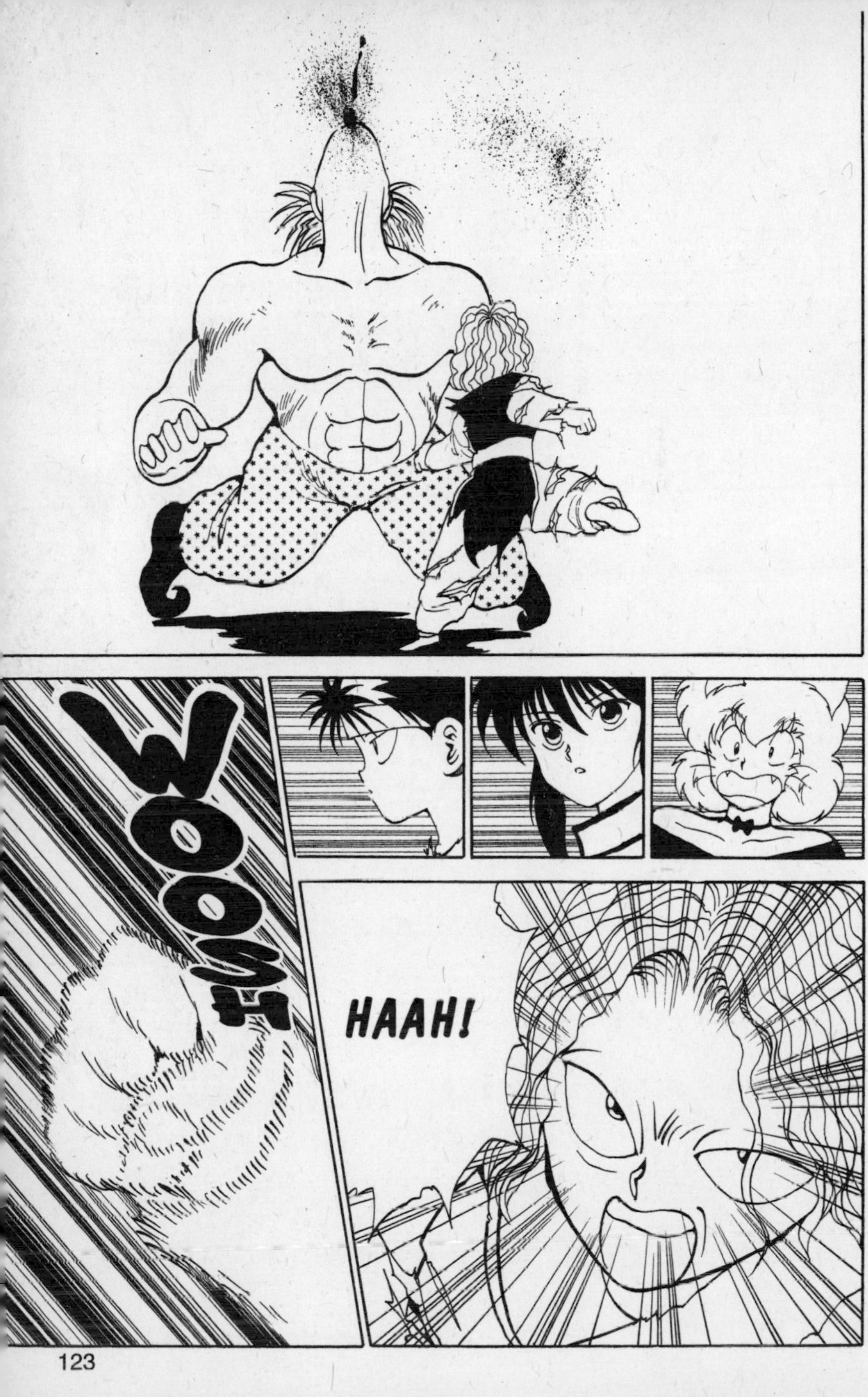
HAAH!
WOOSH

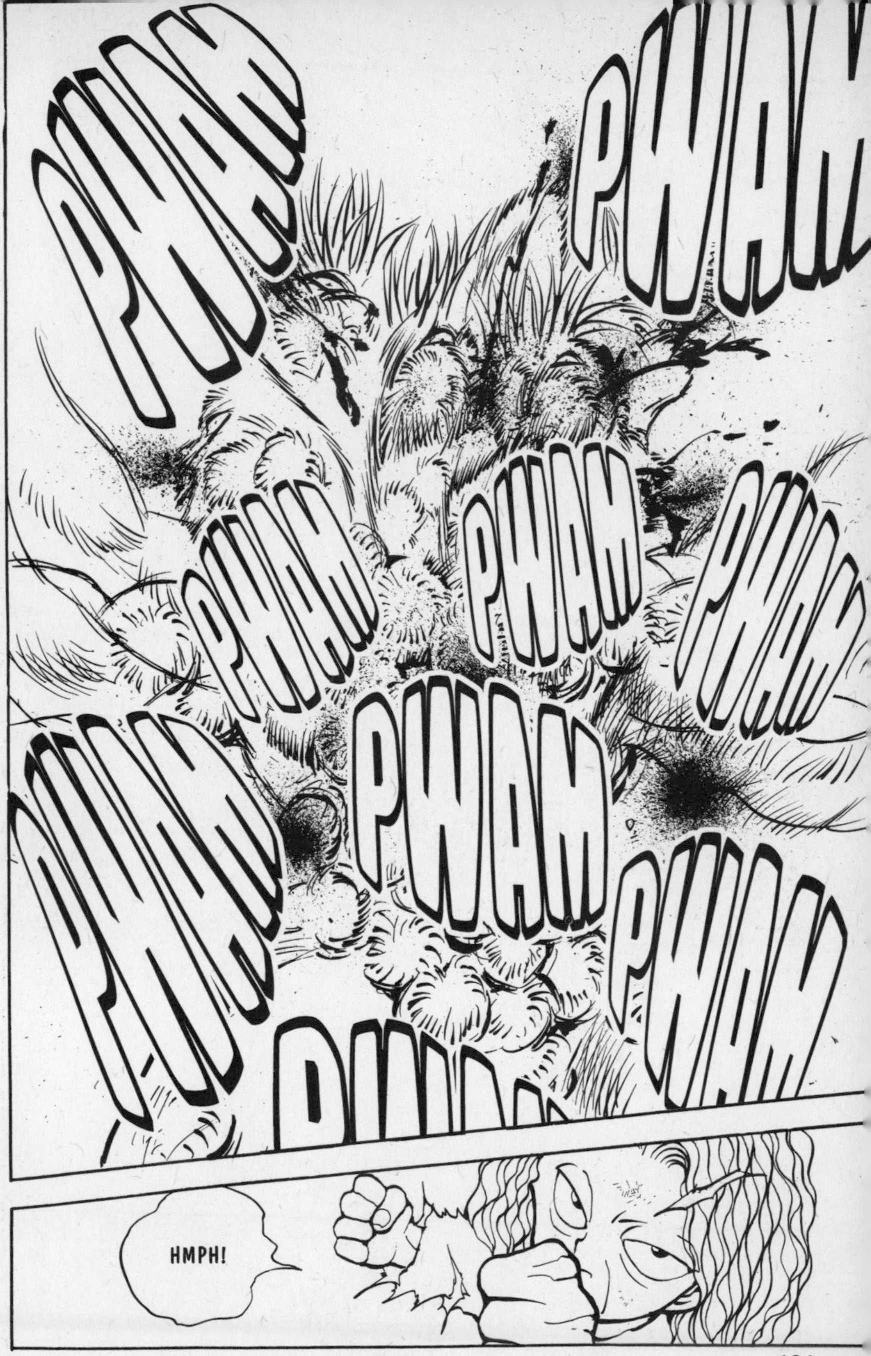
PWAM
PWAM
PWAM
PWAM
PWAM
PWAM
PWAM
PWAM
HMPH!

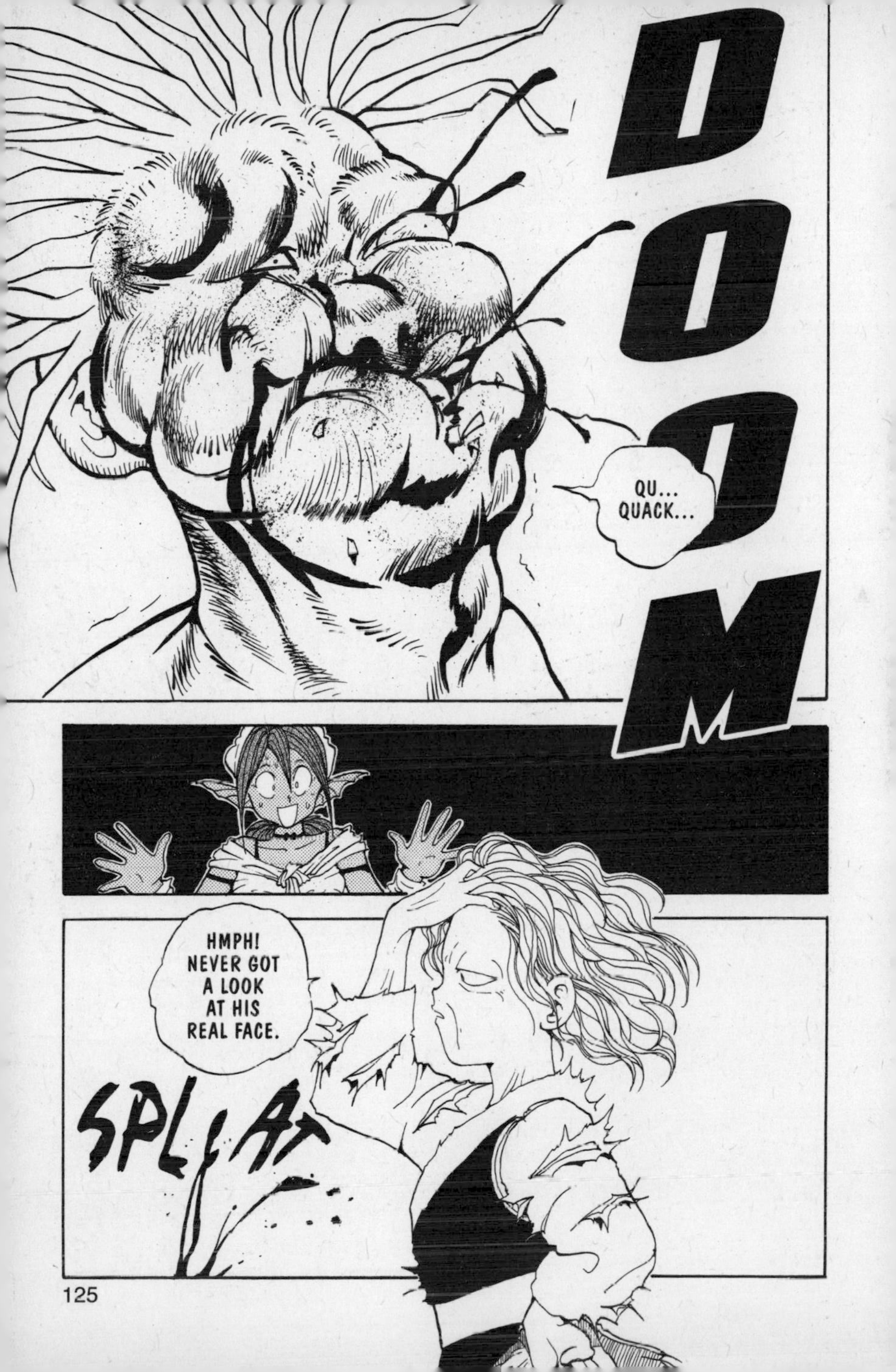
DOOOM
QU... QUACK...
HMPH! NEVER GOT A LOOK AT HIS REAL FACE.
SPLAT

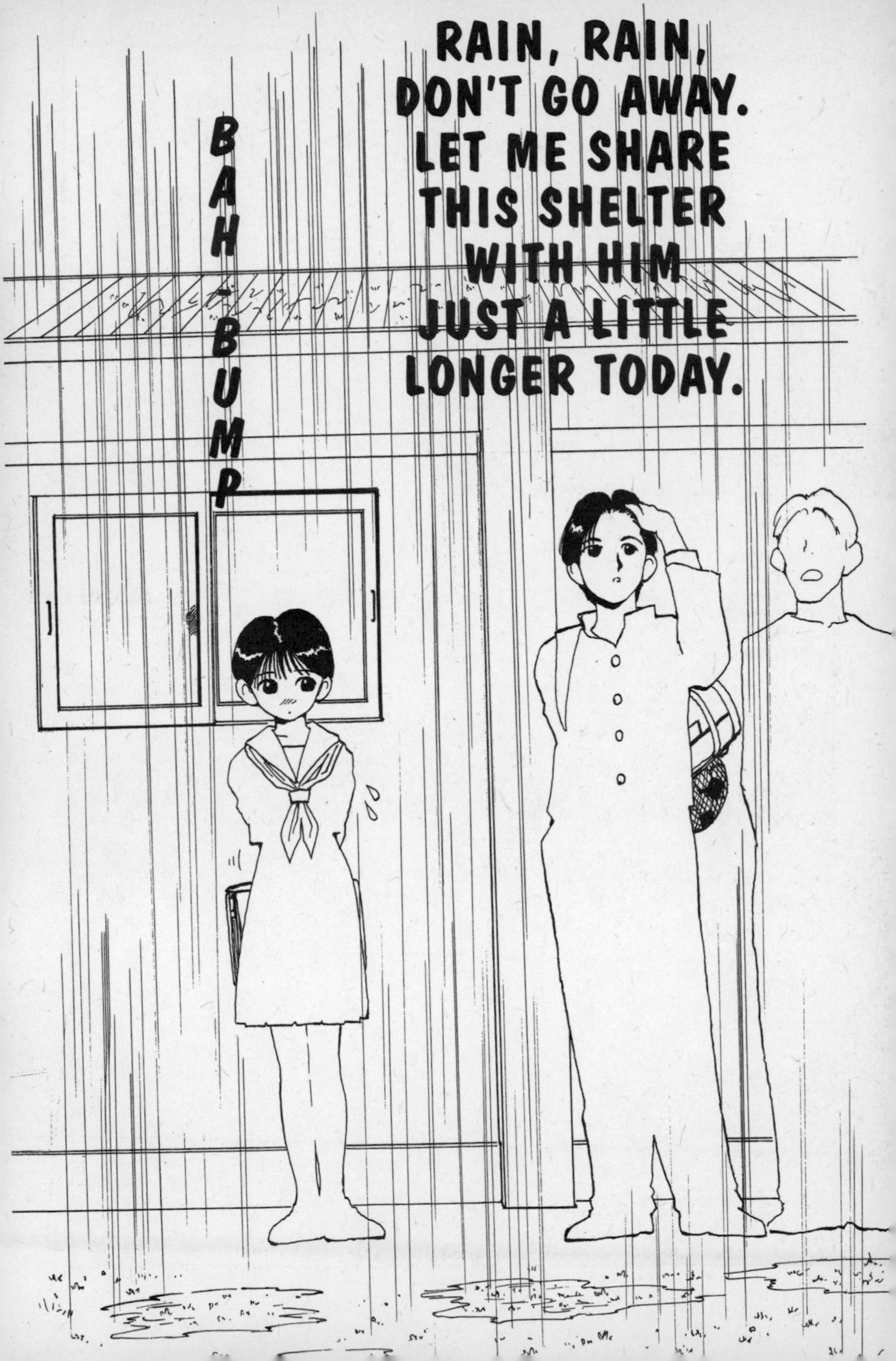
RAIN, RAIN, DON'T GO AWAY. LET ME SHARE THIS SHELTER WITH HIM JUST A LITTLE LONGER TODAY.
BAH-BUMP

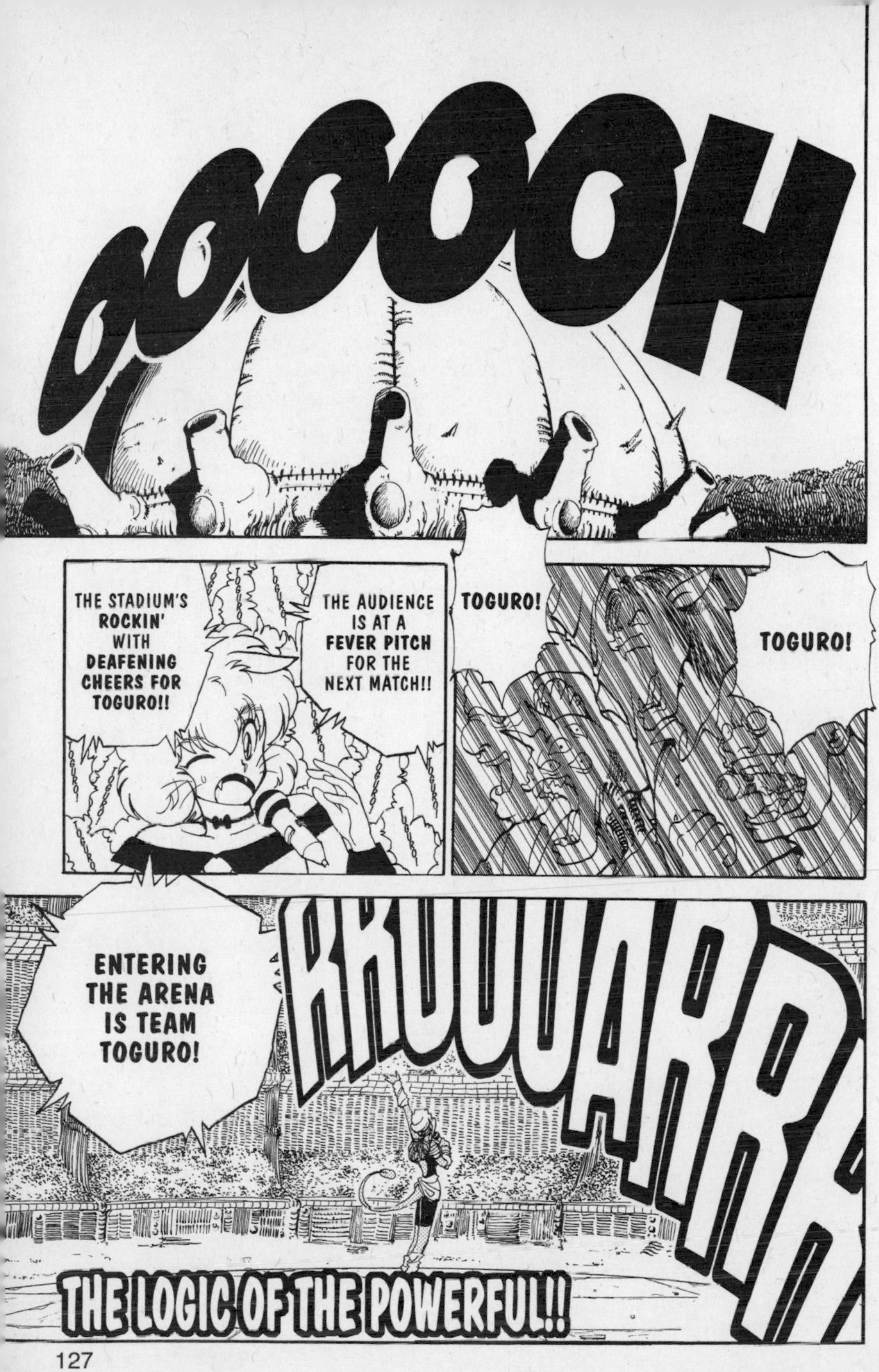
OOOOOH
TOGURO!
TOGURO!
THE AUDIENCE IS AT A FEVER PITCH FOR THE NEXT MATCH!!
THE STADIUM'S ROCKIN' WITH DEAFENING CHEERS FOR TOGURO!!
KRUUUARR
ENTERING THE ARENA IS TEAM TOGURO!
THE LOGIC OF THE POWERFUL!!

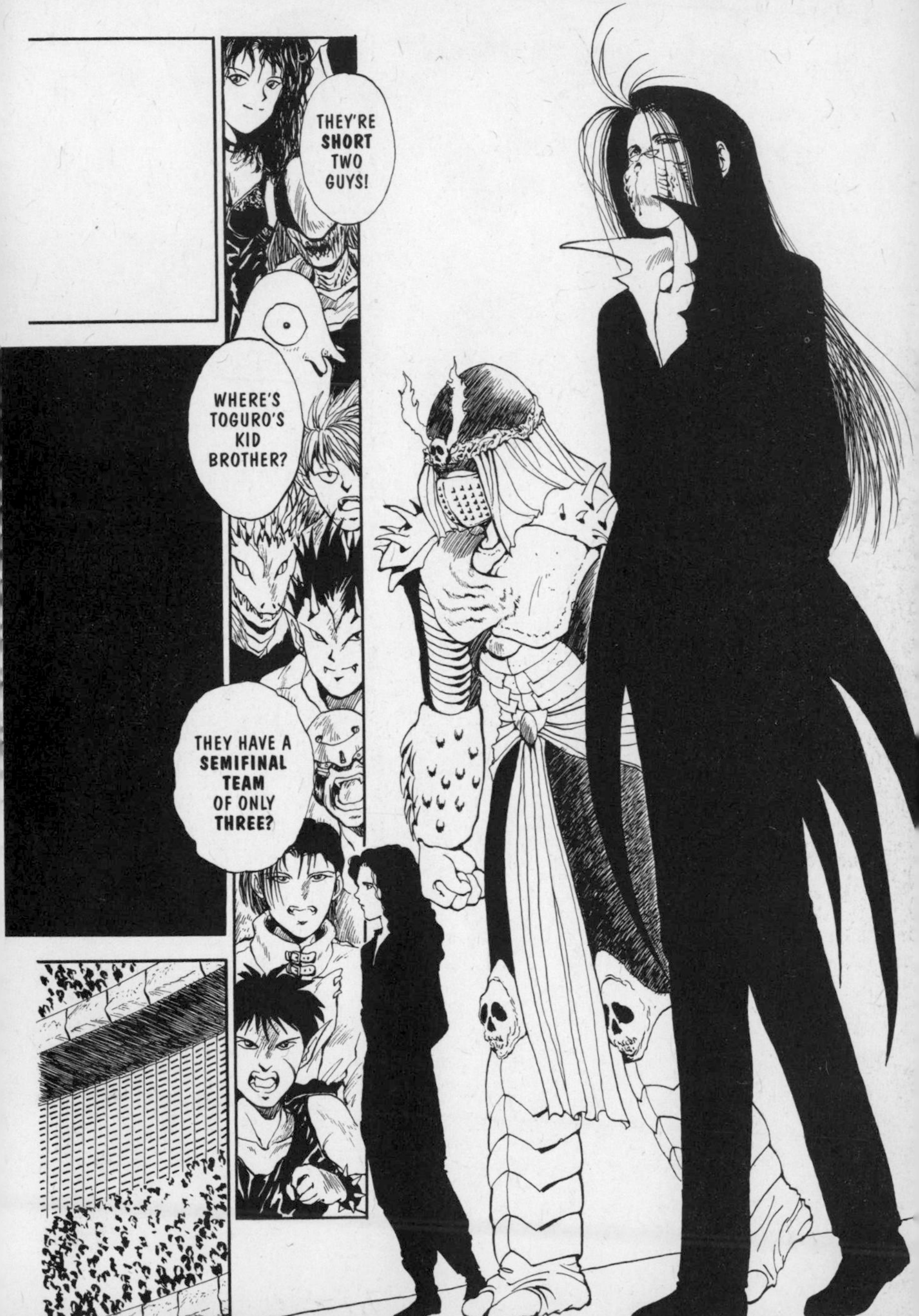
THEY'RE SHORT TWO GUYS!
WHERE'S TOGURO'S KID BROTHER?
THEY HAVE A SEMIFINAL TEAM OF ONLY THREE?

READ THIS WAY

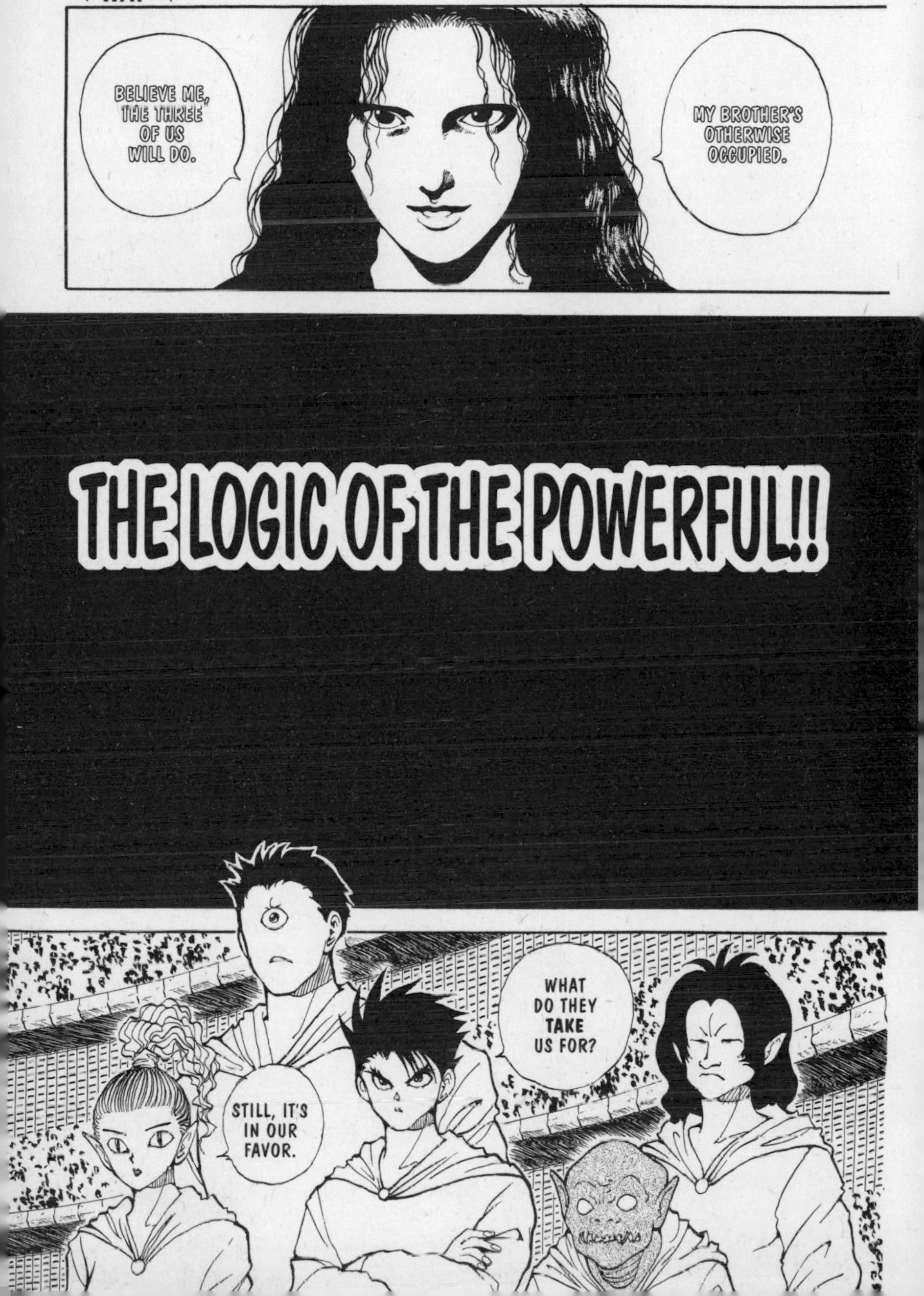
MY BROTHER'S OTHERWISE OCCUPIED.
BELIEVE ME, THE THREE OF US WILL DO.
THE LOGIC OF THE POWERFUL!!
WHAT DO THEY TAKE US FOR?
STILL, IT'S IN OUR FAVOR.

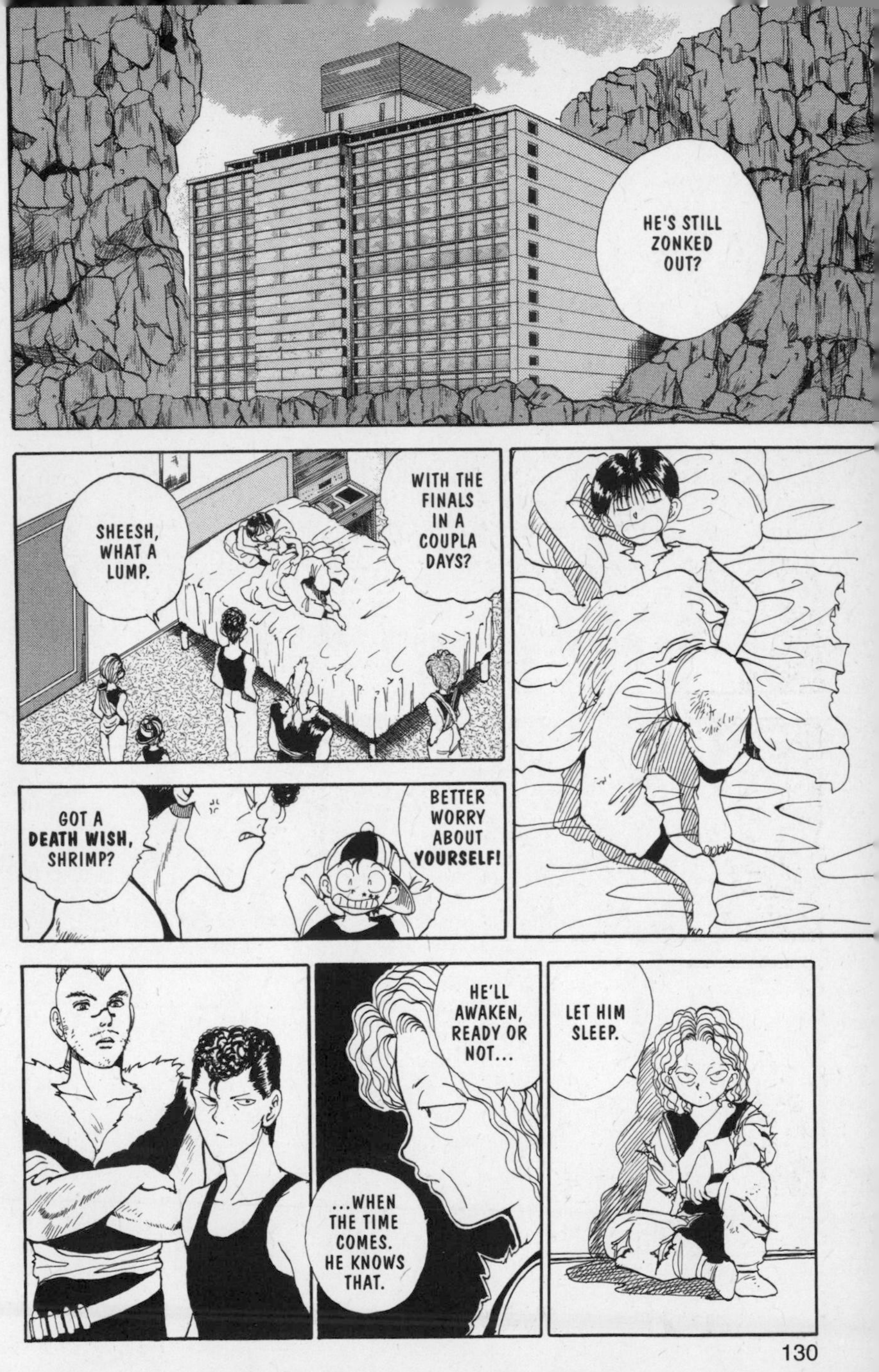
HE'S STILL ZONKED OUT?
WITH THE FINALS IN A COUPLA DAYS?
SHEESH, WHAT A LUMP.
BETTER WORRY ABOUT **YOURSELF!**
GOT A **DEATH WISH,** SHRIMP?
LET HIM SLEEP.
HE'LL AWAKEN, READY OR NOT...
...WHEN THE TIME COMES. HE KNOWS THAT.

READ THIS WAY

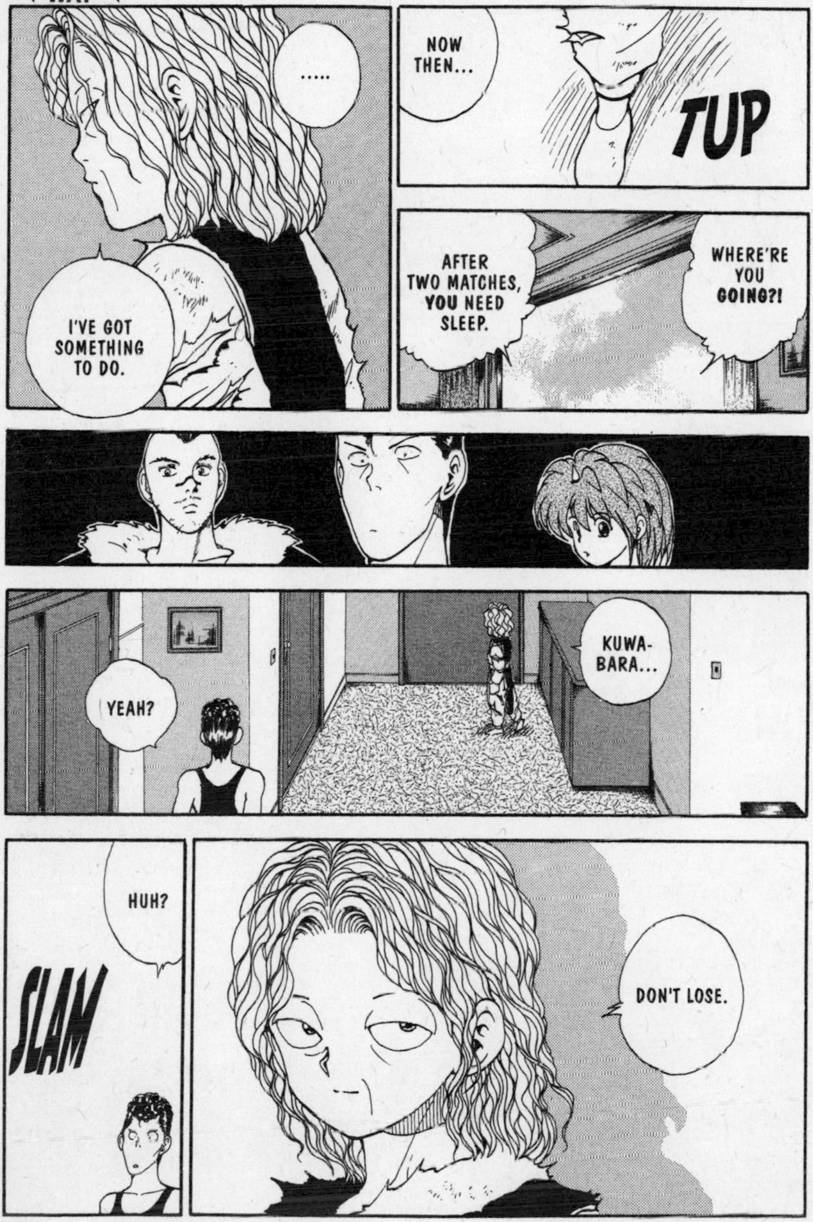

NOW THEN...
TUP
WHERE'RE YOU GOING?!
AFTER TWO MATCHES, YOU NEED SLEEP.
.....
I'VE GOT SOMETHING TO DO.
KUWA-BARA...
YEAH?
DON'T LOSE.
HUH?
SLAM

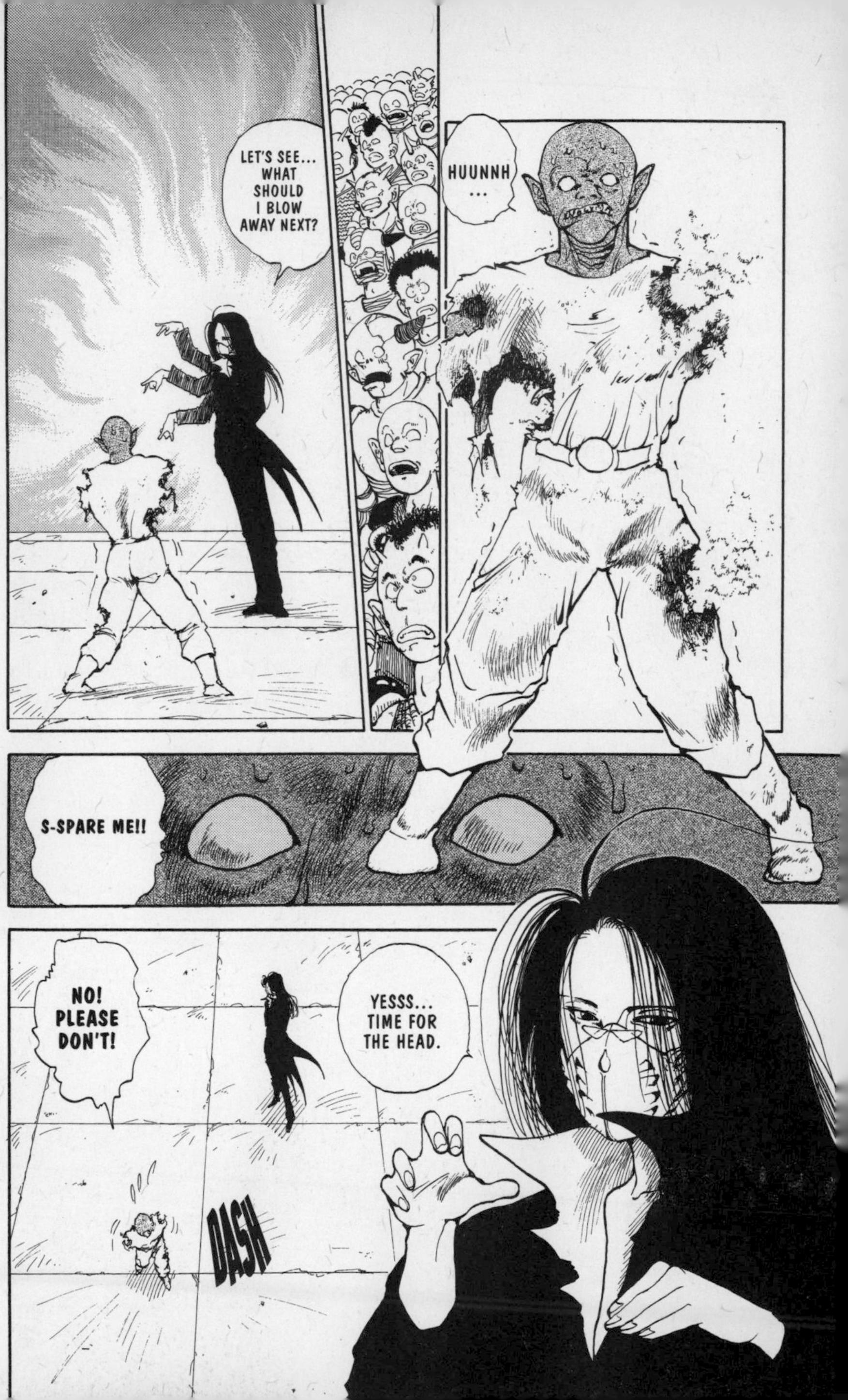
HUUNNH...
LET'S SEE... WHAT SHOULD I BLOW AWAY NEXT?
S-SPARE ME!!
YESSS... TIME FOR THE HEAD.
NO! PLEASE DON'T!
DASH

READ THIS WAY

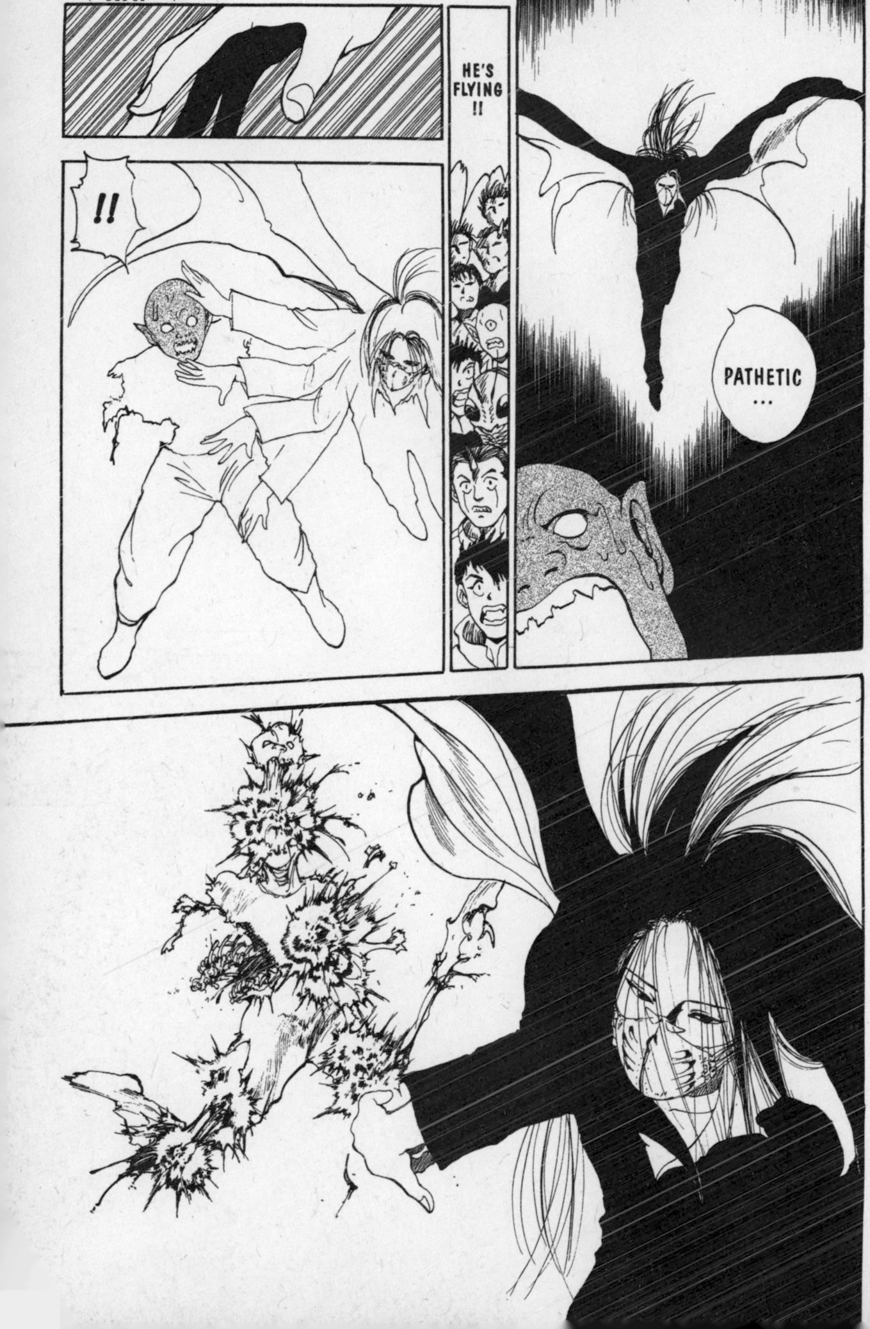
PATHETIC ...
HE'S FLYING !!
!!

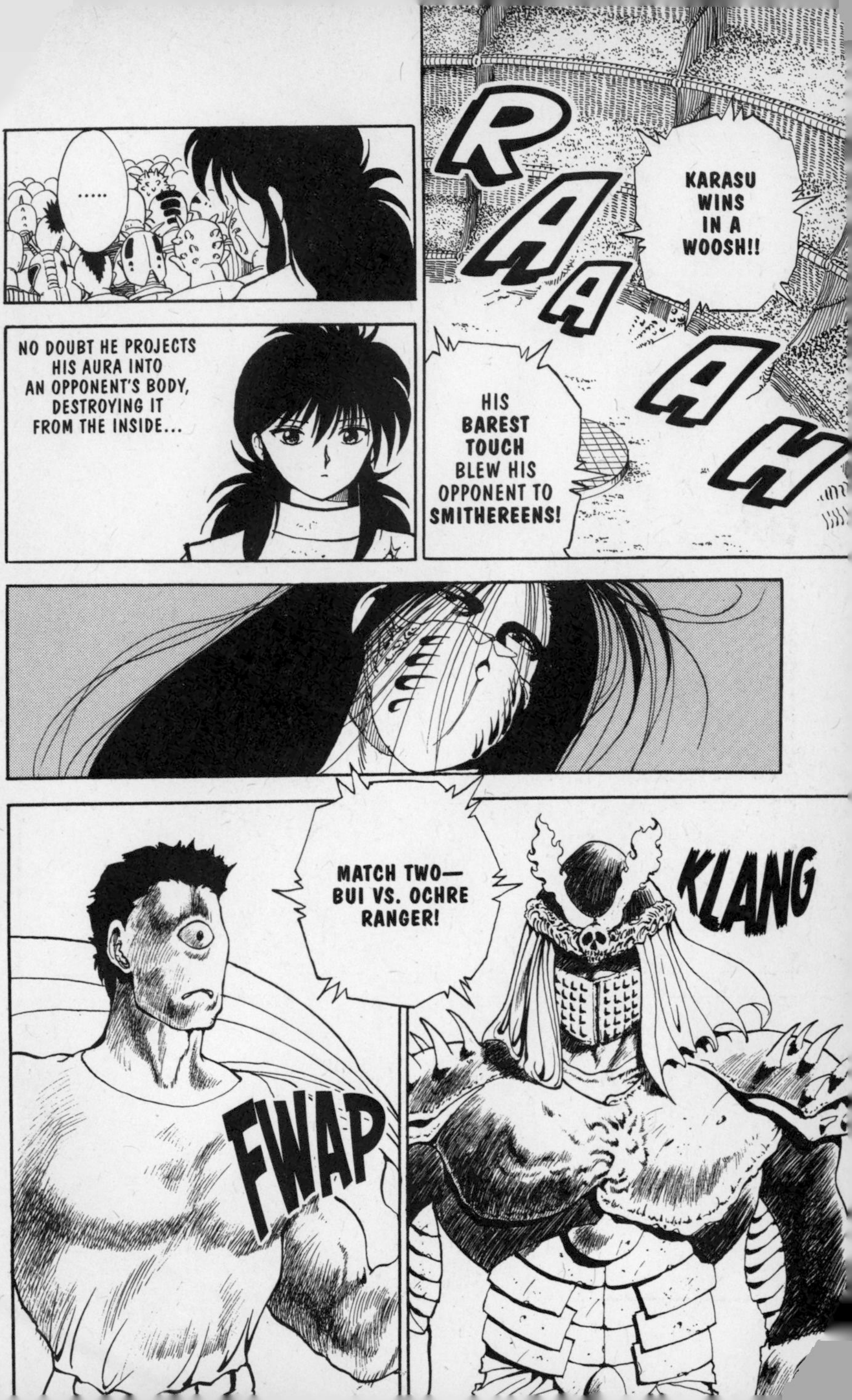
RAAAAH
KARASU WINS IN A WOOSH!!
HIS BAREST TOUCH BLEW HIS OPPONENT TO SMITHEREENS!
......
NO DOUBT HE PROJECTS HIS AURA INTO AN OPPONENT'S BODY, DESTROYING IT FROM THE INSIDE...
KLANG
MATCH TWO—BUI VS. OCHRE RANGER!
FWAP

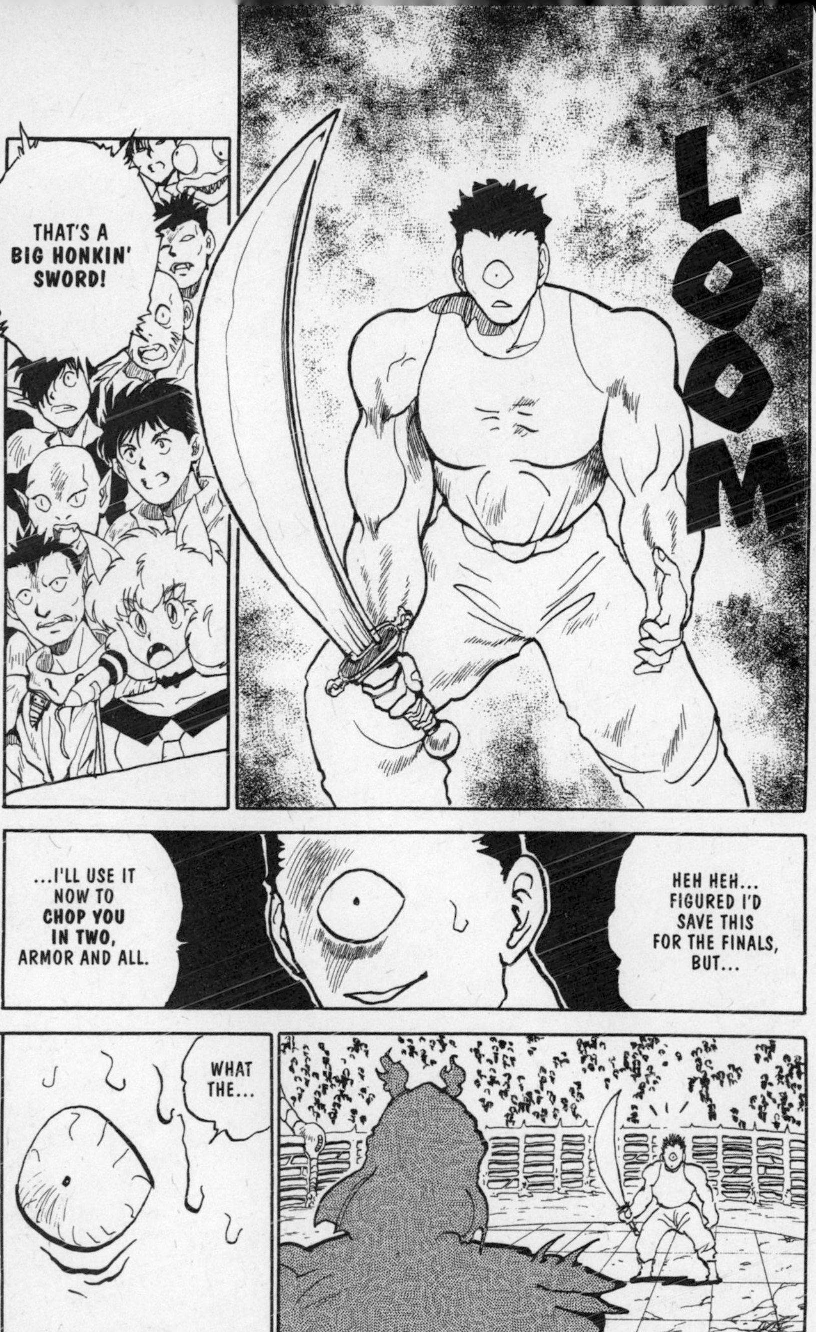
LOOM
THAT'S A BIG HONKIN' SWORD!
HEH HEH... FIGURED I'D SAVE THIS FOR THE FINALS, BUT...
...I'LL USE IT NOW TO CHOP YOU IN TWO, ARMOR AND ALL.
WHAT THE...

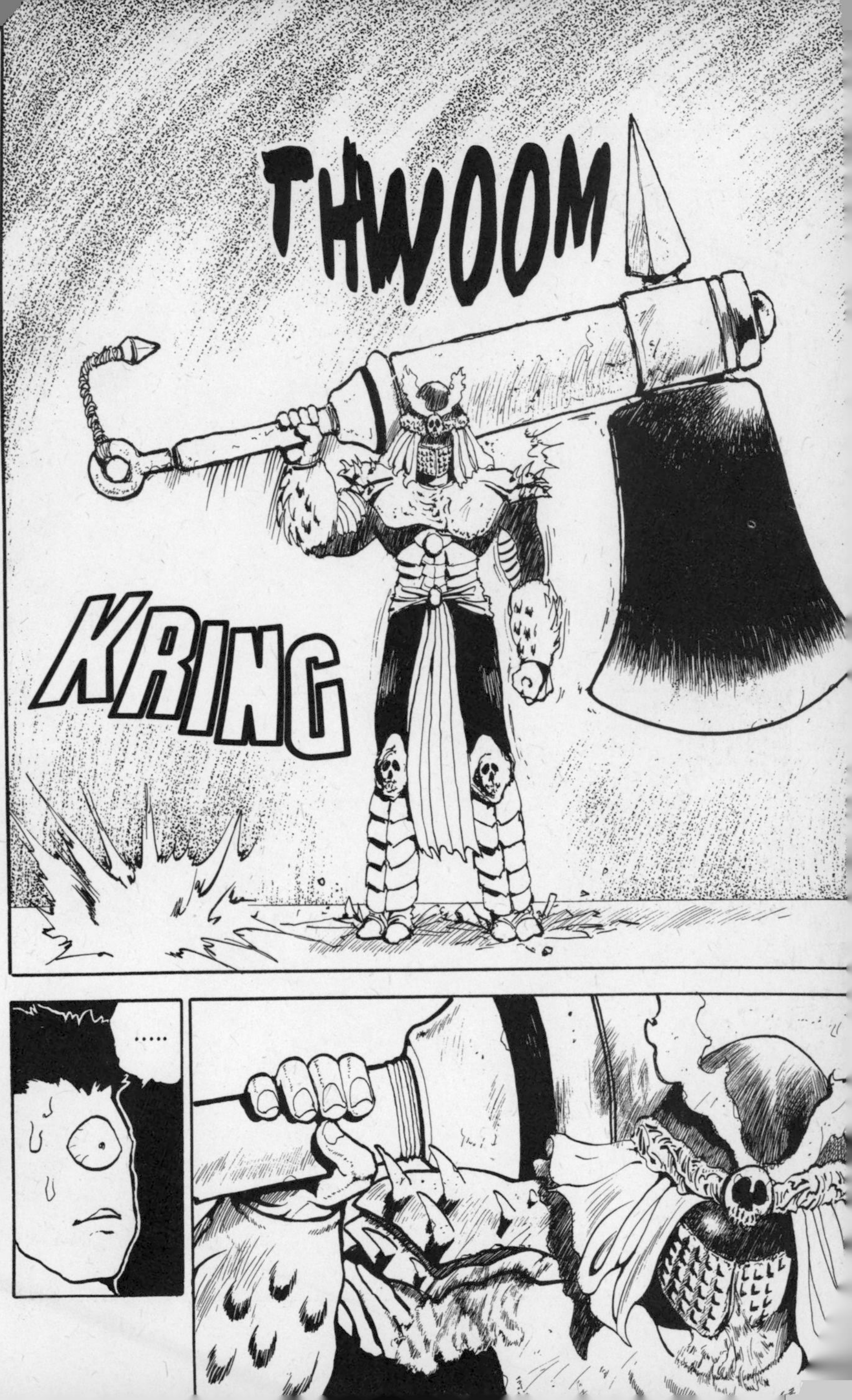
THWOOM
KRING
......

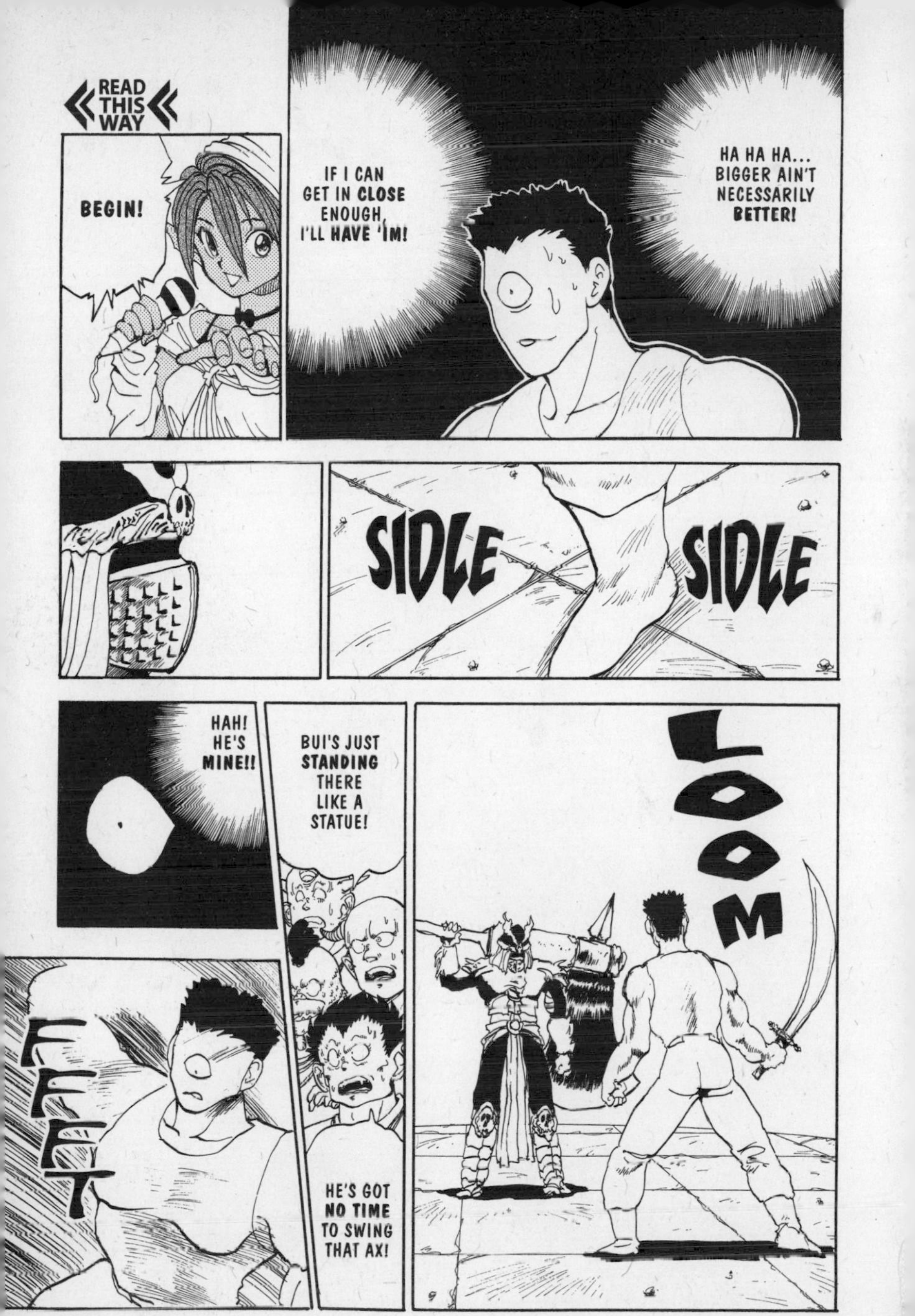
READ THIS WAY
HA HA HA... BIGGER AIN'T NECESSARILY BETTER!
IF I CAN GET IN CLOSE ENOUGH, I'LL HAVE 'IM!
BEGIN!
SIDLE
SIDLE
LOOM
BUI'S JUST STANDING THERE LIKE A STATUE!
HE'S GOT NO TIME TO SWING THAT AX!
HAH! HE'S MINE!!
FFFT

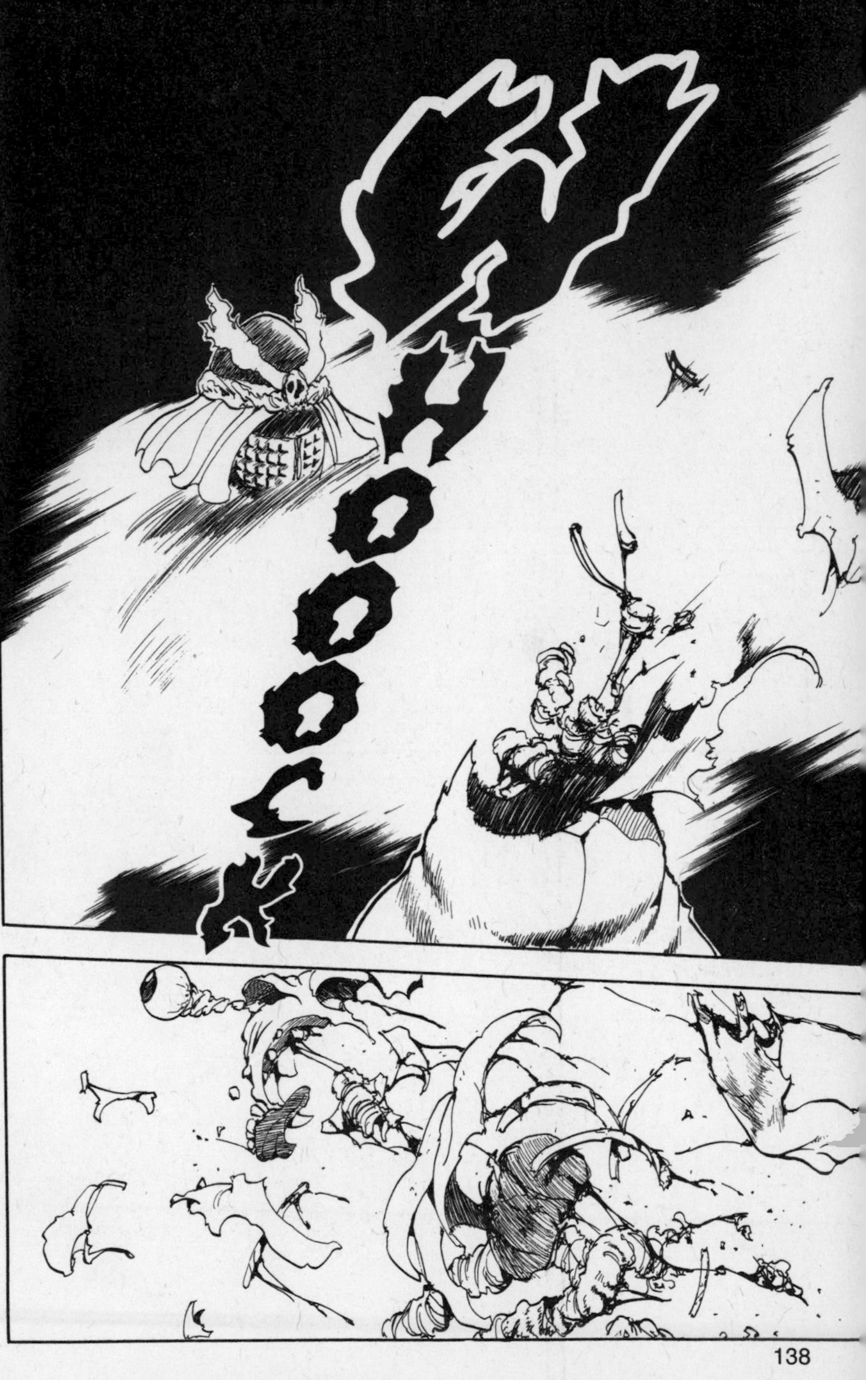

READ THIS WAY

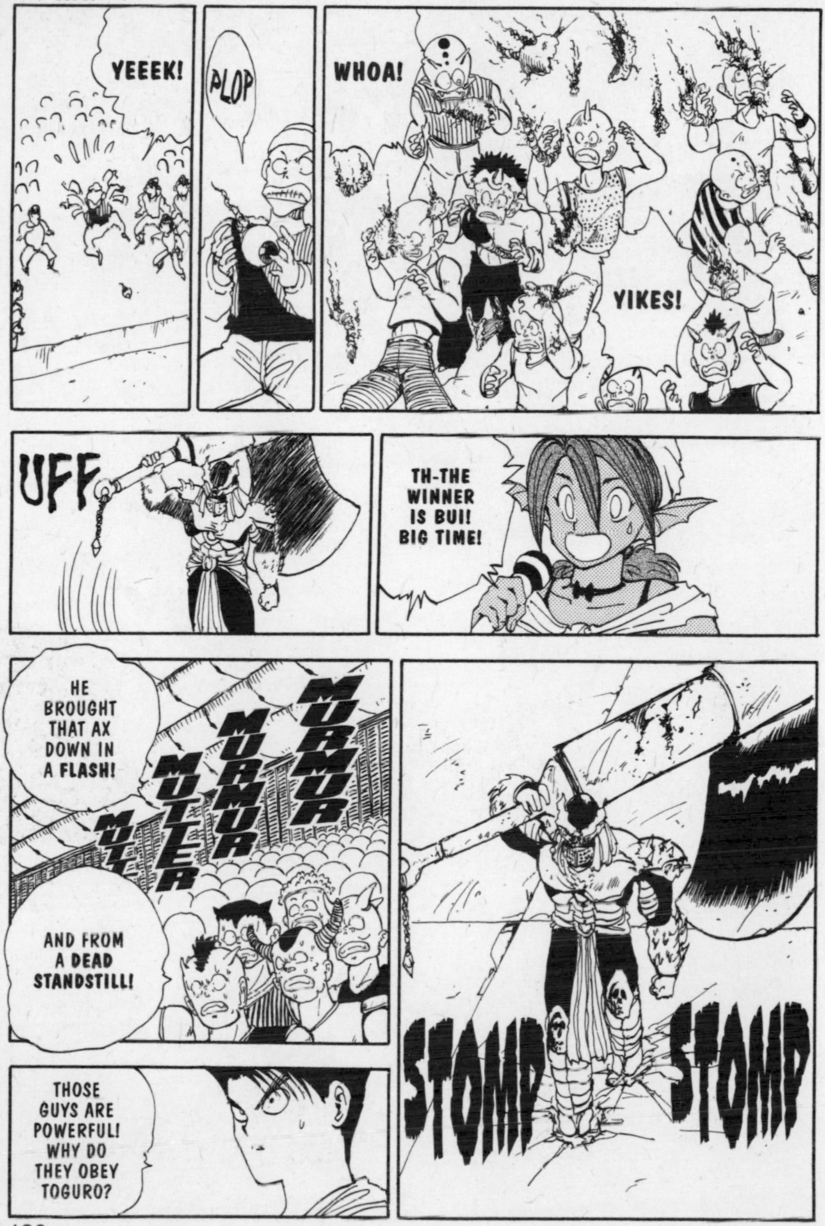
WHOA!
YIKES!
PLOP
YEEEK!
TH-THE WINNER IS BUI! BIG TIME!
UFF
STOMP
STOMP
HE BROUGHT THAT AX DOWN IN A FLASH!
MURMUR
MURMUR
MUTTER
MUTT
AND FROM A DEAD STANDSTILL!
THOSE GUYS ARE POWERFUL! WHY DO THEY OBEY TOGURO?

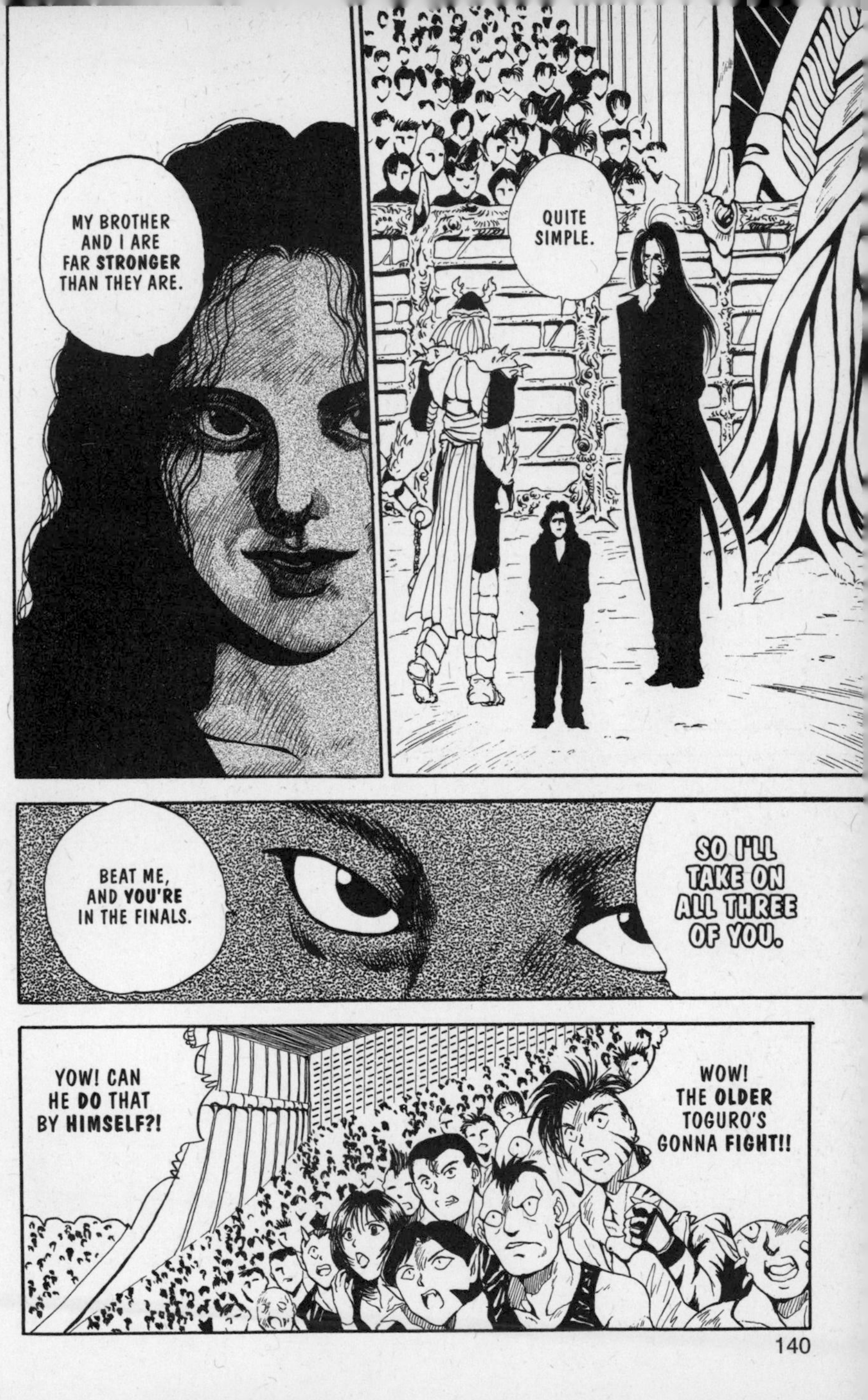
QUITE SIMPLE.
MY BROTHER AND I ARE FAR STRONGER THAN THEY ARE.
SO I'LL TAKE ON ALL THREE OF YOU.
BEAT ME, AND YOU'RE IN THE FINALS.
WOW! THE OLDER TOGURO'S GONNA FIGHT!!
YOW! CAN HE DO THAT BY HIMSELF?!

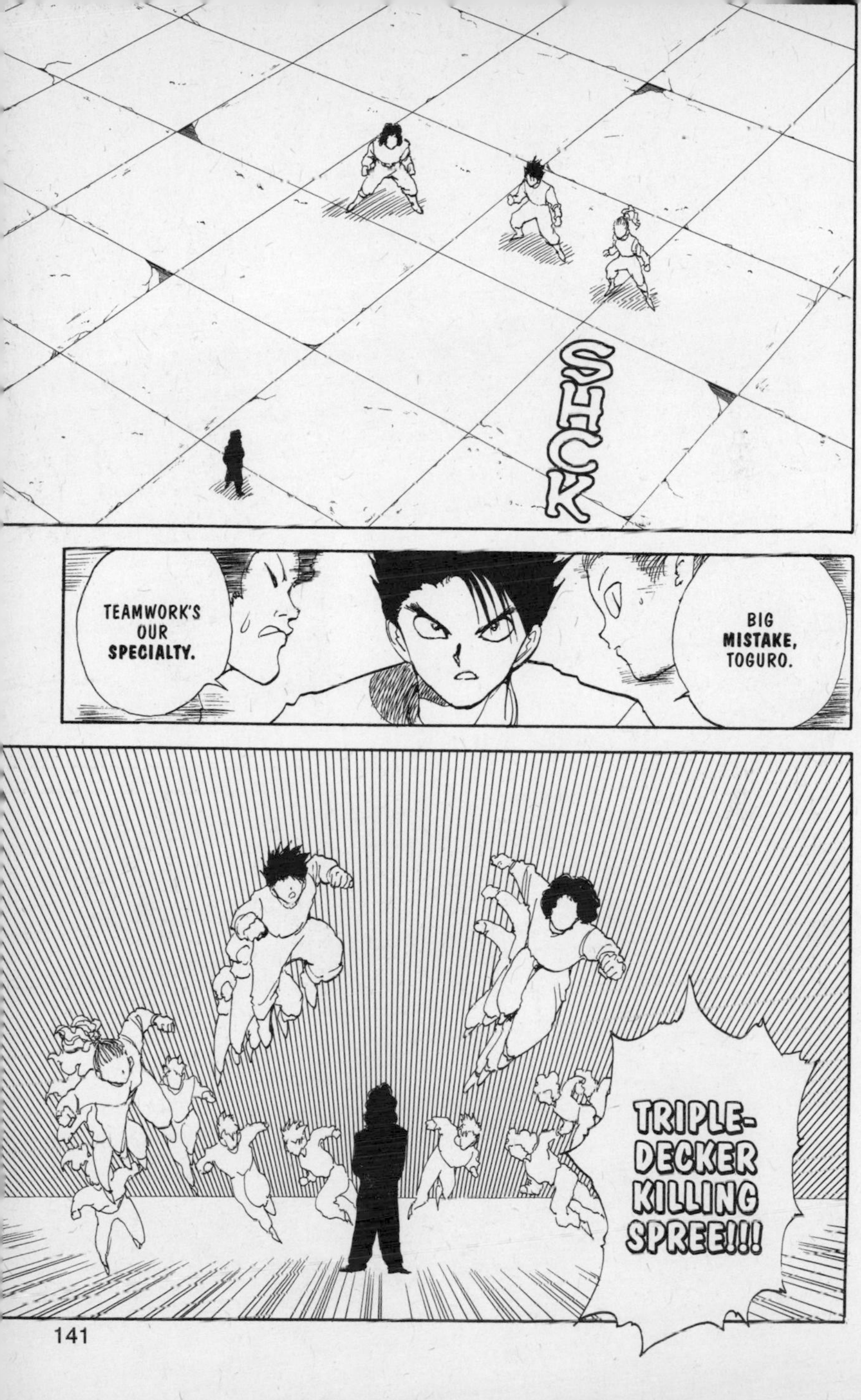
SHCK
BIG MISTAKE, TOGURO.
TEAMWORK'S OUR SPECIALTY.
TRIPLE-DECKER KILLING SPREE!!!

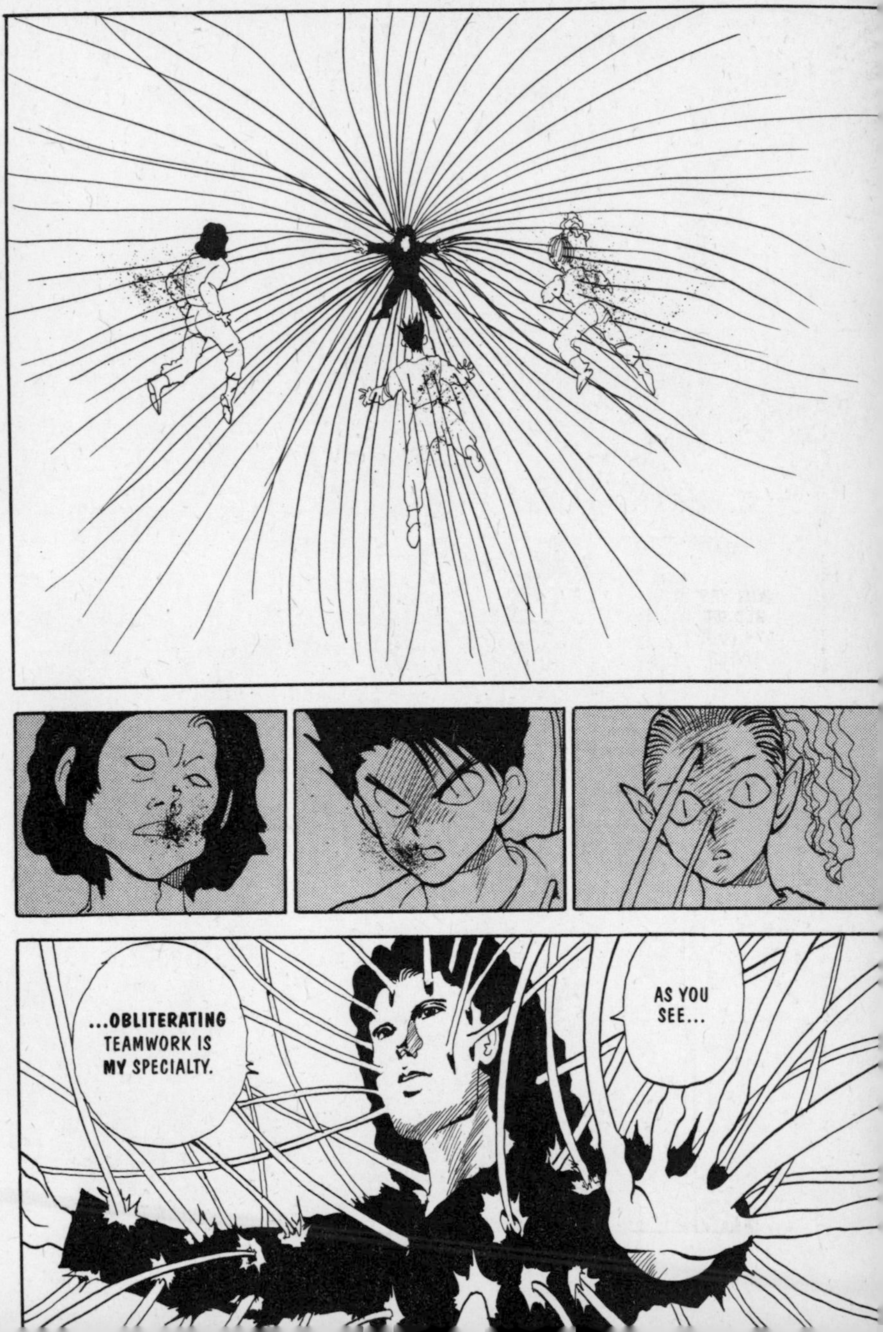
AS YOU SEE...
...OBLITERATING TEAMWORK IS MY SPECIALTY.

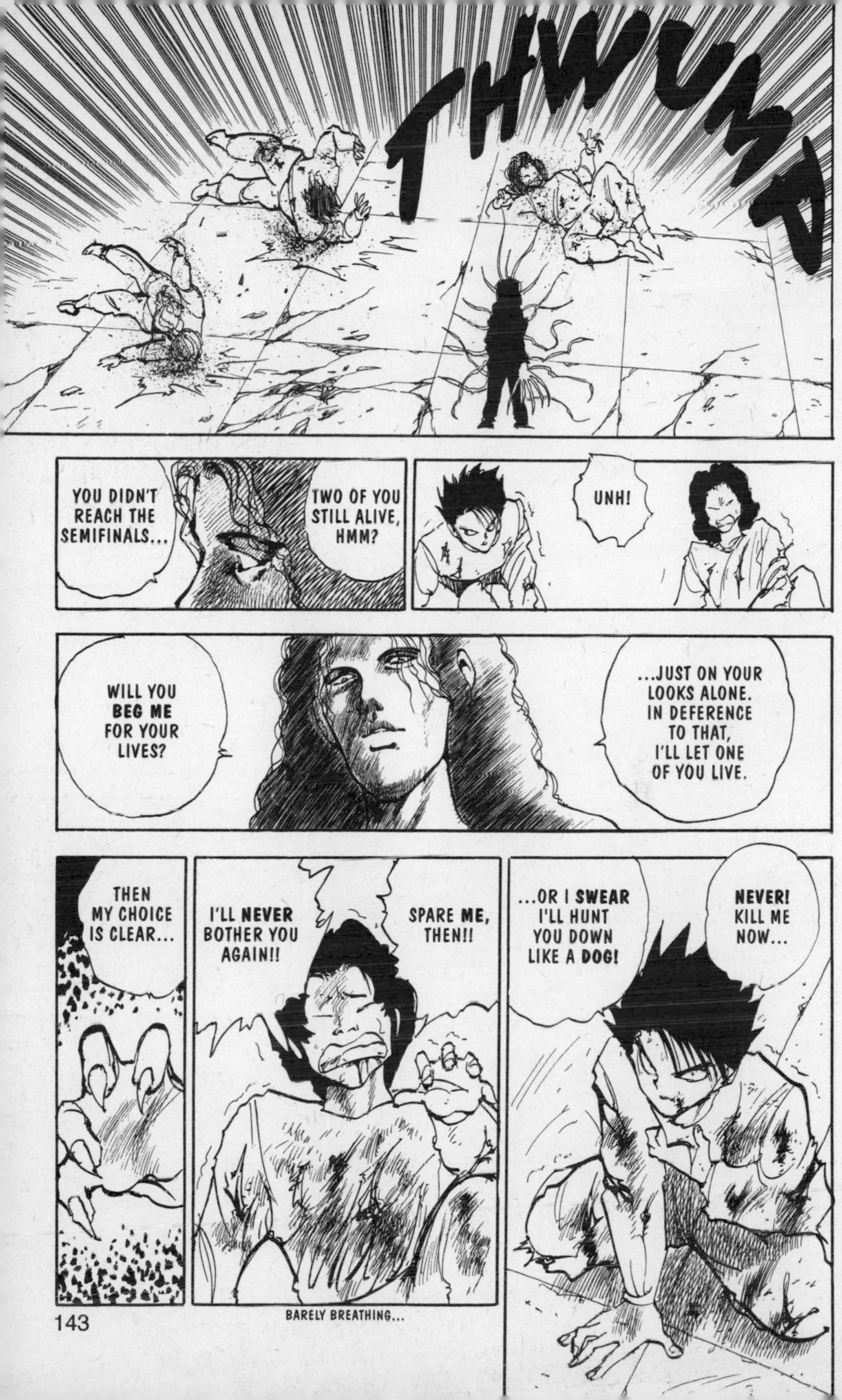
THWUMP
UNH!
TWO OF YOU STILL ALIVE, HMM?
YOU DIDN'T REACH THE SEMIFINALS...
...JUST ON YOUR LOOKS ALONE. IN DEFERENCE TO THAT, I'LL LET ONE OF YOU LIVE.
WILL YOU **BEG ME** FOR YOUR LIVES?
NEVER! KILL ME NOW...
...OR I **SWEAR** I'LL HUNT YOU DOWN LIKE A **DOG!**
SPARE **ME,** THEN!!
I'LL **NEVER** BOTHER YOU AGAIN!!
BARELY BREATHING...
THEN MY CHOICE IS CLEAR...

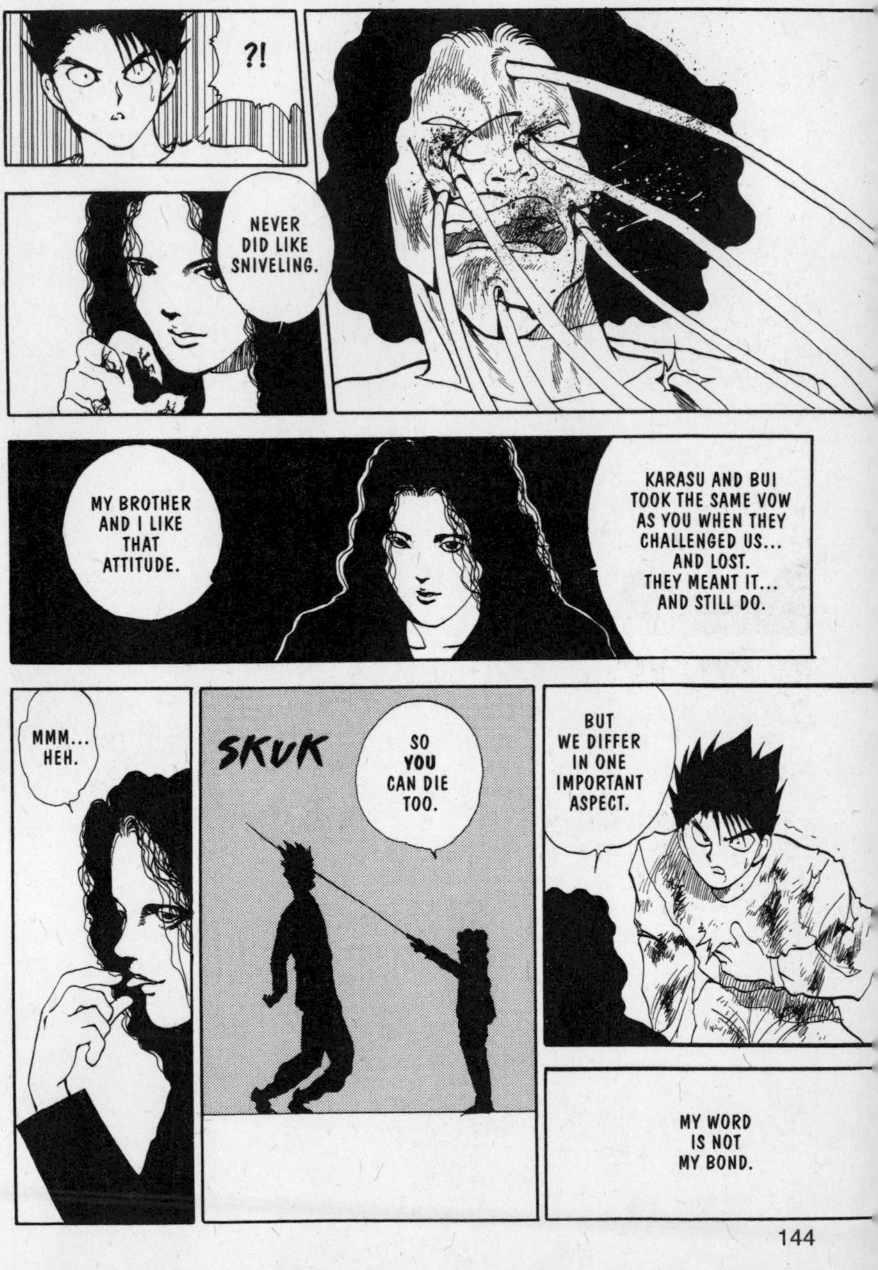
?!
NEVER DID LIKE SNIVELING.
KARASU AND BUI TOOK THE SAME VOW AS YOU WHEN THEY CHALLENGED US... AND LOST. THEY MEANT IT... AND STILL DO.
MY BROTHER AND I LIKE THAT ATTITUDE.
BUT WE DIFFER IN ONE IMPORTANT ASPECT.
MY WORD IS NOT MY BOND.
SKUK
SO **YOU** CAN DIE TOO.
MMM... HEH.

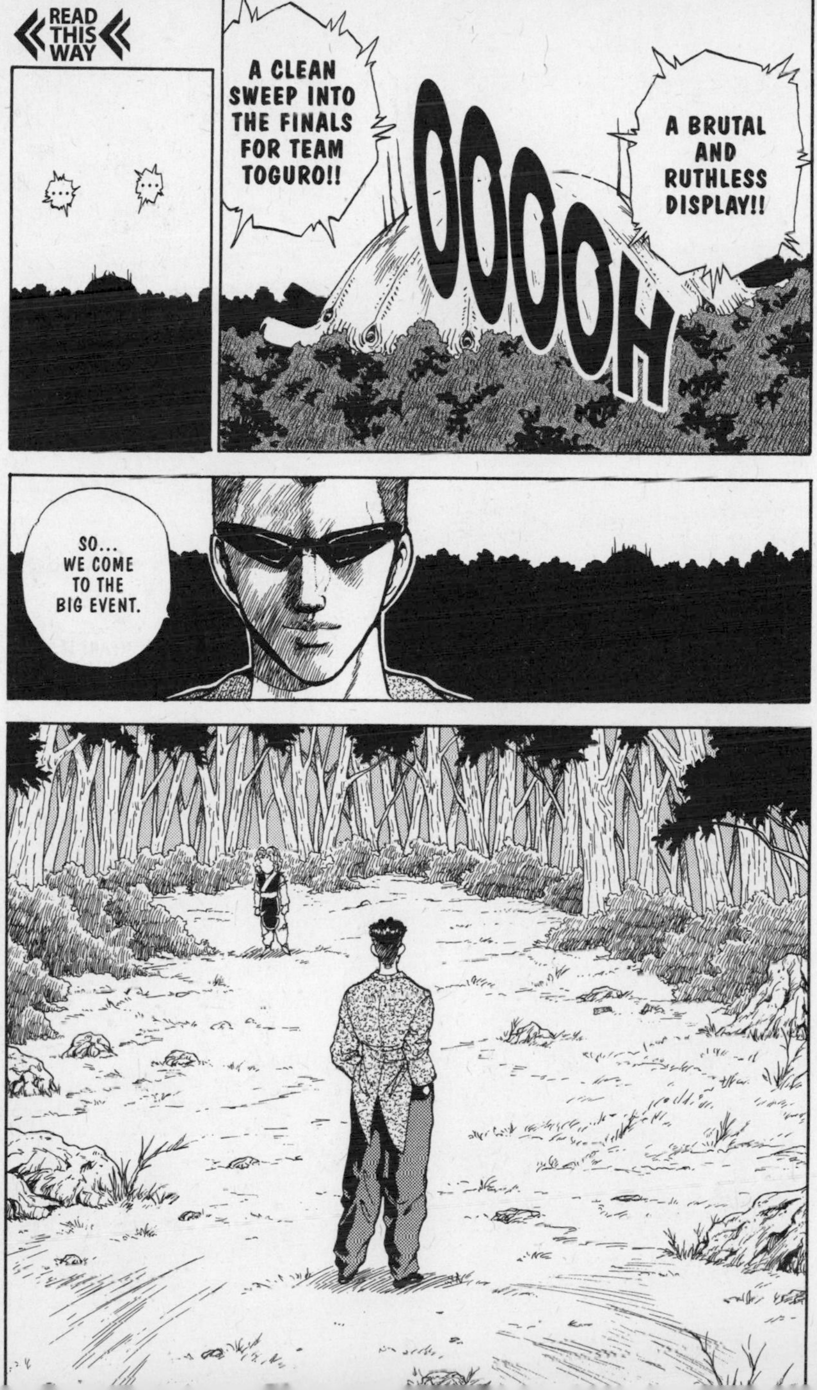
READ THIS WAY
A BRUTAL AND RUTHLESS DISPLAY!!
OOOOH
A CLEAN SWEEP INTO THE FINALS FOR TEAM TOGURO!!
...
...
SO... WE COME TO THE BIG EVENT.

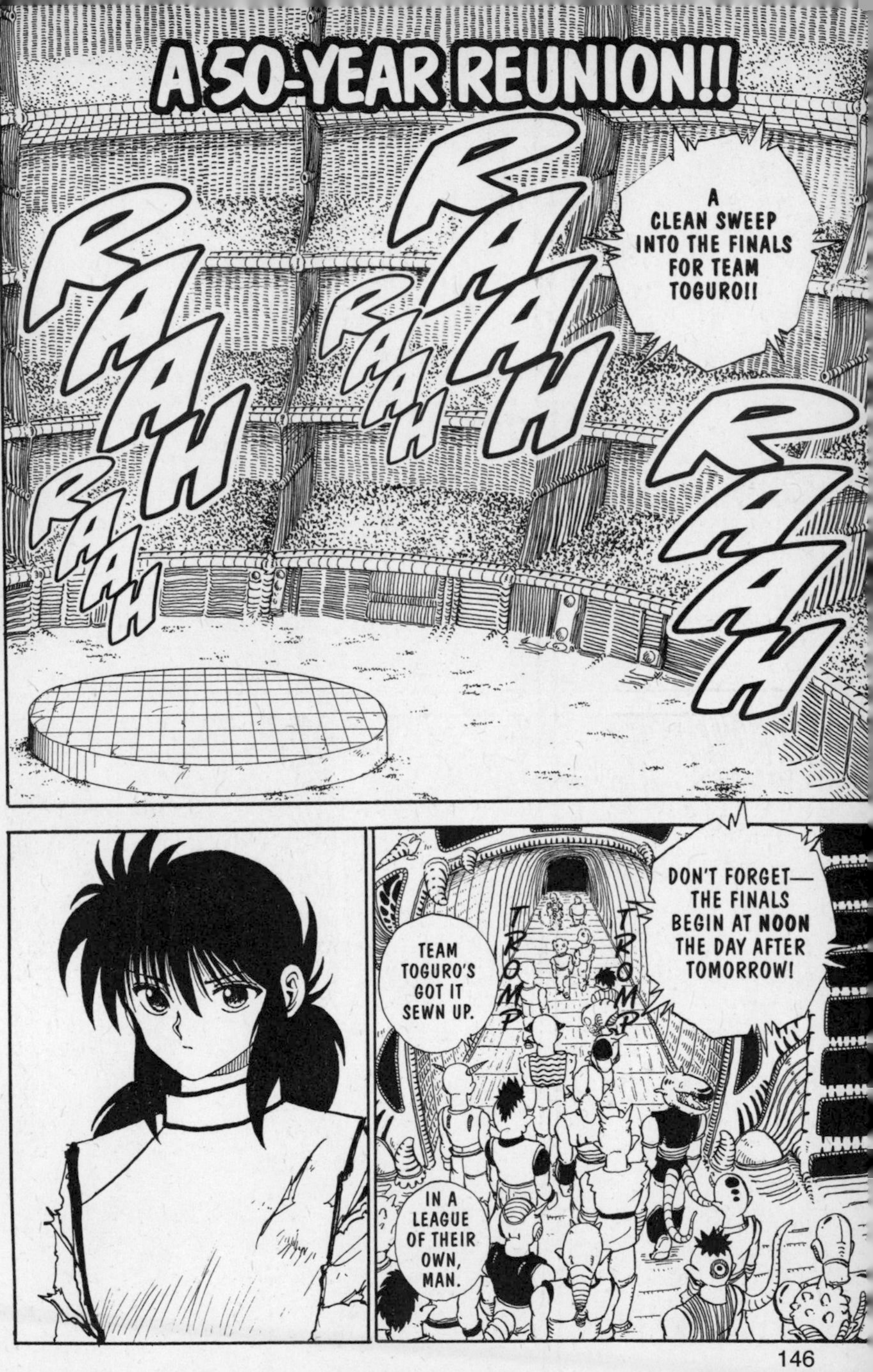
A 50-YEAR REUNION!!
A CLEAN SWEEP INTO THE FINALS FOR TEAM TOGURO!!
RAAH
RAAH
RAAH
RAAH
RAAH
DON'T FORGET— THE FINALS BEGIN AT NOON THE DAY AFTER TOMORROW!
TROMP
TROMP
TEAM TOGURO'S GOT IT SEWN UP.
IN A LEAGUE OF THEIR OWN, MAN.

READ THIS WAY

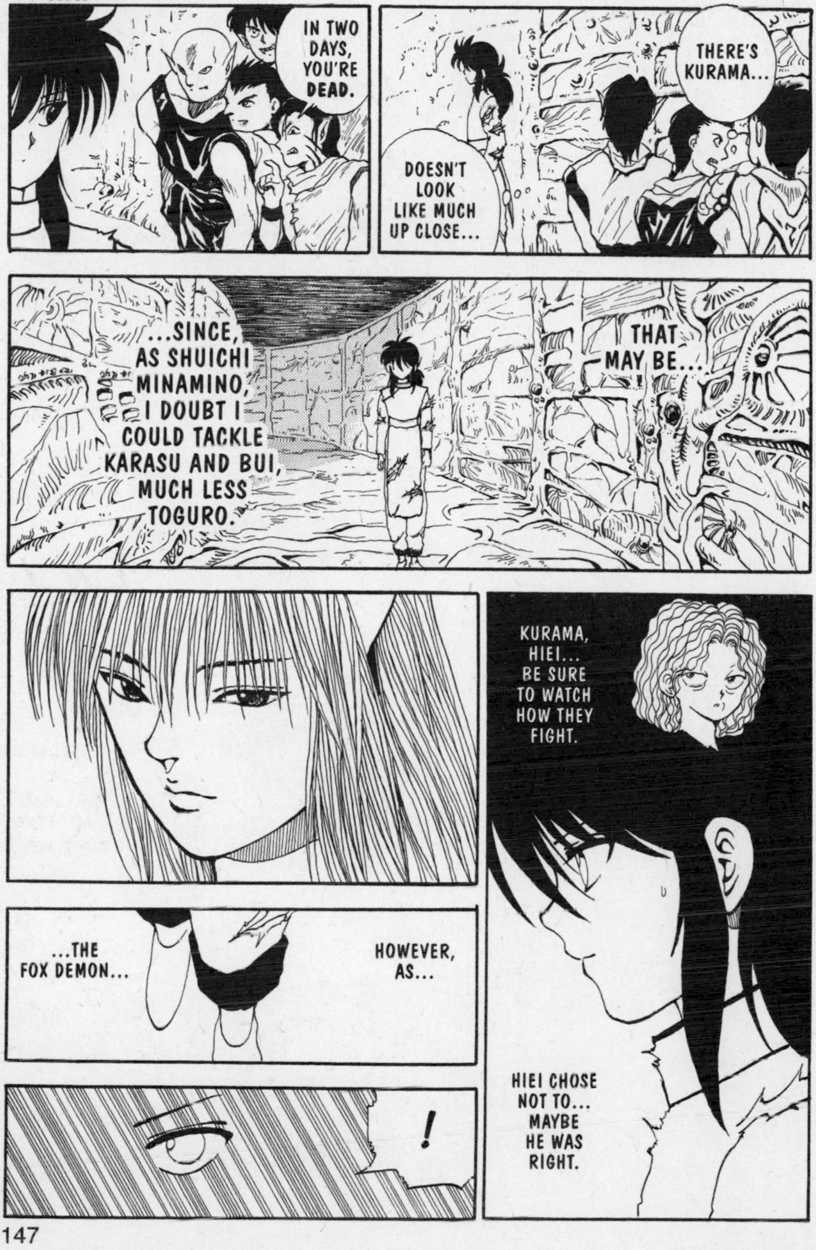

THERE'S KURAMA...
DOESN'T LOOK LIKE MUCH UP CLOSE...
IN TWO DAYS, YOU'RE DEAD.
THAT MAY BE...
...SINCE, AS SHUICHI MINAMINO, I DOUBT I COULD TACKLE KARASU AND BUI, MUCH LESS TOGURO.
KURAMA, HIEI... BE SURE TO WATCH HOW THEY FIGHT.
HIEI CHOSE NOT TO... MAYBE HE WAS RIGHT.
HOWEVER, AS...
...THE FOX DEMON...
!

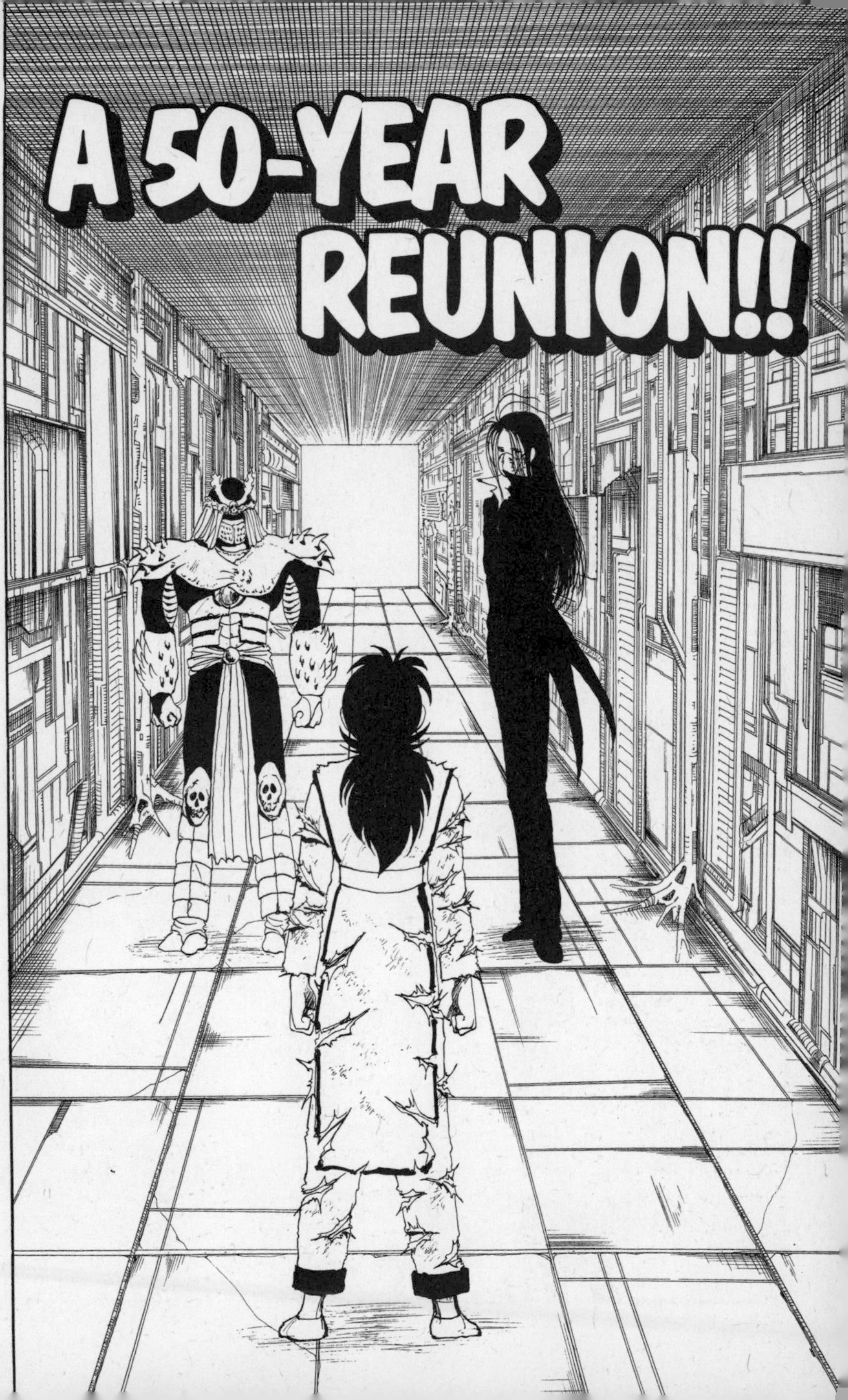
A 50-YEAR
REUNION!!

READ THIS WAY

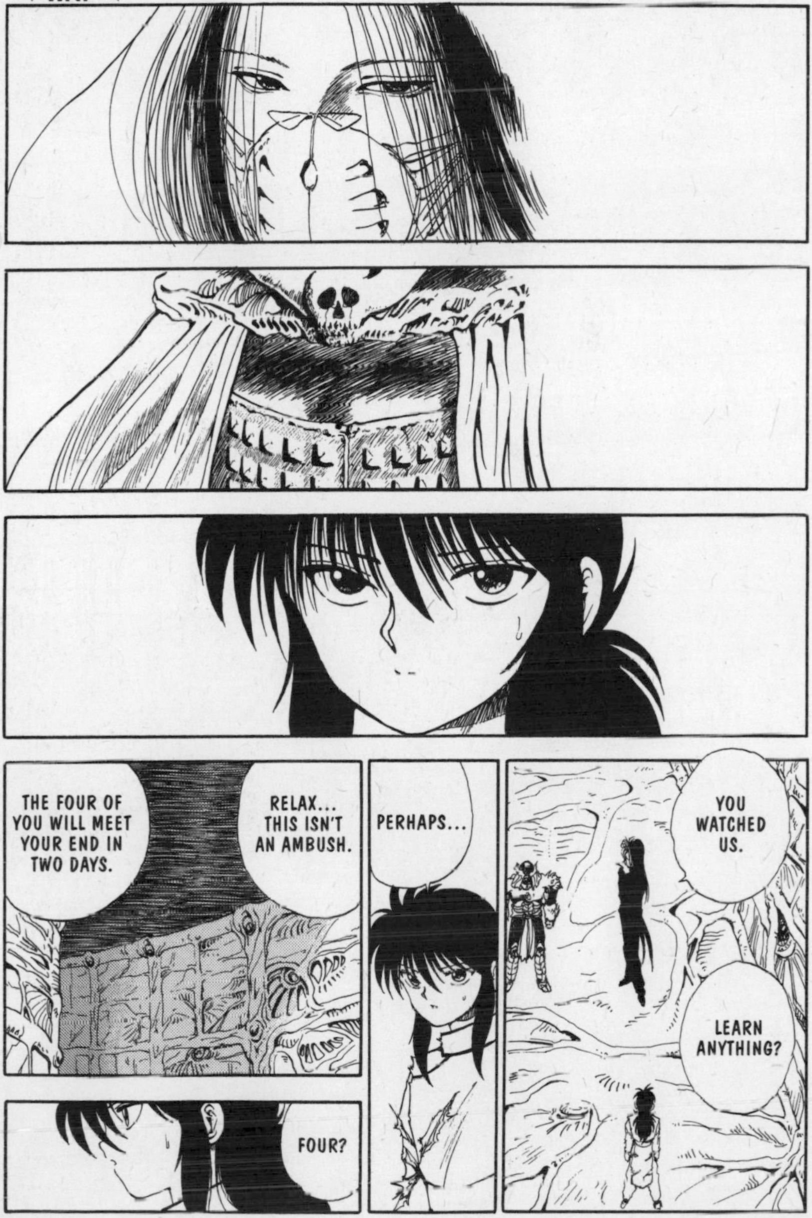
YOU WATCHED US.
LEARN ANYTHING?
PERHAPS...
RELAX... THIS ISN'T AN AMBUSH.
THE FOUR OF YOU WILL MEET YOUR END IN TWO DAYS.
FOUR?

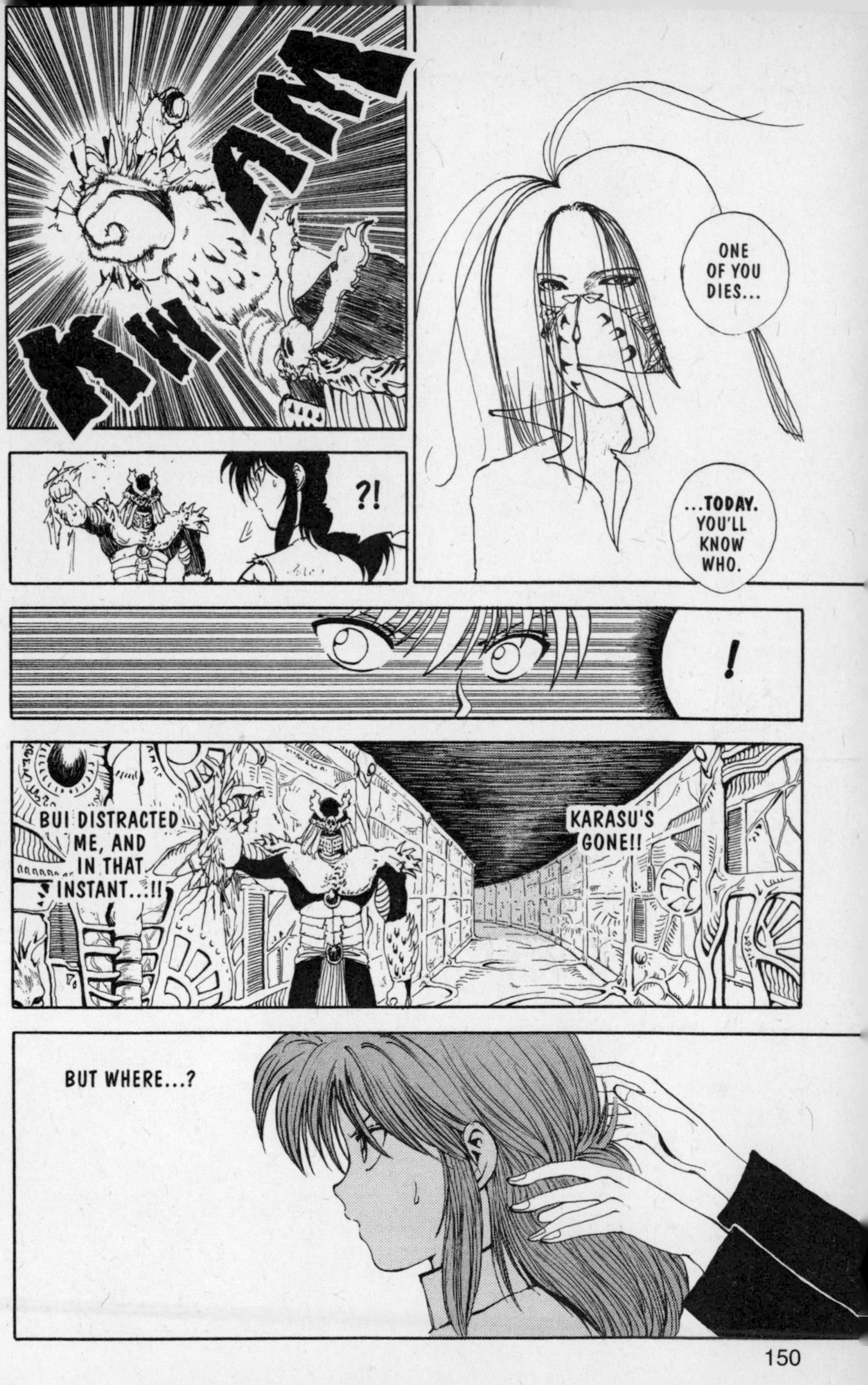
ONE OF YOU DIES...
...TODAY. YOU'LL KNOW WHO.
?!
!
KARASU'S GONE!!
BUI DISTRACTED ME, AND IN THAT INSTANT...!!
BUT WHERE...?

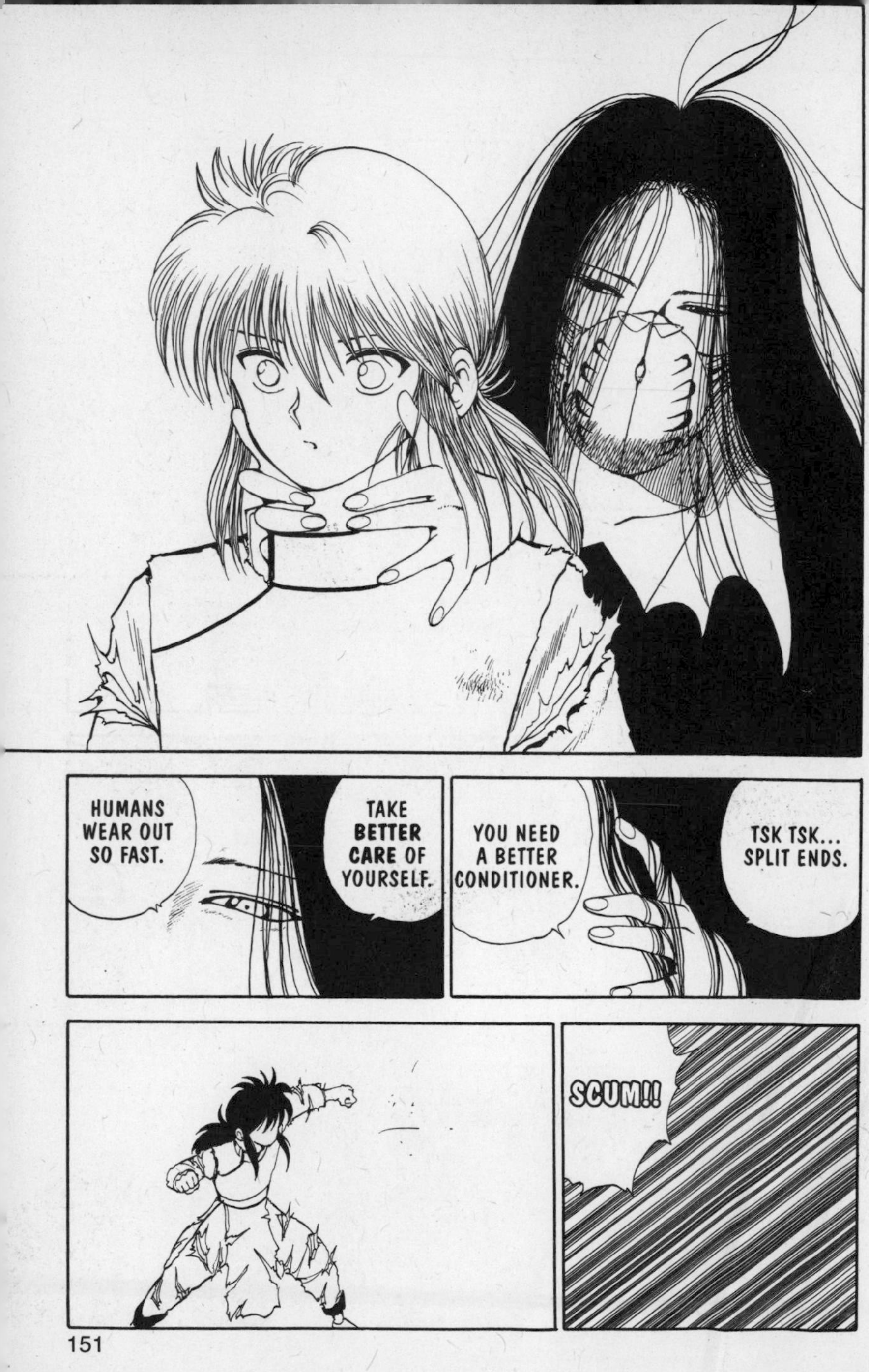
TSK TSK... SPLIT ENDS.
YOU NEED A BETTER CONDITIONER.
TAKE BETTER CARE OF YOURSELF.
HUMANS WEAR OUT SO FAST.
SCUM!!

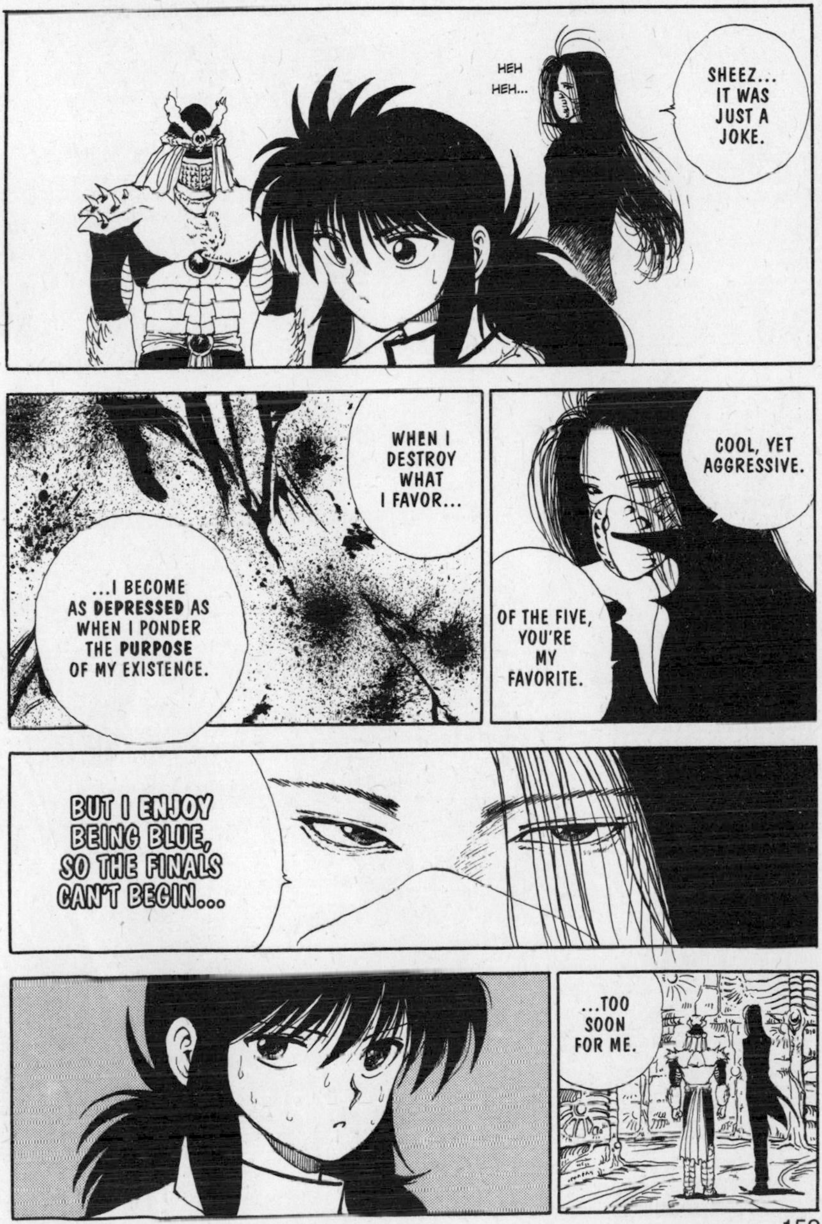
SHEEZ... IT WAS JUST A JOKE.
HEH HEH...
COOL, YET AGGRESSIVE.
OF THE FIVE, YOU'RE MY FAVORITE.
WHEN I DESTROY WHAT I FAVOR...
...I BECOME AS DEPRESSED AS WHEN I PONDER THE PURPOSE OF MY EXISTENCE.
BUT I ENJOY BEING BLUE, SO THE FINALS CAN'T BEGIN...
...TOO SOON FOR ME.

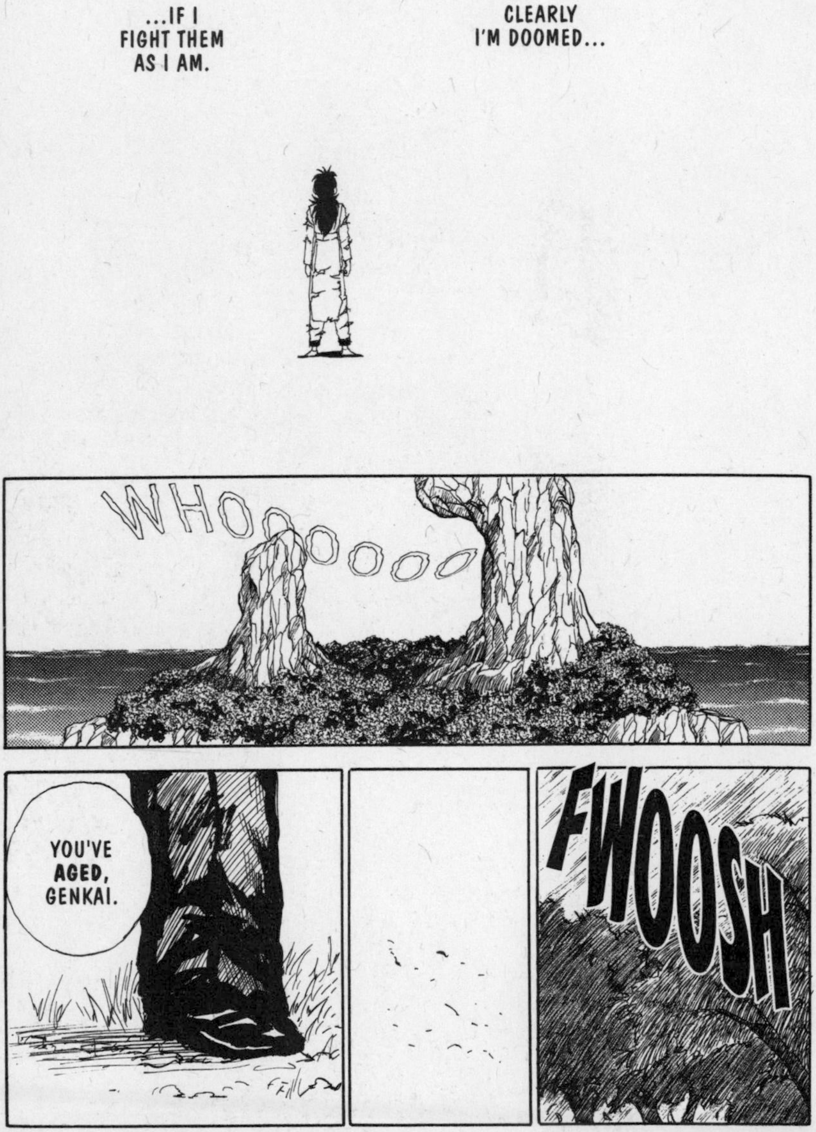
CLEARLY I'M DOOMED...
...IF I FIGHT THEM AS I AM.
WHOOOOOOO
FWOOSH
YOU'VE AGED, GENKAI.

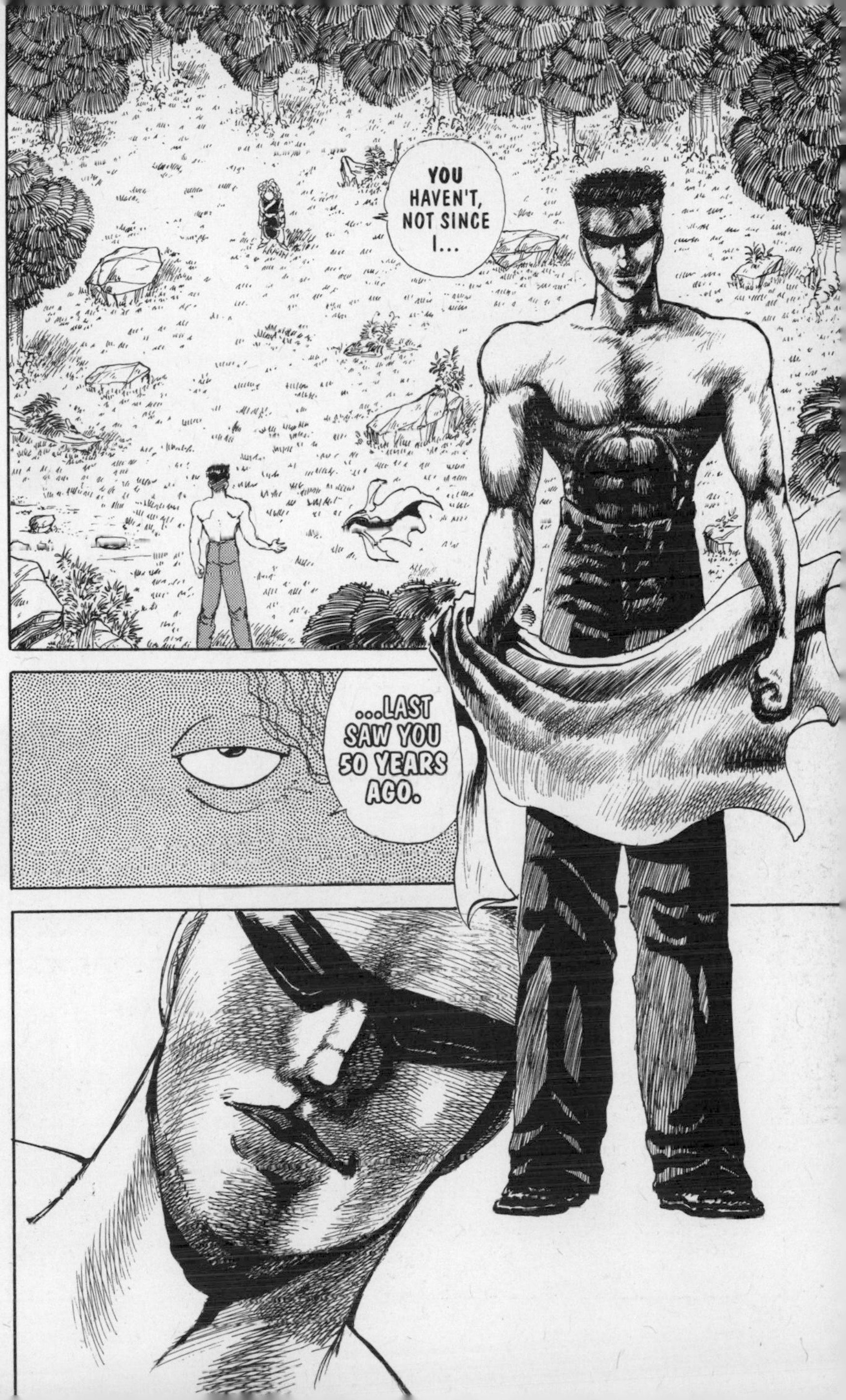
YOU HAVEN'T, NOT SINCE I...
...LAST SAW YOU 50 YEARS AGO.

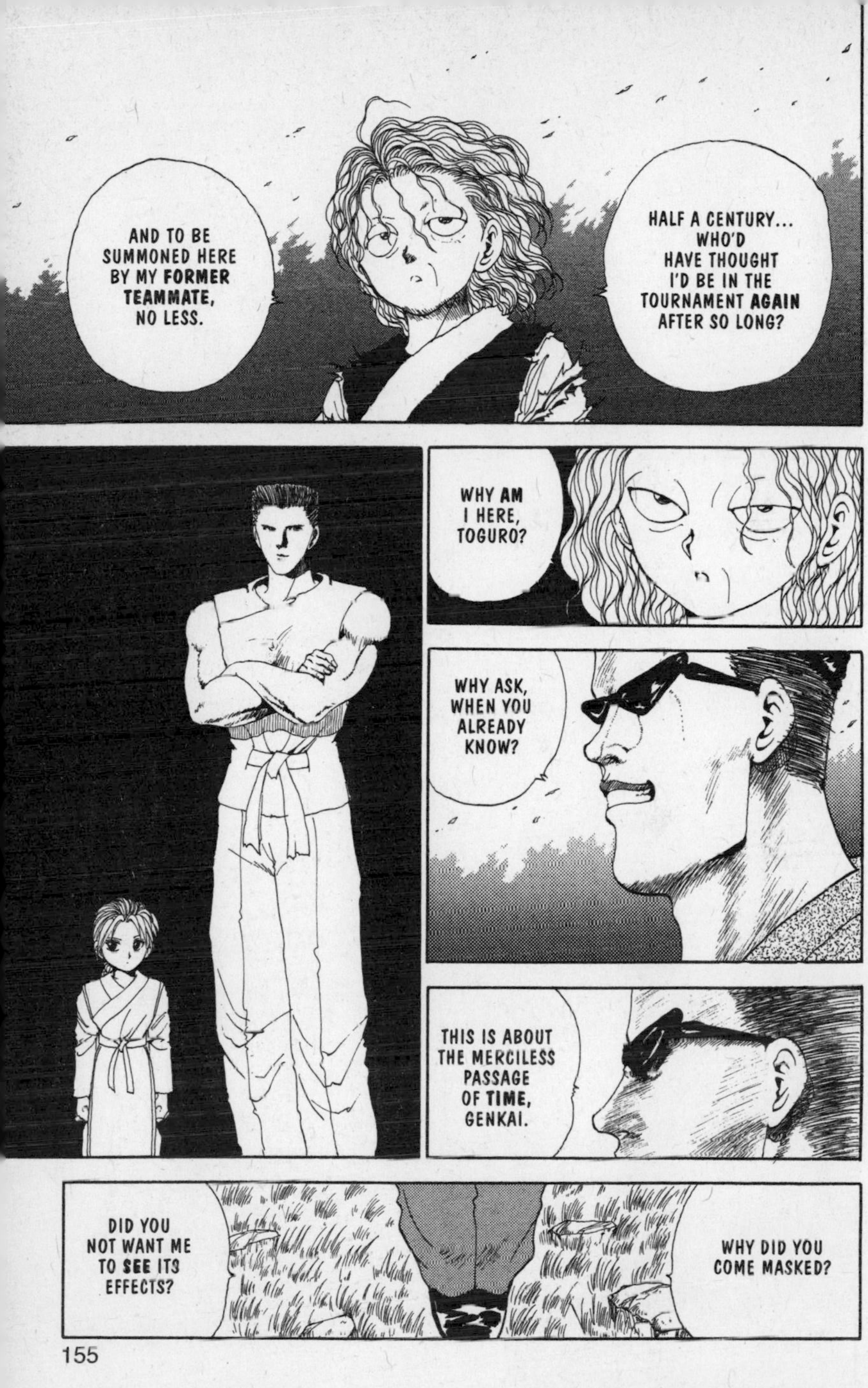
HALF A CENTURY... WHO'D HAVE THOUGHT I'D BE IN THE TOURNAMENT AGAIN AFTER SO LONG?
AND TO BE SUMMONED HERE BY MY FORMER TEAMMATE, NO LESS.
WHY AM I HERE, TOGURO?
WHY ASK, WHEN YOU ALREADY KNOW?
THIS IS ABOUT THE MERCILESS PASSAGE OF TIME, GENKAI.
WHY DID YOU COME MASKED?
DID YOU NOT WANT ME TO SEE ITS EFFECTS?

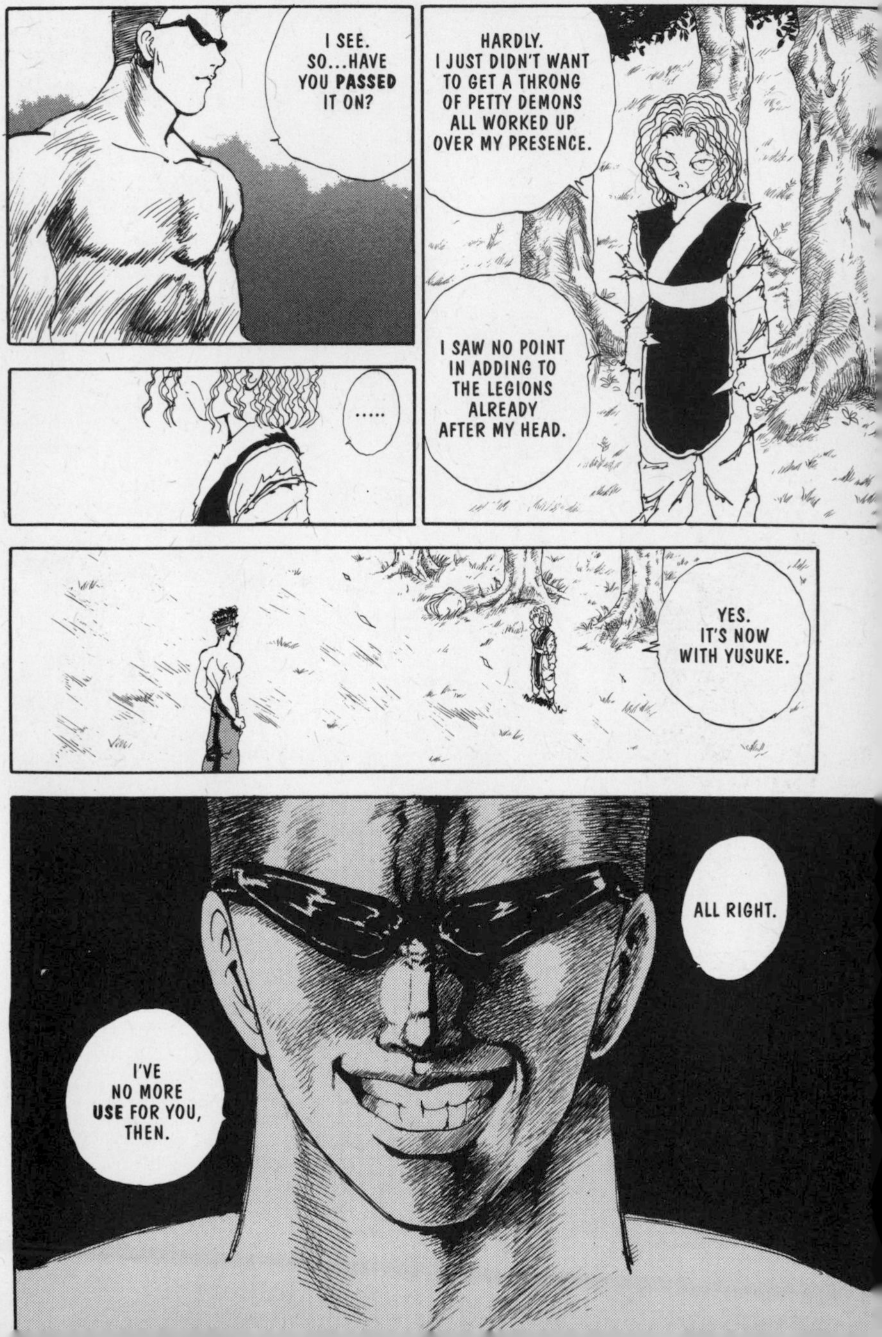
HARDLY. I JUST DIDN'T WANT TO GET A THRONG OF PETTY DEMONS ALL WORKED UP OVER MY PRESENCE.
I SAW NO POINT IN ADDING TO THE LEGIONS ALREADY AFTER MY HEAD.
I SEE. SO...HAVE YOU **PASSED** IT ON?
......
YES. IT'S NOW WITH YUSUKE.
ALL RIGHT.
I'VE NO MORE **USE** FOR YOU, THEN.

READ THIS WAY

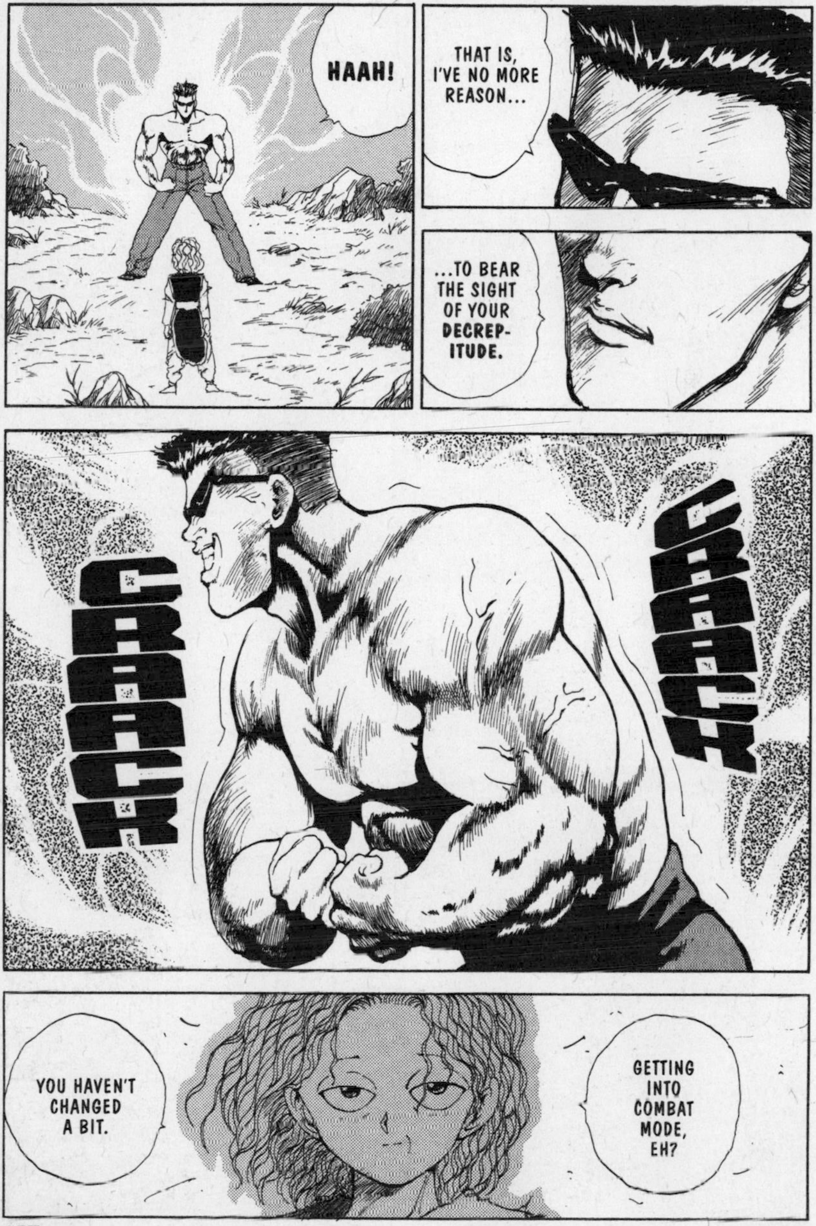
THAT IS, I'VE NO MORE REASON...
...TO BEAR THE SIGHT OF YOUR DECREP-ITUDE.
HAAH!
CRAAACK
CRAAACK
GETTING INTO COMBAT MODE, EH?
YOU HAVEN'T CHANGED A BIT.

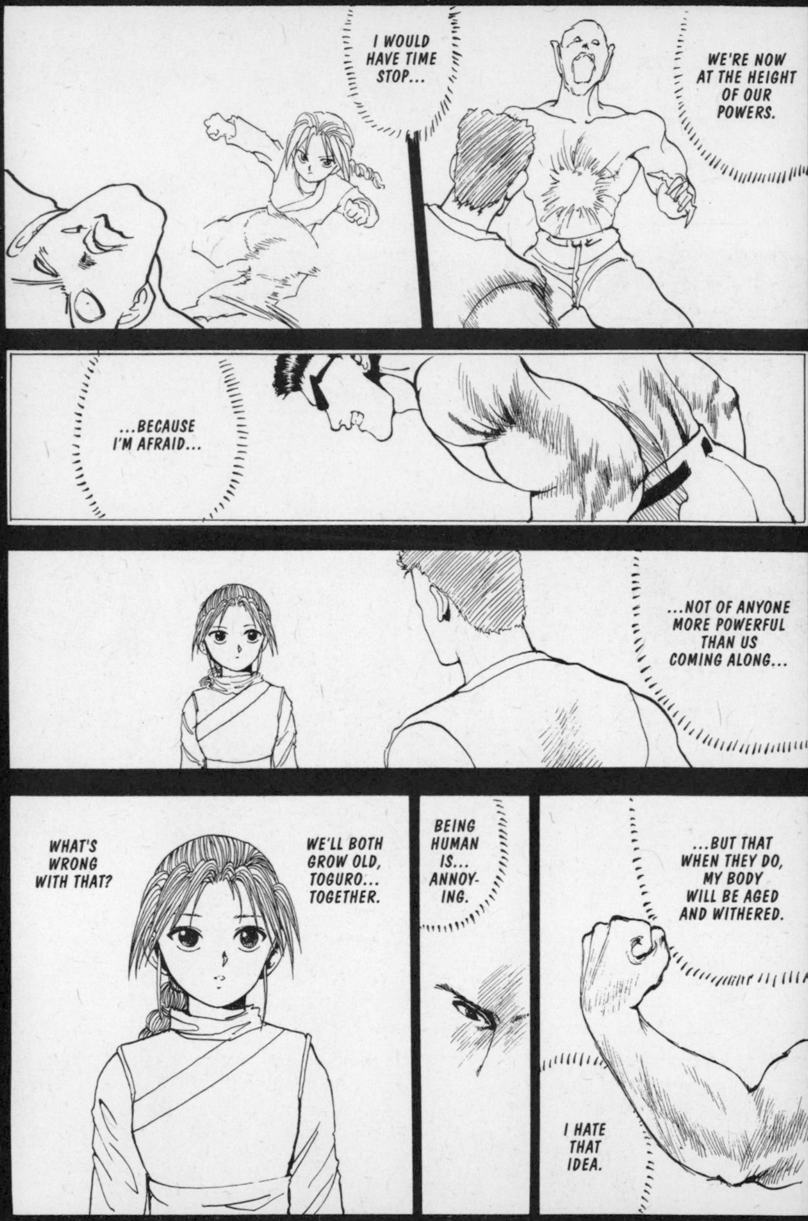
WE'RE NOW AT THE HEIGHT OF OUR POWERS.
I WOULD HAVE TIME STOP...
...BECAUSE I'M AFRAID...
...NOT OF ANYONE MORE POWERFUL THAN US COMING ALONG...
...BUT THAT WHEN THEY DO, MY BODY WILL BE AGED AND WITHERED.
I HATE THAT IDEA.
BEING HUMAN IS... ANNOY-ING.
WE'LL BOTH GROW OLD, TOGURO... TOGETHER.
WHAT'S WRONG WITH THAT?

READ THIS WAY

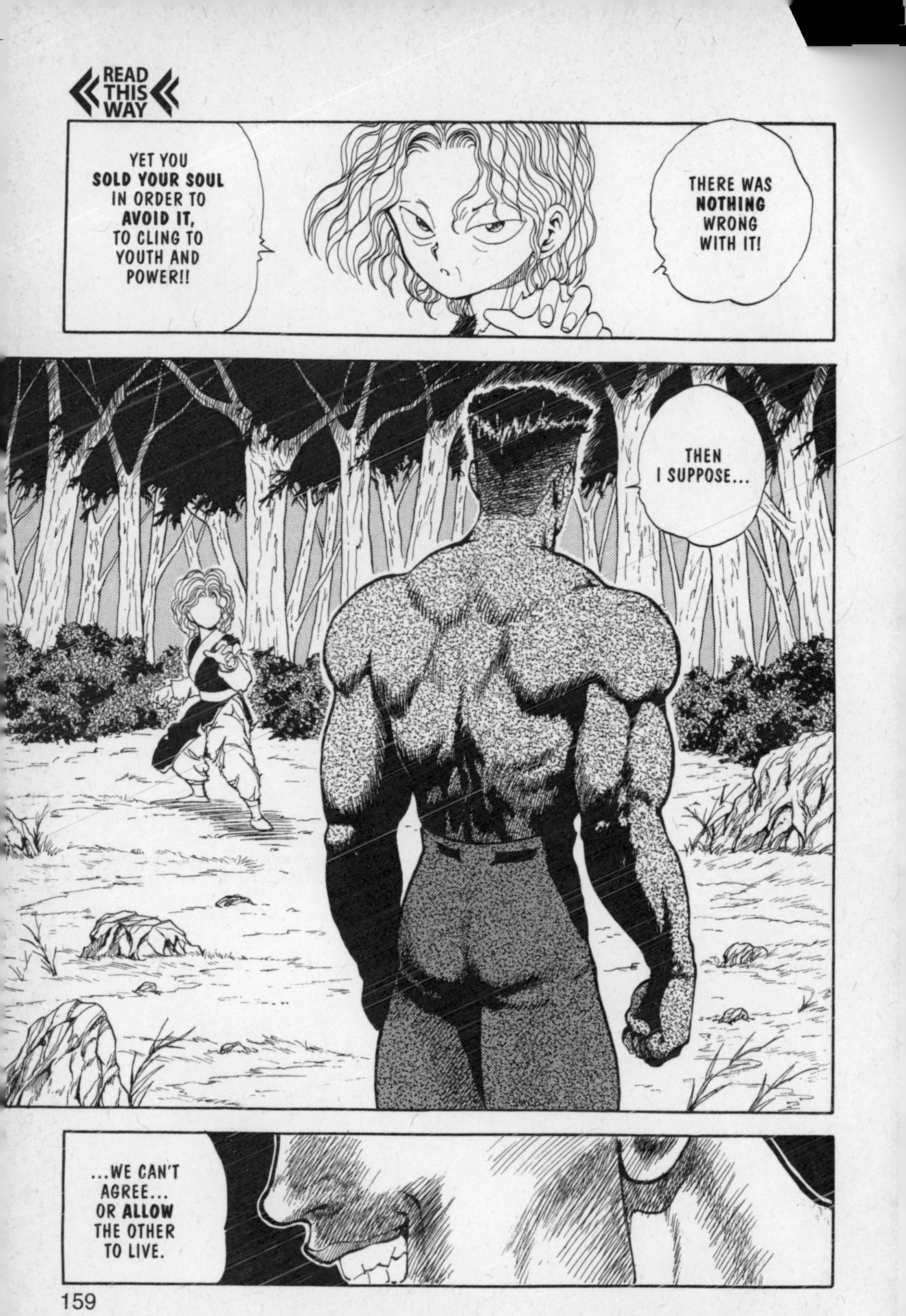

THERE WAS NOTHING WRONG WITH IT!
YET YOU SOLD YOUR SOUL IN ORDER TO AVOID IT, TO CLING TO YOUTH AND POWER!!
THEN I SUPPOSE...
...WE CAN'T AGREE... OR ALLOW THE OTHER TO LIVE.

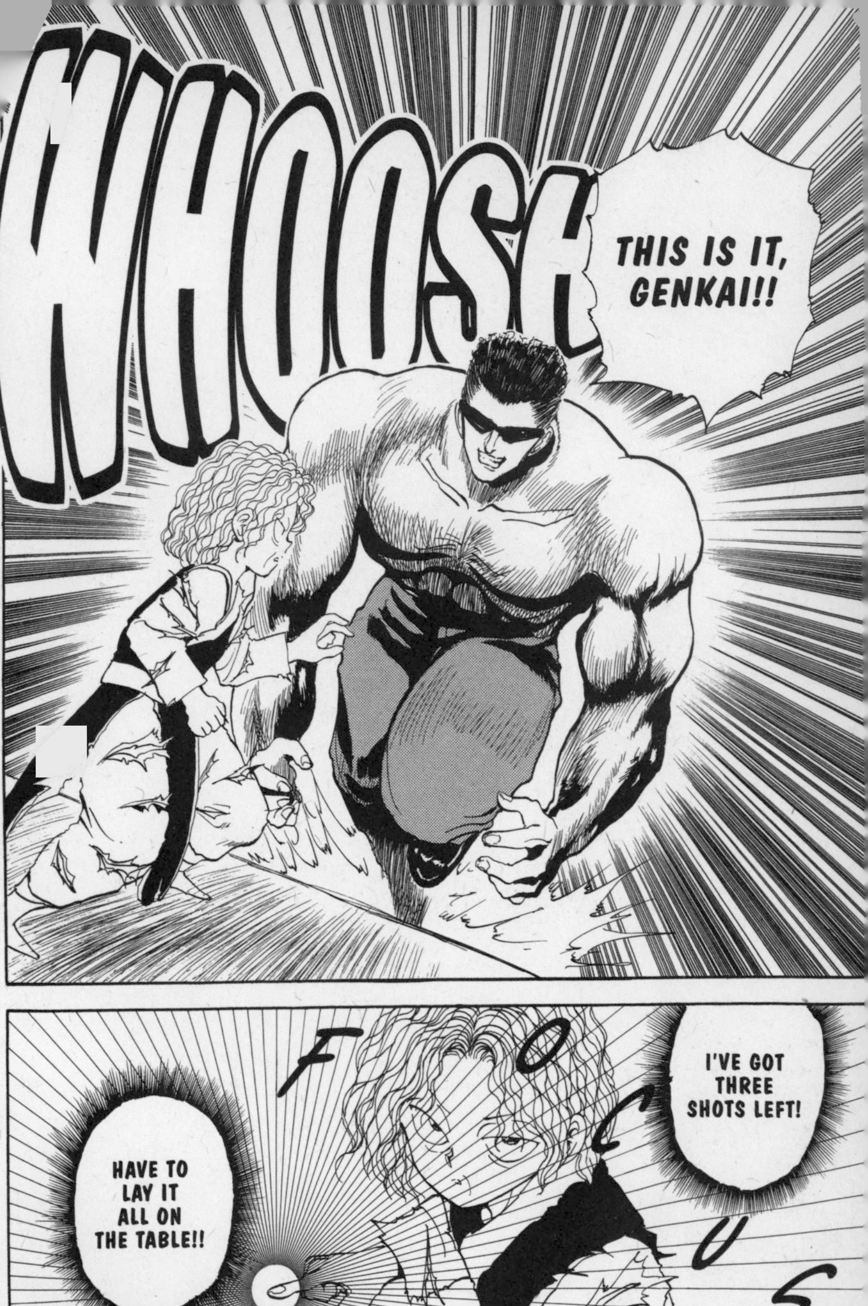
THIS IS IT, GENKAI!!
WHOOSH
I'VE GOT THREE SHOTS LEFT!
FOCUS
HAVE TO LAY IT ALL ON THE TABLE!!

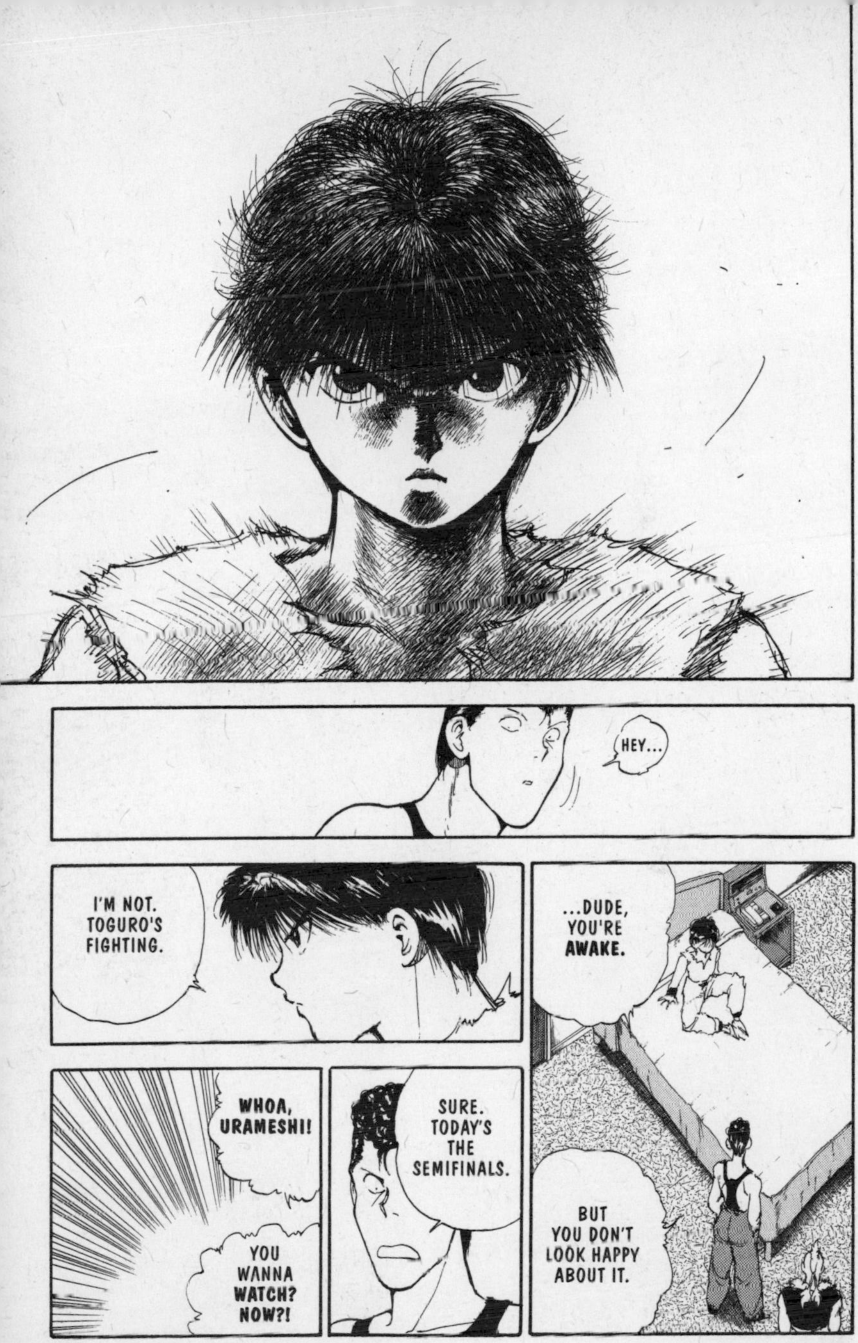
HEY...
...DUDE, YOU'RE AWAKE.
BUT YOU DON'T LOOK HAPPY ABOUT IT.
I'M NOT. TOGURO'S FIGHTING.
SURE. TODAY'S THE SEMIFINALS.
WHOA, URAMESHI!
YOU WANNA WATCH? NOW?!

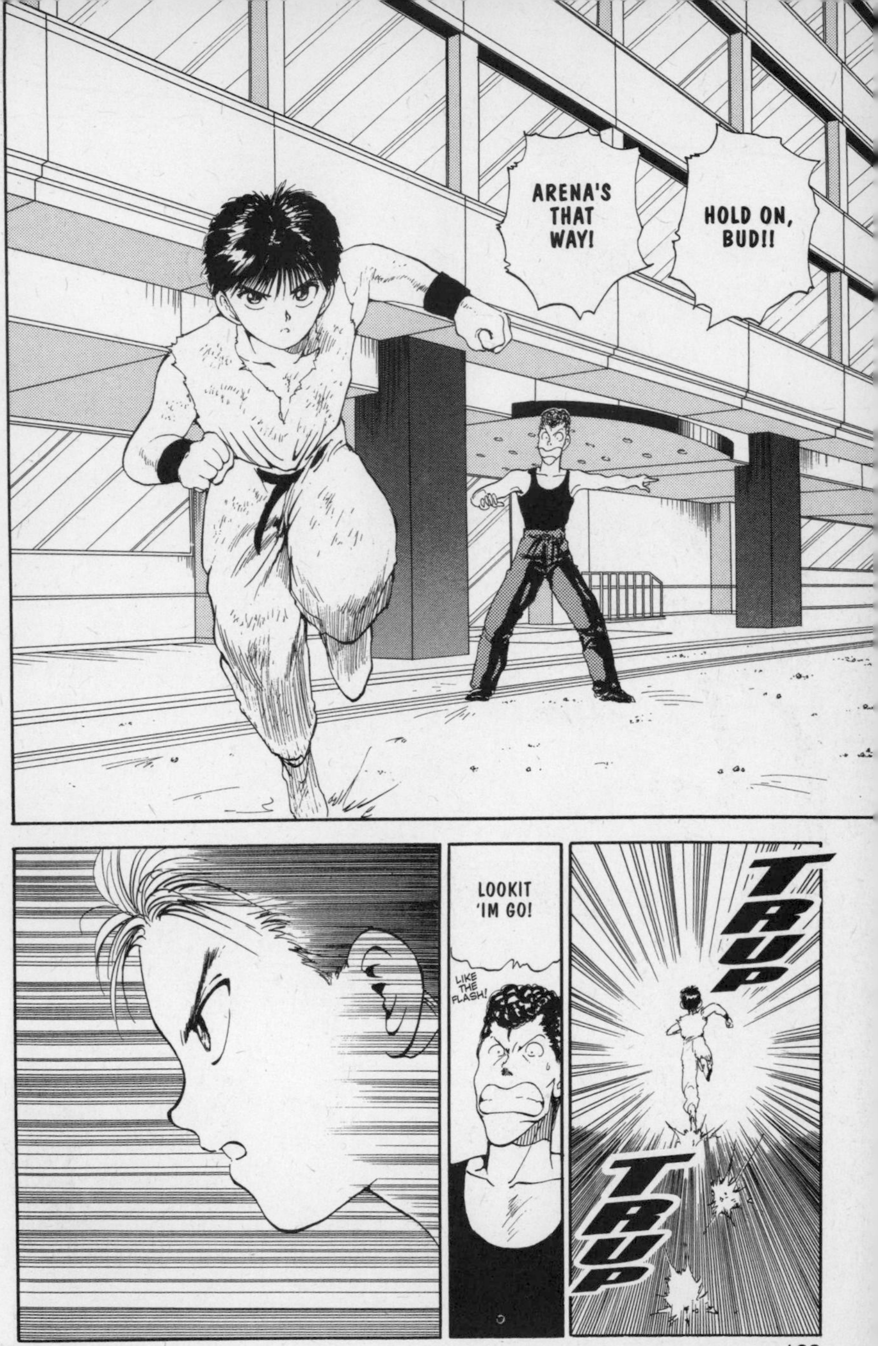
HOLD ON, BUD!!
ARENA'S THAT WAY!
TRUP
TRUP
LOOKIT 'IM GO!
LIKE THE FLASH!

READ THIS WAY

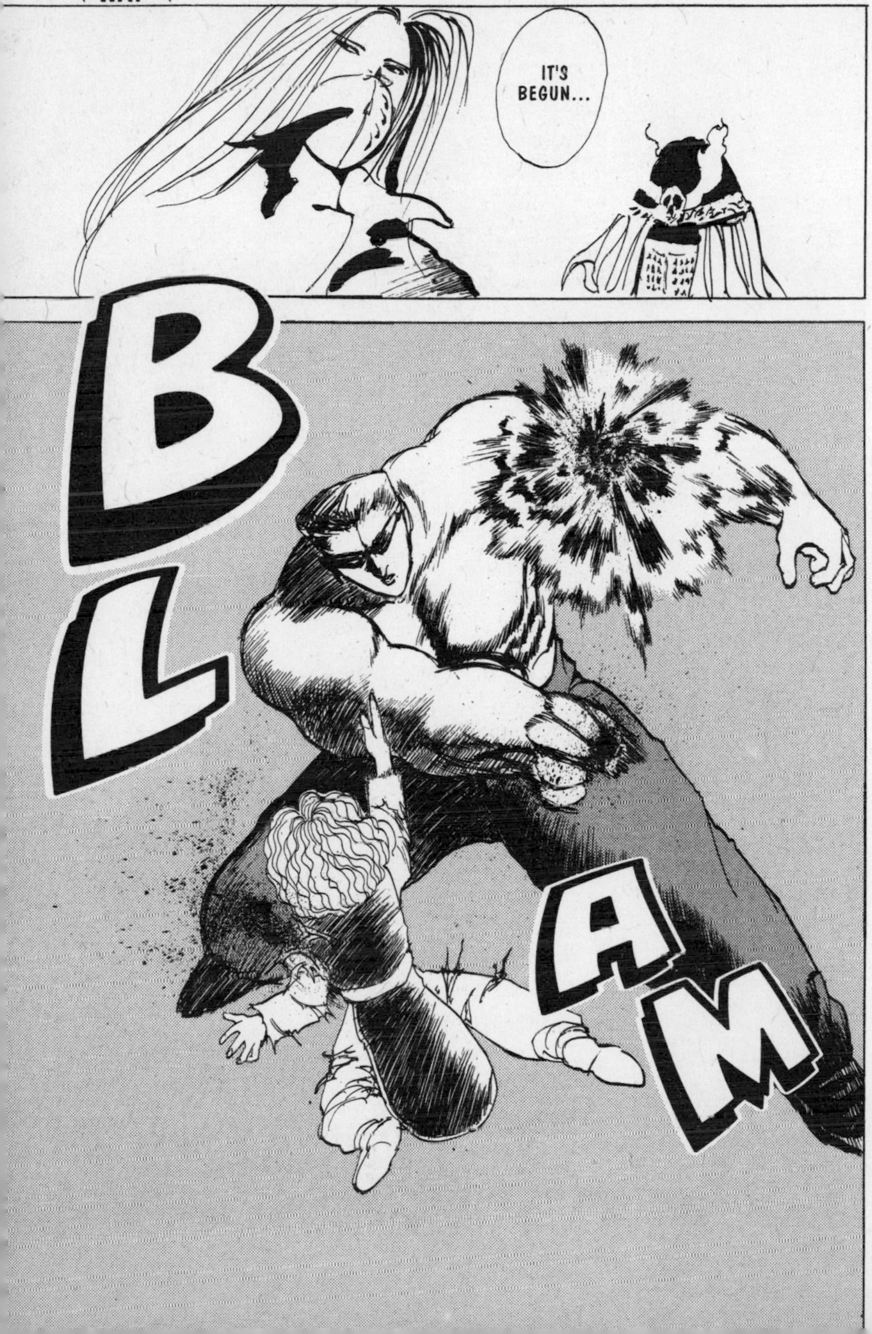
IT'S BEGUN...
BLAM

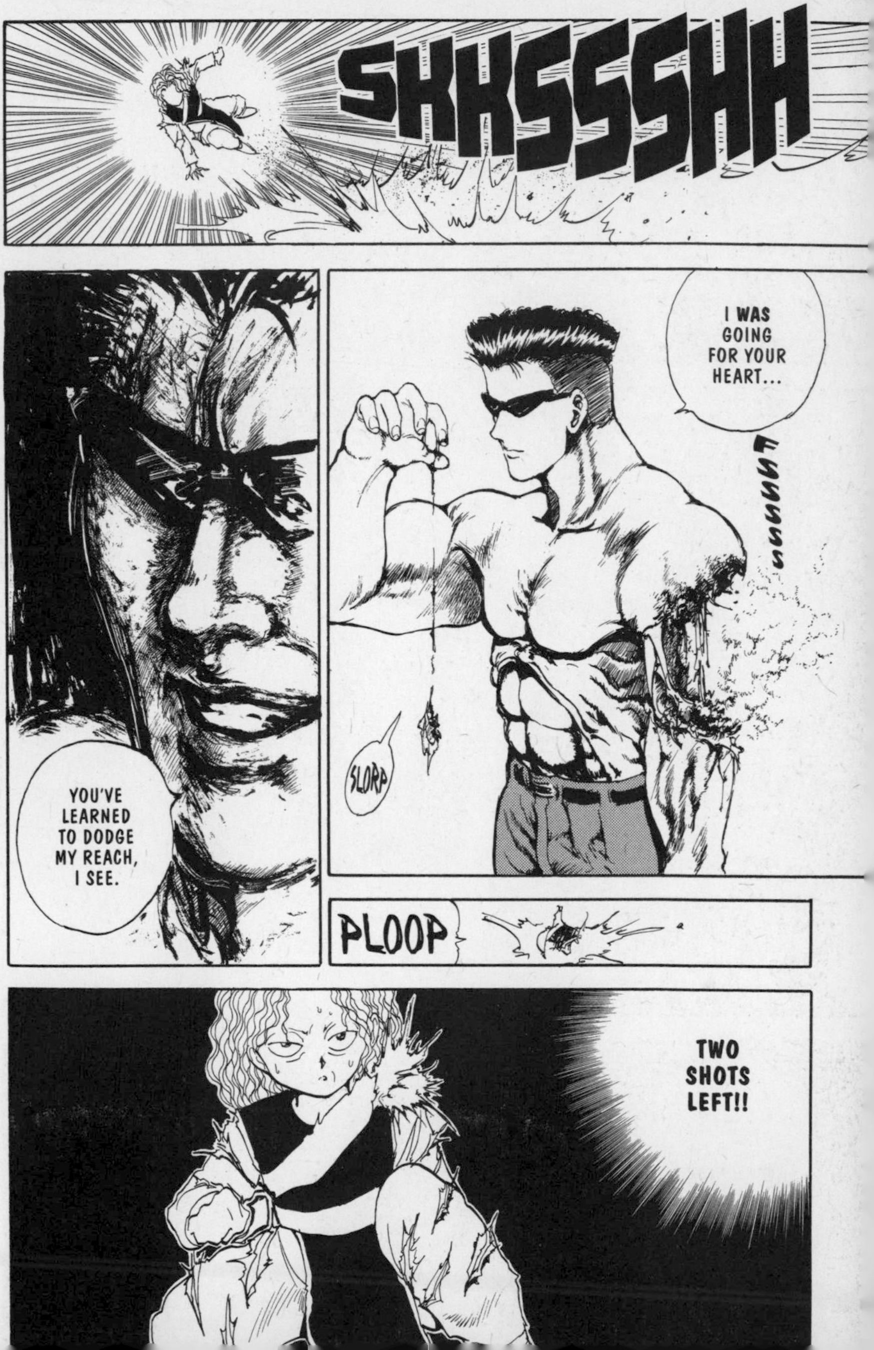
SKSSSSHH
I WAS GOING FOR YOUR HEART...
FSSSSSS
SLORP
PLOOP
YOU'VE LEARNED TO DODGE MY REACH, I SEE.
TWO SHOTS LEFT!!

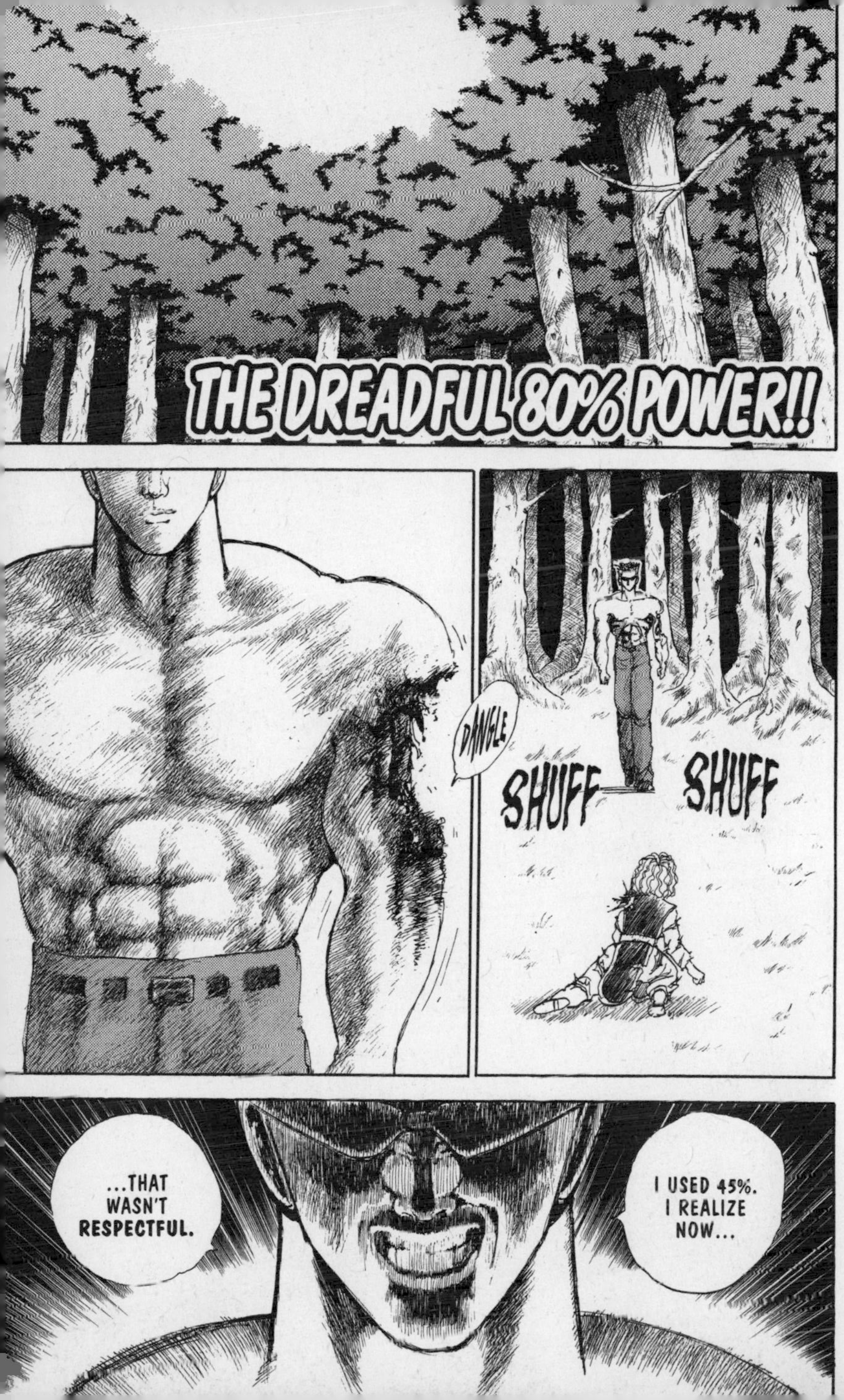
THE DREADFUL 80% POWER!!
SHUFF
SHUFF
DANGLE
I USED 45%. I REALIZE NOW...
...THAT WASN'T RESPECTFUL.

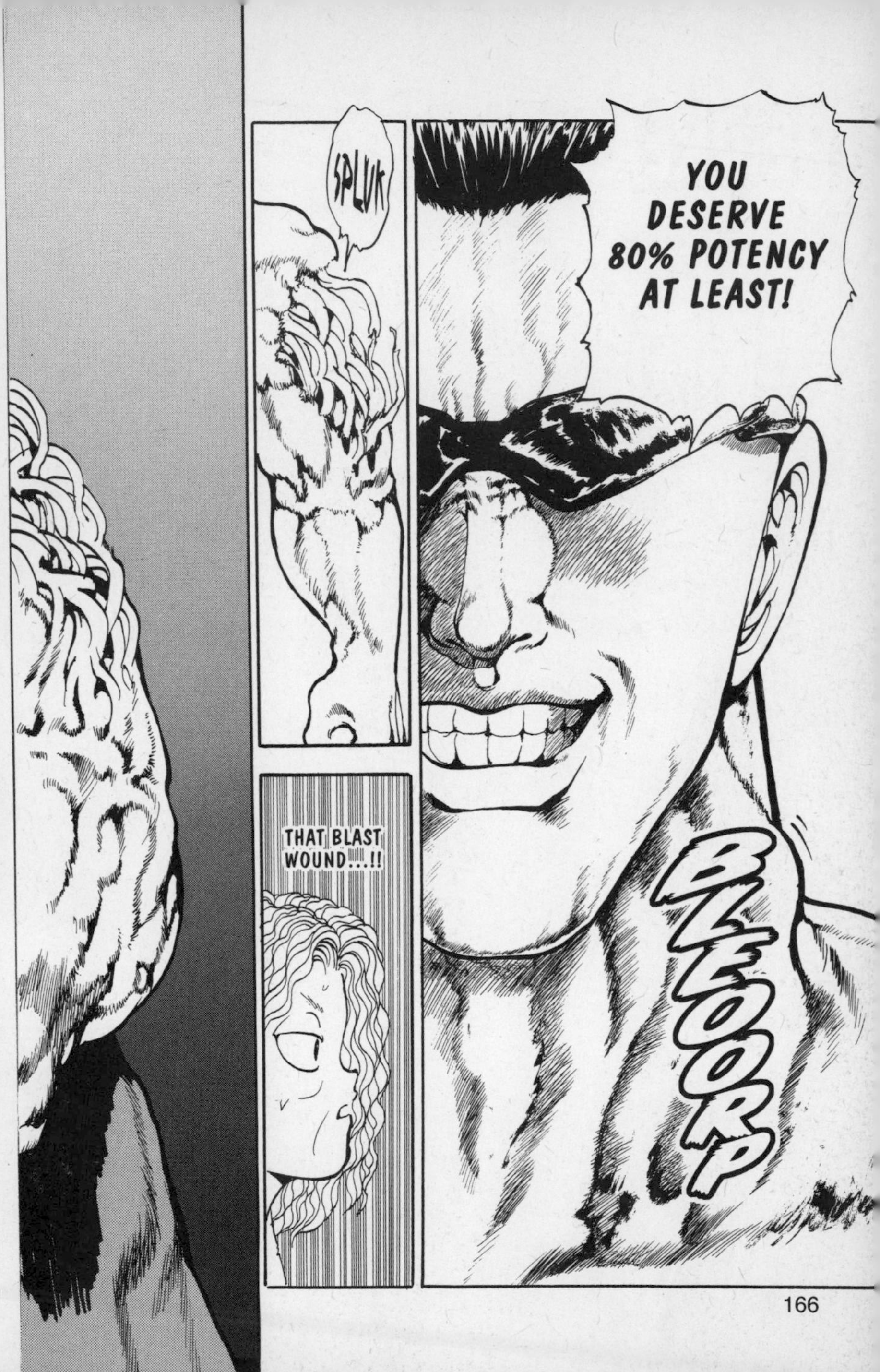
YOU DESERVE 80% POTENCY AT LEAST!
BLOOORP
SPLUK
THAT BLAST WOUND...!!

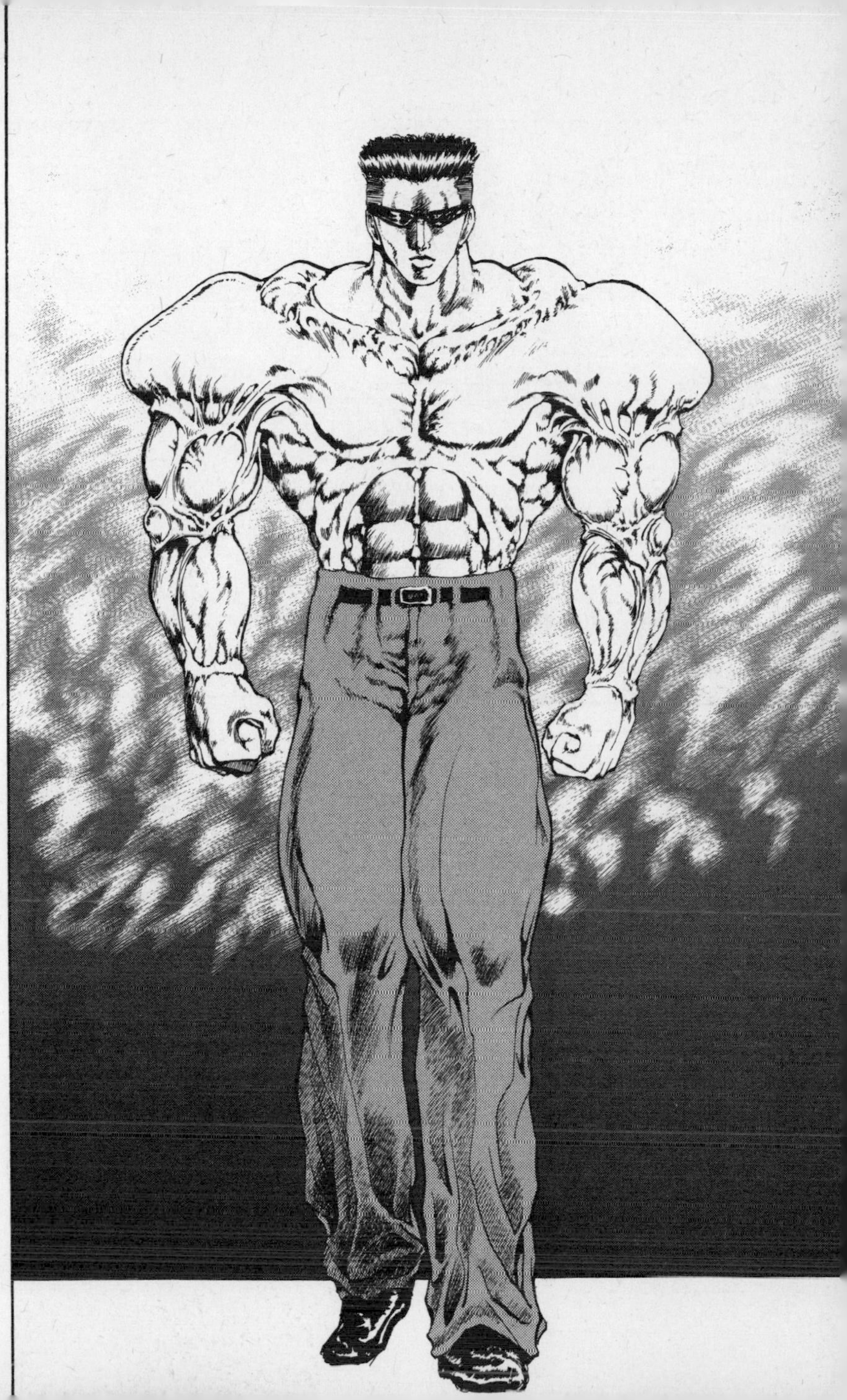

READ THIS WAY

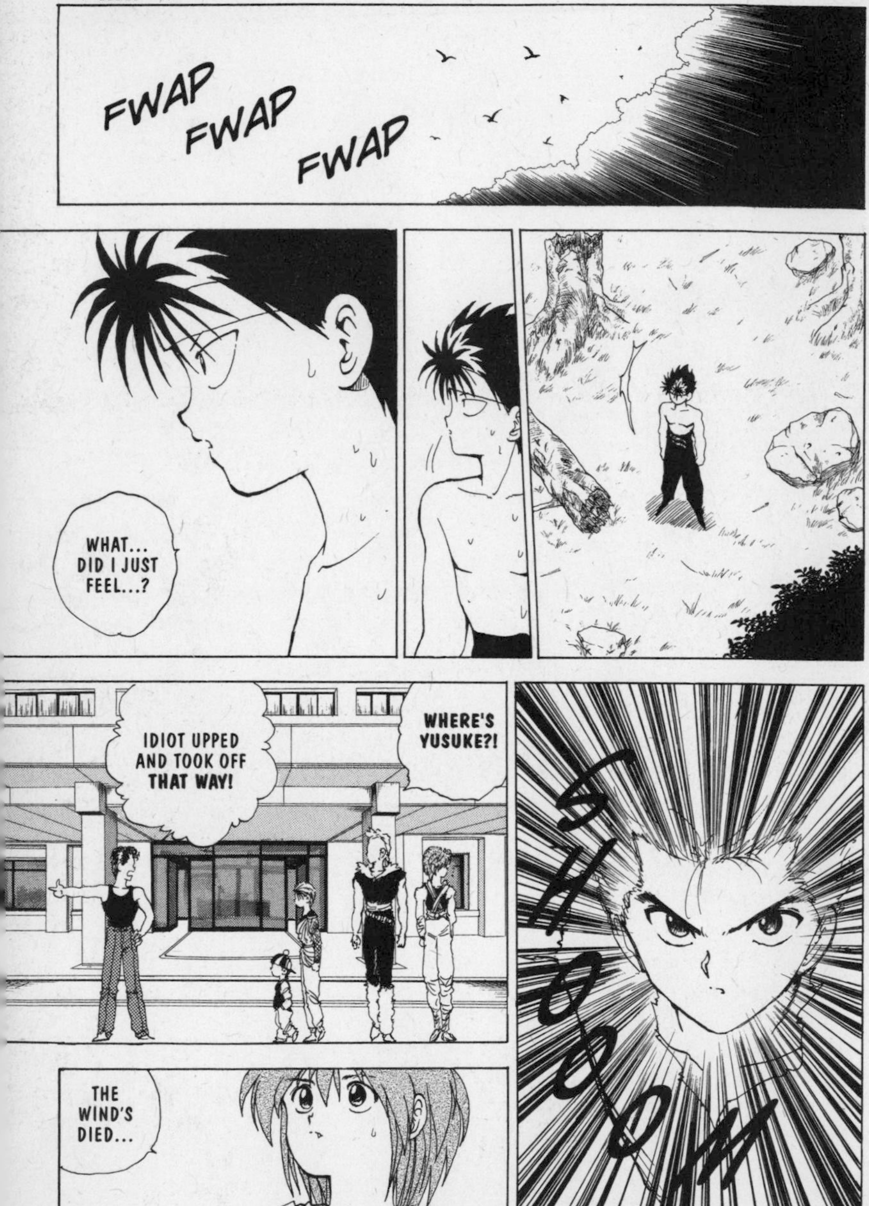
FWAP FWAP FWAP
WHAT... DID I JUST FEEL...?
SHOOOM
WHERE'S YUSUKE?!
IDIOT UPPED AND TOOK OFF THAT WAY!
THE WIND'S DIED...

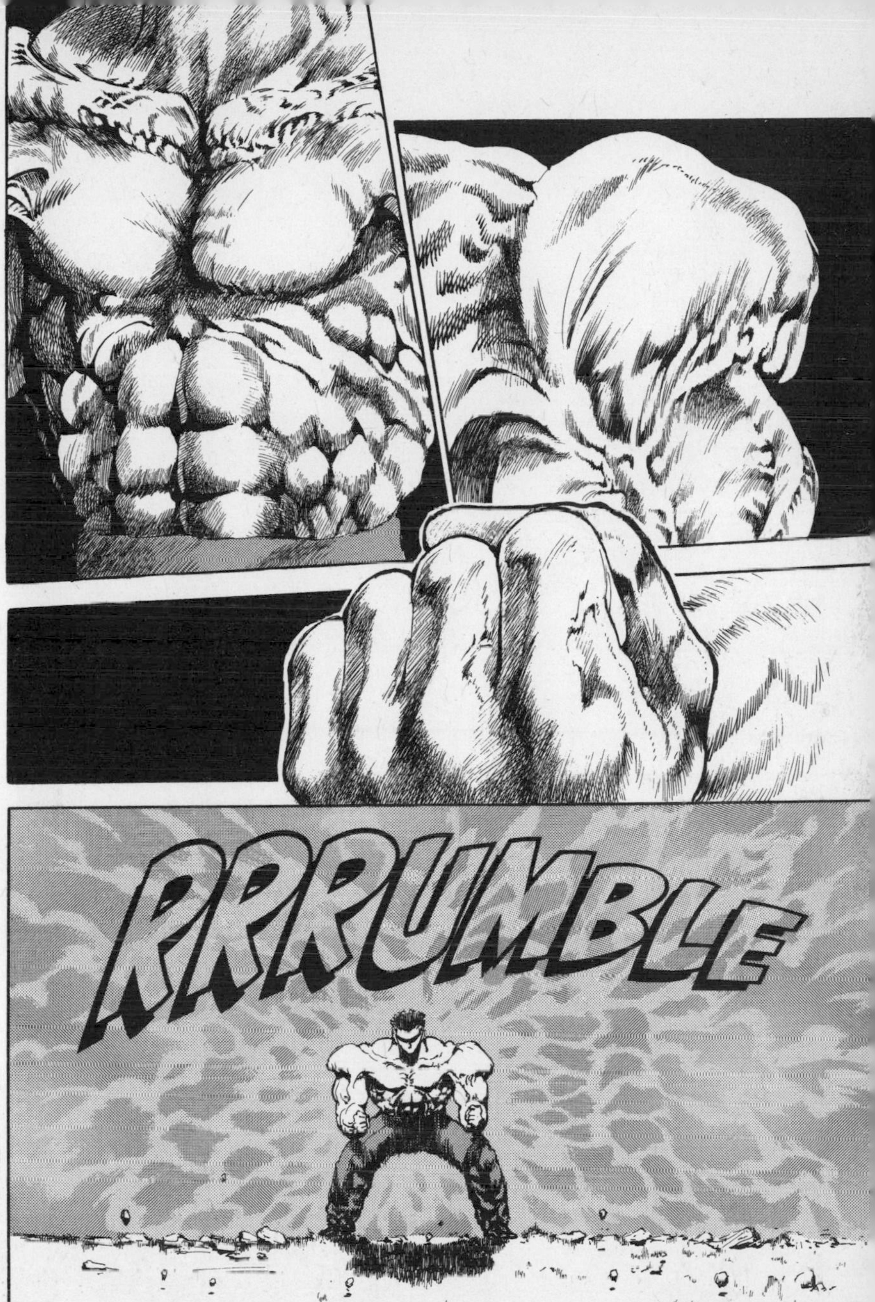
RRRUMBLE

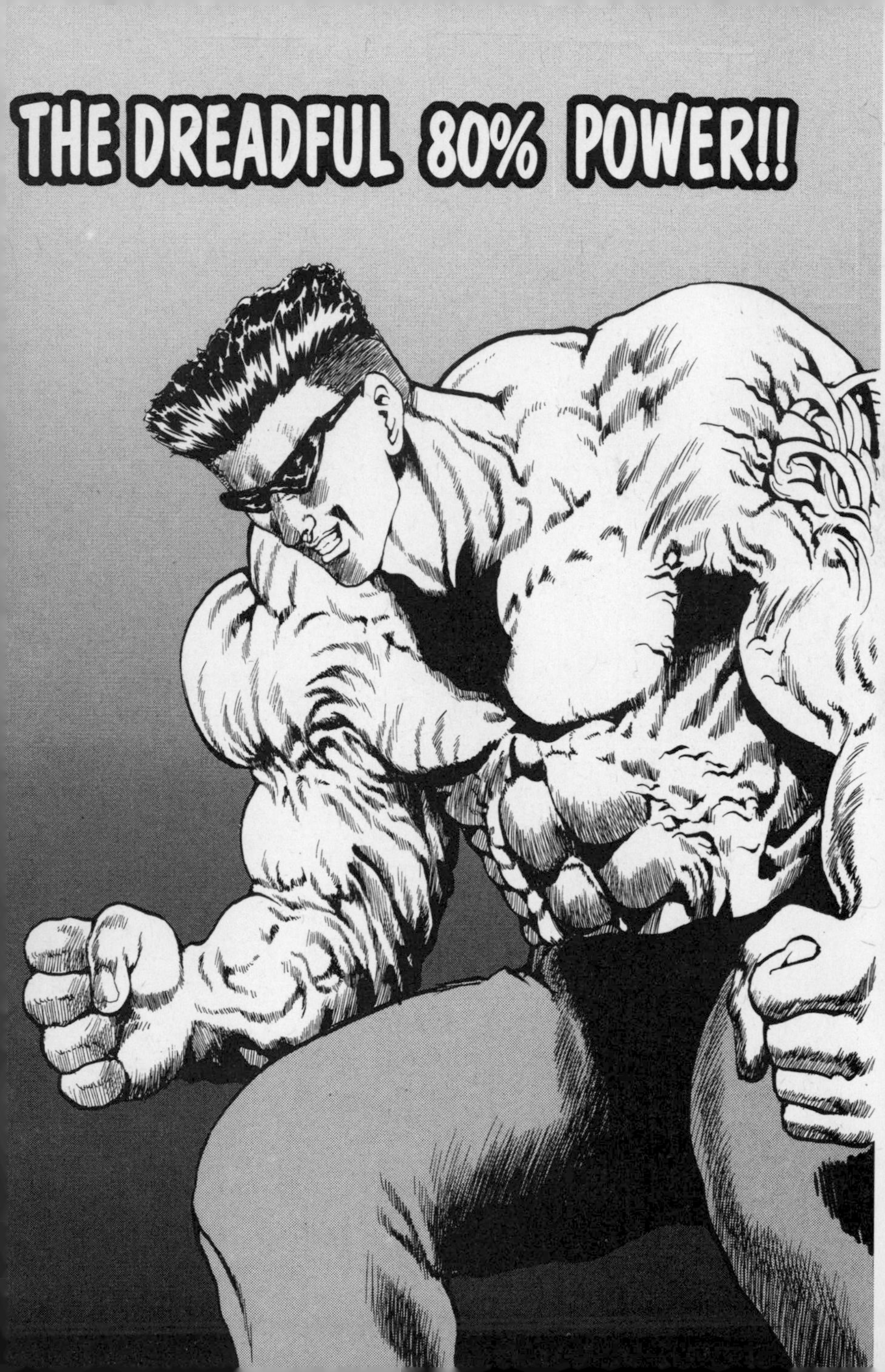
THE DREADFUL 80% POWER!!

READ THIS WAY

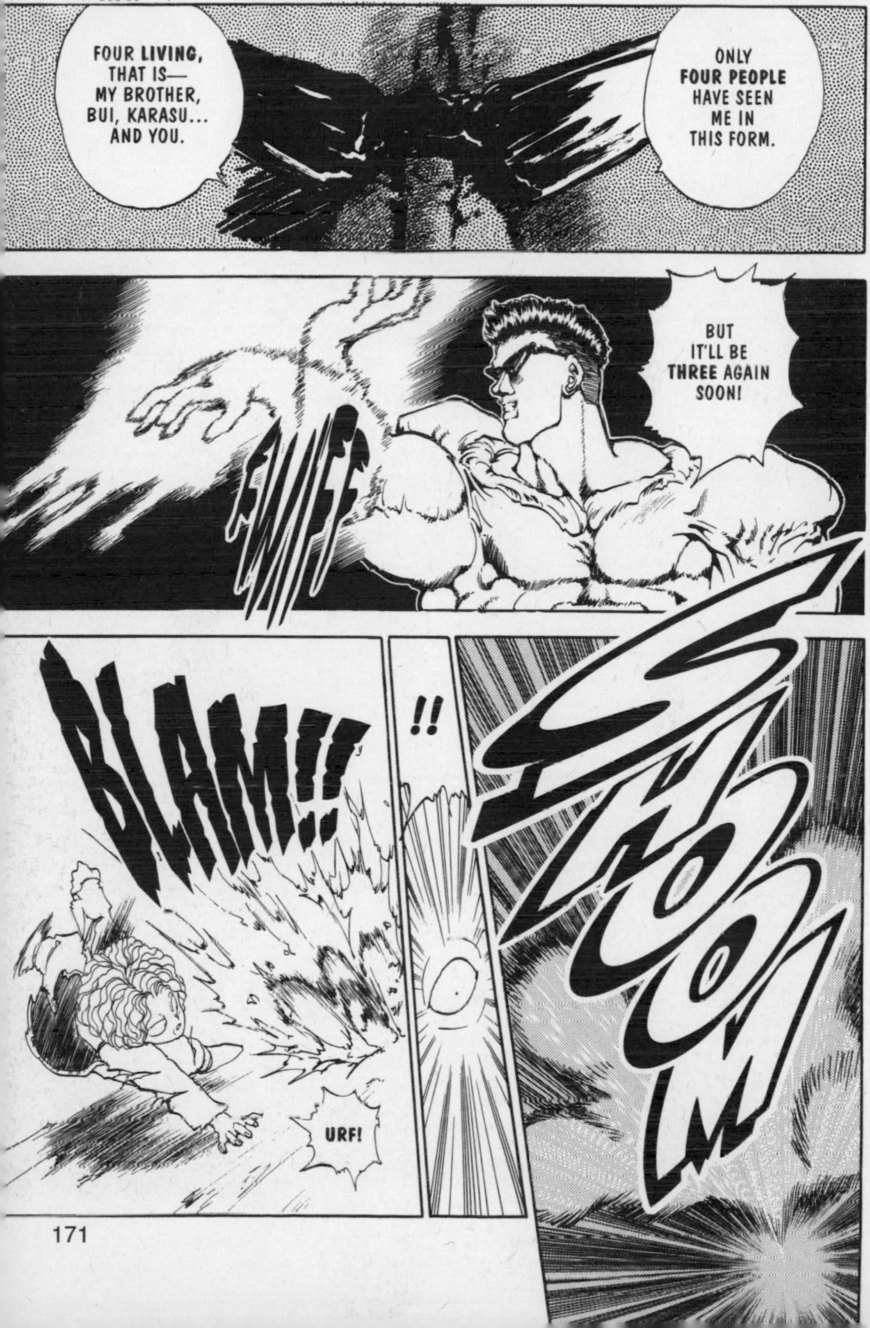
ONLY FOUR PEOPLE HAVE SEEN ME IN THIS FORM.
FOUR LIVING, THAT IS— MY BROTHER, BUI, KARASU... AND YOU.
BUT IT'LL BE THREE AGAIN SOON!
SWIFF
!!
BLAM!!
URF!

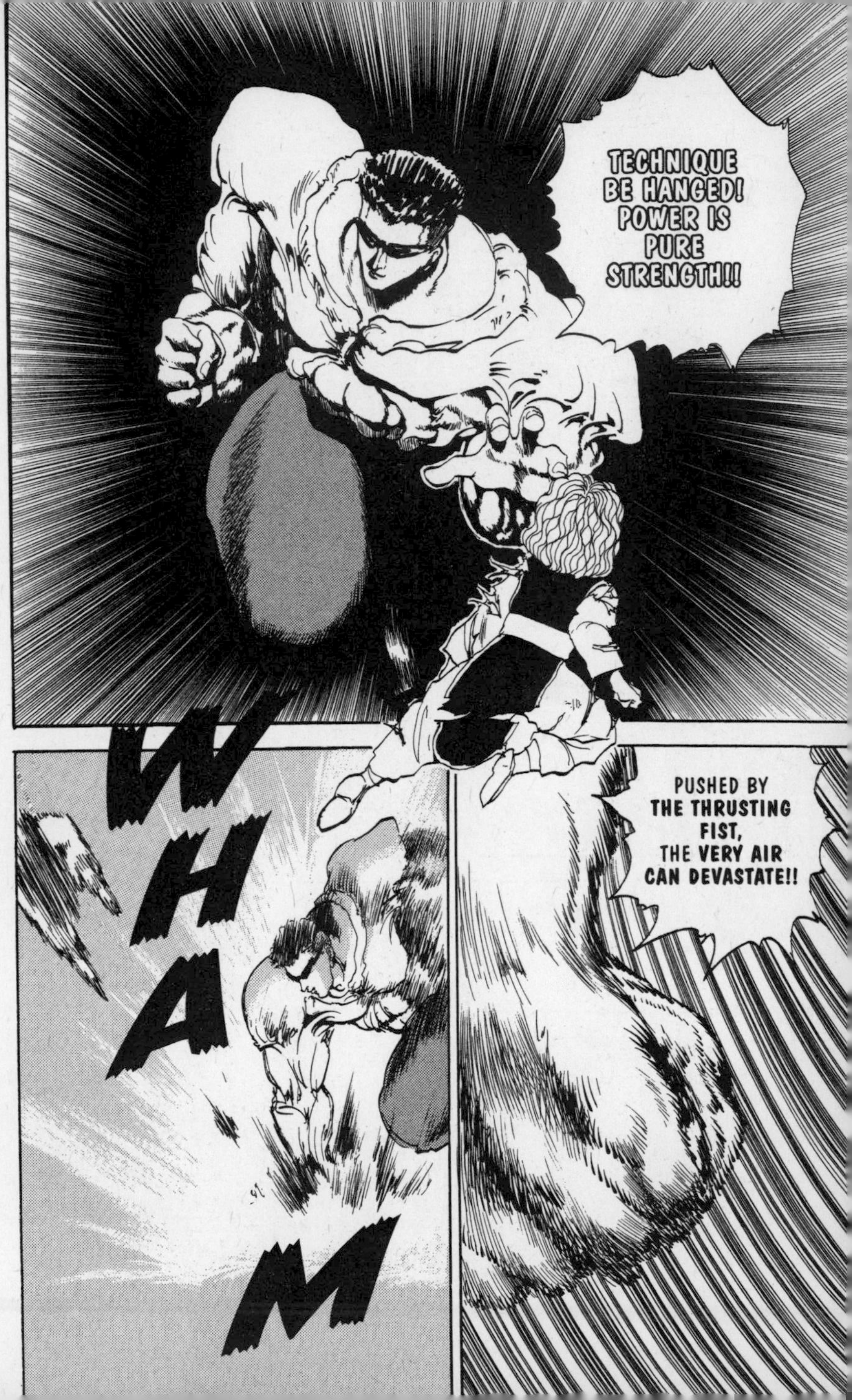
TECHNIQUE BE HANGED! POWER IS PURE STRENGTH!!
PUSHED BY THE THRUSTING FIST, THE VERY AIR CAN DEVASTATE!!
WHAM

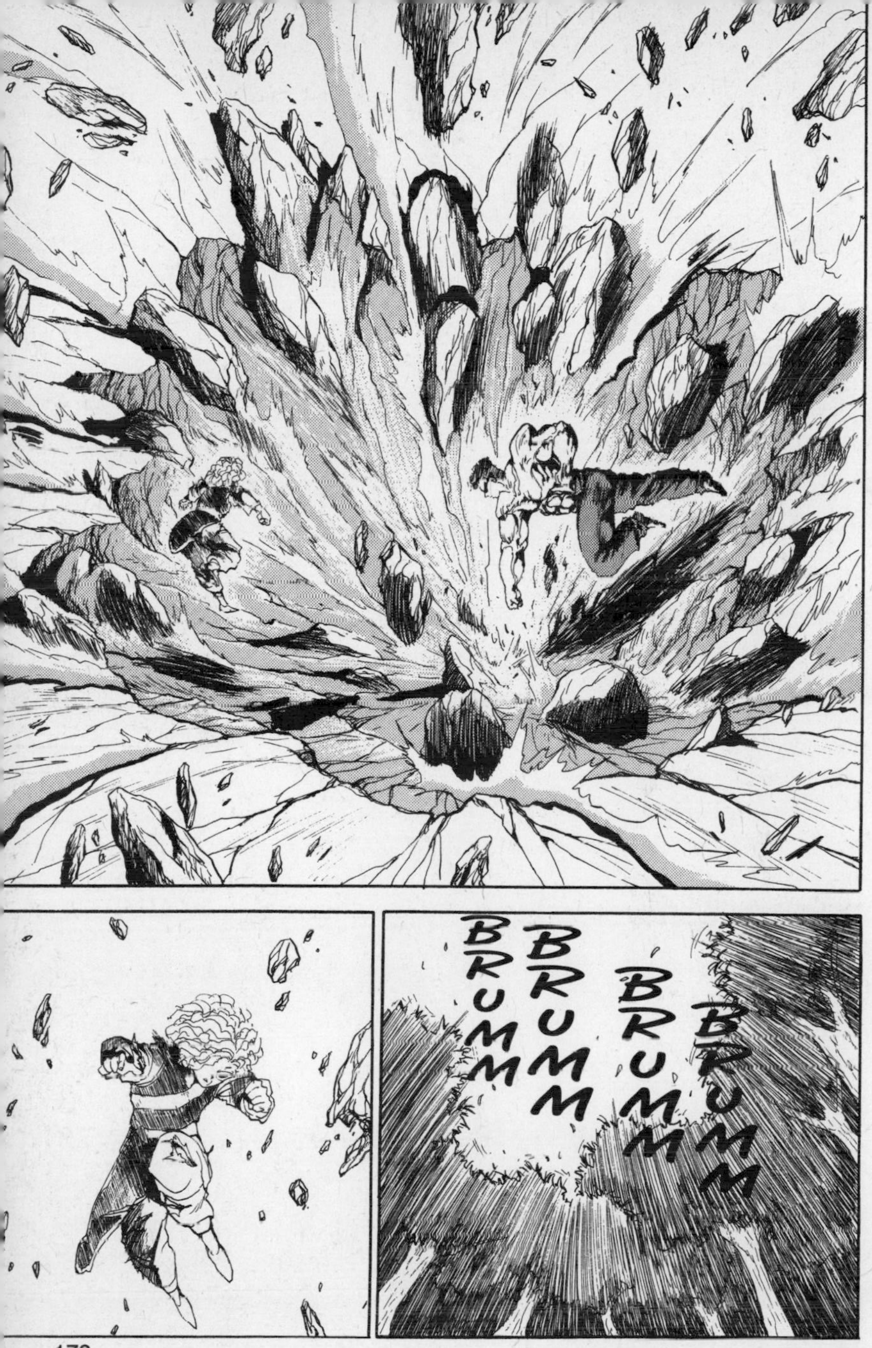
BRUMM
BRUMM
BRUMM
BRUMM

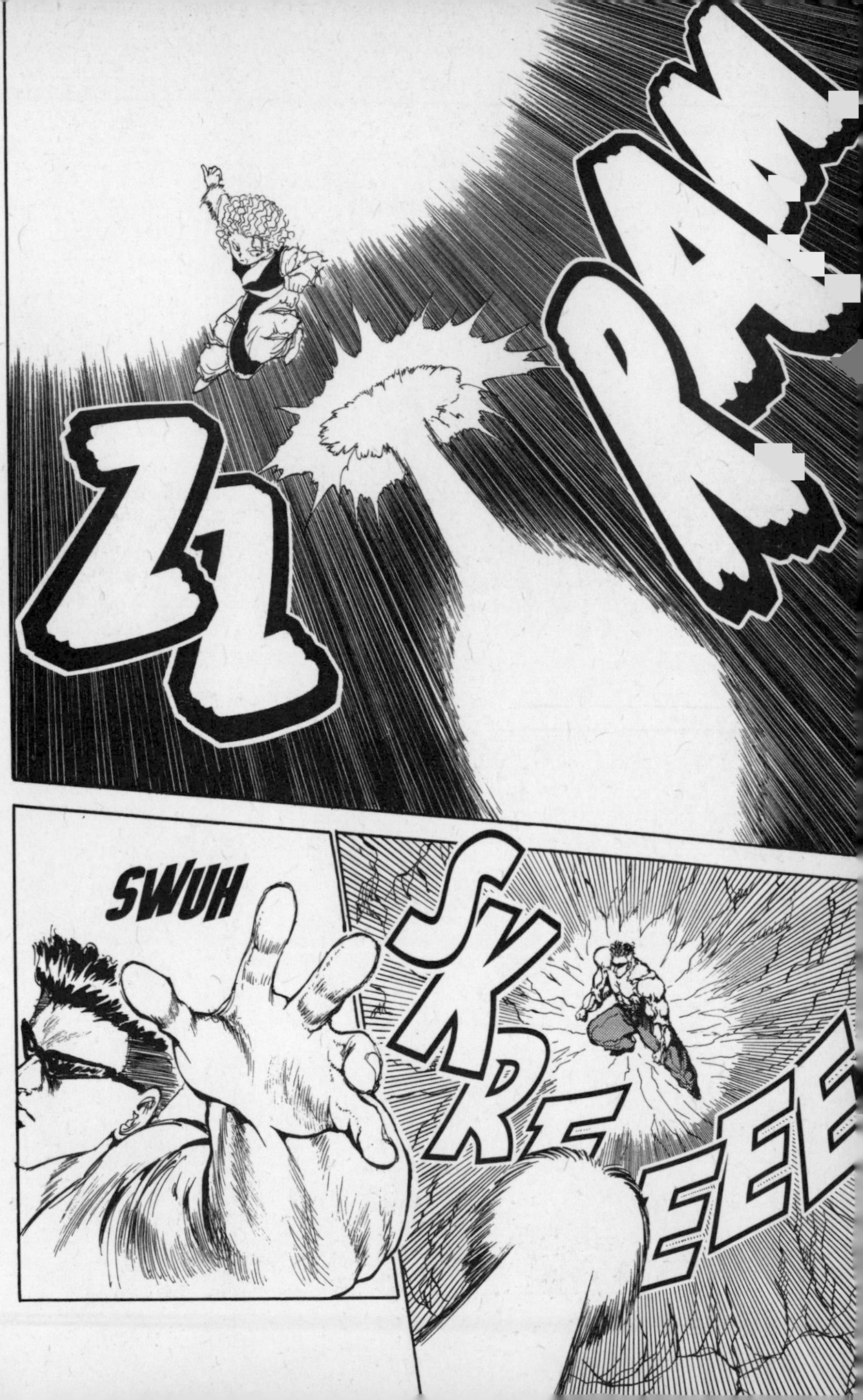
SKREEEE
SWUH

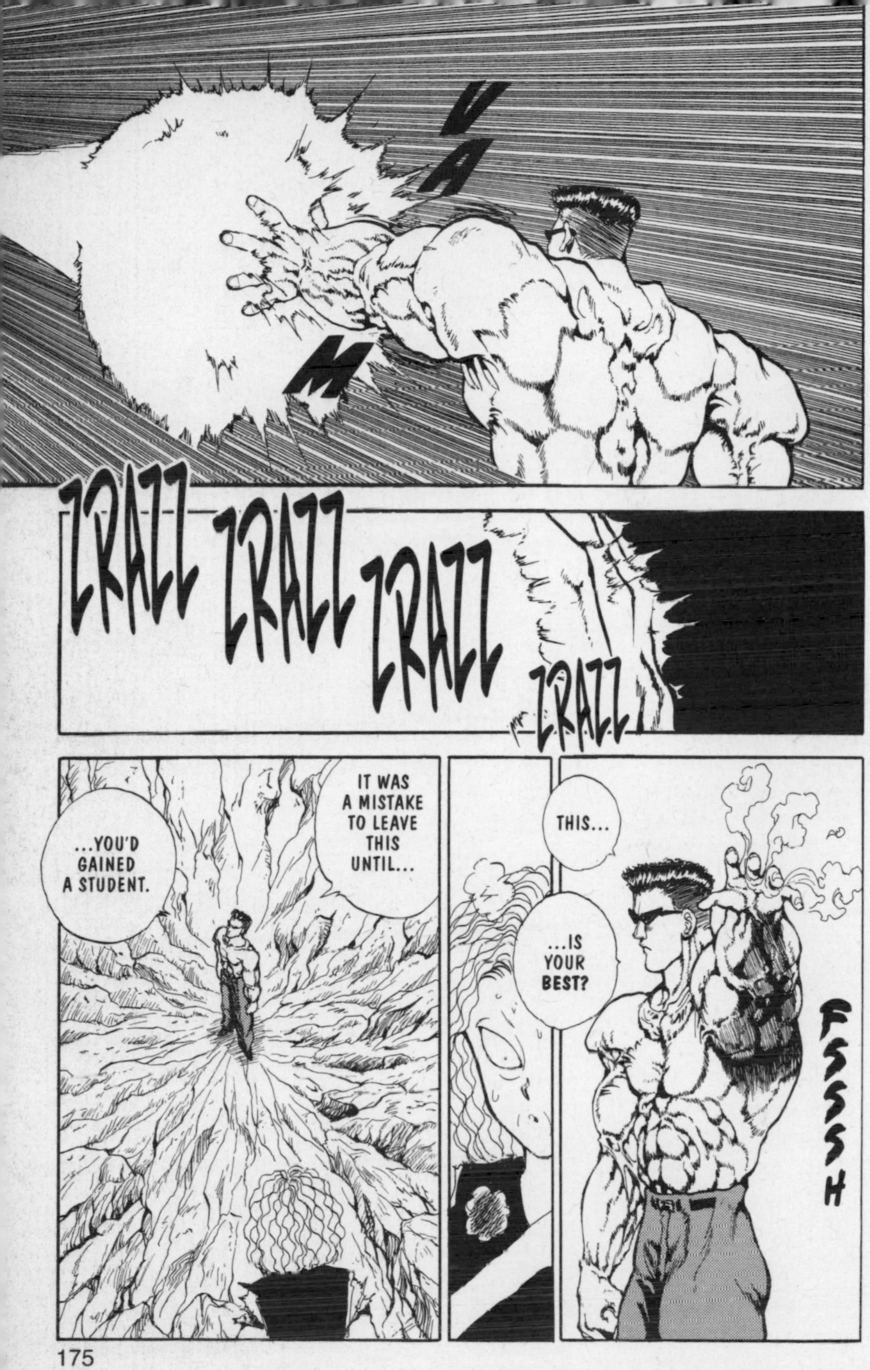
VAM
ZRAZZ ZRAZZ ZRAZZ ZRAZZ
THIS...
...IS YOUR BEST?
FSSSSH
IT WAS A MISTAKE TO LEAVE THIS UNTIL...
...YOU'D GAINED A STUDENT.

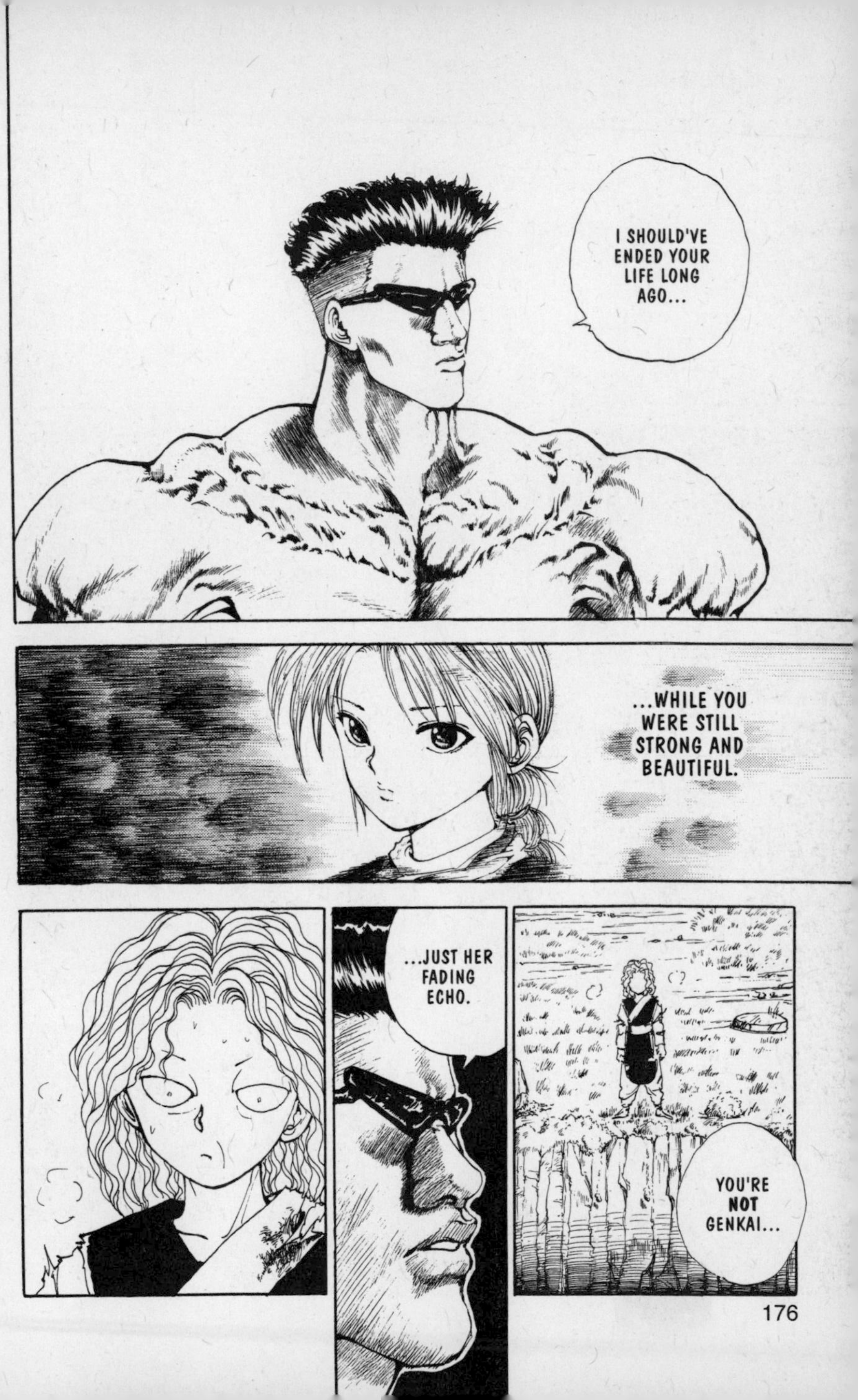
I SHOULD'VE ENDED YOUR LIFE LONG AGO...
...WHILE YOU WERE STILL STRONG AND BEAUTIFUL.
YOU'RE NOT GENKAI...
...JUST HER FADING ECHO.

READ THIS WAY

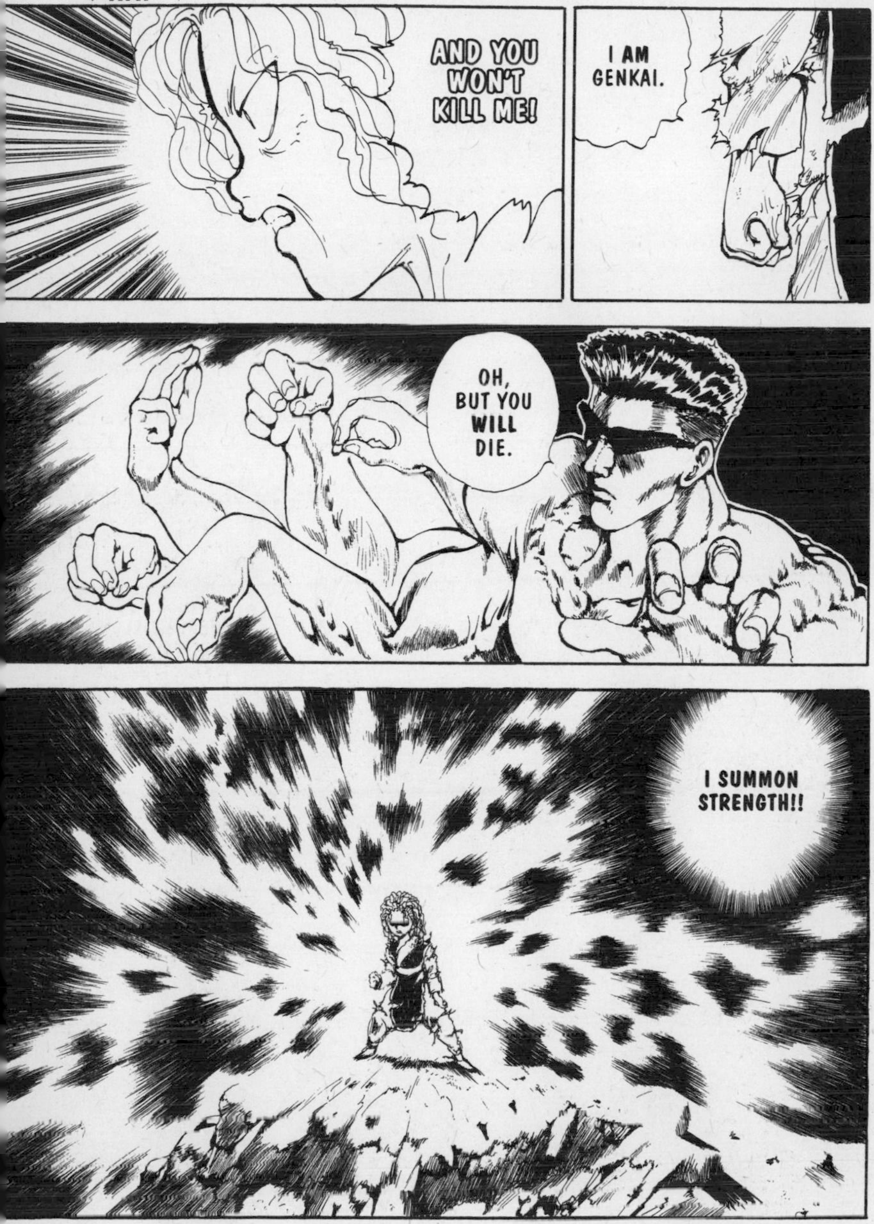

I AM GENKAI.
AND YOU WON'T KILL ME!
OH, BUT YOU WILL DIE.
I SUMMON STRENGTH!!

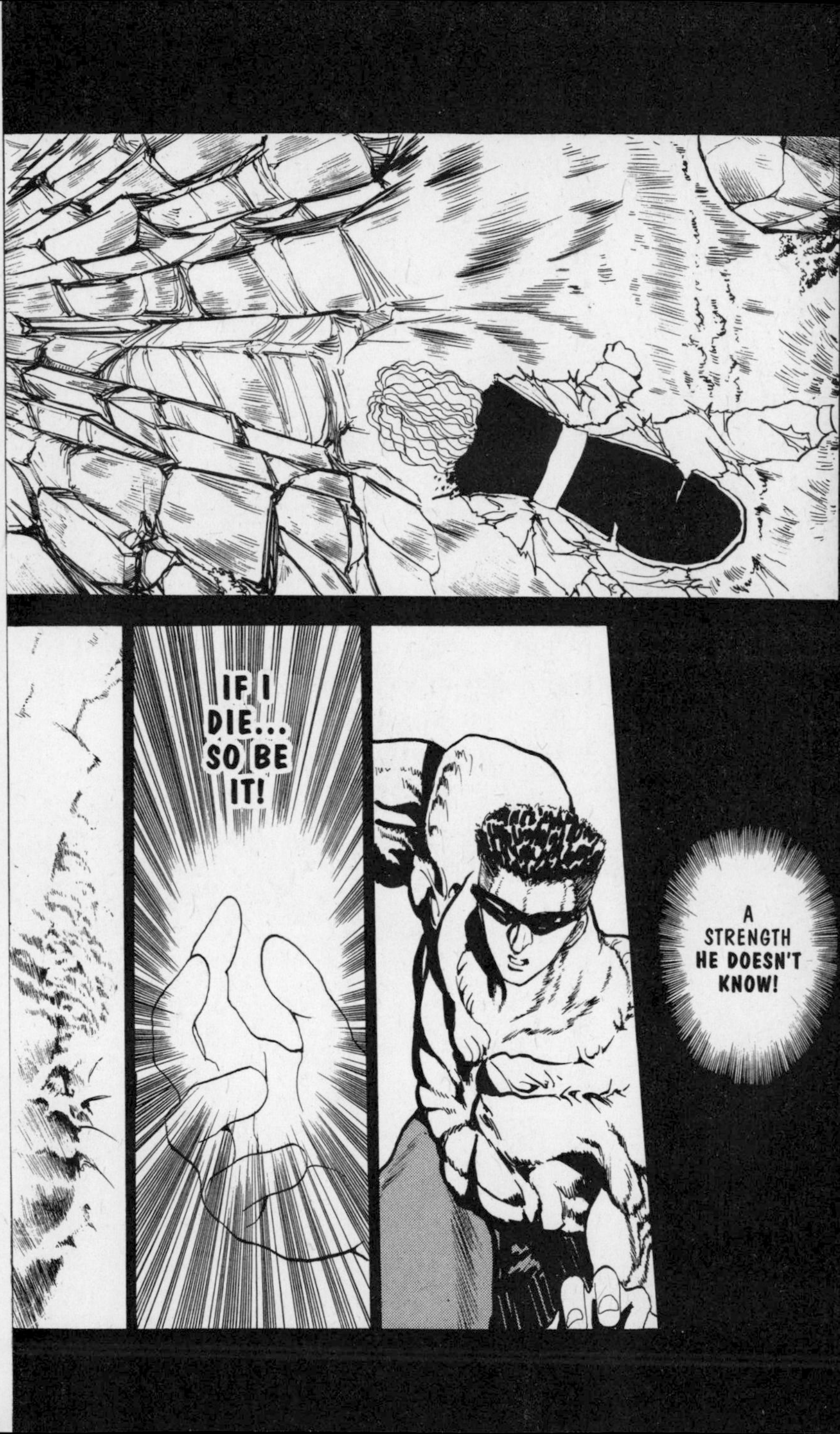
A STRENGTH HE DOESN'T KNOW!
IF I DIE... SO BE IT!

READ THIS WAY

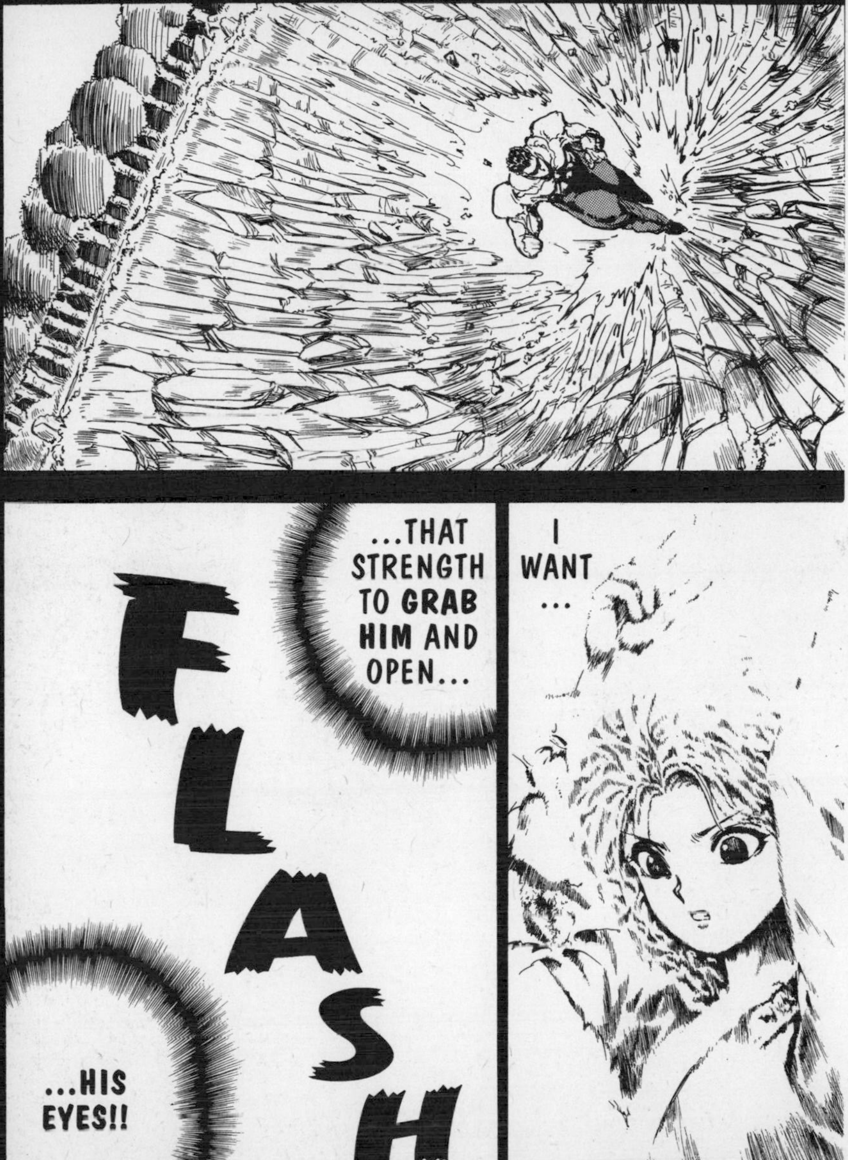
I WANT...
...THAT STRENGTH TO GRAB HIM AND OPEN...
FLASH
...HIS EYES!!

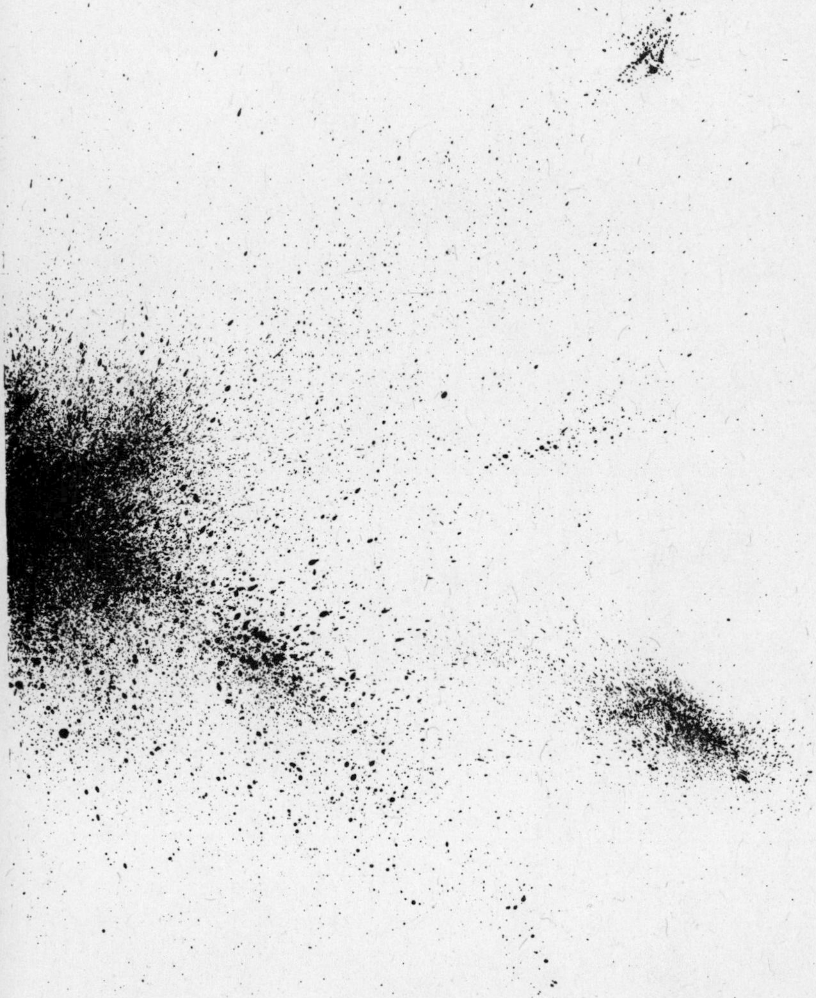

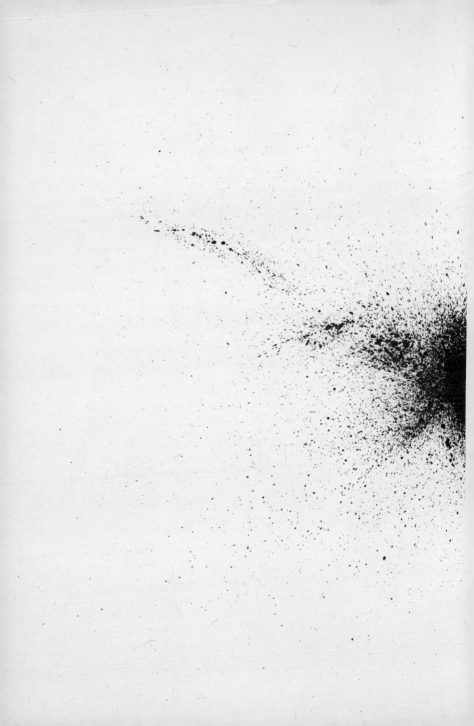

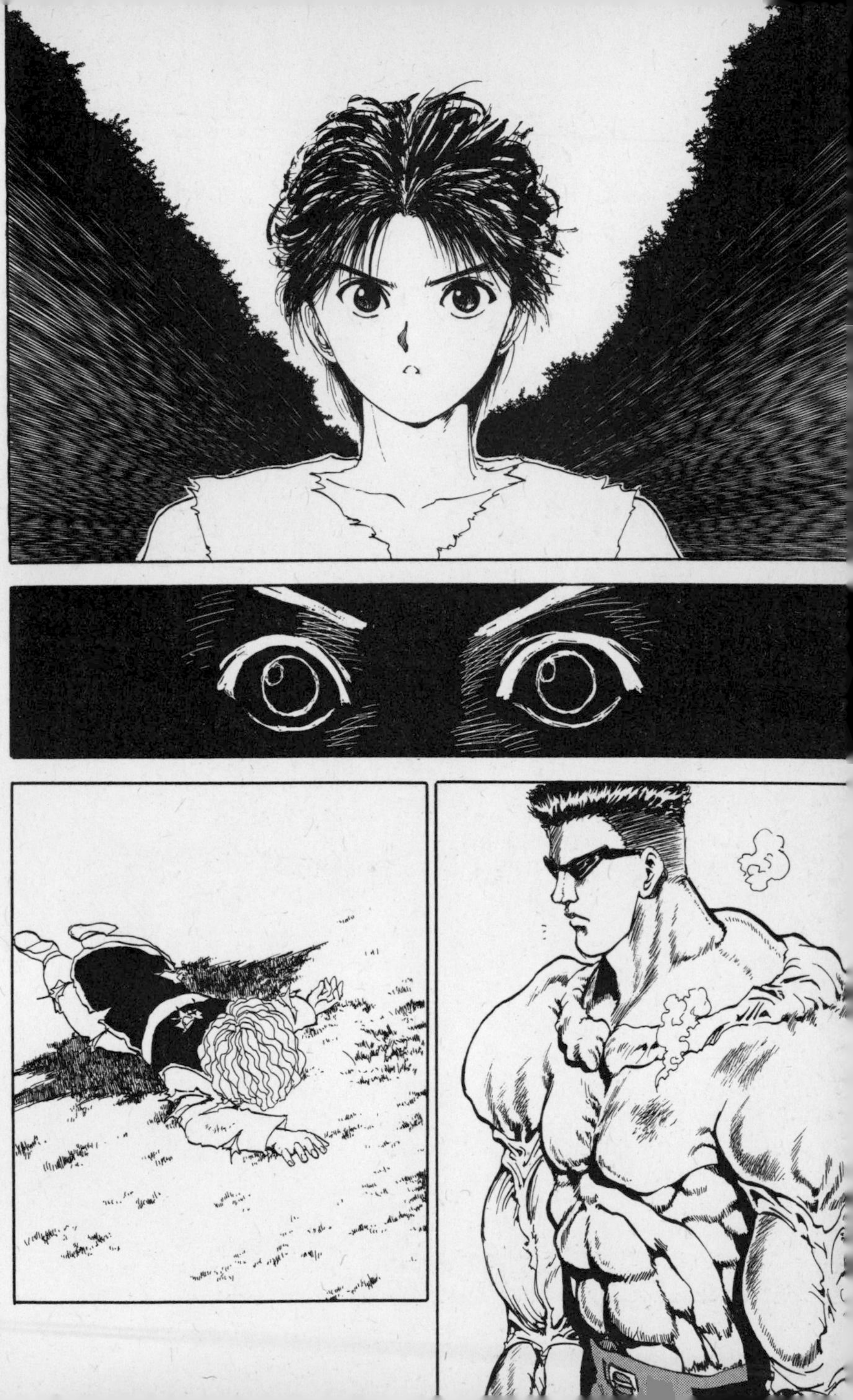

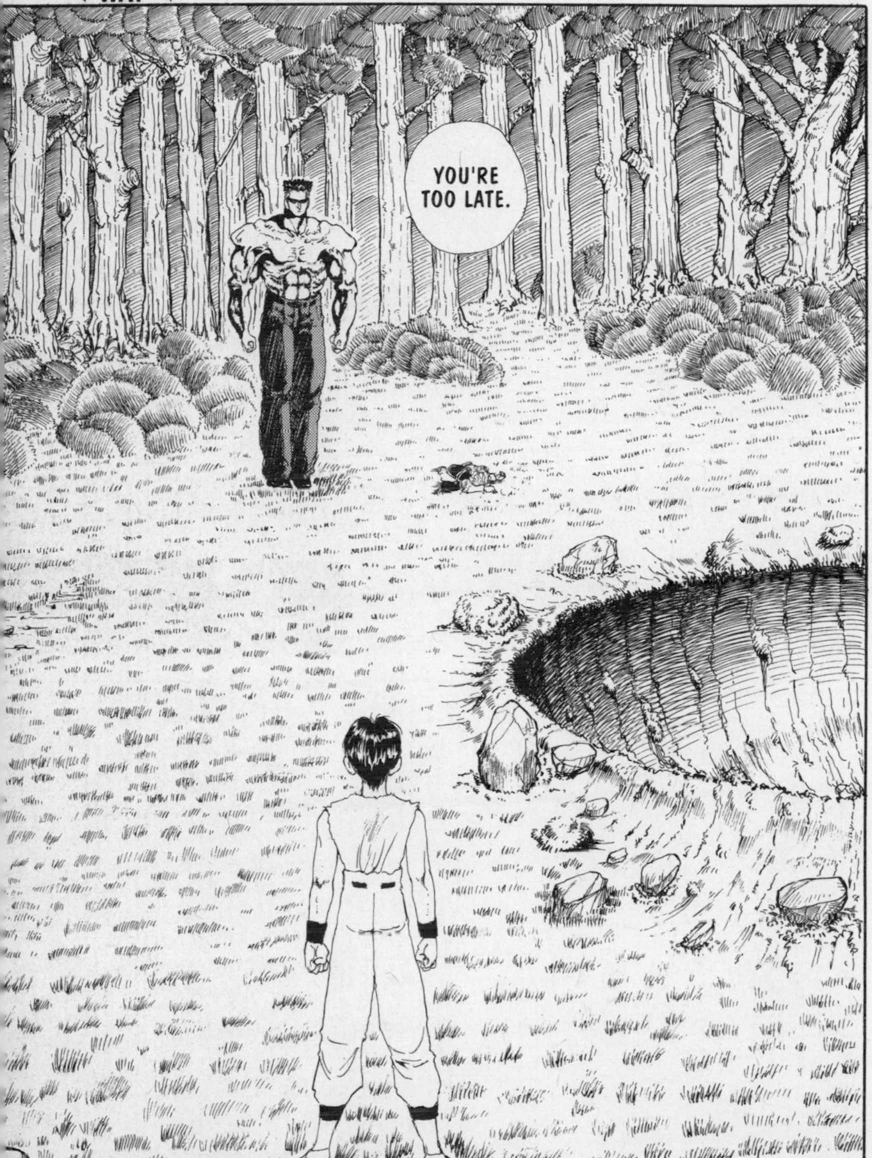
YOU'RE TOO LATE.

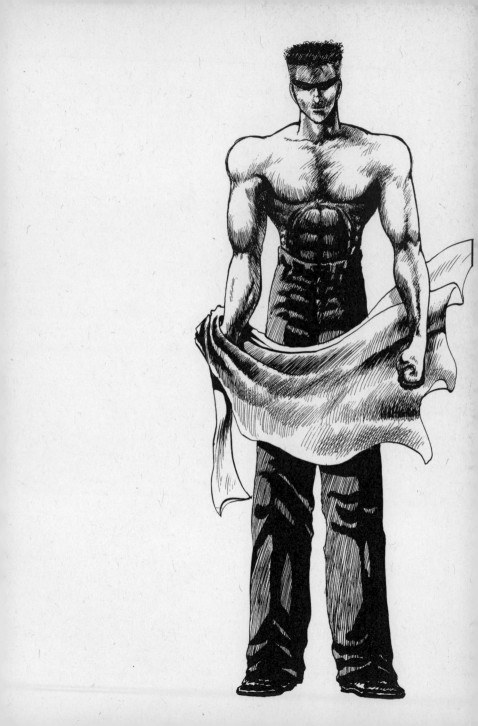

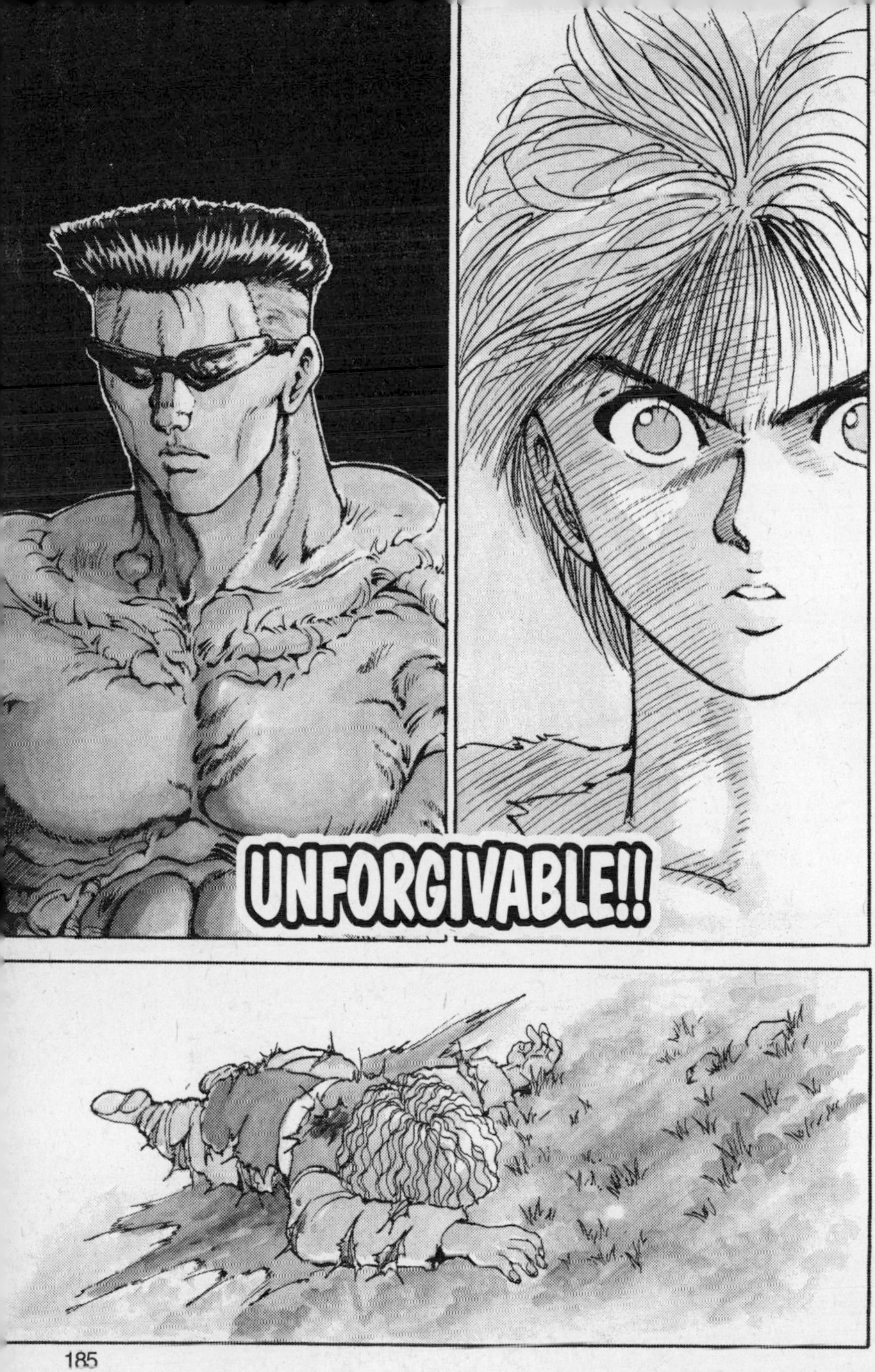
UNFORGIVABLE!!

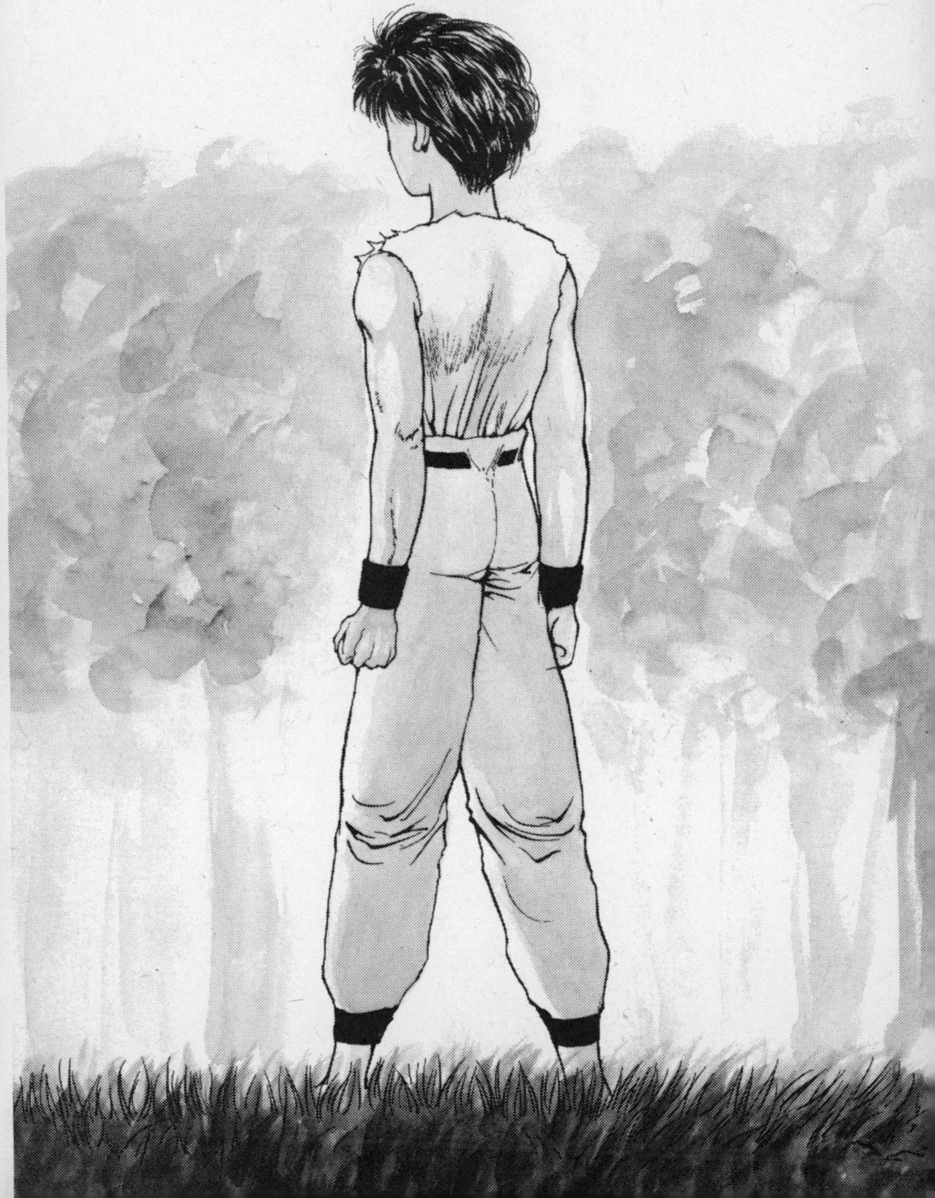

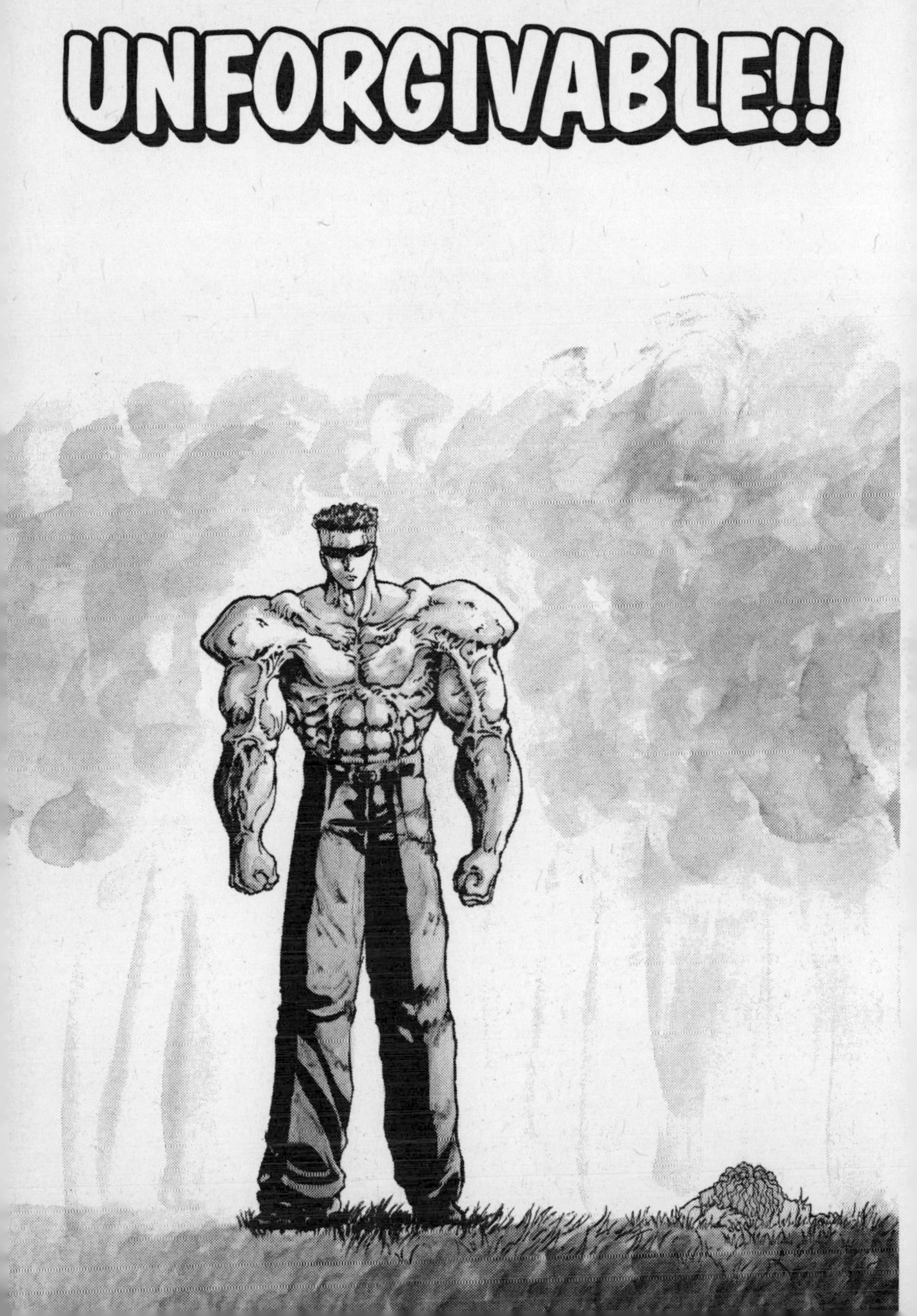
UNFORGIVABLE!!

YuYu HAKUSHO™

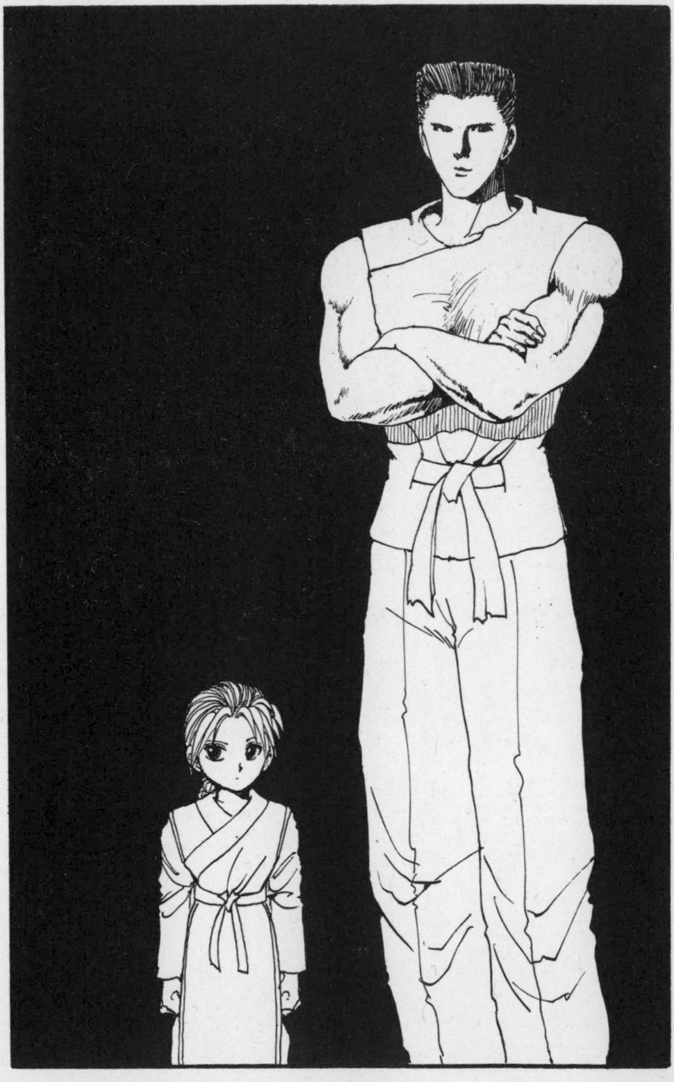

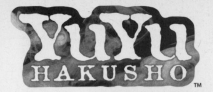

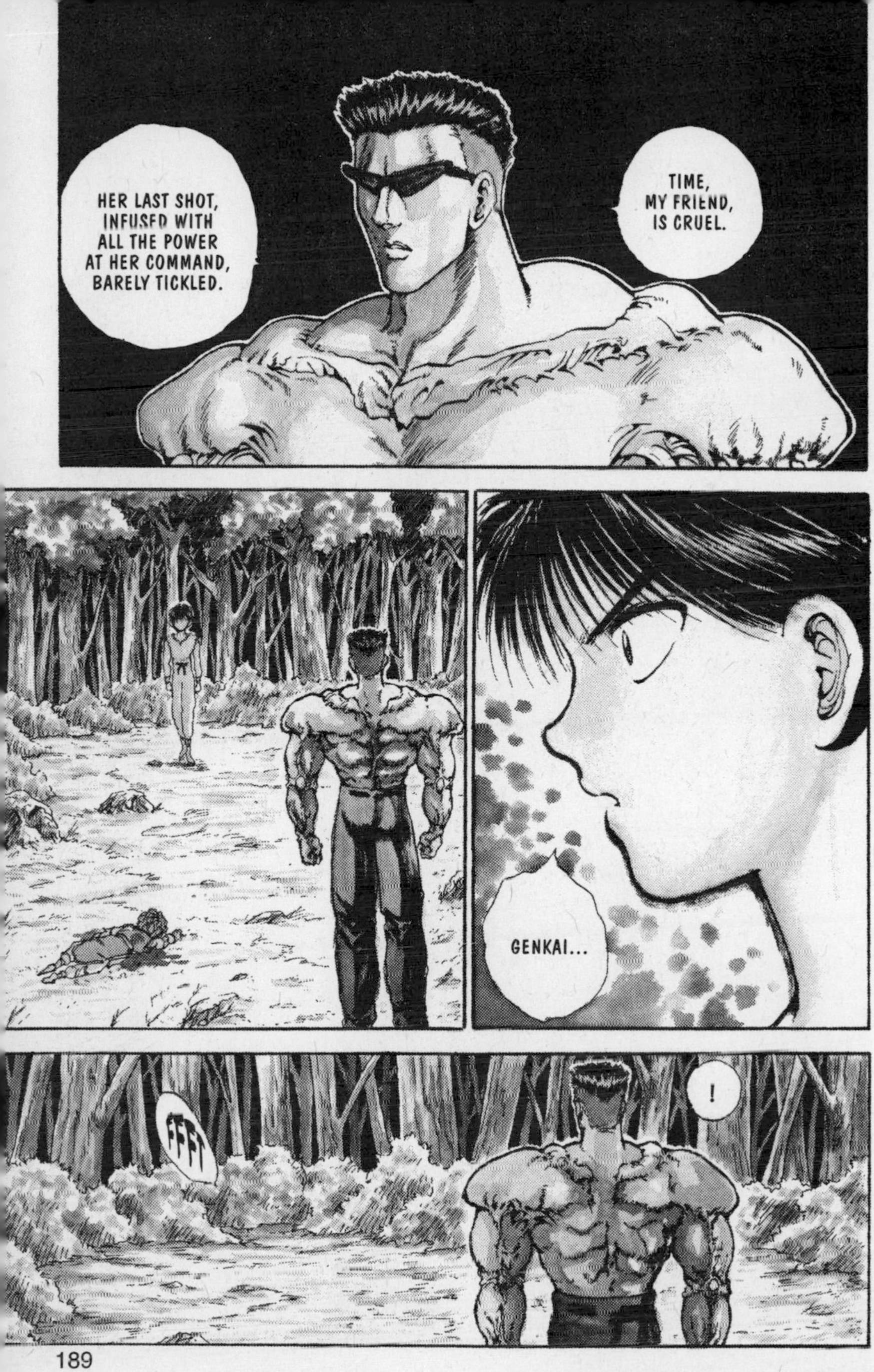
TIME, MY FRIEND, IS CRUEL.
HER LAST SHOT, INFUSED WITH ALL THE POWER AT HER COMMAND, BARELY TICKLED.
GENKAI...
!
FFFT

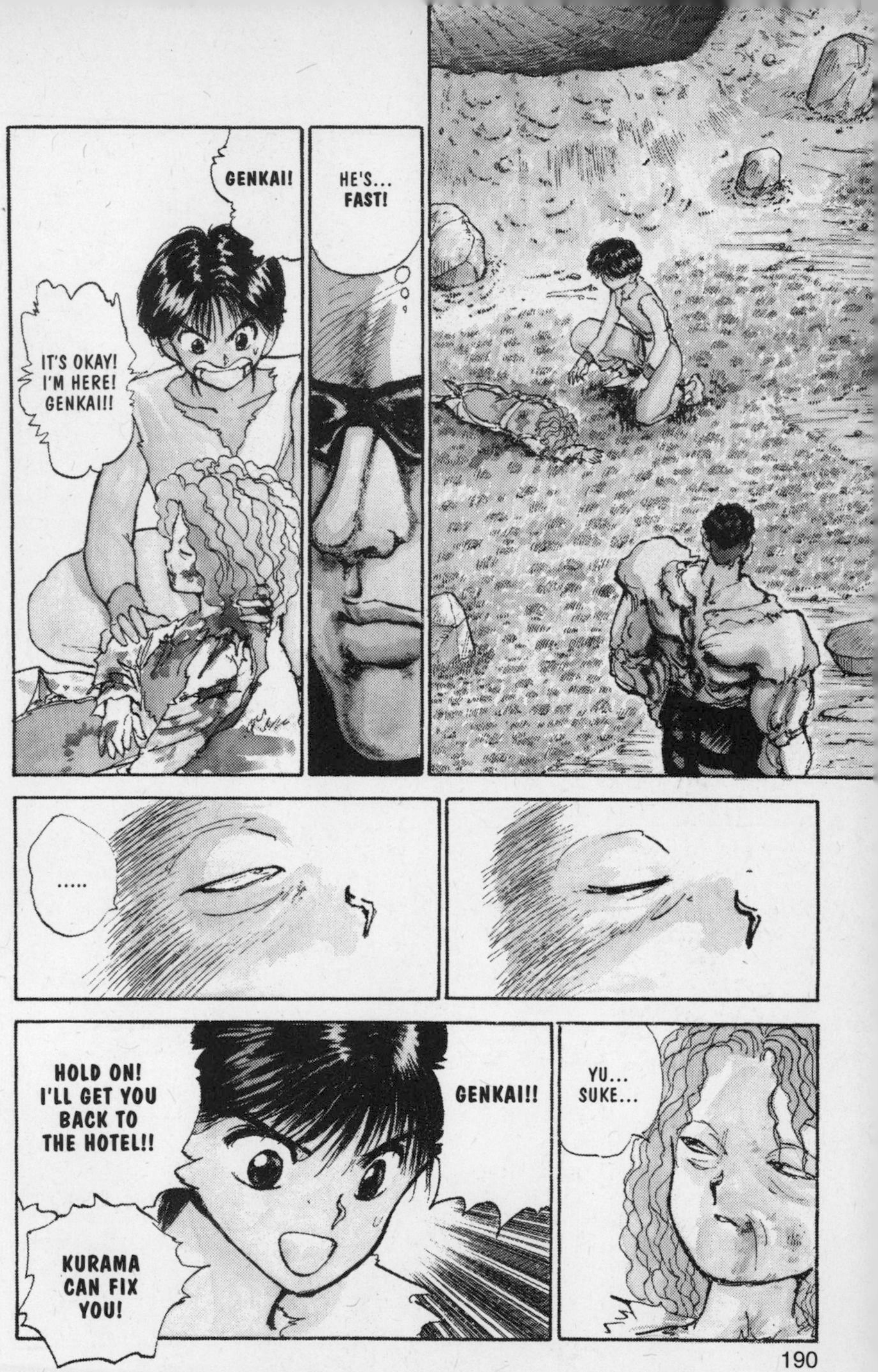
HE'S... FAST!
GENKAI!
IT'S OKAY! I'M HERE! GENKAI!!
.....
YU... SUKE...
GENKAI!!
HOLD ON! I'LL GET YOU BACK TO THE HOTEL!!
KURAMA CAN FIX YOU!

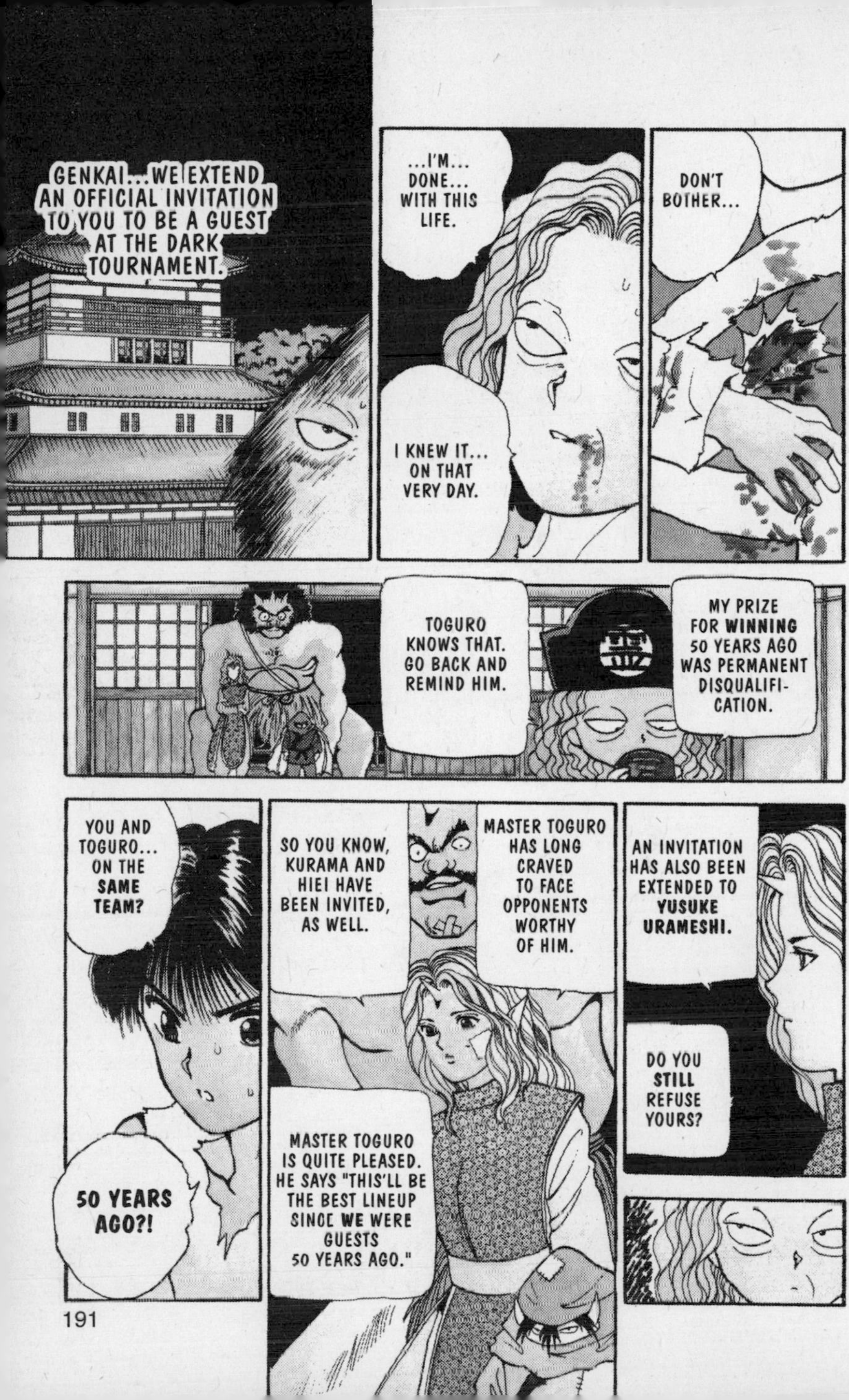
DON'T BOTHER...
...I'M... DONE... WITH THIS LIFE.
I KNEW IT... ON THAT VERY DAY.
GENKAI...WE EXTEND AN OFFICIAL INVITATION TO YOU TO BE A GUEST AT THE DARK TOURNAMENT.
MY PRIZE FOR **WINNING** 50 YEARS AGO WAS PERMANENT DISQUALIFI-CATION.
TOGURO KNOWS THAT. GO BACK AND REMIND HIM.
AN INVITATION HAS ALSO BEEN EXTENDED TO **YUSUKE URAMESHI.**
DO YOU **STILL** REFUSE YOURS?
MASTER TOGURO HAS LONG CRAVED TO FACE OPPONENTS WORTHY OF HIM.
SO YOU KNOW, KURAMA AND HIEI HAVE BEEN INVITED, AS WELL.
MASTER TOGURO IS QUITE PLEASED. HE SAYS "THIS'LL BE THE BEST LINEUP SINCE **WE** WERE GUESTS 50 YEARS AGO."
YOU AND TOGURO... ON THE **SAME TEAM?**
50 YEARS AGO?!

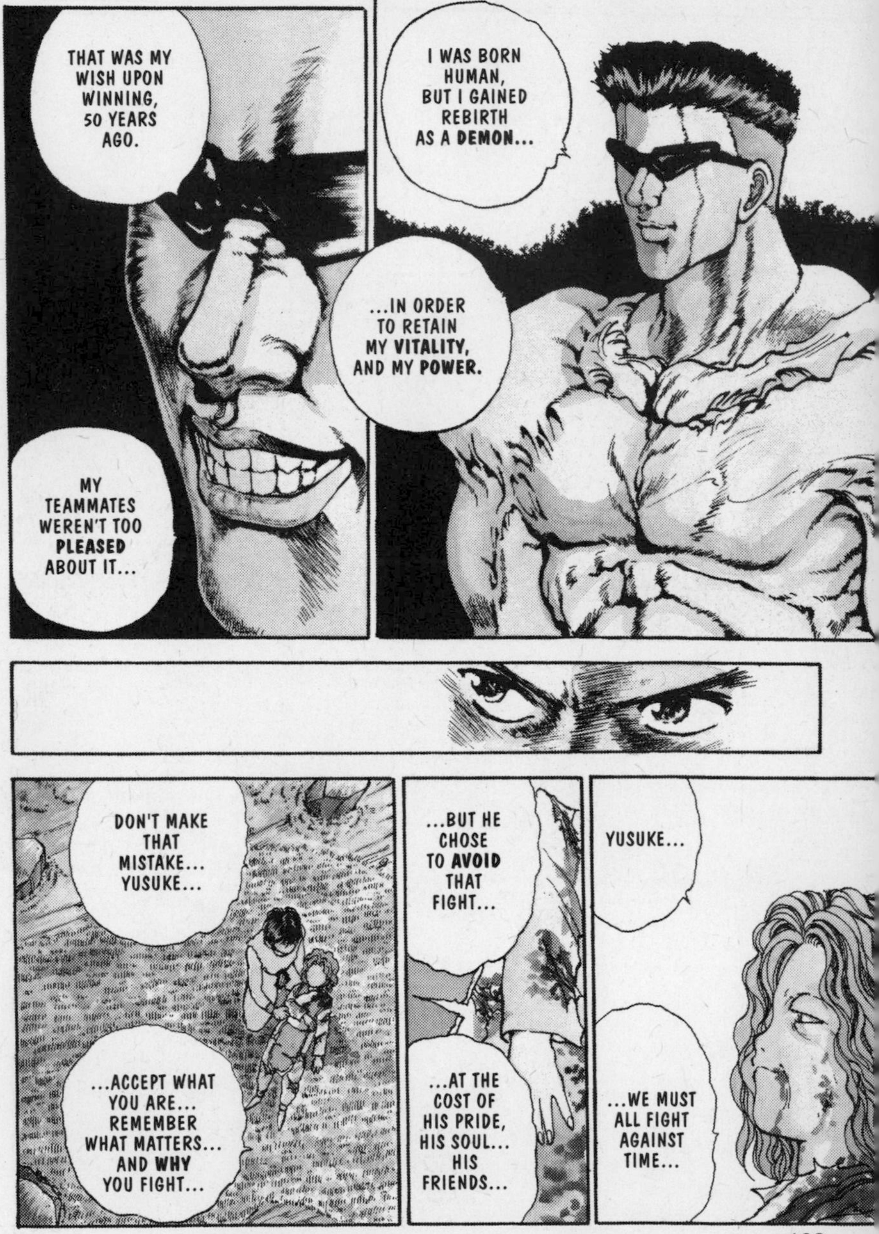
I WAS BORN HUMAN, BUT I GAINED REBIRTH AS A DEMON...
...IN ORDER TO RETAIN MY VITALITY, AND MY POWER.
THAT WAS MY WISH UPON WINNING, 50 YEARS AGO.
MY TEAMMATES WEREN'T TOO PLEASED ABOUT IT...
YUSUKE...
...WE MUST ALL FIGHT AGAINST TIME...
...BUT HE CHOSE TO AVOID THAT FIGHT...
...AT THE COST OF HIS PRIDE, HIS SOUL... HIS FRIENDS...
DON'T MAKE THAT MISTAKE... YUSUKE...
...ACCEPT WHAT YOU ARE... REMEMBER WHAT MATTERS... AND WHY YOU FIGHT...

READ THIS WAY

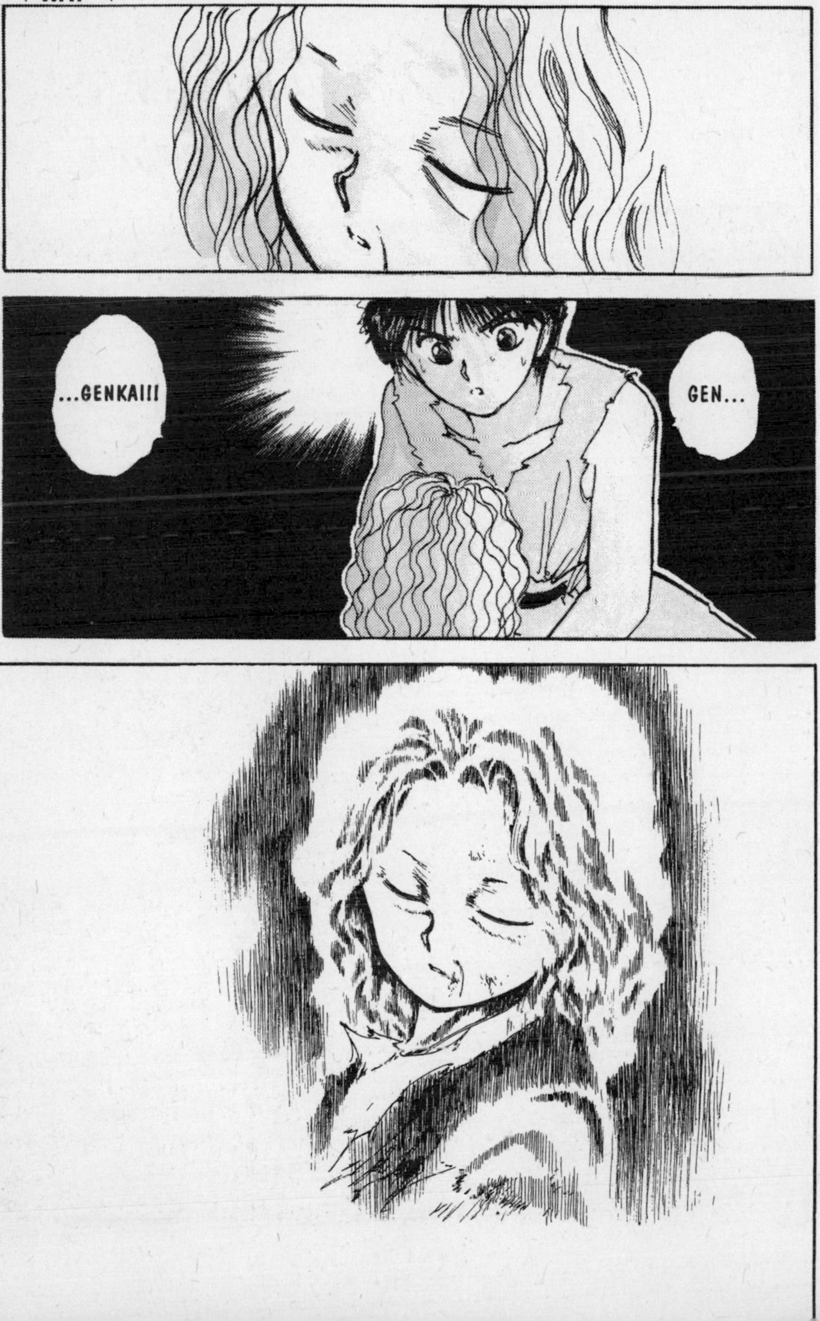
GEN...
...GENKAI!!!

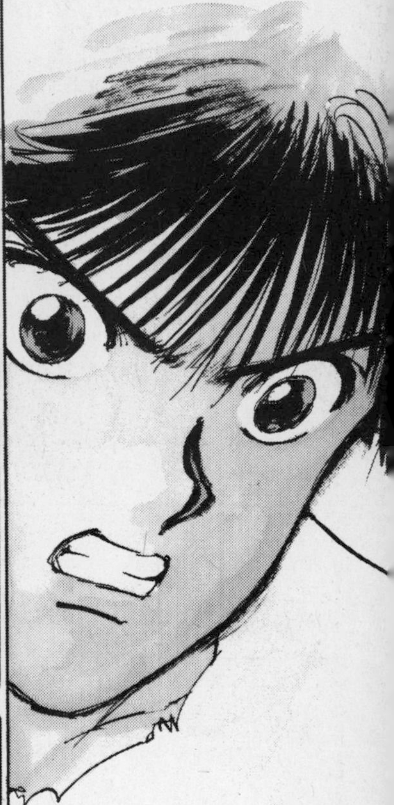

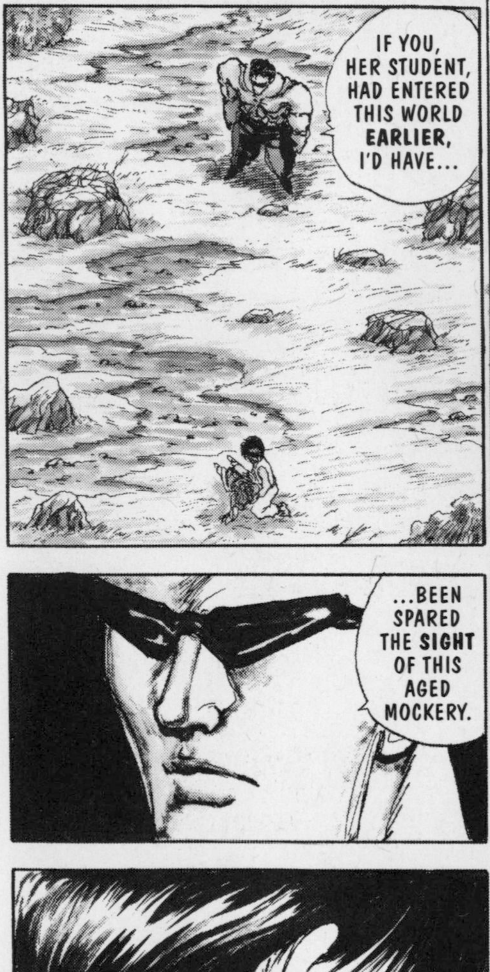
IF YOU, HER STUDENT, HAD ENTERED THIS WORLD EARLIER, I'D HAVE...
...BEEN SPARED THE SIGHT OF THIS AGED MOCKERY.

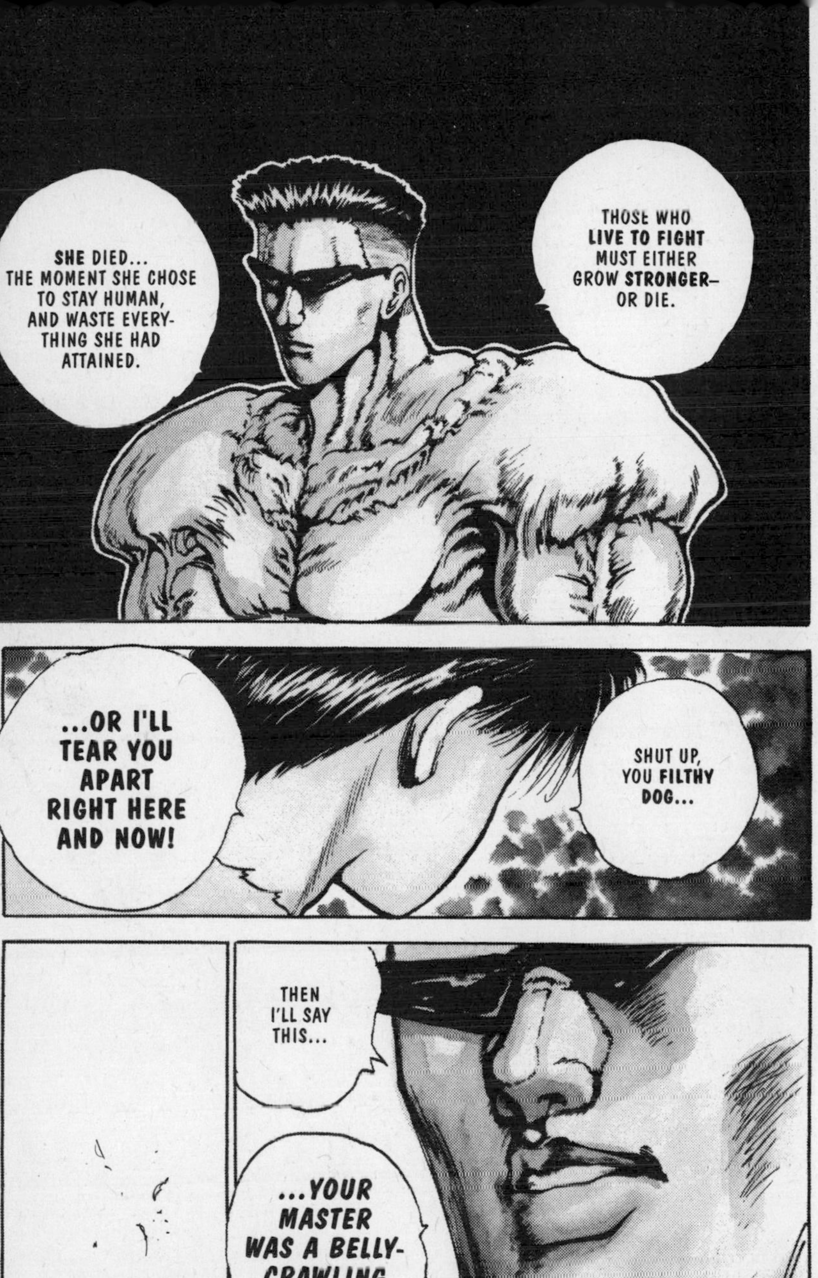
THOSE WHO LIVE TO FIGHT MUST EITHER GROW STRONGER— OR DIE.
SHE DIED... THE MOMENT SHE CHOSE TO STAY HUMAN, AND WASTE EVERYTHING SHE HAD ATTAINED.
SHUT UP, YOU FILTHY DOG...
...OR I'LL TEAR YOU APART RIGHT HERE AND NOW!
THEN I'LL SAY THIS...
...YOUR MASTER WAS A BELLY-CRAWLING MAGGOT!

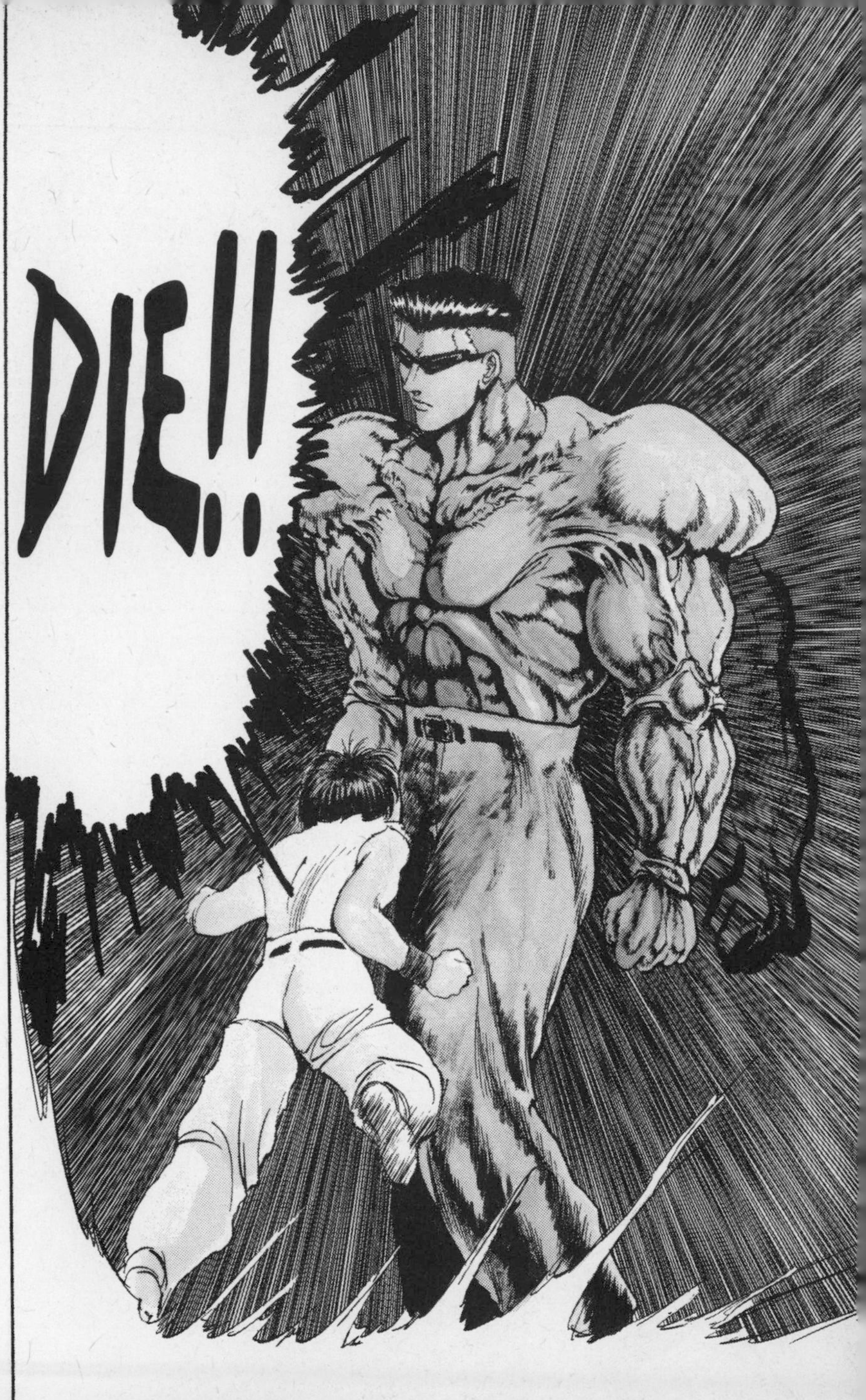
DIE!!

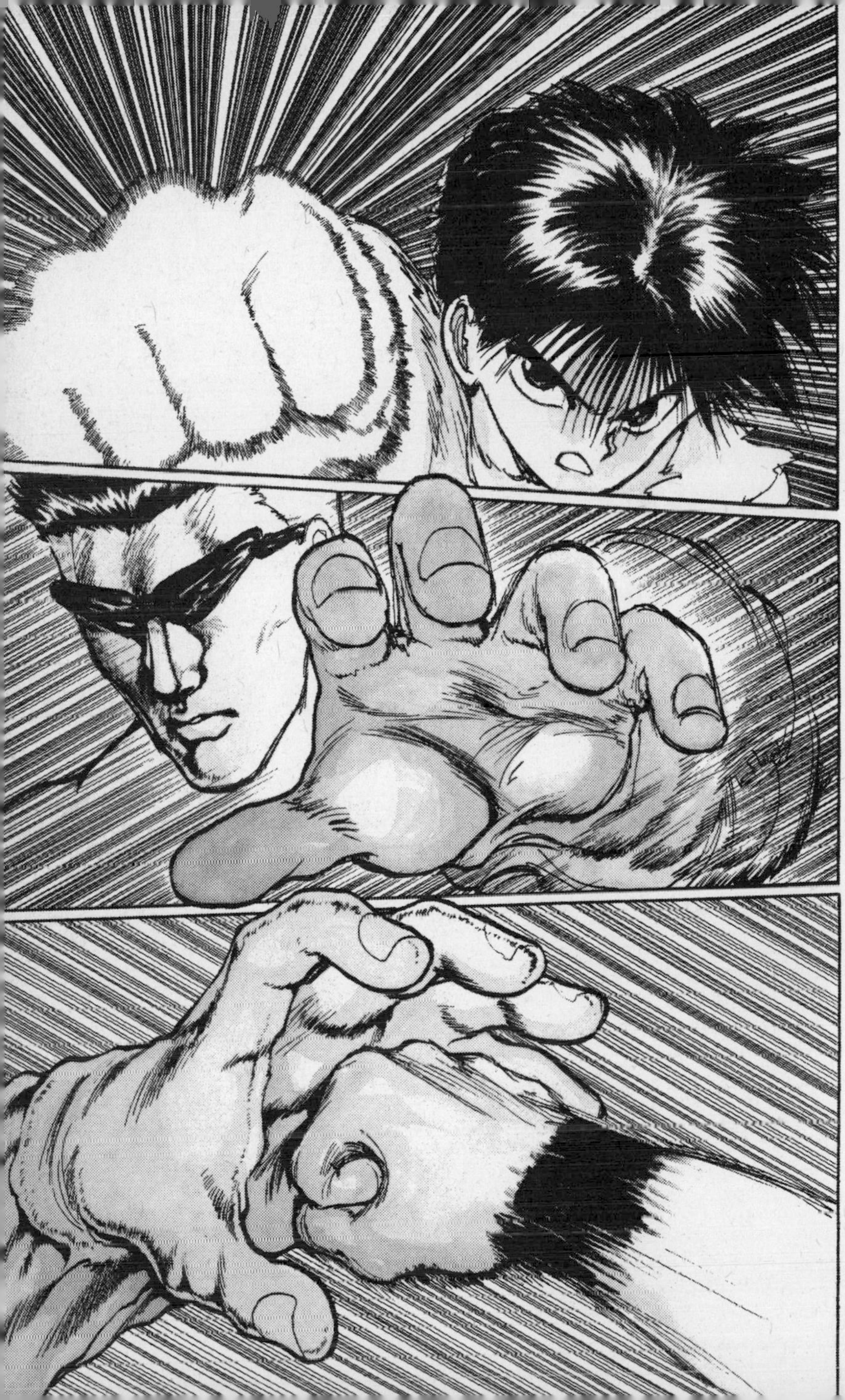

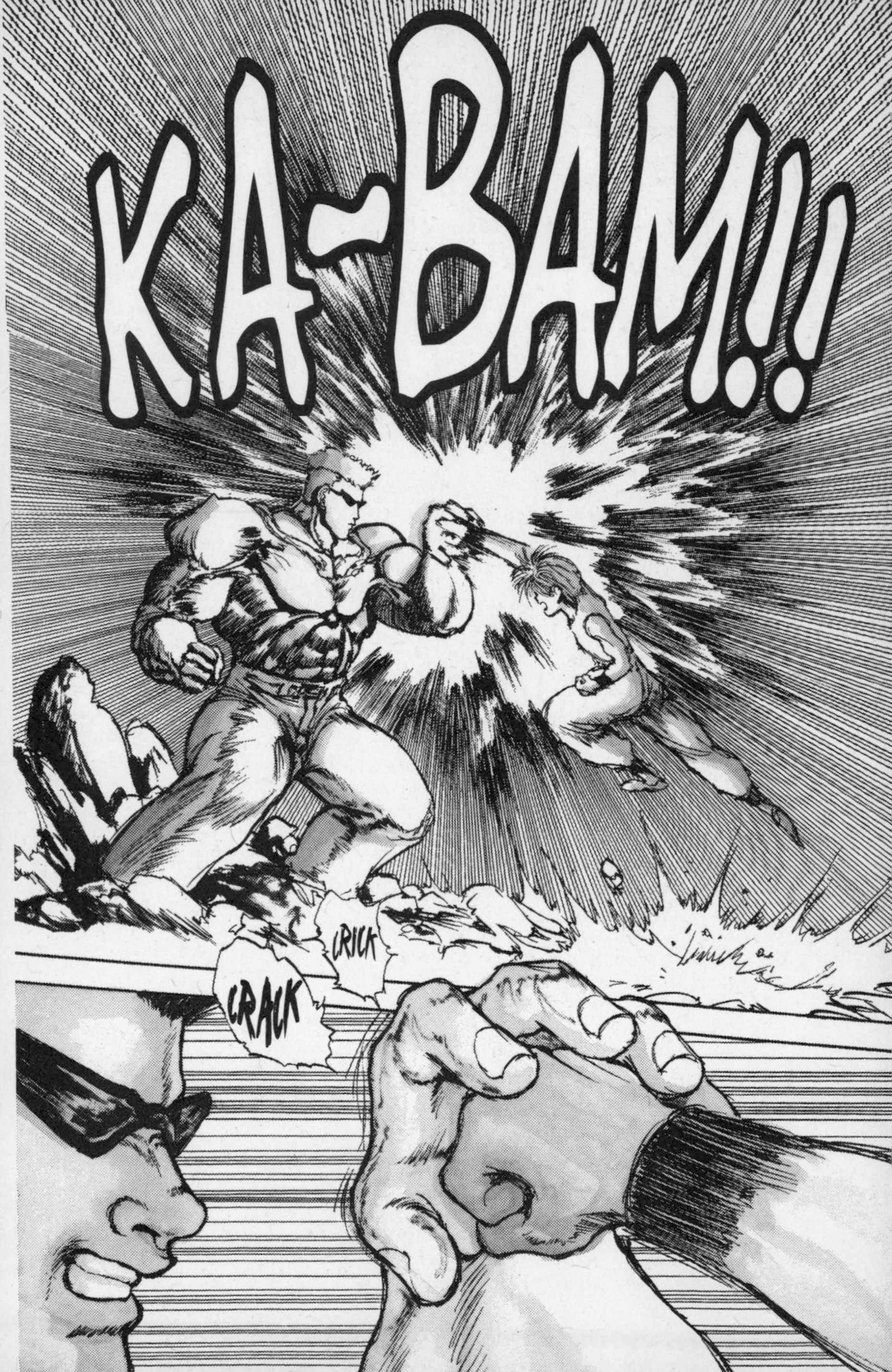
KA-BAM!!
CRICK
CRACK

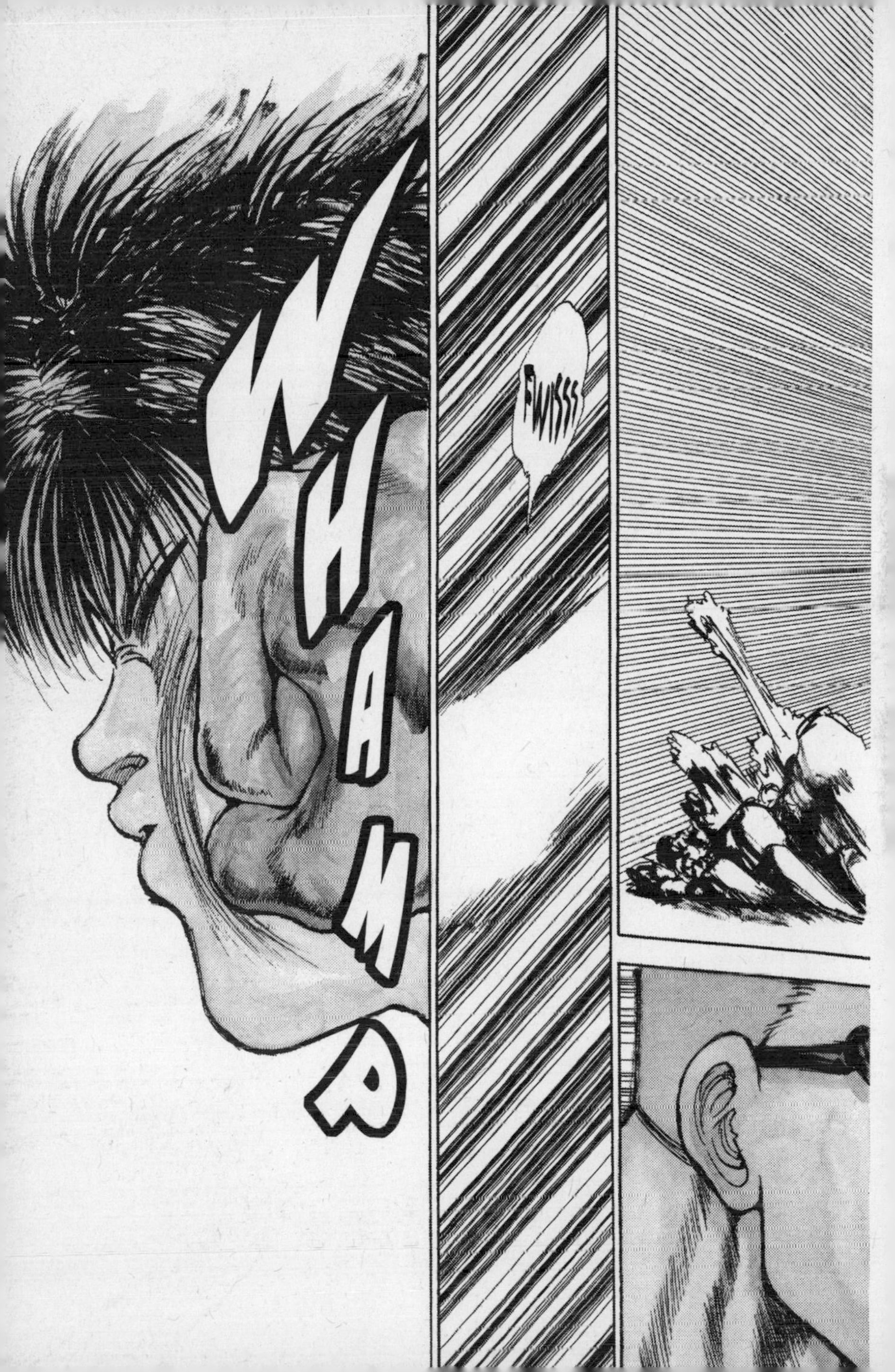
FWISSS
WHAMP

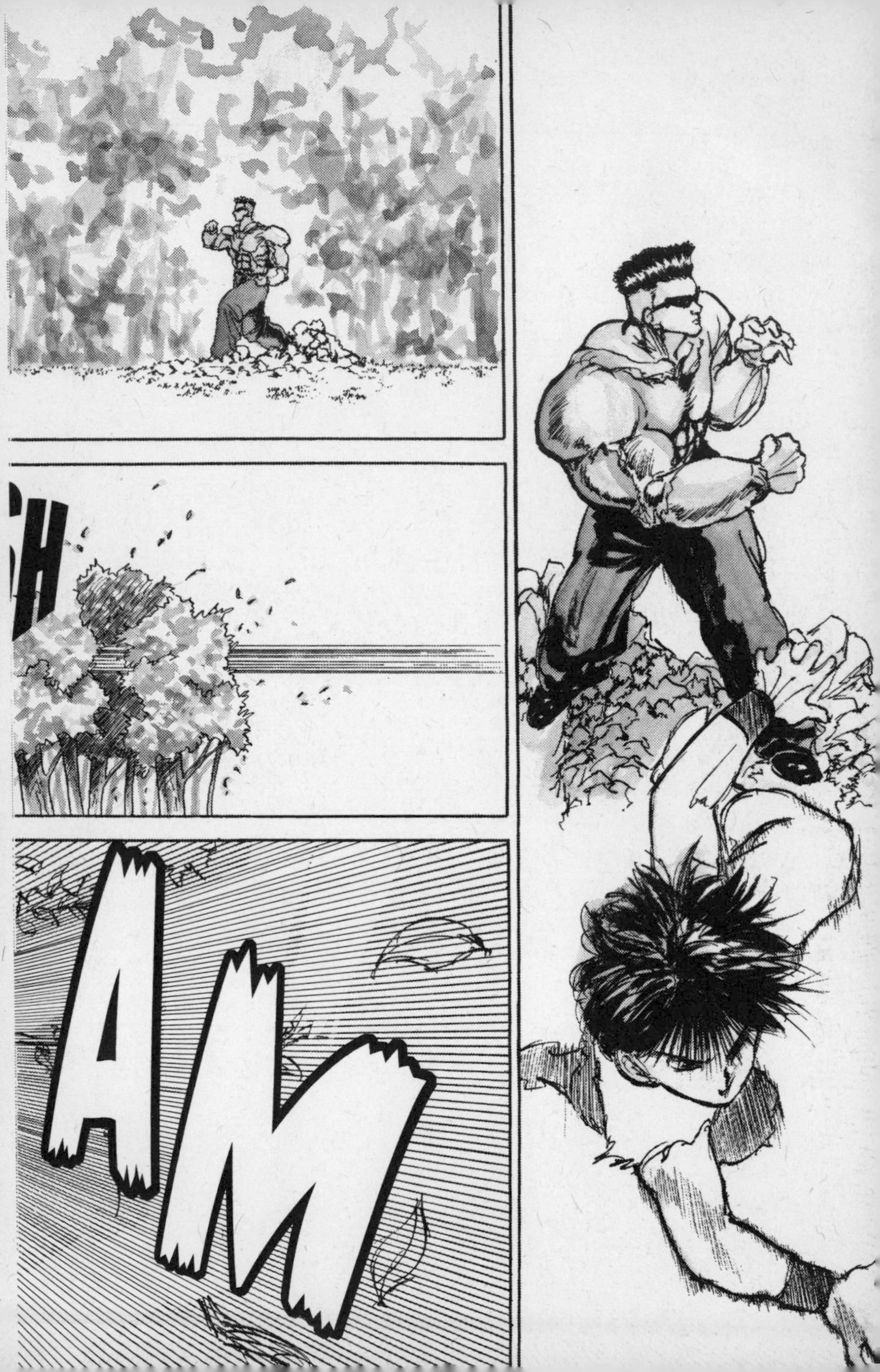
SH
AM

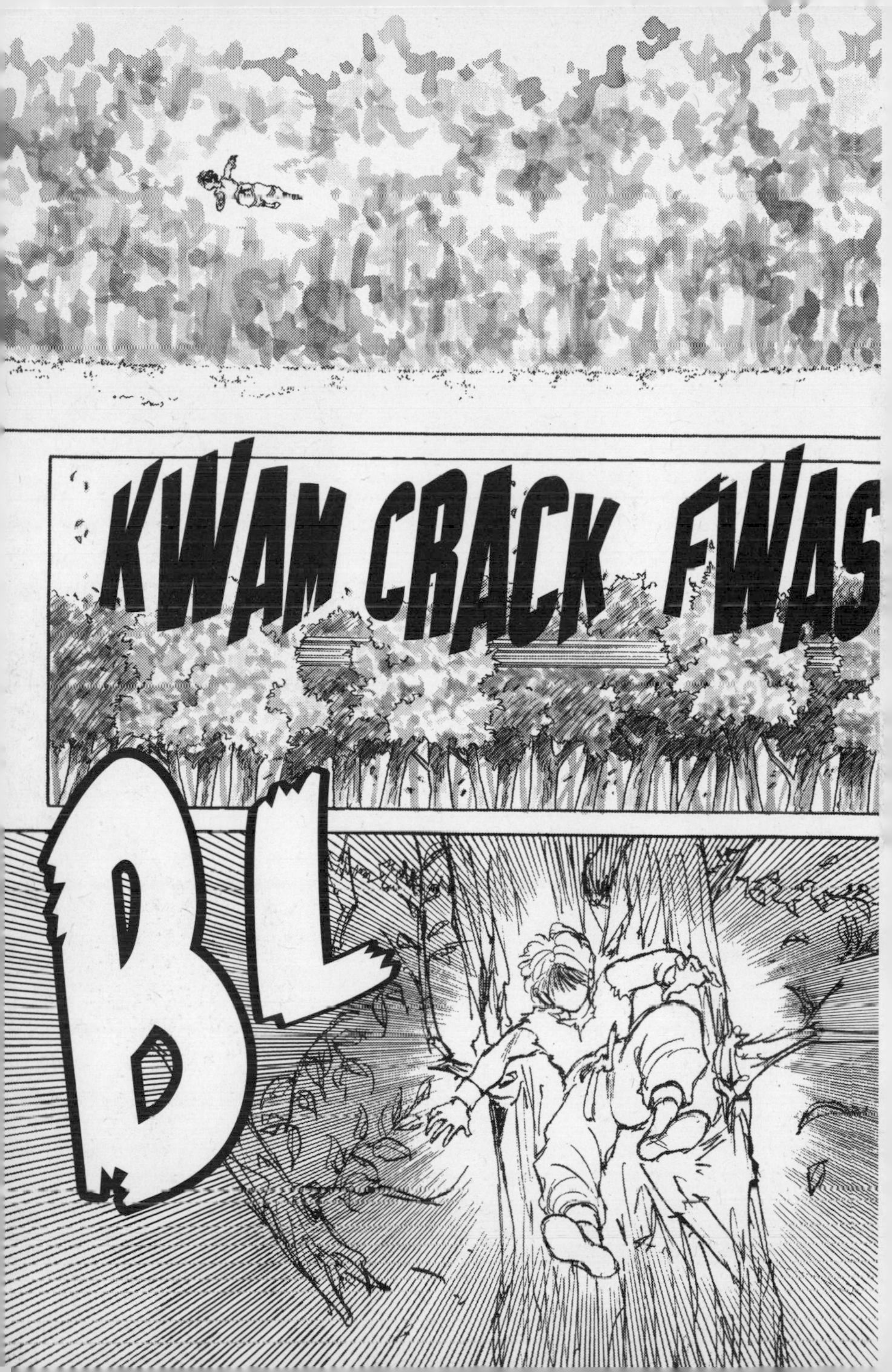
KWAM CRACK FWAS
BL

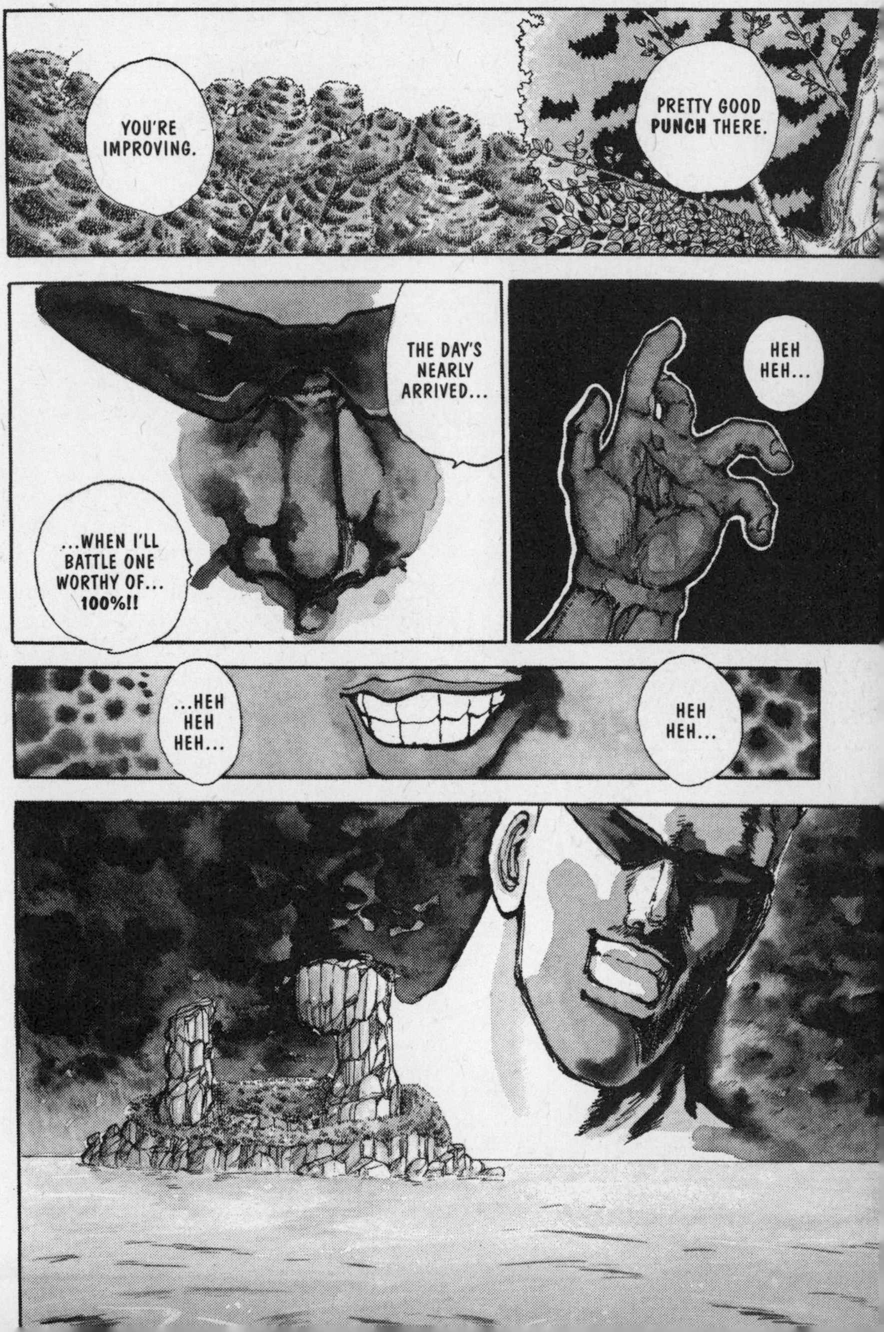
PRETTY GOOD **PUNCH** THERE.
YOU'RE IMPROVING.
HEH HEH...
THE DAY'S NEARLY ARRIVED...
...WHEN I'LL BATTLE ONE WORTHY OF... **100%!!**
HEH HEH...
...HEH HEH HEH...

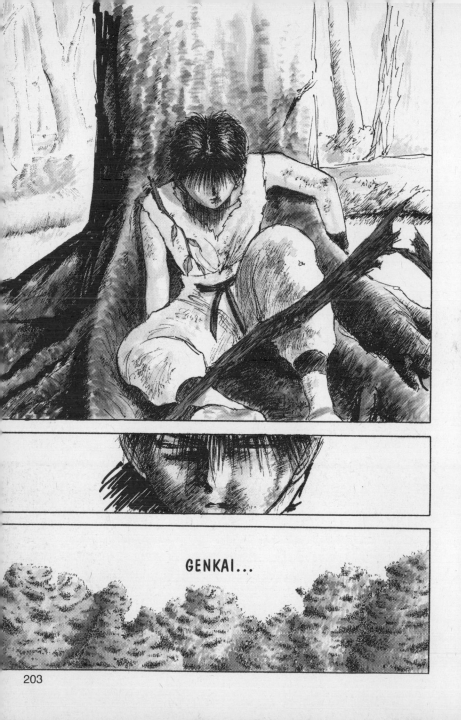

GENKAI...

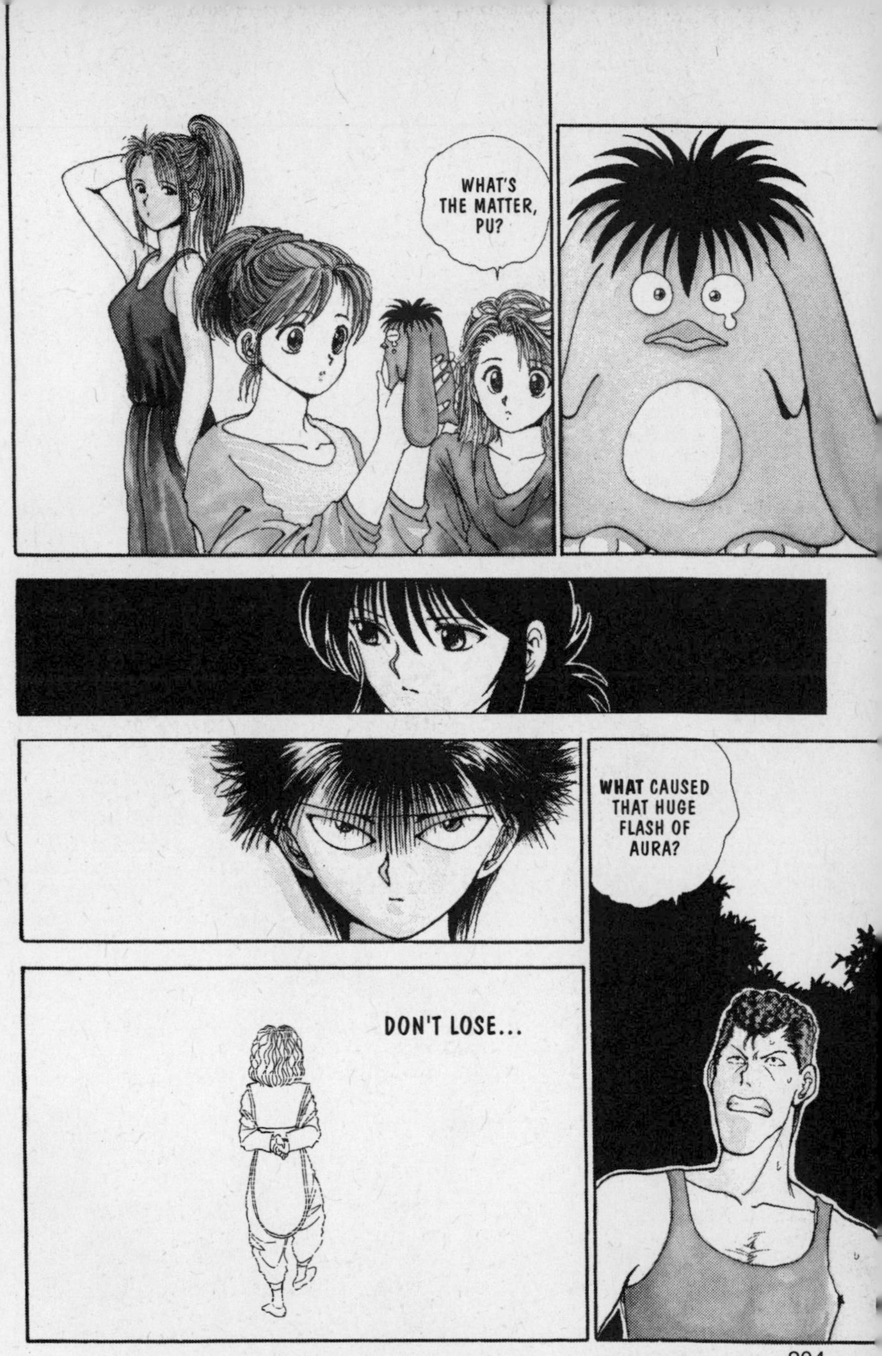
WHAT'S THE MATTER, PU?
WHAT CAUSED THAT HUGE FLASH OF AURA?
DON'T LOSE...

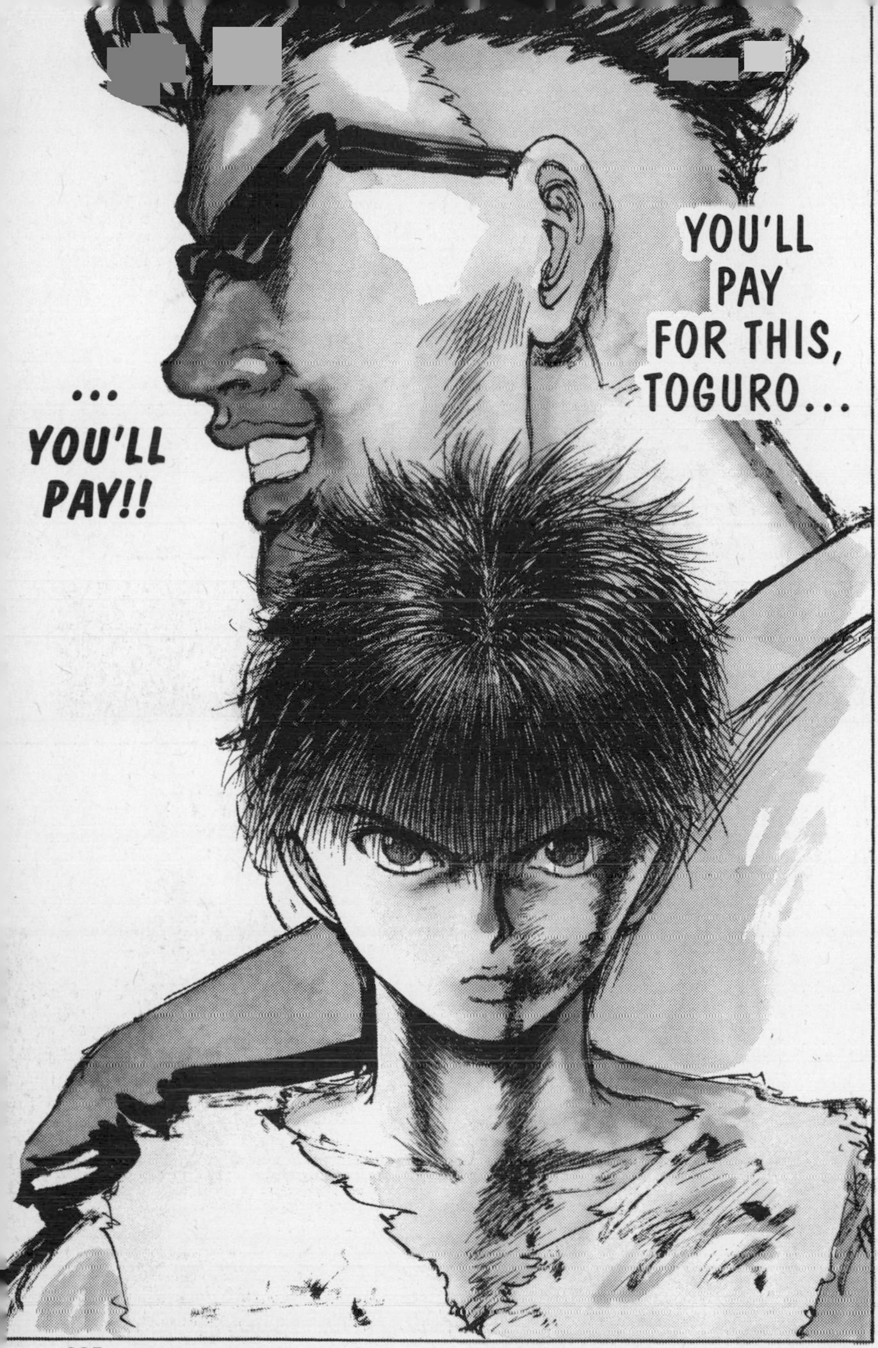
YOU'LL PAY FOR THIS, TOGURO...
... YOU'LL PAY!!

 VOL. 10: END.

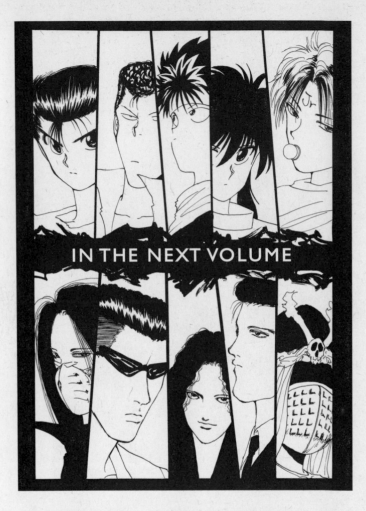

IN THE NEXT VOLUME

The main event has arrived! After one perilous battle after another, Team Urameshi and Team Toguro finally come face-to-face at the Dark Tournament. Meanwhile, evil entrepreneur Sakyo reveals his grand scheme to create a path from the demon plane to the human world. With a portal like that, humans will need all the protection they can get!

Coming December 2006!

Tell us what you think about SHONEN JUMP manga!

Our survey is now available online.
Go to: **www.SHONENJUMP.com/mangasurvey**

Help us make our product offering better!

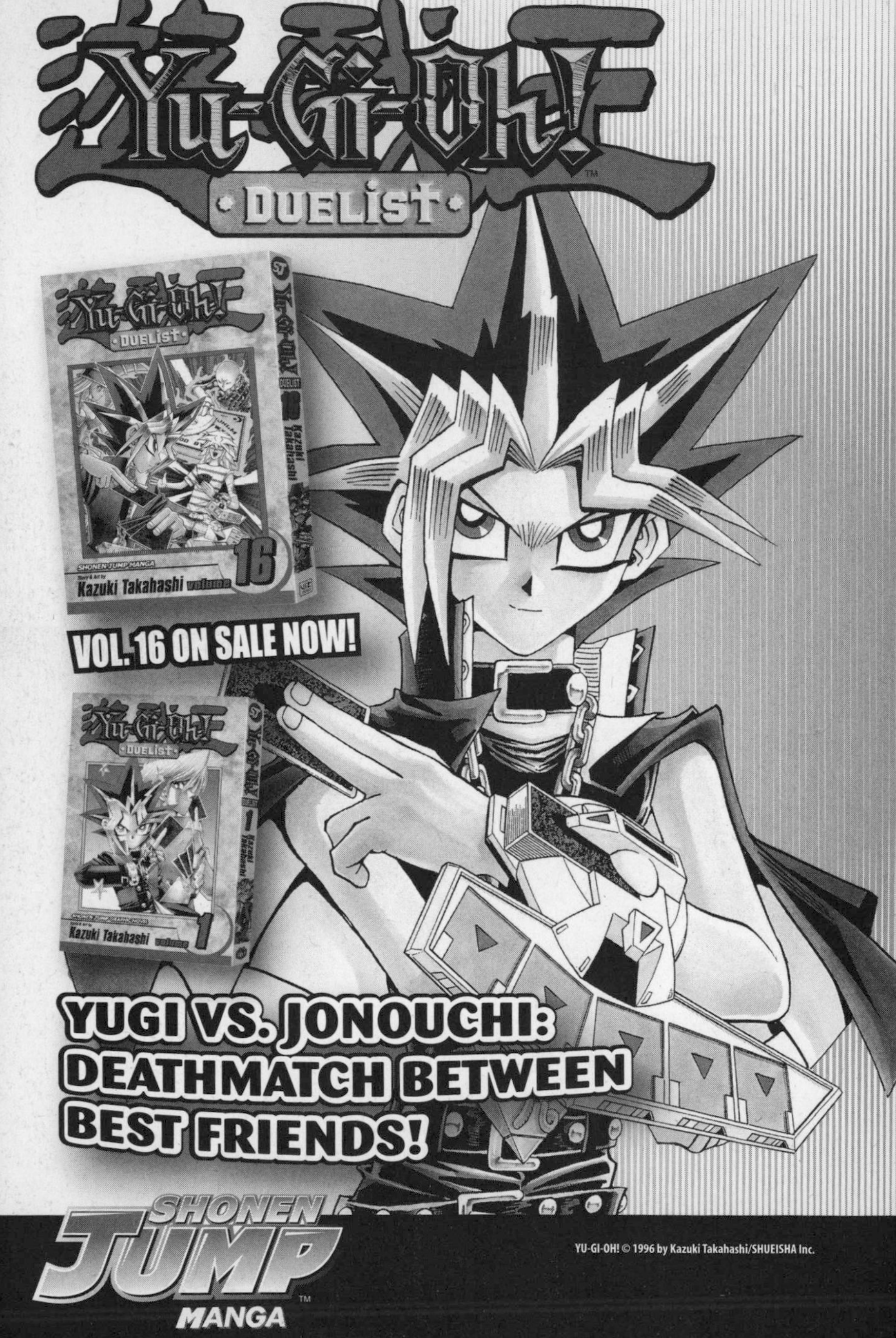

YU-GI-OH!™
DUELIST
SHONEN JUMP MANGA
Kazuki Takahashi volume 16
VOL. 16 ON SALE NOW!
Kazuki Takahashi volume 1
YUGI VS. JONOUCHI:
DEATHMATCH BETWEEN
BEST FRIENDS!
SHONEN JUMP™
MANGA
YU-GI-OH! © 1996 by Kazuki Takahashi/SHUEISHA Inc.

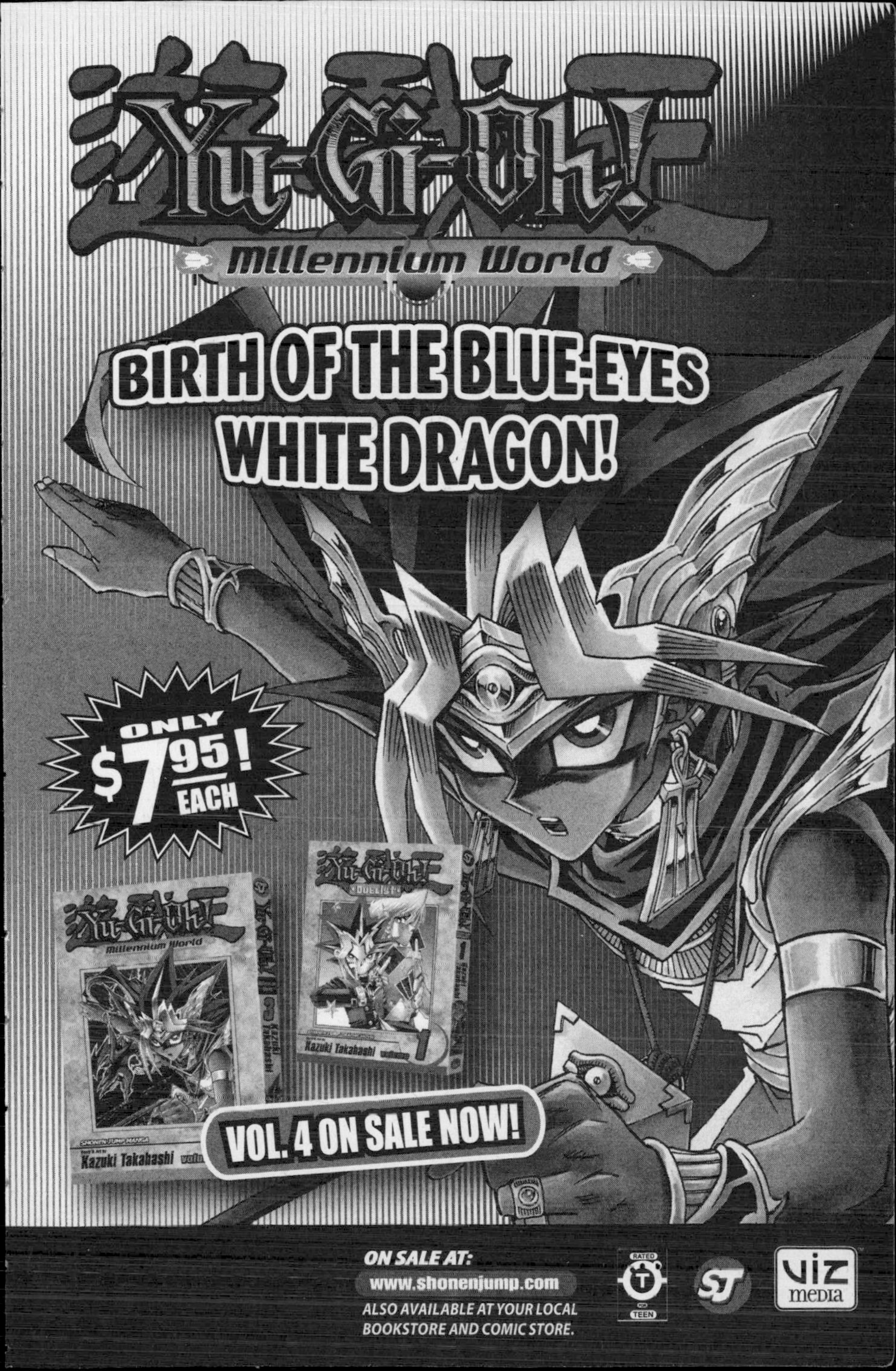

YU-GI-OH!
Millennium World
BIRTH OF THE BLUE-EYES WHITE DRAGON!
ONLY $7.95! EACH
VOL. 4 ON SALE NOW!
ON SALE AT:
www.shonenjump.com
ALSO AVAILABLE AT YOUR LOCAL BOOKSTORE AND COMIC STORE.
RATED T TEEN
SJ
viz media

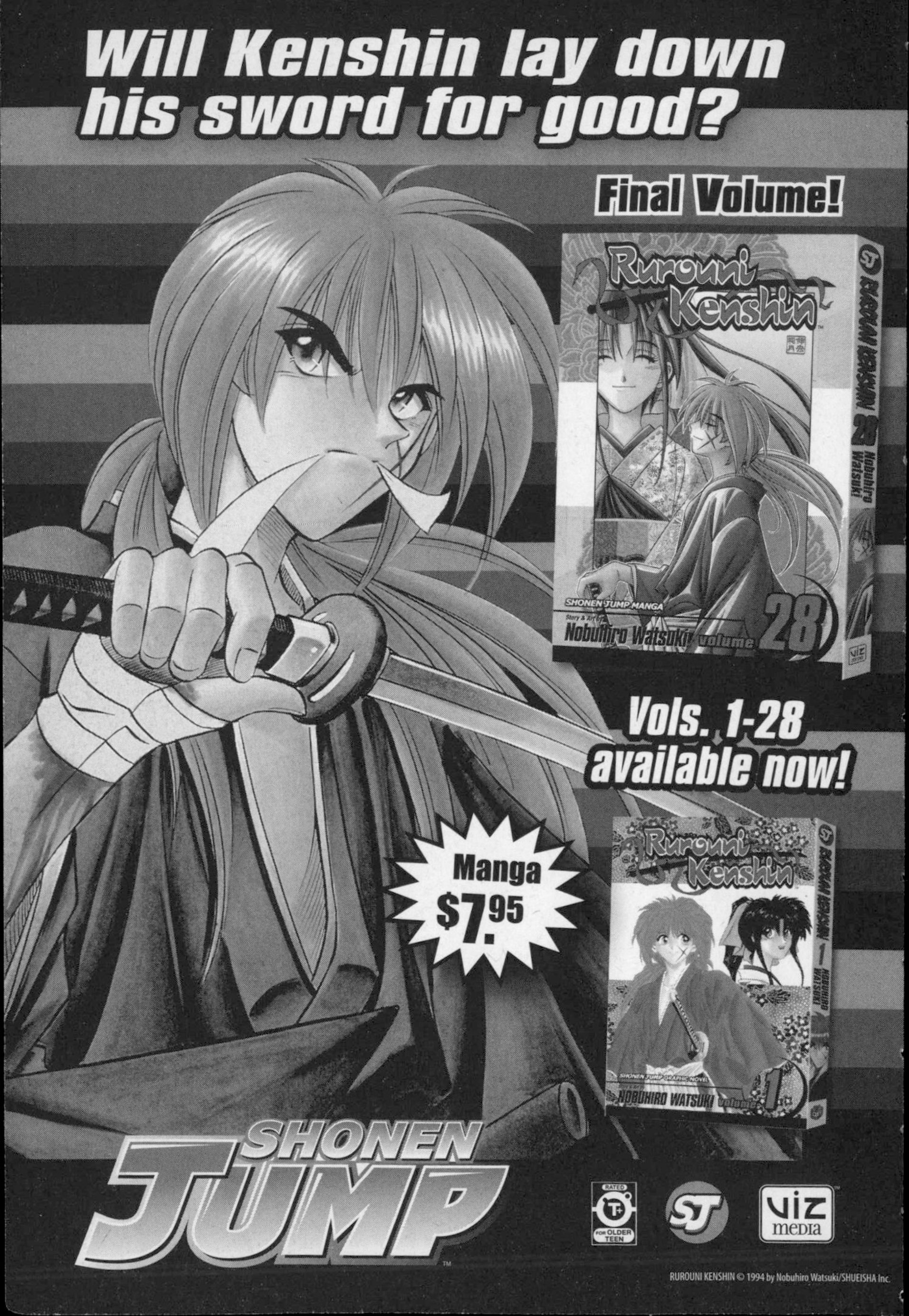

Will Kenshin lay down his sword for good?
Final Volume!
Rurouni Kenshin
SHONEN JUMP MANGA
Nobuhiro Watsuki volume 28
Vols. 1-28 available now!
Manga $7.95
Rurouni Kenshin
NOBUHIRO WATSUKI volume 1
SHONEN JUMP
RATED T+ FOR OLDER TEEN
SJ
VIZ media
RUROUNI KENSHIN © 1994 by Nobuhiro Watsuki/SHUEISHA Inc.

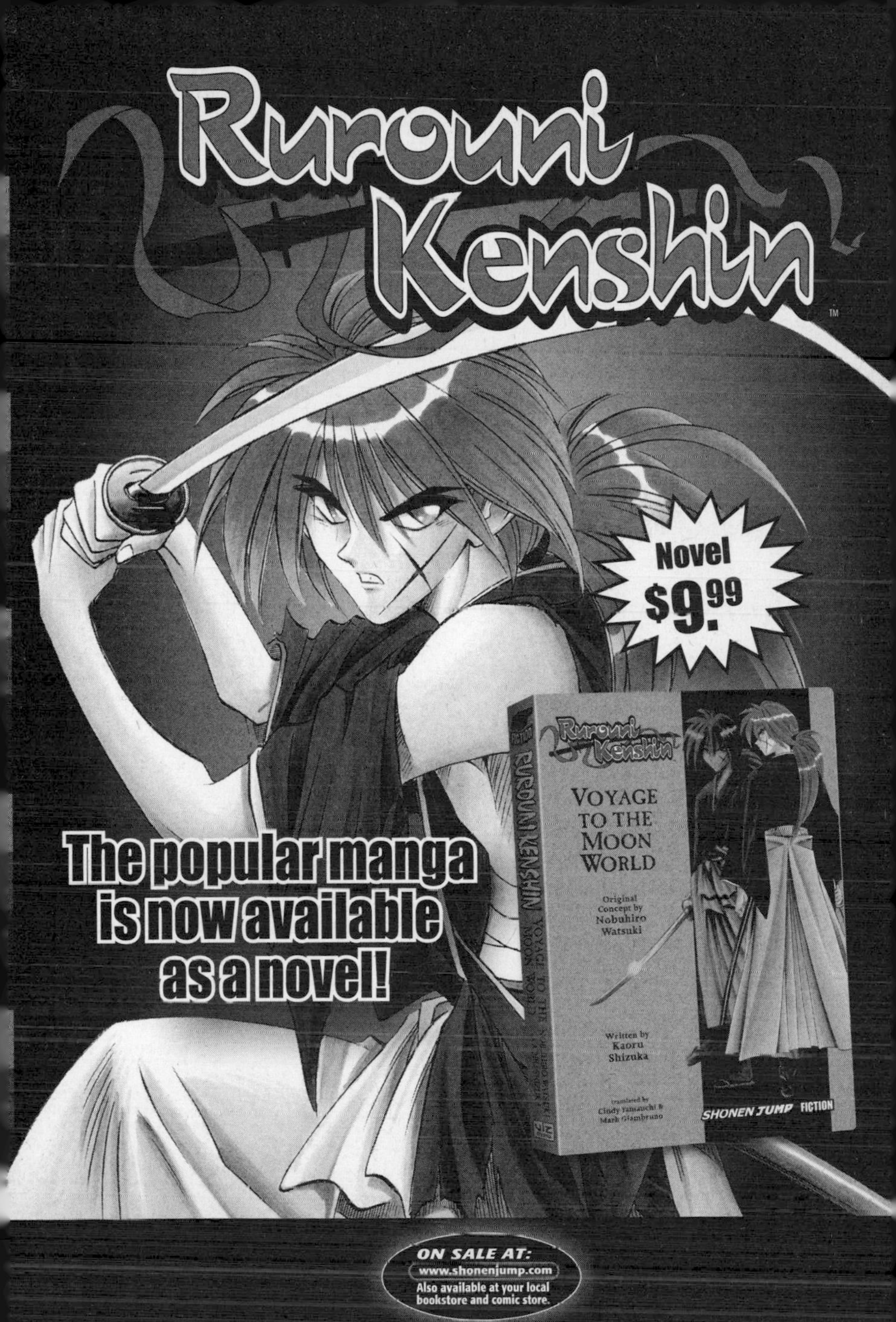
Rurouni Kenshin™
Novel $9.99
The popular manga is now available as a novel!
Rurouni Kenshin
FICTION
RUROUNI KENSHIN VOYAGE TO THE MOON WORLD
VOYAGE TO THE MOON WORLD
Original Concept by Nobuhiro Watsuki
Written by Kaoru Shizuka
translated by Cindy Yamauchi & Mark Giambruno
SHONEN JUMP FICTION
ON SALE AT:
www.shonenjump.com
Also available at your local bookstore and comic store.

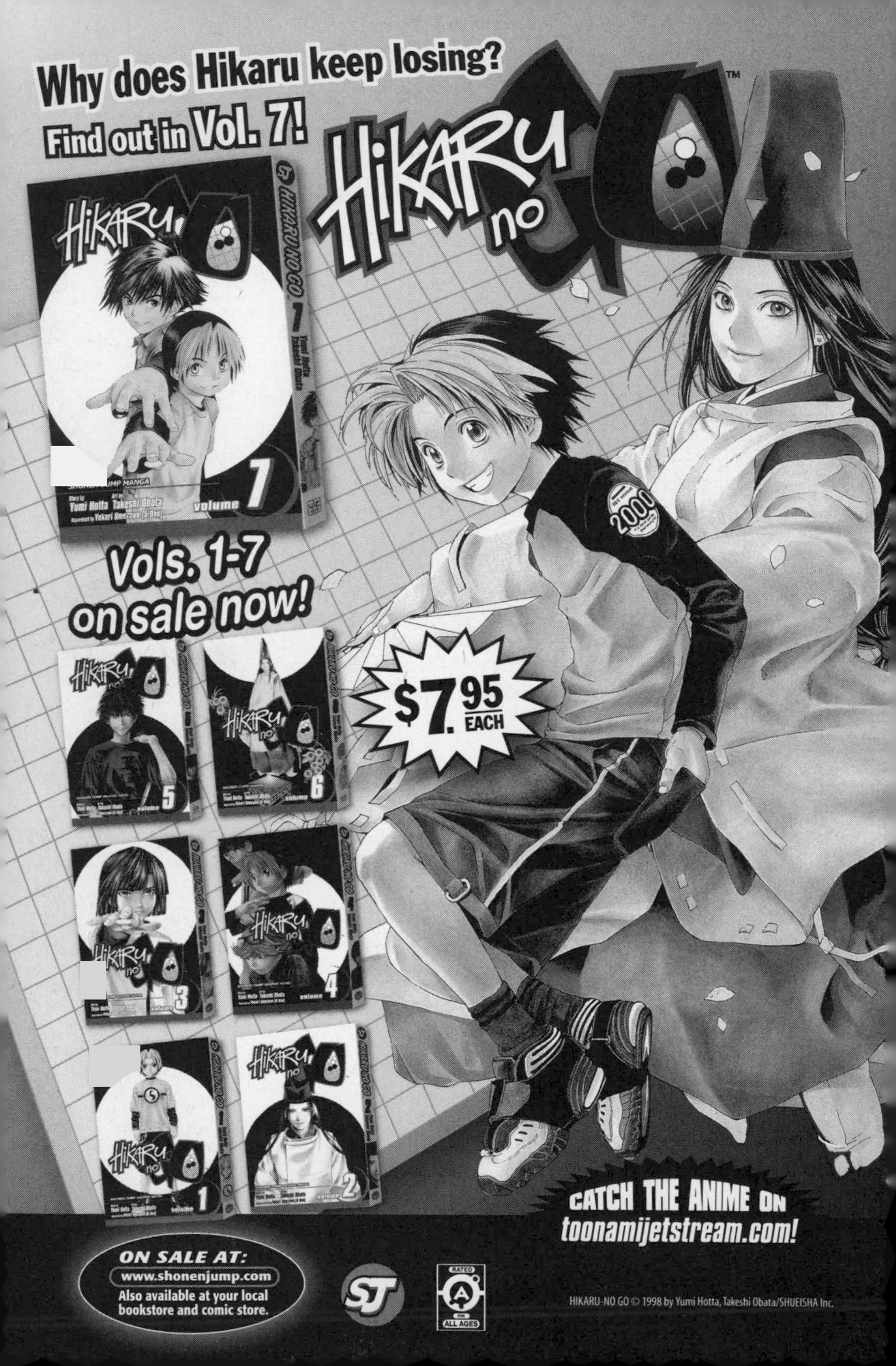
Why does Hikaru keep losing?
Find out in Vol. 7!
HIKARU no GO™
Vols. 1-7
on sale now!
$7.95 EACH
CATCH THE ANIME ON
toonamijetstream.com!
ON SALE AT:
www.shonenjump.com
Also available at your local bookstore and comic store.
RATED A FOR ALL AGES

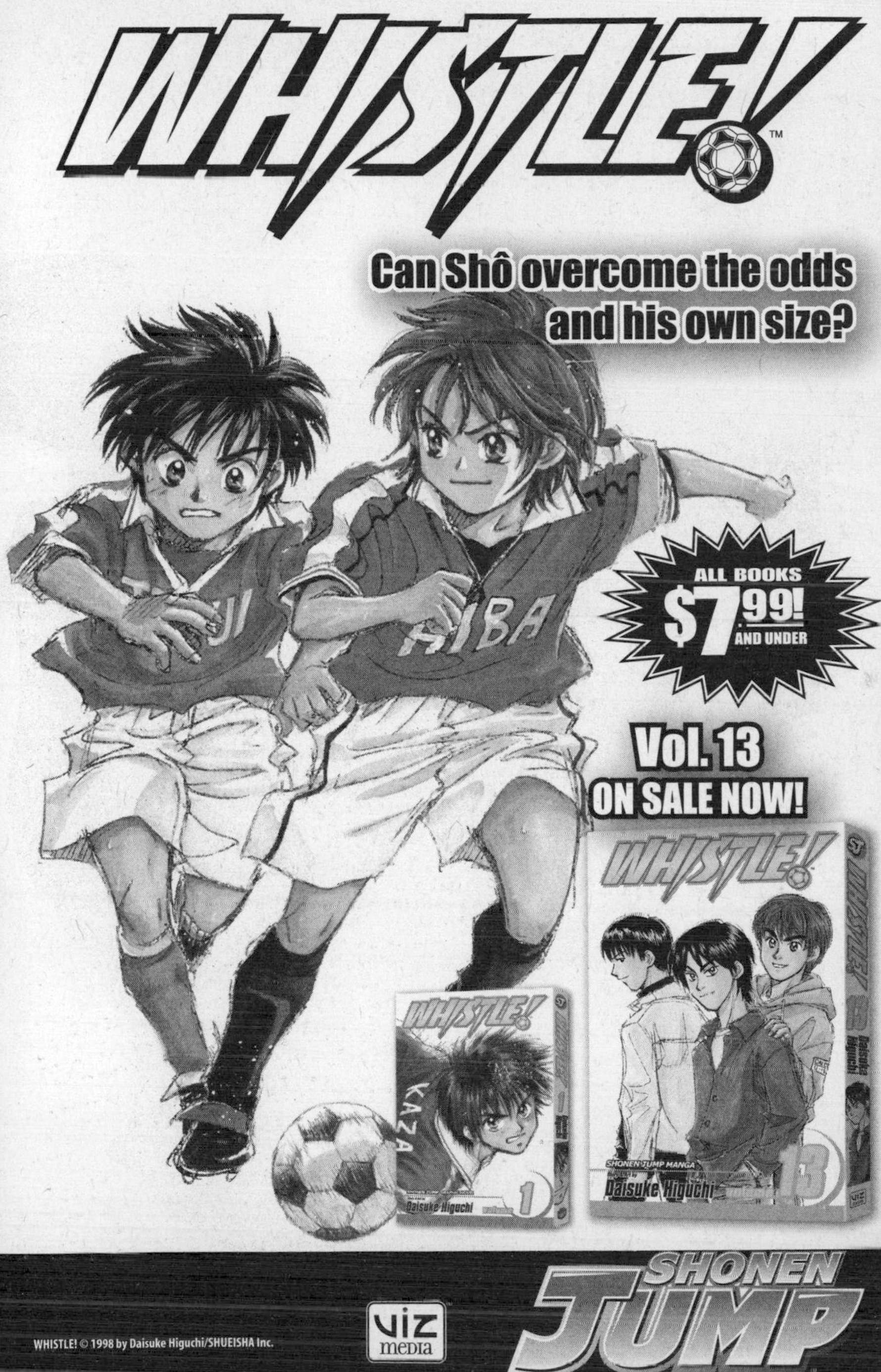
WHISTLE!™
Can Shô overcome the odds and his own size?
ALL BOOKS $7.99! AND UNDER
Vol. 13 ON SALE NOW!
WHISTLE!
Daisuke Higuchi
SHONEN JUMP MANGA
viz media
SHONEN JUMP

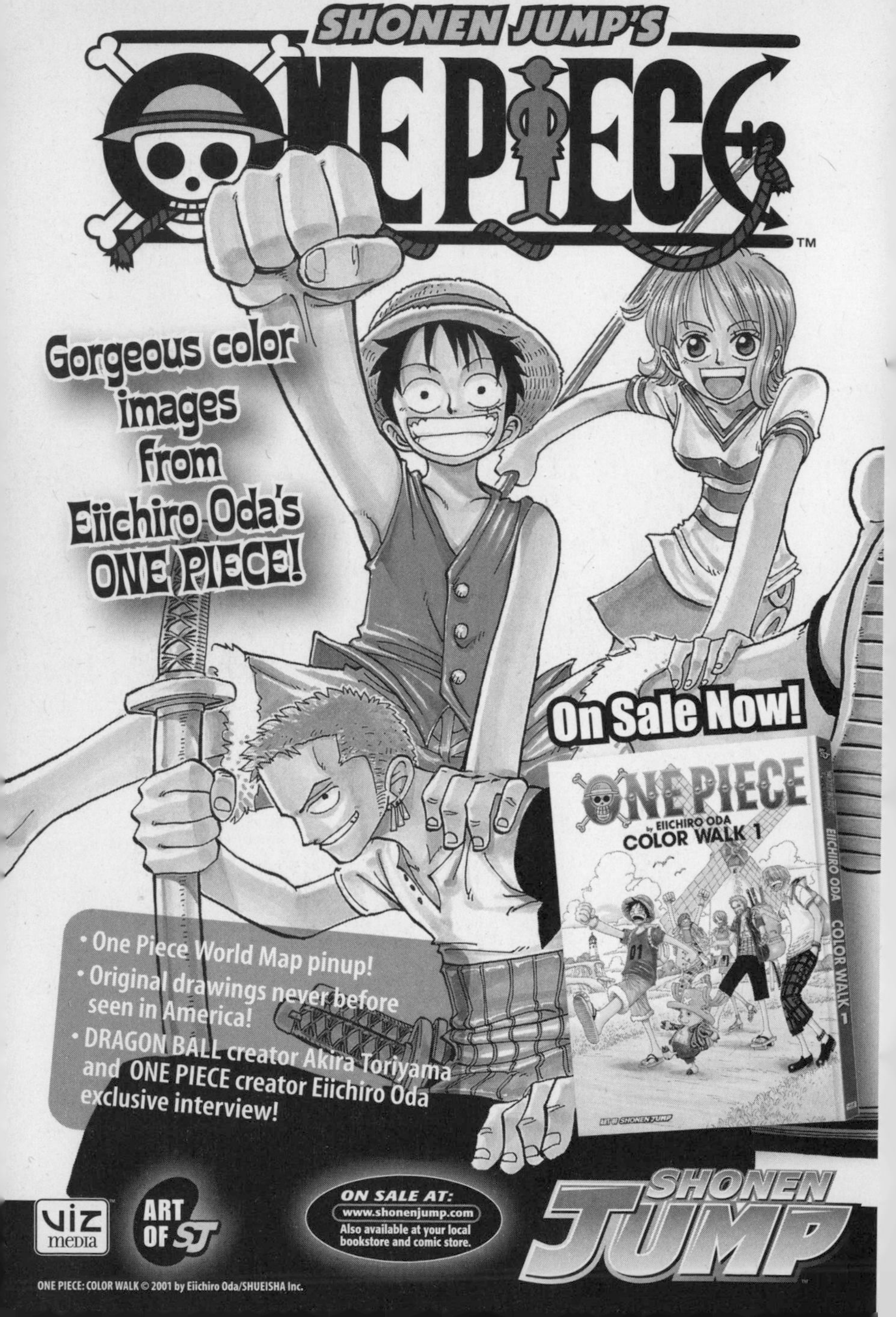
SHONEN JUMP'S
ONE PIECE
TM
Gorgeous color images from Eiichiro Oda's ONE PIECE!
On Sale Now!
ONE PIECE
by EIICHIRO ODA
COLOR WALK 1
EIICHIRO ODA
COLOR WALK 1
SHONEN JUMP
• One Piece World Map pinup!
• Original drawings never before seen in America!
• DRAGON BALL creator Akira Toriyama and ONE PIECE creator Eiichiro Oda exclusive interview!
viz media
ART OF SJ
ON SALE AT:
www.shonenjump.com
Also available at your local bookstore and comic store.
SHONEN JUMP
ONE PIECE: COLOR WALK © 2001 by Eiichiro Oda/SHUEISHA Inc.